RIGGED

RIGGED

AMERICA, RUSSIA, AND ONE HUNDRED YEARS OF COVERT ELECTORAL INTERFERENCE

DAVID SHIMER

ALFRED A. KNOPF NEW YORK 2020

THIS IS A BORZOI BOOK
PUBLISHED BY ALFRED A. KNOPF

Copyright © 2020 by David Shimer

All rights reserved. Published in the United States by Alfred A. Knopf,
a division of Penguin Random House LLC, New York, and distributed
in Canada by Penguin Random House Canada Limited, Toronto.

www.aaknopf.com

Knopf, Borzoi Books, and the colophon are registered
trademarks of Penguin Random House LLC.

Library of Congress Control Number: 2020931325
ISBN 978-0-525-65900-6 (hardcover)
ISBN 978-0-525-65901-3 (ebook)

Jacket design by Tyler Comrie

Manufactured in the United States of America
First Edition

To my teachers

Contents

RIGGED

DEMOCRACY UNDER SIEGE

P resident Barack Obama faced a momentous choice. By the summer of 2016, he knew that Russia was interfering in America's upcoming election. He also knew that Vladimir Putin, the Russian president, was directing this operation. Obama now had to decide whether to retaliate against Putin before or after Election Day.[1]

That summer, Celeste Wallander, the top Russia expert inside the White House, submitted to her superiors a classified memorandum outlining ways to punish Putin immediately, in order to deter further interference in the election.[2] "We wanted to do light deniable countermeasures early, in July," said Victoria Nuland, an assistant secretary of state who collaborated closely with Wallander. "All of my Soviet and Russia training told me we had to deter with a strong set of measures up front and have them calculate the costs of continuing to attack us, particularly with a player like Putin."[3] Nuland, Wallander, and other officials proposed a range of options: sanctioning Russia, leaking damaging information about Putin, even suffocating Russia's economy. James R. Clapper, then the director of national intelligence, recalled considering "all kinds of nasty things we could have done to the Russians," such as "cutting them off from the international financial system."

But, Clapper continued, the risks were too high: "What would the retaliation have been?"[4]

The answer was unknown. Russian intelligence had already stolen and released emails damaging to the Democratic Party, in an effort to influence voters' minds. But Russian hackers had also breached electoral systems, which Washington could not systematically defend. States and localities, not the federal government, purchase and manage America's electoral infrastructure. In some states, voter registration databases were unencrypted and insecure.[5] "[Russia] could have done things as far as voter registration rolls; they could have done things as far as tallies," said John Brennan, then the director of the Central Intelligence Agency (CIA).[6] Jeh Johnson, the secretary of homeland security, worried that Russia "could screw around with voter registration lists to a sufficient degree" to alter the outcome of the election, by making Democrats in swing states like Florida unable to cast their ballots on Election Day.[7]

Retaliating against Putin could provoke him into disrupting the voting process itself. With Hillary Clinton favored to win the presidency, and with Donald Trump alleging that the election would be rigged, Obama delayed punishing Russia. Restraint seemed prudent. Instead, at a summit in China in early September, he warned Putin, "You fuck with us and we'll take you down," as one of his senior advisers put it.[8] Of this encounter, Lisa Monaco, Obama's homeland security adviser, said, "We delivered the message to Putin and others in response to what we were seeing in the state systems. That was our focus."[9]

By October, Russia was still targeting America's electoral infrastructure. Obama's team considered efforts to manipulate these systems "a redline of sorts," said Avril Haines, the deputy national security adviser, and formulated "a series of very significant responses in the event that the Russians engaged in vote tampering." On Election Day, parts of the federal government secretly braced for such an assault. "We did, in fact, have an entire crisis team set up in the White House," said Michael Daniel, Obama's cybersecurity coordinator. "There were teams at all of the respective agencies," he continued, monitoring for a Russian cyberattack.[10]

The worst-case scenario did not arrive: Voting unfolded without interruption. But Russia's operation had by no means failed. Hacked emails had already dominated the news cycle for months, and Russian propaganda had reached tens of millions of Americans on social media. Obama had prioritized protecting the ballot box from direct manipulation, but at a cost: Russia had brazenly manipulated voters' minds. Victoria Nuland lamented the White House's redline mentality. "That is what they were focused on," she said, regarding the threat of vote alterations. "They were not focused at all on what we knew had been very effective elsewhere: the influence campaign, changing public opinion."[11]

Obama, near the end of his presidency, retaliated against Russia with economic and diplomatic countermeasures.[12] Too little, too late, many of his advisers now say. "We did not do enough, at an early enough point in our tenure," said Jon Finer, then the State Department chief of staff. "I would have done more sanctions sooner." The then deputy secretary of state Tony Blinken said that, as he has learned more about Russia's operation, he has asked himself: "Did we do enough in terms of punishment? And I think clearly, we didn't." Even James Clapper said it was a mistake to impose costs on Russia only in December: "I would have preferred that been done before the election."[13] (President Obama, through a representative, declined to be interviewed for this book.)

By waiting to retaliate, Obama effectively permitted a degree of foreign interference in an American election to avoid making an already-bad situation worse. A previous generation of U.S. policy makers—who themselves interfered in many elections overseas—would have found such a scenario unimaginable: the United States, the world's most powerful democracy, unable to secure its own elections. But Obama was operating in a new world, a digital one, that had left America vulnerable.

—

The story of Russia's attack on the 2016 election is, in part, a story of difficult choices, made inside the Situation Room based on imperfect information and incomplete intelligence. In this environment, Obama had settled for a policy of managed interference, working to contain but not stop Russia's operation. Rather than impose costs on Putin in real time, he had focused on preventing one form of electoral interference—changing actual votes—while neglecting another: changing minds.

In these critical months, Obama had tried but failed to preserve America's sovereignty. The theorist Hans Morgenthau described sovereignty as the "impenetrability" of the nation; others have argued that sovereignty means being "free from all foreign authority" and is "violated when external actors influence or determine domestic authority structures."[14] Covert electoral interference targets a democracy's process of succession and therefore targets the *electoral sovereignty* of that democracy. When such activity is discovered, the benefiting candidate is plagued with *electoral insecurity,* or a fear that citizens will consider him illegitimate and indebted to a foreign actor.

Can a democracy maintain its electoral sovereignty in the twenty-first century? Obama's intelligence chiefs are skeptical. "It would have been impossible, given the nature of this world, for the Obama administration to do something that would have led to a complete cessation of Russian efforts," John Brennan insisted. "It's not the way the world works. It's not the way the Russians work."[15] Other officials disagree. "Bullshit. That's just bullshit," said one of Obama's senior advisers, who requested anonymity to speak freely, when presented with Brennan's argument. "There were things we could have done to protect U.S. national security that [Obama] chose not to do."

———

Since 2016, Russia's operation has received ceaseless attention, but much of it remains misunderstood. Basic questions have been left unanswered: What is covert electoral interference? For how long have states executed such operations? When did America's elections become so exposed? Just how exposed *is* America? And, in the digital age, what can democracies do to defend themselves?[16]

This book seeks to answer these questions by analyzing not just interference in America's 2016 election but also what came before. Politicians, policy makers, and commentators today often act as though Putin were the first leader to manipulate a foreign election. In this vacuum, covert electoral interference *is* Russian interference in the 2016 election, in favor of Donald Trump. This ignorance is dangerous. To understand what Russia achieved in 2016, and to prepare for what's ahead, this book looks beyond the daily news cycle. After Trump won, high-profile investigations into his campaign distracted from the issue that spawned them: a massive foreign operation to undermine a presidential election.

Back in the summer of 2016, Avril Haines and other senior Obama administration officials sought a more complete picture. They requested a report on Moscow's previous attempts to covertly influence U.S. elections.[17] The briefing they then received, presumably from the U.S. intelligence community, remains classified.

This book can be understood as the unclassified and expanded version. Traveling across six countries, I spoke with foreign heads of state and intelligence chiefs, eight former CIA directors and many more CIA officers, twenty-six former advisers to President Obama and eleven former advisers to President Trump, and a host of leading journalists and technology experts. I also learned from the work of historians and other scholars, and I analyzed hundreds of pages of KGB and Stasi archives, many thousands of pages of declassified CIA files, and as many government reports, official testimonies, and meeting transcripts as I could get my hands on.

My aims are twofold: to examine a century's worth of covert electoral interference, and to analyze Putin's 2016 operation as the evolution of a practice rather than its creation. For democracies today, the stakes of grappling with this hidden and revelatory history could hardly be higher. The twin processes of globalization and digital connectivity have empowered hostile actors to manipulate democracies everywhere. The evolving threat of covert electoral interference is a symptom of a still more momentous challenge: the exposure of democracies in the age of the internet. "[Russia] is taking advantage of our free and open societies in using these capabilities," said H. R. McMaster, Trump's former national security adviser. "It's important for us to develop better means of defending ourselves against this kind of sustained, really sustained campaign of political subversion."[18] If democracies do not meet this challenge, foreign actors—for now Russia, but soon others—will erode them from within.

—

Some definitions are needed to keep my arguments precise. The words "covert," "interference," and "electoral" determine the scope of this book. An operation is *covert* only if the hand of the interfering actor is meant to be hidden; a public endorsement by a foreign leader, for example, does not qualify, but stolen emails released by a third party do. An operation amounts to *interference* only if the foreign actor deploys active measures, defined as "activities intended to influence a person or government that are carried out in coordination with, or at the behest of, political leaders," including through the "establishment or funding of a front group . . . covert broadcasting . . . media manipulation . . . disinformation and forgeries . . . funding agents of influence . . . [and] assassinations."[19] And an operation qualifies as *electoral* only if it targets a vote that determines who becomes another country's leader. Covert electoral interference can thus be defined as *a concealed foreign effort to influence a democratic vote of succession*. Staged coups d'état do not involve votes of succession and therefore fall outside the bounds of this book.

"Democracy is a procedure to change rulers," writes historian Timothy Snyder. "Democracies die when people cease to believe that voting matters. The question is not whether elections are held, but whether they are free and fair."[20] Many factors can undermine an election, from voter suppression to voter intimidation. My focus is on *foreign* disruptions to electoral processes and on the power those operations have to corrupt democratic governments.

This book advances four core arguments. First, the story of covert electoral interference is, above all, a story of Washington and Moscow. This story has spanned the past century, beginning with the end of World War I, when old empires collapsed and vulnerable democracies emerged. The Soviet Union, but not the United States, seized the opportunity to manipulate elections overseas. A break occurred between 1941 and 1945, as a result of a U.S.-Soviet alliance during another world war. The next phase of this history arose thereafter as Moscow rigged elections in Eastern Europe, and the world witnessed an explosion of covert electoral interference. Between 1948 and 1991, the CIA and the KGB, competing in a global Cold War, targeted elections aggressively and frequently. After the Soviet Union collapsed, a divergence took place. The United States moved away from covert electoral interference as a policy option, while Putin's Russia, empowered by the internet, doubled down on the practice, marking its second global explosion. Today, as in 1919, Moscow is covertly interfering in elections abroad while Washington sits on the sidelines—only now Russia possesses a digital arsenal to which the United States is profoundly vulnerable.[21]

Second, American operations to interfere in elections are comparable but not identical to Russian efforts to do the same. Every instance of covert electoral interference can be understood across two planes. One has to do with *individual change:* whether the intention of an operation is to promote a friendly candidate, defeat an unfriendly candidate, or exhibits no preference. The other has to do with *systemic change:* whether the intention of an operation is to strengthen, weaken, or not at all impact the internal functions of a democracy. Washington and Moscow are equivalent across the first plane. Both have used covert electoral interference to advantage specific candidates. But Moscow and Washington are not equivalent across the second plane. Putin and his predecessors have long believed they could use covert electoral interference to weaken foreign democracies, while American presidents, sometimes wrongly, have long believed they could use covert electoral interference to strengthen foreign democracies.

Some operations detailed in this book exclusively involved individual change, as when the KGB supported major-party candidates in Cold War–era U.S. elections, not to weaken American democracy, but to promote friendlier American governments. Other operations exclusively involved systemic change, as when Russia covertly spread propaganda in favor of the Leave campaign in the United Kingdom, in order to weaken British democracy. And certain operations involved both systemic and individual change, as when the CIA, in 2000, supported the opposition to Slobodan Milošević, a murderous tyrant, not just to establish a more conciliatory Serbian government, but also to strengthen Serbian democracy. "The guy was a war criminal," President Bill Clinton told me, in explaining why he authorized the CIA to interfere in this election. "I didn't consider Milošević to be a democracy candidate; I thought he was trying to get rid of democracy."[22] In this sense, covert electoral interference is a more tense policy option for Washington—which has purported to manipulate democracies in order to solidify those democracies—than for Moscow, which has manipulated democracies in order to tear them apart.

Third, Russian interference in the 2016 election marked a direct continuation of old ideas. Covert electoral interference has always taken two forms: changing ballots and changing minds. The former can range from falsifying vote counts and buying votes to blackmailing voters and hacking into voting systems; the latter, from influencing foreign media and disseminating propaganda to leaking salacious information and funding political campaigns. The purpose of Russia's 2016 operation is not new, either: assisting a friendly candidate, undermining a threatening candidate, and sowing discord within a foreign democracy. Voters, once aware of a covert campaign to influence them, have always struggled to accept that they might have been played. And across history, as in 2016, the mere discovery of such an operation can divide a nation. From Britain's 1924 election, to Chile's 1964 election, to America's 2016 election, this book recognizes and learns from these patterns.

Fourth, the digital age has irrevocably enhanced the weapon of covert electoral interference. The internet has enabled hostile actors to penetrate the ballot box in new and more accessible ways, as Barack Obama learned in 2016. It has also empowered interfering actors to target voters based on their personal profiles. A new battlefield has emerged in social media, where foreigners can suppress, turn out, and frighten voters while avoiding real-time detection and sidelining traditional news outlets. Today, the press has less influence over what information—and, importantly, disinformation—reaches citizens.[23] "We're no longer the filter we once were," said Peter Baker, the chief White House correspondent for *The New York Times*.[24] Platforms like Facebook and Twitter don't just enhance modern interference operations; they enable them. "The truth is Facebook did fuck up [in 2016]," said Alex Stamos, then the company's chief security officer, "but we fucked up in the context of a lot of [other] people making mistakes."[25]

Newer democracies were once more vulnerable to covert electoral interference than their more established counterparts. The internet has leveled the playing field. All democracies are exposed.

In this anarchic environment, Putin foments discord as an end in itself. Valery Gerasimov, a top Russian general, has commented that "the information space opens wide asymmetrical possibilities for reducing the fighting potential of the enemy."[26] Gerasimov and his colleagues have weaponized the digital sphere to strike at the heart of democracies: their elections.

The democratic model is not guaranteed to exist. It is a human creation maintained by human actors. Today, Moscow is working to corrupt democracies by assisting illiberal and divisive candidates of any political leaning. This campaign is unfolding not by land, sea, or air but across the internet.[27] The first part of this book, spanning chapters 1 through 8, tracks the origins and evolution of covert electoral interference, from Vladimir Lenin's creations, to the battles of the Cold War, to Putin's modern strategy. The second part, spanning chapters 9 through 13, examines Russian interference in the 2016 election, illuminating President Obama's struggle to defend America's electoral sovereignty, as well as President Trump's refusal to recognize this threat.

Central to this book is an idea: that the lessons of the past can and must be used to protect democracies in the present.

Part One

THE HIDDEN HISTORY

Chapter 1

ENTER LENIN

In 1952, Oleg Kalugin, then seventeen years old, graduated from a Soviet high school seeking meaning, adventure, and the chance to combat capitalism. So he joined the KGB, his state's security and intelligence service. Kalugin spent the next six years training at spy facilities in Leningrad and Moscow, after which he moved to America. He was stationed in New York until 1964 and then, after a brief interlude, was transferred to Washington, D.C., where he worked through 1970, eventually as acting station chief. (As his cover story, Kalugin presented himself as an inquisitive foreign correspondent.) He then returned to Moscow, rising to become the chief of counterintelligence and, in 1974, the KGB's youngest-ever general. His job was to penetrate the "intelligence and security organizations of the world," he told me, "and, of course, number one was the United States."[1]

One summer day in 2019, I spent four hours with Kalugin in Rockville, Maryland, about sixteen miles from the White House. His home is modest, nestled in a quiet neighborhood. Paintings and memorabilia line the walls. On display are a photograph with William Colby, a former CIA director, and a signed copy of a book by Michael Hayden, another former CIA director. Since Vladimir Putin came to power in Russia, Kalugin has criticized aspects of his regime. The feeling is mutual: In 2002, a Russian court tried Kalugin for treason and sentenced him in absentia to fifteen years in prison.[2] If Kalugin lived in any other country, he coolly pointed out, Putin would have him killed.

Sitting in his living room, however, Kalugin had many stories to tell about covert electoral interference. The roots of such operations run deep, he explained—back to the very founding of the Soviet Union. To any leader in Moscow, foreign elections present opportunities to redirect nations. The democratic process of succession practically invites interference. "What we did all around the world," Kalugin said, "was provide money and support to people who we thought would be friendly and would change the foreign and domestic policies of their countries."[3]

The Soviet Union first targeted foreign elections a century ago. The historian Tony Judt argued that the Cold War began in Europe after World War I, when Vladimir Lenin consolidated control over the ruins of the Russian Empire and Communist Moscow first clashed with Western democracies.[4] Lenin, who distrusted the United States, possessed a comparative advantage in the area of covert action: Unlike Moscow, an isolationist Washington had no peacetime foreign intelligence agency.[5] As Americans looked inward, Lenin surveyed the globe. His grand ambition was for foreign Communists to seize power, shed their preexisting governments, and abolish their nations' borders. Through covert electoral interference, he could help.

—

Secret funding is perhaps the oldest form of covert electoral interference. It enables political campaigns to better target, turn out, and manipulate the masses. In March 1919, Lenin laid the groundwork for such operations at a pivotal conference in Moscow. The summit attracted delegates from more than two dozen countries, who together established the Communist International (Comintern), a transnational organization charged with uniting the Communist Parties of the world—and fomenting revolution abroad. "Particularly for the majority of the western European countries, spreading of the soviet system is a most important task," Lenin told his guests. "America is the country that is most ripe . . . for a real socialist revolution," said Boris Reinstein, the only American citizen present.[6] The attendees, despite their limited means, had set their sights on a historic end: toppling the international system.

"The purpose of the [Communist] International is shown to be to propagate revolution and communism throughout the world," warned a front-page *New York Times* article in 1920. That year, as the Red Army marched westward, the Comintern's Second Congress attracted over two hundred representatives from thirty-seven countries.[7] Lenin seemed poised to change the world.

The Comintern's mission was publicly known, but its finances were shrouded in mystery. We now know that its Department of International Communication covertly distributed directions, propaganda, and money to foreign Communist Parties. The Soviet government provided the funds. In return, Lenin expected obedience. "Any person taking money" from the Comintern, Lenin said, "is warned that he is obliged to implement absolutely scrupulously all instructions of the [Executive Committee of the Communist International]."[8] Beginning in the spring of 1919, the Comintern financed various Communist groups, including in the United States, Hungary, Czechoslovakia, Germany, Italy, Yugoslavia, Austria, Poland, Holland, and Britain.[9]

But a global Communist revolution was not, in fact, imminent. The Comintern's early operations coincided with an ongoing war between Polish and Soviet soldiers. In August 1920, the Red Army lost at Warsaw, preventing Lenin's forces from advancing across Europe. The Treaty of Riga instead forced the Soviet Union to establish itself as a state with defined borders. Western democracies, meanwhile, had not abandoned their political model for Lenin's. Now seeking to deter foreign interference in its affairs, Soviet intelligence spread disinformation exaggerating the strength of its military.[10] With this deception campaign under way, Lenin died in January 1924, not knowing where his Communist experiment would lead.

Lenin's successor, Joseph Stalin, initially forbade foreign Communist Parties to ally with social democrats. This strategy proved self-defeating. In parliamentary democracies, politicians often obtain power through coalition building. By insisting on ideological purity, Stalin inadvertently empowered his rivals by isolating his friends. In Germany's July 1932 and March 1933 elections, for example, Adolf Hitler's National Socialists succeeded at the ballot box in part because Germany's Communist Party would not stand with the Social Democrats.[11]

After Hitler's rise, the Comintern shifted its strategy: It began supporting electoral alliances against fascists. At its Seventh Congress in 1935, the Comintern endorsed so-called popular front coalitions of antifascist parties. Some successes followed. In Spain, the Communist Party, whose Comintern representative had written Moscow requesting its "promised sum . . . for the [1936] electoral campaign," joined a Popular Front coalition, which prevailed at the polls in February of that year.[12] In France, where the Comintern was funding as much as one fourth of the Communist Party's budget, a Popular Front that included the Communist, Socialist, and Radical Parties also won in 1936. Outlawed Communist groups received covert assistance, too, as the Comintern smuggled funds into fascist Italy and Germany.[13]

—

Still, the Comintern struggled. None of its foreign Communist Parties, with the exception of China's, had more than thirty thousand or so members.[14] In the interwar period, the specter of Russian interference thus mattered more as an idea than as an actual mechanism for change. "The call of the Comintern," writes the historian Odd Arne Westad, "was heard throughout a world that was tired of war and colonial oppression." The Soviet Union was founded on the premise of catalyzing global revolution; the Comintern sought to execute this mission. As foreign governments searched for signs of its meddling, prudence gave way to paranoia. In the United States, the first Red Scare unfolded from 1919 to 1920.[15] A few years later, a similar crisis enveloped the United Kingdom.

Four days before Britain's 1924 election, the *Daily Mail* published a letter that Grigory Zinoviev, the head of the Comintern, had allegedly sent the British Communist Party (which the Comintern had been covertly funding for years).[16] Taken at face value, the letter constituted direct interference in the affairs of another nation. It instructed Communist Party officials to "strain every nerve in the struggle for the ratification" of a treaty between the Soviet government and that of Ramsay MacDonald, the first-ever

Labour Party prime minister, and to "stir up the masses of the British proletariat." The *Daily Mail* ran the headline "Civil War Plot by Socialists' Masters . . . and Mr. MacDonald Would Lend Russia Our Money!"[17]

When covert interference is uncovered, the beneficiary is put on the defensive, regardless of whether he solicited the help. Because Zinoviev favored Labour, the right swiftly labeled MacDonald an instrument of Moscow and linked his party with foreign influence. MacDonald was left to fight for his political life. "All I say is this: So far as I know, the letter might have originated anywhere," he said two days before the election. "How can I, a simple-minded, honest person who puts two and two together, avoid the suspicion—I will not say the conclusion—that the whole thing is a political plot?"[18]

MacDonald was right: Historians now consider the Zinoviev letter a forgery. To this day, it is a mystery who wrote it. But none of this was clear in 1924, so when the Conservative Party won the election, Labour attributed its defeat to the Comintern's apparent interference in British politics (although scholars like A. J. P. Taylor are certain that Labour would have lost anyway).[19] Regardless of whether the letter swung the election, it certainly divided voters. MacDonald's opponents had cast Labour as sympathetic to Moscow, and the party's supporters felt unfairly attacked as such. The mere *appearance* of covert interference had polarized a nation. Almost a century later, the legacy of the letter lingers. "This document—which may never have existed in the form of an original letter and was almost certainly not written by Zinoviev—has haunted politics, especially Labour politics, in the United Kingdom ever since," writes Gill Bennett, the former chief historian of the British Foreign and Commonwealth Office.[20]

Foreign democracies assumed the Comintern had powers that it did not. By overtly calling for world revolution, the organization had developed an outsized reputation. The Comintern could not catapult Communists into power globally, but it could sow discord within democracies. A single letter had thrown British politics into upheaval. The Comintern's perceived influence, though, came at a cost: It isolated Moscow on the international stage. Elected leaders distrusted the Comintern and, therefore, Stalin.

—

As Hitler strengthened Germany, Moscow needed allies. The Comintern, however, had alienated democracies like the United Kingdom and the United States. Lenin's creation had become Stalin's liability. "It would therefore be in the interest of Russia itself to dissolve the Comintern and to prove, by scrupulous abstention from interference abroad, that it can be treated on an equal footing with those democratic powers whose ideals it professes to share," urged Franz Borkenau, an Austrian political theorist, in 1939.[21]

Stalin chose a different path. That August, he entered into a nonaggression pact with Germany. The German Wehrmacht and the Soviet Red Army then invaded, divided, and annexed Poland. The United Kingdom and France responded by declaring war on Germany. World War II had begun, but the treaty that kicked it off did not last. In June 1941, Hitler betrayed Stalin and invaded the Soviet Union. Fascism once again became the enemy of Communism. Stalin, now allied with democracies, provided the Comintern with fewer and fewer resources "for rendering assistance to foreign parties."[22]

Stalin finally abolished the Comintern in 1943, as a gesture of goodwill toward Washington. "The dissolution of the Communist International is proper," Stalin told Reuters, "because . . . it exposes the lie of the Hitlerites to the effect that Moscow allegedly intends to intervene in the life of other nations."[23] There was, of course, no lie to expose. The Soviet Union had interfered in foreign elections and would continue to do so. The Comintern's fatal flaw was not its covert activities but its public mission, which had disturbed Moscow's wartime allies and made its existence untenable.

—

The outcome of World War II left Stalin with means of which Lenin had only dreamed. During the interwar period, the Soviet Union had controlled its own territory, and the Comintern had funded foreign Communist Parties, but those parties were, for the most part, unpopular, illegal, or both. Moscow's ability to shape other countries was limited. The results of the war changed what was possible. Four great powers—Nazi Germany, the Empire of Japan, the United Kingdom, and France—were either destroyed or severely weakened, creating a power vacuum for the Soviet Union and the United States to fill.

As the Red Army marched toward Berlin, its forces occupied the countries of Eastern Europe, which became a testing ground for electoral interference. After the war, most of these states held elections, but Moscow manipulated them so intensively that they hardly qualified as competitive. Whereas the power of the Comintern was its reputation, the power of these postwar operations was their scope, scale, and ambition. In East Germany, the Soviets directed the campaign of the Socialist Unity Party (SED), a coalition of Communists and Social Democrats. "All of the SED's decisions," a Soviet official said at the time, "must be agreed upon by the leadership of the Soviet Military Administration." Moscow bolstered the SED's electoral prospects through a variety of tactics, such as enabling its leaders to print more than a million leaflets and posters. But in October 1946, the SED still underperformed relative to Moscow's expectations, so more aggressive forms of interference—arrests, intimidation, and threats—followed. In December 1947, the Soviets forced the resignation of Jakob Kaiser, the head of the rival Christian Democrats. He then went into exile in West Berlin.[24]

A similar story unfolded elsewhere as a mix of covert and overt tactics determined the outcomes of supposedly free elections. In Poland, ahead of the January 1947 election, opposition leaders were arrested, Communist officials falsely alleged that a rival candidate had died, and soldiers monitored polling places as voting unfolded. The Soviet-supported "democratic bloc" achieved an overwhelming victory, in part because ballots were falsified in its favor.[25] Meanwhile, in Hungary, Mátyás Rákosi, the Communist leader, used so-called salami tactics to slice off his opposition. In February 1947, Soviet soldiers arrested Béla Kovács, the secretary general of the popular Smallholders Party, whose colleagues then went into exile. For the election that summer, hundreds of thousands of voters were purged from the rolls; many thousands more were too intimidated to turn out. On Election Day, special brigades traveled from district to district, some riding in Soviet vehicles, visibly stuffing ballot boxes. The Communist Party triumphed and, as in Poland and East Germany, consolidated control.[26] More than four decades would pass until these countries again held contested elections.

The brazenness of these electoral operations was extraordinary. The Red Army's physical presence enabled their most aggressive components, such as Béla Kovács's arrest. But other tactics, like manipulating voter rolls, altering vote counts, and disseminating propaganda, have since remained central to Moscow's approach to covert electoral interference.

American policy makers worried that the Red Army would push farther, past Berlin and into Western Europe. Stalin did little to assuage such concerns. In October 1947, just four years after dissolving the Comintern, he established another international body with the express purpose of uniting foreign Communist Parties. The Communist Information Bureau (Cominform), as it was called, was scathing in its rhetoric. In one communiqué, the organization denounced Americans as "imperialist warmongers" working toward the "forcible establishment of Anglo-American world domination, the enslavement of foreign countries and peoples, the destruction of democracy and the unleashing of a new war."[27]

—

In practice, the Cominform was more bark than bite. It rarely met, and it lacked the resources, mandate, or infrastructure to support foreign political parties. While Lenin's Comintern had been outward facing, aiming to catalyze world revolution, Stalin's Cominform faced inward; its purpose was to help solidify his sphere of influence across Eastern Europe.[28] Moscow would henceforth use its main intelligence service, renamed the KGB, rather than an international institution to interfere in elections overseas.[29]

From America's perspective, the fall of Eastern Europe prompted alarm. Stalin's plans were unknown; seemingly nothing was off-limits. "The idea was to eventually advance the Soviet system across the world," said Oleg Kalugin, the former KGB general.[30] Having mostly sat on the sidelines after World War I, Washington had to decide whether, and how, to lead abroad after World War II.

Chapter 2

THE CIA IN ITALY

Present Harry Truman's administration responded to the Soviet threat with a strategy of containment: structuring its foreign policy around preventing the further spread of Communism.[1] Some of the initiatives that followed were well-known, from massive aid programs to a sustained military presence in Western Europe. Others were meant to be hidden. In 1947, Truman authorized the newly formed Central Intelligence Agency to engage in covert action. The White House, like the Kremlin, finally had a peacetime intelligence service capable of deploying active measures abroad.[2]

From world war had emerged a global competition for influence; elections, more than anything, drew its dividing lines. As Moscow established Communist regimes across Eastern Europe, Washington charted a different course in Western Europe, where a set of democracies developed and soon prospered. The openness of America's allies meant that any of their elections could become a contest between East and West.

The first of such battles took place in Italy, where, in 1948, a fight for security and ideological alignment unfolded in the country's general election. Italy's economy was struggling, and its Communist Party was surging.[3] In Washington, the Truman administration hoped to preserve Italy's centrist government. What followed was a novel idea: electoral interference executed, in part, by the CIA.

—

In early 1948, Huntington Smith, a *New York Times* correspondent, traveled to Gravina, a small town in southern Italy. He found a village in disarray. Residents had stable jobs only three months each year, during the olive harvest. Families lived in cramped, filthy quarters. Tuberculosis was common. Smith visited a bedroom in which ten people, including a baby, lived with a man dying of the disease; two shared his bed. "We are all Communists here," one woman told Smith, gesturing to the deteriorating walls around her.[4]

These poor conditions were an aftereffect of World War II, when the Allied powers had occupied fascist Italy and forced its surrender. The fighting was over, but low incomes, inflation, and basic supply shortages still ravaged Italy. Working-class families spent more than 90 percent of their monthly paychecks on food alone.[5] In villages like Gravina, widespread impoverishment empowered left-wing politicians.

By 1946, Italy had become a democracy, and its Communist Party, with some two million members, was the largest in Western Europe. In an election that year, the centrist Christian Democratic Party received 35 percent of the vote, compared with a combined 40 percent for the Communist Party (which received 19 percent) and the Socialist Party (which received 21 percent). Also in 1946, the Italian people voted to replace their monarchic system with that of a republic, further breaking with their political past.[6] Ahead of the next election, in 1948, much of what made Italy vulnerable to foreign interference was the newness of its political institutions, as well as the polarized nature of its electorate.

The United States and the Soviet Union each had a horse in this race. The White House favored the Christian Democrats and their leader, Alcide De Gasperi, who, while visiting Washington in early 1947, had met with Truman and told reporters that Italy and America were "bound by so many ties of history and civilization."[7] Joseph Stalin, meanwhile, exerted influence over the Italian Communist Party, which did not hide its affinity for Moscow.[8] One Communist campaign poster, for example, contrasted depictions of American imperialists and Soviet friendship.[9]

At first, De Gasperi led an antifascist coalition that included his Christian Democrats, the Communists, and the Socialists. But this arrangement proved dysfunctional. In May 1947, De Gasperi dissolved Italy's governing coalition and established a new one that excluded the left. Chaos followed. Palmiro Togliatti, the Communist Party leader, called for an "intensification of agitation against the Government." By the end of 1947, more than eleven hundred strikes had taken place across Italy. Responding to this instability, Truman successfully lobbied Congress for an emergency aid package, partially for Italy, which he signed into law in December.[10]

The Italian Communist Party, already formidable, announced at the start of 1948 that it would stand with the Socialist Party in the April election as a popular front, echoing the Comintern strategy of the mid-1930s.[11] Togliatti aimed to take control of the government through coalition building. It seemed as if he might prevail. "It is not outside the bounds of possibility that the Communists and left-wing Socialists plus a few minor left-wing parties and groups may succeed in obtaining 51 percent or more of the votes at the next general election," *The New York Times* reported. "It must be admitted that at present the Communists are riding high, wide and handsome."[12]

From Italy, James Clement Dunn, the U.S. ambassador, cabled Secretary of State George Marshall, a war hero and five-star general, that the "present electoral situation justifies grave concern and calls for serious consideration." The Front's strategy, Dunn explained, was to corral specific constituencies—youth, veterans, labor, and farmworkers—and to inspire voters, especially women, to turn out.[13] Dunn also believed the Soviets were covertly funding the Front's campaign. He told Marshall the Communists had "unlimited funds" as a direct "result of Soviet support."[14] The CIA concurred. "The Communist Party of Italy was funded, in the first place, by black bags of money directly out of the Soviet compound in Rome," F. Mark Wyatt, a CIA officer stationed in Italy in 1948, said decades later.[15]

—

For Washington, electoral interference seemed necessary precisely because the worst-case scenario—a Communist victory—seemed so plausible. In one classified memorandum, the CIA warned that the Communist Party was planning an "all-out" election effort involving "legal and semi-legal methods."[16] In another, the CIA elaborated upon the perceived stakes of the election. In the Cold War's emerging battle of ideas, a Front victory would mark the "first instance in history of a communist accession to power by popular suffrage and legal procedure" (discounting, presumably, recent elections across Eastern Europe as illegitimate). Were the Front to win, the memorandum continued, civil war might ensue. Matters would only worsen once the Communists took office, because the Soviet Union would establish influence over Italy's foreign policy, economy, and military bases, from which Moscow could then threaten shipping across the Mediterranean. Ultimately, the CIA portended, Italian democracy would collapse "by processes made familiar in Eastern Europe," replaced by "a fully developed police state under open and exclusive Communist control."[17]

The call to action was evident; the question was how the Truman administration would respond. On December 14, 1947, Major General Lawrence C. Jaynes and America's other remaining soldiers in Italy—some 1,600 in all—completed their scheduled withdrawal from the country. The troops set sail from Livorno for Brooklyn, following a ceremony in which an American flag was lowered and replaced with an Italian one. General Mark W. Clark, formerly the U.S. commander in Italy, transmitted a farewell message that read, in part, "I decry, as do my countrymen, the evil influences at work both from outside and from within Italy to foist upon her yet another 'ism'—communism." As America's forces departed, Truman issued a statement renewing his commitment to "the preservation of a free and independent Italy."[18]

In his statement, Truman had said that if necessary he would "consider what measures" to take in Italy's defense.[19] Secret plans were, in fact, already in motion. The National Security Council (NSC), in its first-ever directive, dated November 14, 1947, had concluded that America "has security interests of primary importance in Italy" and that "measures . . . to safeguard those interests should be strengthened without delay," including to "combat Communist propaganda in Italy by an effective US information program and by all other practicable means."[20] For this mission, U.S. officials recommended covert action. Dwight D. Eisenhower, then the army chief of staff, suggested that a list of possible Italian assets be assembled for future operations.[21]

But who would oversee them? Until this point, America had possessed no formal mechanism for covert action during peacetime. Italy inspired change. Initially, the State Department was to carry out covert operations, but Marshall refused the mandate. He believed such programs would be uncovered and thus undermine his department's work elsewhere.[22] Marshall, at least, understood the risks of manipulating a foreign election covertly while advocating liberal ideals publicly.

Truman next turned to the CIA. During World War II, the Psychological Warfare Branch of the Office of Strategic Services (OSS) had spread propaganda across Italy. As the OSS's ultimate successor, the CIA would now do the same. In December 1947, as America's troops left Italy, the White House issued directive NSC 4-A, which authorized the CIA to "initiate and conduct . . . covert psychological operations" abroad.[23] Truman also sanctioned secret shipments of arms to Italy.[24] A generation later, the U.S. Congress would conclude that NSC 4-A "was the President's first formal authorization for covert operations in the postwar period," and that "it was used to undertake covert attempts to influence the outcome of the 1948 Italian national elections."[25]

The starting point of CIA covert action would be electoral interference.

—

While the CIA manipulated Italy's election in secret, the State Department did the same in the light. Overt interference inevitably provokes a backlash—because it is visible and attributable, the benefiting party can be portrayed as a foreign puppet—but Dunn, the ambassador, still felt that such action was worthwhile. In February, he told Marshall that the "full implementation of US policy is essential to an electoral decision by the Italian people for democratic as against totalitarian government." Italians valued America's economic support, Dunn explained, and wanted it to persist. "The issue of friendship with the US will in Italy play fully as great a role in the forthcoming elections as will the internal domestic situation," he wrote. "Every action of the US will have a direct bearing on the outcome."[26] Marshall agreed, cabling that he "concur[s] US actions will have direct bearing on elections, and will take all feasible steps to evince firm US friendship toward Italy."[27]

Much of Washington's leverage came from the European Recovery Program, a massive economic program for Western Europe. Marshall had announced the policy, today known as the Marshall Plan, in June 1947. The Front's leaders claimed that if they won, Italy could still take part in the initiative, even though the Soviet Union had declined to participate and ordered its Eastern European satellites to do the same. In early 1948, Dunn urged Marshall to rebut the Front's claims publicly and loudly, and, in the process, turn the Marshall Plan into a tool of electoral interference.[28]

After receiving Dunn's cables, Marshall declared in a March speech at the University of California, Berkeley, that a Communist-led Italy would *not* receive Marshall Plan aid. "If [the Italian people] choose to vote into power a Government in which the dominant political force would be a party whose hostility to this program has been frequently, publicly and emphatically proclaimed," Marshall said, "this Government would have to conclude that Italy had removed itself from the benefits of the European Recovery Program."[29]

Marshall's message reverberated across Italy, reaching impoverished voters who believed a better future was contingent upon American assistance. "His language is crystal clear," observed Italy's *Il Tempo* newspaper, which reported that a Front victory would result in the "suspension of American aid with resulting economic catastrophe in Italy." Italy's left-leaning publications reacted scathingly. "Marshall's language clearly shows how [the] US intends to use aid as electoral weapon of blackmail against [the] Italian people," read the Communist-affiliated *l'Unità* paper. For the Christian Democrats, Marshall's speech was a political gift. The Italian government worked with American officials to produce six million posters and, with the Vatican's approval, ten million prayer cards about the benefits of American aid.[30]

Italian voters had a choice: America's open hand or its closed fist. Back in Washington, other parts of the government raised the stakes still higher. In conjunction with Marshall's announcement, the Department of Justice, citing a decades-old law, announced that it would not permit Italians who supported the Communist Party to enter the United States. "There sh[oul]d be no doubt left [in the] minds [of] Ital[ian]s that policy [in] this regard [is] unchanged," Marshall wrote to the U.S. embassy in Italy. This rule had the potential to influence millions of voters; the State Department estimated that as many as fourteen million Italians wanted to move to the United States.[31]

With these sticks also came carrots. American aid continued to flood Italy. In February, Dunn urged Marshall to ensure that the United States kept providing Italy with wheat; otherwise, De Gasperi's government would have to reduce bread rations. The following month, Truman signed an order transferring twenty-nine merchant ships to the Italian government. As more and more assistance arrived, Dunn, recognizing its psychological power, personally welcomed every hundredth delivery.[32]

This overt interference had costs, which Marshall recognized. In a cable to Dunn's embassy, he emphasized the importance of "offset[ting] possible communist attacks against US 'interference.' " De Gasperi often had to rebut accusations that he was a tool of the United States. On one occasion, he told Italian lawmakers that "there is nothing servile in accepting American aid," which he described as a "free gift." Directing his comments at Communist politicians, De Gasperi said, "You should explain this to the working masses. If, after giving them the facts, you should decide to do without American help, you should say so and assume full responsibility for your attitude."[33] Italy's struggling economy offered De Gasperi much-needed cover.

But there were limits to what Washington could accomplish overtly. All of its tactics had a common weakness: None targeted voters personally, based on their individual views and biases. The State and Justice Departments, at least, lacked the means to engage in such behavior.

—

Italian Americans picked up the slack. Between 1876 and 1930, five million Italians had immigrated to the United States; many retained connections to their native country.[34] As April approached, the sizable Italian American community became a weapon of electoral interference, participating in a project that at the time seemed spontaneous.

The public face of this effort was Generoso Pope, the owner of the largest Italian-language newspaper in the United States. Ahead of Italy's April election, Pope executed a clever idea: to use his newspaper to influence Italian voters. He urged readers to mail anti-Communist letters back home, into the mailboxes of their friends and relatives. "I knew that the only way to beat the Communists was to have the people of Italy know the truth," Pope said at the time. "I started the campaign, realizing that the people of Italy would believe the truth when it was told by a brother, or a friend, or a blood relation."[35]

The idea spread quickly. Other non-state actors, from the Roman Catholic Church to more Italian-language newspapers, pressed their followers to take part in what became known as the "Letters to Italy" initiative. Victor Anfuso, a New York–based lawyer and OSS veteran, distributed 250,000 pre-written form letters for Italian Americans to sign and mail home. Anfuso's letter read, in part, "We implore you not to throw our beautiful Italy into the arms of that cruel despot Communism." Another form letter, distributed in New Jersey, warned, "If you should vote for the Communists or the Left-wing Socialists you will become the slaves of Russia."[36]

—

As letters poured into Italy, American officials were euphoric. Even the typically pessimistic Dunn was uplifted. "Surge of letters and packages mainly to southern Italy from America definitely is harming Front vote prospects to extent that loud protests have been made," he told Marshall on April 7. The State Department encouraged Italian Americans to keep writing letters, and just before the election the U.S. government expedited mail deliveries to Italy.[37]

In all, Italian Americans sent an estimated *ten million* messages to Italy. In one town in New York, more than 40 percent of

Italian American residents took part in the campaign. John Ellis, a Republican politician who traveled to Italy in April, found that the letter writing was "heard all over" the country, in what can best be understood as a primitive form of micro-targeting. In 1948, loved ones could influence voters on a personal basis. The major cost of the initiative, as with Marshall's speech, was that it was not a secret. Italy's Communist leaders swiftly denounced the letter writing as foreign interference.[38]

The letter writers were not alone in influencing Italy's politics. In an open statement, luminaries such as Eleanor Roosevelt and Henry Stimson expressed solidarity with Italians struggling against "the threat of oppression and slavery." Famous Italian Americans like Frank Sinatra, Rocky Graziano, and Joe DiMaggio broadcast similar messages across Italy. (One Christian Democratic campaign poster read, "Even Hollywood stars are against Communism.") And private American companies sent anti-Communist films to cinemas in Italy. Just before the election, an estimated five million Italians were watching them each week.[39]

Italians' psyches were under assault from all angles as a result of American efforts to influence their opinions ahead of the election. In their mailboxes were letters begging them to vote against the Front; in their theaters were anti-Communist productions; on their radios were celebrities urging them to back De Gasperi; and in their newspapers was a clear warning: Voting Communist meant sacrificing Marshall Plan aid and the ability to enter the United States.

—

Events beyond Washington's control shaped aspects of foreign interference in Italy's election. The most important had unfolded in February 1948, when Communists staged a coup d'état in Czechoslovakia. The value of the Italian lira plummeted in reaction to fears that Italy's Communist Party would similarly seize power. Christian Democrats used these concerns to highlight the stakes of the election. The party's manifesto stated, in part, that the "recent tragic experiences" of Eastern European countries had elucidated the treachery of Communism and that Italians had to decide between "Bolshevik totalitarianism and sincerely democratic parties."[40]

In the United States, the Czechoslovak coup assured the passage of the Marshall Plan. Truman urged a joint session of Congress to approve the plan, citing "the tragic death of the republic of Czechoslovakia" as well as the ongoing effort of a "Communist minority to take control" of Italy. Lawmakers voted in favor of the bill, and on April 3 Truman signed it into law at a high-profile ceremony, just fifteen days before Italy's election.[41]

The Czechoslovak coup also alarmed the Roman Catholic Church, which, alongside the United States, had been influencing Italy's election. Not only did the Vatican instruct its clergy to vote, but Church leaders also encouraged their followers, especially women and nuns, to turn out on Election Day in opposition to the Front.[42] On March 10, Pope Pius XII issued a directive to priests. "In this grave moment," he said, "it is your right and duty to draw the attention of the faithful to the extraordinary importance of the forthcoming elections." All citizens who could vote, he stressed, must do so. "Anybody who abstains, especially because of laziness or cowardice, commits a grave sin—a mortal transgression."[43] The pope had "placed the whole weight and influence of the Catholic Church behind the Christian Democratic party," *The New York Times* reported. On March 28, in his Easter address, the pope gave what the U.S. media described as "one of the most political speeches he has ever uttered." Appearing in St. Peter's Square, he told more than 150,000 worshippers that "the great hour of Christian conscience has struck."[44]

The interests of Washington and the Vatican were aligned. Moscow saw only conspiracy. A leading Soviet newspaper reported that "the subversive activity of the Vatican is inspired in every way by American military authorities in Italy." Knowing the Roman Catholic Church held immense influence in Italy, the Christian Democrats took advantage of its support. One of the party's slogans was "God can see you in the secrecy of the election booth, but not Stalin."[45]

The CIA, meanwhile, closely tracked this confluence of overt electoral interference. The agency recorded internally how the Vatican and the State Department were working against the Front. One CIA report said that "to assure the defeat of the Communists," Dunn wanted America to send more supplies to Italy in support of

De Gasperi's government. Another explained that the State Department had recommended taking "every opportunity" to illustrate the "close support being given to the Italian people by the western powers."[46] When overt and covert mechanisms are deployed jointly, intelligence officers often study the former to enhance the latter.

—

Behind the scenes, CIA officers—with limited time, experience, and tradecraft—were interfering in the election covertly. By the end of 1947, the CIA had dispatched a special operations team to Italy. "We very hastily moved to support the Christian Democrats," F. Mark Wyatt, who participated in this effort, said in retirement. In January 1948, Defense Secretary James Forrestal pushed Roscoe Hillenkoetter, the CIA director, to expand operations in Italy.[47] The CIA's methods had to be unattributable; otherwise, they would backfire. "The United States saw fit to conduct a covert operation in Italy," Clark Clifford, then the White House counsel, later testified. "Had they done so openly, it not only would have been counterproductive, but I think it would have assured a Communist victory."[48]

What the CIA did in Italy during those crucial months has long been kept secret. More than seven decades later, many files relating to the operation remain classified. Inside the CIA, however, the History Staff has full access to these documents. The head of this department is David Robarge, who became the CIA's Chief Historian in 2005. Robarge spends much of his time writing classified histories based on classified sources. One summer morning in 2019, he met me at a coffee shop near Langley, Virginia, where we spent several hours discussing the CIA's history of electoral interference, including and especially in Italy.

As our conversation progressed, it became clear that the CIA had been intimately involved with overt tactics that had appeared spontaneous. When asked about the makeup of the CIA's operation, Robarge cited initiatives that ostensibly had nothing to do with the agency: "the letter-writing campaign from the U.S." and "working with the church." In March 1948, an NSC directive had said to "immediately initiate in this country . . . [a] letter-writing campaign by private citizens, regarding the political issues in Italy."[49] But still, wouldn't the letter-writing initiative have happened without the CIA? "I can't say whether anybody would have either come up with the idea or reinforced it the way we did," Robarge responded, since the CIA was "facilitating it through American contacts, principally the church, but also the ethnic communities in New York and Boston and elsewhere."[50]

The same went for the Roman Catholic Church's propaganda campaign. The church opposed the Communist Party on its own initiative, Robarge said, but the CIA "piggybacked" on its efforts by "making them more expansive [and] more robust." To Robarge, it was this synergy between the overt and the covert that made the CIA's operation more effective than any funding from the Soviet Union. "Ours is much more tactically savvy because of the tradecraft," he explained. "The Communists did not have a letter-writing campaign, the Communists did not work with the Catholic Church, etc., etc. You can just baldly see the differences."

And then, of course, there was cash—lots of it. "We had bags of money that we delivered to selected politicians, to defray their political expenses, their campaign expenses, for posters, for pamphlets," F. Mark Wyatt has said. With these funds, Christian Democrats and other anti-Front politicians could better reach and manipulate voters. "We bought that election," Donald Gregg, who worked for the CIA from 1951 to 1982, told me. "It is a classic example of how really interfering in another country's political system can pay off, if you're convinced that it needs to be done, as we were."[51]

Some historians have claimed that the CIA expended as much as $10 million interfering in Italy's 1948 election (roughly $107 million in 2020 values), although no known source corroborates this figure. One report by the U.S. Congress in the mid-1970s pegged spending at just $1 million, far less. The truth, Robarge said, is in the middle. "It was several million," he maintained. "It was a very high-priority operation and one that the U.S. was committed to seeing through."[52]

Much of the propaganda that the CIA funded had a specific purpose: to frighten. "Mainly it was to scare the Italians into not voting for the Communists," Robarge said, including by spreading disinformation. Some pieces of propaganda warned that the Communists would stage a coup d'état in Italy, as they had in Czechoslovakia.

Others raised the specter of the Soviet military inside the country. "The point here was to get out the vote, in part by scaring people," Robarge explained. "It was spending a lot of money, sending people to do the work to get people to vote: knock on doors, organize rallies to stir up pro-western voter centers, and scare people against the Communists."[53]

In executing this operation, Wyatt claimed that the CIA worked directly with De Gasperi, the Italian prime minister. "Certainly, De Gasperi was witting and engaged with us," Robarge confirmed. "He's certainly aware the funding is coming in, he knows where it's going, he's approving its use and its distribution. . . . We haven't recruited him, we don't control him, but [there's] a relationship." The agency also collaborated with lower-ranking Christian Democratic officials. "You have an effective party with a ground structure, why not use it?" Robarge asked. The CIA relied on its party contacts, he explained, for "passing the money around, making sure it got into the right hands, letting us know about upcoming rallies, letting us know that they were in touch with certain media individuals, that kind of synchronization of activities."[54] The U.S. embassy was operating alongside the CIA. In the weeks preceding the vote, Dunn's team functioned, by his own account, as a "political action committee" working to defeat the Front.[55]

The CIA focused on manipulating the psyches of Italian voters. Today, billions of people have uploaded their psyches onto the internet, exposing them to targeted manipulation. The platform is new, but the goal of shaping people's views is not. For renowned diplomats like George Kennan, whose writings had provided a foundation for the strategy of containment, psychological tactics held immense promise.[56] At a public lecture prior to Italy's election, he said, "It would be a mistake to consider psychological measures as anything separate from the rest of diplomacy."[57]

—

The CIA did have limits, though: Its officers focused on changing minds rather than changing actual ballots. The CIA has "hardly ever" altered votes directly, Robarge said, and the agency did not stuff ballot boxes or bribe election officials in Italy.[58] With the

CIA's operational files still classified, some of the agency's work has undoubtedly escaped the historical record. What is certain, though, is that the CIA enhanced overt tools, spread misleading and incendiary propaganda, and funneled millions of dollars into De Gasperi's campaign.

—

But would it be enough? Because the CIA was influencing voters rather than altering votes, its work brought no guarantees. This uncertainty unnerved Kennan, who, during the Italian campaign, was serving as the State Department's first-ever director of policy planning. On March 15, 1948, he sent Marshall, his boss, a top secret cable proposing even bolder action. "It would clearly be better that elections not take place at all than that Communists win in these circumstances," he wrote. The message continued,

> I question whether it would not be preferable for Italian Government to outlaw Communist Party and take strong action against it before elections. Communists would presumably reply with civil war. . . . This would admittedly result in much violence and probably a military division of Italy; but we are getting close to the deadline and I think it might well be preferable to a bloodless election victory, unopposed by ourselves, which would give the Communists the entire peninsula at one coup and send waves of panic to all surrounding areas.[59]

For Kennan, the question was how, not whether, to manipulate Italy's democracy. His proposal—basically, to cancel the election—lacked the subtlety of electoral interference. His colleagues felt that such rash action would prove self-defeating. John Hickerson, a senior State Department official, scribbled onto Kennan's memorandum the many reasons why he opposed this "drastic" and "unwise" recommendation. "Instead, U.S. Govt. should do everything it properly can to strengthen non-communist forces and parties," Hickerson wrote, endorsing electoral interference anew.[60] Kennan's idea was a nonstarter, but it reflected Washington's priority at the time: to defeat the Communists and maintain its influence over Italy, even if that meant violating the country's electoral sovereignty.

Kennan's letter points to a broader issue for interfering actors: the need for contingency planning. In any election that attracts foreign attention, the question lingers of what will come after the vote of interest. In this case, American officials feared that Italy's Communists would claim in defeat that the race was "not free," stage riots, and mount a coup d'état. Italians, too, braced for chaos. "There is no doubt that the Communists intend in the more or less distant future to plunge Italy into a frightful civil war," the *Tempo* newspaper reported just before the election.[61]

There was also the possibility that the United States would stage a coup d'état if the Front prevailed. Kennan had already proposed canceling Italy's election. In February, the left-wing *l'Unità* and *Avanti!* newspapers alleged that the Italian government intended to call off the contest. A CIA memorandum from March 1948 read that if the Front won, its "actual accession to power might be prevented by falsification of the returns or by force." On Truman's orders, the United States had been smuggling arms and supplies to the Italian military. "The CIA has its emergency plans," Victor Marchetti, a Cold War–era CIA officer turned agency critic, later said, for if Italy's leftist parties won a national election. "Support to Italian colonels would not be lacking."[62]

—

Italy's election had become a dual contest: one between the Front and the Christian Democrats, and the other between Moscow and Washington. TASS, the Soviet news agency, emphasized American "interference" in the election. From the other side of the world, *The New York Times* summed up the dynamic with the headline "The Great Issue in Italy: Russia or the U.S." Inside Italy, this superpower competition had become a key campaign issue. Communist politicians warned that "every vote for De Gasperi is a vote for Truman," while Christian Democrats retorted that "every vote for Togliatti is a vote for Stalin." To increase turnout, the Vatican rescheduled church services so that its followers could get to the polls. Come

Election Day on April 18, a remarkable 92 percent of eligible voters cast their ballots.[63]

In the end, it wasn't even close. The Christian Democrats triumphed with 48.5 percent of the vote, compared with just 31 percent for the Front. "Most interpret results primarily as striking defeat for communism," Dunn reported. And critically, the Front's leaders announced that they would respect the results. (Soviet officials had, behind the scenes, discouraged Togliatti from resorting to violence.) The right-wing *l'Ora* newspaper ran the headline "No to Stalin!," while *The New York Times* declared that the "U.S. has scored over Russia in worldwide battle."[64]

Reactions were swift and emotional. Pope Pius XII announced his "profound joy." Truman celebrated publicly. At a news conference, he said, "I know that free peoples everywhere will be encouraged by the outcome of the recent Italian elections." A few weeks later, Italy received its first Marshall Plan delivery.[65] Towns like Gravina reaped the benefits.

Members of the Italian Left fumed. Togliatti attributed his defeat to "the intervention of foreign powers and the Vatican," while *l'Unità* accused the Catholic Church of manipulating its followers. Pivotal elections can divide a country, especially when a foreign actor involves itself in the contest. Much of America's operation had been overt, exposing its hand and, in the process, polarizing Italy's electorate. Many Front voters felt they had been tricked into participating in an unfair election.[66]

Some Americans, too, protested Washington's interference. Just before the election, about eighty individuals, including a U.S. senator, had sent a joint telegram to Truman requesting "an end to all outside interference with democratic electoral procedure" in Italy. "The Italians are not a savage people who need to be taught what to do," they wrote. "No American would tolerate Italian interference in American elections." Foreign interference in a U.S. election, though, was unthinkable at the time. Washington was operating from a position of strength: As a well-established democracy, its elections seemed impenetrable.[67]

The most consequential reactions to De Gasperi's victory unfolded in CIA headquarters. For America's intelligence officers, the outcome had confirmed the value and potential of covert electoral interference. "It was very, very exciting," Wyatt recalled. "I mean, we were euphoric: 'We've won this one, and we'll win others.'" Within the U.S. government, this operation became legend and inspiration. "Italy was always raised as one of the successes that we had staged," said Bobby Inman, the CIA's deputy director in 1981 and 1982. John Negroponte, the U.S. deputy national security adviser toward the end of the Cold War, likewise said, "The policy makers of the next generation, they all remembered Italy, and the threat of Communists taking over, and the huge effort we made to prevent that from happening, when we went in big-time to influence things."[68]

When an interfering actor's preferred electoral outcome is achieved, it is tempting to attribute the result to covert action. But the historical record paints a more uncertain picture. The CIA was in its infancy in 1948. It lacked not only a playbook but also experience. After the election, CIA officers, while triumphant, had no evidence that their tactics, which were just part of a broader operation, had made the difference. Maybe Marshall's speech was the decisive factor, or maybe De Gasperi would have won unassisted. "We still argue about it," Robarge said. "The best we can say, even at this late date, is that we probably gave the [Christian Democrats] enough of a margin [of victory]—a big margin—to be able to say the election was honest, the Communists lost fair and square, and there's no reason for them to take to the streets."[69]

Robarge's assessment is entirely plausible but, in tracking the development of American foreign policy, largely irrelevant. In Washington's collective imagination, the CIA had rescued Italy's democracy. The CIA's work "resulted in the Christian Democrats essentially dominating Italy for the next fifty years," commented Joseph Wippl, a Cold War–era CIA officer, "and certainly it was in our interests to support them." When I pressed Wippl, though, he recognized that he did not know if the agency had accomplished what he had just claimed it did. "If you were to ask me, 'Joe, can you prove that that $10 million we spent in that election actually resulted in the election result?' I can't. It maybe would have happened anyway."[70]

No proof was needed. America's preferred party had won. And influential voices noticed. After 1948, Averell Harriman, a close adviser to Truman, and Allen Dulles, the CIA's powerful deputy director, pressed for further interference in Italy's elections.[71] Dulles, in 1951, warned that the Italian Communist Party "constituted a continuing threat to democratic government and even to the security of the NATO forces in Western Europe." Dulles further argued that the Christian Democrats—whom he described as "complacent and somewhat feeble"—would not act boldly on their own. "They may be prepared, however, with some backing from us and if persuaded by our seriousness, to take on, one by one, a series of measures to cripple the Communist Party."[72] Psychological warfare applies not only to the masses: Often, covert interference involves manipulating friendly officials, too.

Dulles advocated an aggressive posture. He called for a surge in covert support for "patriotic citizens" in the "press, radio, motion pictures and like media," as well as efforts to "break the strength" of Communist-aligned labor unions. At the end of his cable, he concluded that "it should be a major point of American and of NATO policy to cripple these Communist Parties, to uncover their true intentions, to sow discord in their ranks and promote defection, to deprive them of privilege and respectability, and to drive them underground."[73]

The CIA went to work. After 1948, it funneled almost $65.2 million into Italy (roughly $582 million in 2020 values) over the course of twenty years. Nearly 84 percent of those funds, or $54.6 million went to the Christian Democrats and related organizations, while the rest went to "other non-Communist parties and affiliates."[74] Dunn, for his part, suggested in 1951 that "a most effective way of combating Communism is . . . in such a way that the workers are approached on a personal basis."[75] But by then, targeted forms of interference had become difficult to execute. No future election elicited as much emotion as that of 1948, making another letter-writing campaign unfeasible. America needed a new playbook for a new moment.

The CIA picked William Colby, a young and ambitious intelligence officer, for the job. In 1953, he moved to Rome, where he spent the next five years manipulating Italy's elections. In his memoirs, he described the effort as "by far the CIA's largest covert political action program undertaken until then or, indeed, since—an unparalleled opportunity to demonstrate that secret aid could help our friends and frustrate our foes without the use of force or violence." America's preferred parties used the CIA's money to execute newsletter, leaflet, and poster campaigns, as well as to organize public rallies, membership events, and voter registration drives— all to reach and influence the masses. "More was needed than the sporadic election year support," Colby explained, "especially since Moscow was covertly pouring in massive support to the Italian Communists."[76]

Colby was especially passionate about the media. While in Italy, he recruited a newspaper editor to whom he could feed anti-Communist stories, which other outlets then reproduced. Thomas Fina, an embassy official in Rome, later said that the United States had "the tilting power to shift decisions marginally one way or another" in Italy, including by "subsidizing the publication of books, the content of radio programs, subsidizing newspapers, [and] subsidizing journalists."[77] Colby rarely contacted the recipients of CIA funds directly. Most of the time, he worked through third parties, or cutouts, which protected both the agency and its beneficiaries.[78]

—

America was intent on keeping its hand hidden. Dulles wanted measures deployed against Italy's Communists to "be covert not overt" and "presented to the people as independent" developments.[79] Dunn, the ambassador, likewise concluded that "the most effective action in influencing the Italian people away from Communism would be that taken . . . without too much evidence of American participation."[80] His attitude had evolved since 1948, when much of America's operation was visible and attributable. The second-term Truman administration, convinced that overt tactics would backfire, informed as few people as possible about the CIA's work. This secrecy stretched across presidencies. In January 1953, the CIA director, Walter Smith, briefed Dwight D. Eisenhower, Truman's successor, on world affairs. During the briefing, one of Eisenhower's advisers said the "remarks of our aiding the Italian elections" should not be shared with members of Congress—a suggestion promptly "agreed upon" by the room.[81]

The CIA equated its effectiveness with which party led Italy. By this measure, every election was encouraging. The Christian Democrats governed through 1994, by which point the Cold War had ended. The perception inside Washington was that the CIA had changed Italy's future. "Our accomplishments could not be measured in short-term ways," Colby acknowledged in his memoirs. But he insisted that in the long term the CIA had strengthened the Christian Democratic Party, divided the Front, and therefore "did succeed." He then launched into a passionate defense of covert electoral interference:

> The charge has been leveled that the United States and, most certainly, the CIA have no business "interfering" in the domestic political affairs of another sovereign nation, that their assistance to one side or another in an election there is not only illegal but immoral. . . . [If] military "interference" is accepted, then surely lesser forms of interference can be justified under the same conditions. The test involves both ends and means. The end sought must be in defense of the security of the state acting, not for aggression or aggrandizement, and the means used must be only those needed to accomplish that end, not excessive ones. In this moral and philosophical framework, assistance to democratic groups in Italy to enable them to meet the Soviet-supported subversive campaign there can certainly be accepted as a moral act. It was clearly for the defense of the United States and its NATO allies against the danger of Soviet expansion, and the financial and political support given was plainly a low-key and nonviolent means of acting for that end. This framework cannot justify every act of political interference by CIA since 1947, but it certainly does in the case of Italy.[82]

Figures like Colby, who went on to direct the CIA, had come to believe in covert electoral interference, just as the Cold War expanded in scope and intensity. In 1950, Truman's foreign policy team filed NSC 68, a top secret document advocating, in part, the need for "operations by covert means in the fields of . . . political and psychological warfare."[83] Covert action, initially limited in use, became central to American foreign policy. In 1953 alone, the CIA executed hundreds of covert action projects across forty-eight countries.[84] Electoral operations were central to this web of activity. Miles Copeland, who joined the CIA in 1947, later summarized this evolving dynamic: "In an election in such-and-such a country, the Soviet KGB backs a candidate, the CIA backs a candidate, and the CIA candidate wins."[85]

Decades later, in 1984, William Colby married Sally Shelton, his second wife and a former ambassador, eight years after retiring as CIA director. Colby suggested a destination wedding, with a specific location in mind: Venice, Italy.

"I think he wanted somehow to reconnect with Italy through marrying me, given our respective backgrounds, since we both loved Italy and both spoke Italian," Shelton-Colby told me, reminiscing about her late husband. "He had a thing for Italy, a certain fascination for the country," she recalled, as his time there "was one of the highlights of his career."

Colby forever felt attached to the country he thought he had saved. Not long after their wedding, he and Shelton-Colby traveled there again. While strolling on a side street, Colby noticed a poster for the Democratic Party of the Left, the successor to the Communist Party, which had disbanded. He asked his wife to photograph him next to it. "We did it," Colby told her, staring at the poster, tears in his eyes. "The U.S. did it."[86]

Chapter 3

THE EXPLOSION

From Italy emerged an era of covert electoral interference. The Italy operation became "a template," explained David Robarge, the CIA's chief internal historian, for what the agency then did "in many, many countries around the world."[1] The appeal of this tactic was obvious: The costs were manageable, the loss of life was zero, and the payoff seemed substantial. Influencing an election to the detriment of a certain politician was also more palatable than, say, staging a coup d'état against that politician (as both Moscow and Washington did, in select cases, including CIA operations to topple the elected leaders of Iran and Guatemala in the early 1950s).

Manipulating democratic elections in the name of democracy might seem contradictory. But during the Cold War, in what felt like an existential battle with the Soviet Union, the ends appeared to justify the means. "It was 100 percent ensuring that you got a government that was pro-U.S. as opposed to pro-Soviet," said Bobby Inman, the CIA's deputy director in 1981 and 1982. "Everything was seen in the light of bipolar: You are either with us or you are against us."[2] American policy makers feared that Communist politicians, once in power, would abandon the democratic model, as they had in East Germany, Hungary, Czechoslovakia, Poland, and elsewhere in Eastern Europe. These precedents provided officials in Washington with a moral rationale for covert electoral interference: better to undermine undemocratic candidates at the ballot box than let those candidates take power and unravel their democracies from within. Manipulating voters in the short term, the argument went, protected the rights of those same voters in the long term.

While the CIA escalated its covert operations, the KGB did the same, targeting democracies everywhere. "The Cold War affected everyone in the world," writes historian Odd Arne Westad, and without it "Africa, Asia, and possibly also Latin America would have been very different regions today."[3] It should be said that comparing the CIA with the KGB is a fraught business. Domestically, there is no comparison: The KGB terrorized its citizens in a way that America's equivalents never did. But on electoral matters, after 1948, both Soviet and American intelligence had entered "the game," as various CIA officers put it. "This issue of intervening in elections was part of a comprehensive strategy, which both sides were doing," said Arturo Muñoz, who joined the CIA in 1980. "We were a mirror image of each other."[4]

Colby and Wyatt, while in Italy, had suspected that Moscow was bankrolling the Front, but lacked conclusive evidence. Now it seems all too clear. In the 1980s, the Soviet Union, despite its economic struggles, still used the KGB to distribute $200 million (roughly $480 million in 2020 values) to the Communist Parties of eighty countries.[5] Although Italy's Communist Party never took power, the KGB kept supporting its campaigns. Plan A was a Communist victory, but Plan B was what happened instead: Communist candidates receiving significant popular support. In foreign elections, America's sole measure of success was whether its preferred parties triumphed. Moscow, by contrast, saw advantages to performing well in defeat. The robust standing of Italy's Communist Party—in 1976, it received more than 12.5 million votes—lent Moscow influence abroad and propaganda at home. State-sponsored news outlets could advertise that in Italy, a country entrapped in America's sphere of influence, millions of citizens still desired Communist rule.

For Moscow, covert electoral interference was a win-win. So the KGB provided Italy's Communists with $6.2 million in 1972 and $6.5 million in 1976, hoping for victory but reaping benefits regardless.[6] Beyond bankrolling campaigns, the KGB funded news outlets, bribed journalists, and spread disinformation. Ahead of the 1974 election in France, where the Communist Party boasted considerable support, the KGB carried out dozens of "significant operational measures" designed to advantage François Mitterrand, the head of the left-wing coalition, over Valéry Giscard d'Estaing, his right-wing rival; one such measure involved circulating a fake document connecting Giscard's policies with the murder of one of his relatives. Mitterrand narrowly lost, but the interference persisted. In 1979 and 1980, the KGB's Paris station planted 287 news articles, held 146 "influence conversations," spread disinformation verbally seventy-eight times, and disseminated leaflets, books, and forgeries. The money also kept flowing. Ahead of another election, the French Communist Party received $2 million from Moscow, but its leader, Georges Marchais, was not yet satisfied. He wrote Mikhail Gorbachev, the Soviet leader, requesting more "emergency financial aid." The KGB dutifully delivered another $1 million.[7]

Compared with their American counterparts, Soviet intelligence possessed an advantage—a lack of boundaries and accountability—and a disadvantage: They had no background in professional campaigning. The Soviet Union never held a competitive election, so the initiatives that the CIA concocted in Italy, like voter registration drives, were unfamiliar to the KGB. But Moscow made up for its lack of experience with sheer will.

Targeted countries had at least one feature in common: They held competitive elections. Much of the world did not, and the countries that did were typically in America's sphere of influence. For the CIA, unlike the KGB, manipulating an election often meant manipulating an ally.[8] Such was the case with Japan, the target of a three-pronged electoral interference operation executed by the CIA in the 1950s and 1960s. The first component involved delivering money and campaign advice to key members of the right-wing Liberal Democratic Party (LDP). The motivation was familiar—to preserve a friendly government—as was the method: The CIA used cutouts, or middlemen, to transfer the funds. "In effect the LDP was kind of in our pocket," Robarge said. The second component, authorized in 1959, was to sow division within Japan's leftist bloc. And third, the CIA ran a well-funded propaganda operation aimed at manipulating Japanese citizens.[9]

Each of these tactics had originated in Italy and had since become a part of the CIA's playbook: subsidizing campaigns, dividing the opposition, and influencing voters' minds. The effort appeared successful. The LDP governed without interruption from 1955 to 1993. "The principle was certainly acceptable to me," U. Alexis Johnson, a former U.S. ambassador to Japan, said in 1994. "We were financing a party on our side."[10]

In certain instances, Washington used covert electoral interference to establish rather than merely preserve its influence over another country. Before Guyana's 1964 election, the CIA, hoping to unseat Cheddi Jagan, the country's left-wing leader, provided the opposition with money and counsel. "Jagan must be defeated in the next election," Dean Rusk, then the secretary of state, cabled President Lyndon B. Johnson. The operation, again, seemed to pay off. Forbes Burnham, America's preferred candidate, was able to form a majority coalition. But as was so often the case, CIA-led interference in Guyana did not end with a single contest.[11]

As the next election approached, the CIA worked to "assure" Burnham's continued success at the polls.[12] In this instance, the United States, while influencing voters, also showed a tolerance for altering the actual vote count. In 1968, Burnham won the election by a wide margin—by cheating. Policy makers in Washington had known about his plans in advance. "When the U.S. Government learned that Burnham was going to use fraudulent absentee ballots to continue in power in the 1968 elections, it advised him against such a course of action, but did not try to stop him," the State Department recently acknowledged. In all, from 1962 to 1968, the CIA spent more than $2 million on its covert action programs in Guyana, which Burnham ruled until his death in 1985.[13]

In Washington, covert electoral interference had earned a reputation for effectiveness. When the CIA got involved, America's preferred candidate always seemed to win. Henry Kissinger, a famed practitioner of realpolitik, advocated such operations while serving as national security adviser, a position he assumed in 1969. A German refugee with a PhD from Harvard, Kissinger was known for identifying hidden opportunities to advance America's interests. In 1970, he told President Richard Nixon about an "excellent" CIA memorandum detailing "covert programs to offset the threat of

Communist election victories in the Free World," from Chile to Guyana.[14] Kissinger then sent Nixon the full document, part of which read,

> There have been numerous instances when, facing the threat of a Communist Party or popular front election victory in the Free World, we have met the threat and turned it successfully. Guyana in 1963 and Chile in 1964 are good examples of what can be accomplished under difficult circumstances. Similar situations may soon face us in various parts of the world, and we are prepared for action with carefully planned covert election programs when U.S. policy calls for them.[15]

The case of Chile—top of mind for both the CIA and Kissinger— was unique in several respects. At a time when Moscow and Washington were targeting elections globally, CIA interference in Chile proved unusually extensive and unusually representative of the tools the agency used to interfere in elections. And because the U.S. government has declassified many of its Chile files, the CIA's work there can be examined in exceptional detail.

While Italy marked the beginning of CIA-led electoral interference, Chile marked its peak.

—

Porter Goss much prefers to discuss his work as CIA director under President George W. Bush than his work as an intelligence officer a generation earlier. What Goss saw and did for the CIA is legend within the agency. After graduating from Yale in 1960, he joined the CIA's clandestine service. "It was men from Yale, Harvard, Princeton, gentleman-type organizations, working with extremely loose rules in terms of gentlemen knowing what was right or wrong," Goss told me on his porch in the Florida Keys. Even now, Goss speaks, thinks, and acts like a spy. "You see a nice thing that happened," he proposed excitedly. "Maybe it's an election; maybe the good guys win an election. If nothing that you can observe seems out of the ordinary, 'oh, isn't that a good thing, and it just happened,' well, guess what: It happened because of covert action."[16]

Goss recalled why the CIA became so involved in Chilean politics. "It was worries about what was going on in our hemisphere, defending the Monroe Doctrine, are Communists moving into our quarters, do we have stable governments," and, above all, it was about *Allende.*

In interviews with Goss and his contemporaries, the same name always arose: that of Salvador Allende, a Chilean politician whom the CIA relentlessly worked to undermine. Allende was born to privilege in 1908 in the town of Valparaíso. As a young man, he was twice jailed for his political activism while pursuing his medical degree. A year after graduating, he founded the Chilean Socialist Party alongside fellow Marxists. He spent his adult life operating at the highest levels of Chilean politics. Well educated, deliberate, and ambitious, he was elected to the Senate in 1945. He first ran for president in 1952 but lost resoundingly. Six years later, in 1958, he ran again and came within thirty-three thousand votes of victory. Many Chilean analysts had anticipated that Allende would perform well, as a result of a decline in real wages, entrenched wealth inequality, and swelling resentment of the American companies that controlled copper mines in Chile. Washington, though, was caught off guard: A self-described Marxist had nearly won an election in the Western Hemisphere.[17]

Then, in 1959, Fidel Castro seized control over Cuba.[18] Allende soon visited and met with Castro, to whom he became personally close. The CIA warned internally that "Communist influence has been rising in Latin America," threatening "all aspects of US-LA relations—diplomatic, economic, and cultural." The KGB, meanwhile, drew inspiration from Castro's rise. Oleg Kalugin, then based in New York, said that "isolating America" from countries in its hemisphere was a "major strategic part of the anti-America battle."[19]

In this environment, Chile's 1964 election, in which Allende would again compete, captivated Washington. As in Italy, the logic of containment applied to Chile. The U.S. embassy in Santiago assessed that an Allende administration would pursue the "drastic reduction [of] US influence in Chile and the Hemisphere," marking a "defeat for US policy" and prompting "alarms from the U.S. press and business interests."[20] The loss of Chile would also reflect poorly on the Alliance for Progress, America's massive aid program for Latin America, for which Chile was meant to be the showcase.[21]

Worst of all, Allende sought to take power through a competitive election. "Another 'Castro' in the Hemisphere, particularly one who achieved power through the democratic process in a country where we have invested the highest rate of per capita assistance, would be awfully tough to handle," reported a U.S. embassy official in mid-1964. A *Time* article similarly warned that Chile would be the first country in the Western Hemisphere to elect a Marxist president. The CIA feared other countries would then follow suit.[22]

———

As America plotted in secret, the Soviet Union did as well. Washington suspected what the KGB archives now confirm: Allende was cooperating with Soviet intelligence. Svyatoslav Kuznetsov, a KGB colonel, established contact with Allende in 1953 and assigned him the code name "Leader." Through the 1950s, they met in various Latin American countries and established a "friendly and trusting" bond.[23] Moscow began providing Chile's Communist Party—which belonged to Allende's coalition—with an annual subsidy, ranging from $50,000 to $400,000.[24] The KGB recorded that, in 1961, a "trusting relationship" as well as "systematic connection" with Allende had been "solidified." The archives read,

> In that period, Allende declared his readiness to confidentially cooperate and provide necessary help since he considered himself a friend of the Soviet Union. He readily shared political information and, at the KGB's request, took direct actions to protect Cuba and took steps to establish diplomatic relationship between Chile and the USSR.[25]

Moscow hoped Chile would enter its orbit. Kalugin explained, "We were trying just to widen and strengthen the pro-Cuban left-wing—any movement in Latin America or Central America which would be friendly toward Fidel Castro, and thus be a pro-Soviet regime."[26] The CIA was convinced that both the Soviet Union and Cuba were supporting Allende covertly. In March 1964, President

Lyndon B. Johnson's daily intelligence briefing conveyed that Cuba had "agreed to provide funds" for Allende's campaign. The next month, the CIA relayed that Che Guevara, a revolutionary in Cuba, "obviously believes that Allende, who has visited Cuba often and is being bankrolled in part by Havana, will win the presidential election in the fall."[27]

With Allende again on the ballot in September 1964, and with America's adversaries backing him, the stage was set for a massive operation of CIA-led electoral interference.

—

The CIA enjoyed considerable autonomy in its early years. The agency could approve internally covert action programs it deemed "low risk" and "low cost." For more sensitive operations, the CIA director would deliver classified proposals to a committee, or Special Group, of senior government officials. Members included the chairman of the Joint Chiefs of Staff, the deputy secretary of defense, the undersecretary of state for political affairs, and the national security adviser. The Special Group acted as judge and jury. It could authorize covert operations without alerting Congress or even the president. Richard Helms, CIA director from 1966 to 1973, later explained that this arrangement provided plausible deniability. "The mechanism . . . was set up," he said, "to use as a circuit breaker so that these things did not explode in the president's face and that he was not held responsible for them."[28]

Covert electoral interference requires advance planning. The CIA laid the groundwork for operations in Chile in 1961, when it established relationships with select political parties, as well as networks through which to distribute propaganda. By March 1964, with the election seven months away, McGeorge Bundy, the national security adviser, was under pressure to formulate an actual strategy.[29] The election had effectively become a two-way contest between Eduardo Frei, a Christian Democrat, and Allende's Popular Action Front, a coalition of Socialists, Communists, and smaller left-wing parties. Allende was campaigning on a policy gambit that Frei had rejected as risky and provocative: nationalizing U.S.-controlled copper mines.[30]

For Washington, the path forward was clear: Support Frei, and keep Julio Durán of the Radical Party in the race as a third-party candidate. Durán stood no chance of victory, and the CIA believed his candidacy would benefit Frei more than it would Allende.[31] "Generally speaking, we should simply do what we can to get people to back Frei," Gordon Chase, a White House aide, told Bundy, lest Allende win the presidency, nationalize the copper mines, and, in the process, increase Moscow's influence over Chile.[32]

In the Christian Democratic Party, America found a willing partner, as it had in Italy. In late March, Frei's advisers visited the U.S. embassy in Santiago, where they painted a grim portrait: His political operation was struggling to cover its $100,000 monthly expenditures but needed to spend three times that to run a winning campaign. The Chileans then requested $1 million in assistance. Embassy officials left the meeting with two impressions: first, that Washington could and should provide the funds but, second, that this assistance should be delivered covertly and through third-party cutouts. Direct contact would invite unnecessary risks. The embassy urged the Special Group to ensure that funding for Frei's campaign "not seem to come from U.S. sources."[33]

At 3:30 p.m. on April 2, the members of the Special Group gathered in the White House Situation Room to consider a CIA proposal to interfere in Chile's election. The plan, budgeted at $750,000, included eight specific steps. Some concerned high politics, such as bribing certain politicians to back Frei. Others involved financing specific organizations—such as women's, peasant, youth, and labor groups—and executing "specialized propaganda operations, some of which will be black, to denigrate Allende." Both of these tactics revolved around manipulating voters' minds. More aggressively still, the proposal authorized a more direct form of interference: "in the latter stages of the campaign to buy some votes outright if required."[34]

The Special Group approved the CIA's plan. Its members also settled a contentious question: whether to keep the agency's hand hidden from Frei himself. Embassy officials in Santiago had advocated non-attributability; the CIA felt otherwise. The agency's top priority was to secure a Frei victory. Its secondary priority, though, was to develop influence over his government. Achieving victory was thus a means to a still further end: for Frei to know to whom he owed his power. "An effort should be made to achieve greater influence over [Frei] by modifying the Special Group restriction on non-attributability," Joseph King, a senior CIA official, had urged. "Funds could be provided in a fashion causing Frei to infer United States origin of funds and yet permitting plausible denial."[35]

The Special Group sided with the CIA. "Attribution of U.S. support would be inferred but there should be no evidence of proof," the committee decided.[36] In this operation, the CIA would attempt to manipulate the masses *and* the benefiting candidate.

—

To oversee the operation, the CIA, White House, and State Department formed an interagency electoral interference committee. Its members included Thomas Mann, an assistant secretary of state; McGeorge Bundy, the national security adviser; Ralph Dungan, his special assistant; and Desmond Fitzgerald, a CIA official. A parallel committee worked out of the U.S. embassy in Santiago. Its members included the CIA station chief, the U.S. ambassador, and senior embassy officials.[37]

The chain of command reached the very top. On April 29, the CIA director, John McCone, and Secretary of State Dean Rusk spoke twice about Chile's election. A few weeks later, Bundy forwarded a memorandum about the CIA's operation to Lyndon B. Johnson, along with a brief cover note. "In essence, the problem we face is that a very popular and attractive candidate, named Allende, who has thrown in his lot with the Communists, has more than a fighting chance to win," Bundy wrote. "We have a coordinated Government-wide program of action to strengthen his opponent. . . . [W]e will be watching it very closely, but I do think you ought to know about it yourself."[38] On a subsequent call with Mann, Johnson sought more information, evidently balancing a desire for plausible deniability with the need to manage his own intelligence services. "What are our problems now?" the president asked. "What are the hot ones?

You got an election in Chile." Mann asserted back, "We're going to win this election in Chile, things look good, we've done a hell of a lot of work on that."[39]

The CIA's covert operation ran on two tracks: directly supporting Frei's campaign, and disseminating propaganda among the masses. For Frei's campaign, the agency provided money and helped conduct polls, register voters, and get out the vote. It was an American-like campaign, exported to Chile. As for propaganda, the CIA circulated films, pamphlets, posters, leaflets, and mailings. Some of the information spread was standard fare; some, less so. " 'Disinformation' and 'black propaganda'—material which purported to originate from another source, such as the Chilean Communist Party—were used," the U.S. Congress has acknowledged.[40]

Taking a page out of its Italy playbook, the CIA invested heavily in another scare campaign, spreading depictions of Soviet tanks and the Cuban armed forces. This fearmongering especially targeted women, who had overwhelmingly opposed Allende in the last presidential election. One poster warned, "Chilean Mother: Fidel Castro sent 15,000 children to Russia, tearing them from their mothers' arms. If you don't want to lose your children, vote for Durán."[41]

The CIA also corrupted Chile's media, recruiting reporters, columnists, and editors. Some planted anti-Allende stories, while others suppressed anti-American articles. The CIA financed wire services, magazines, and a weekly newspaper. By the end of June, a single CIA-funded propaganda group was producing twenty radio spots, issuing five news broadcasts, and distributing three thousand posters per day—all to persuade Chilean voters to oppose Allende.[42] This wide-ranging effort was not cheap. Between May and July, the Special Group—renamed the 303 Committee—approved another $1.75 million for the operation. The CIA also transferred three more officers to its Santiago station.[43]

Targeting voters' minds was, as always, a gamble. Frei might win; he might lose. Still, Bundy left as little as possible to chance. One of his advisers put it well: "We can't afford to lose this one, so I don't think there should be any economy shaving in this instance. We assume the Commies are pouring in dough; we have no proofs.

They must assume we are pouring in dough; they have no proofs. Let's pour it on and in."[44]

All told, the CIA spent $3 million (roughly $25 million in 2020 values) on its operation, a remarkable amount, given that fewer than three million Chileans would actually vote in the election. More remarkably still, the United States funded over half of Frei's campaign.[45] In the pre-digital era, manipulating an election at scale required substantial investment.

Washington remained publicly silent as the CIA carried out its covert operation. In August, Chile severed its diplomatic ties with Cuba. Bundy promptly informed Johnson that "our friends in Santiago" hoped the White House would provide no comment. "If we look as if we are interfering in any way," Bundy explained, "it will be bad for our friend Frei."[46] The CIA had forecast in various memoranda that Allende would lose the election, and that his supporters might "resort to violence" in defeat. At a National Security Council meeting, Dean Rusk predicted that Frei would triumph "partly as a result of the good work of CIA."[47]

—

Then came September 4: Election Day. The Santiago embassy sent hourly updates to the State Department, which forwarded them to the White House. The CIA's projections proved prescient. At 9:10 p.m., Allende conceded. He then urged his followers to accept the outcome. Fears of violence abated.[48]

Frei had not just won; he had won in a landslide, receiving 56 percent of the vote compared with Allende's 39 percent and Durán's 5 percent. For the first time in decades, a Chilean presidential candidate had secured an outright majority. "Frei, Victor in Chile, Vows Cooperation with the U.S.," read a front-page *New York Times* headline. In his inaugural address, Frei called for renewed commitment to the Alliance for Progress.[49] America's man indeed.

In Washington, the credit for Frei's performance went to the CIA, in what appeared to be yet another success for covert electoral interference. The agency bragged internally about Frei's "smashing" victory. The CIA had secured Frei's majority, John McCone told the 303 Committee, and this outcome had delighted certain American businessmen. Today, the CIA's best assessment, according to David Robarge, is that "Chile '64 and Italy '48 are somewhat analogous" in that the CIA had "provided a cushion for Frei."[50]

Regardless of the effectiveness of the CIA's operation, Johnson—himself competing in an election—reaped political benefits from Frei's victory. In a news conference, he declared the outcome a victory for democracy. Johnson also made sure to specify that the contest "was an internal matter in which the people of Chile were the only judges of the issues." In private, Frei thanked the U.S. ambassador in Santiago for Johnson's comments and for the American embassy's "discretion and cooperation" during the campaign.[51]

The new leader of Chile was indebted to a foreign nation. He hoped this debt would remain hidden. John McLaughlin, a Cold War–era CIA officer who later directed the agency, explained, "You always had to weigh the question of whether by interfering in an election you would be exposed and that would play to the disadvantage of the side you were favoring, because you'd make them appear like puppets."[52]

Such was the case with Frei. The scale and scope of the CIA's operation in Chile proved too significant to go unnoticed. *Time* and *The New York Times* had both reported that it was "no secret" that America favored Frei. And just before the election, Radio Moscow had alleged that Chile was "swamped with agents of the CIA."[53] Rumors that Frei was an American puppet dogged his presidency and tarnished his electoral legitimacy. "In Chile in 1964, there was simply too much unexplained money, too many leaflets, too many broadcasts," Congress later found. "That the United States was involved in the election has been taken for granted in Latin America for many years."[54]

—

In defeat, Allende remained a political force, ready and waiting to pursue the presidency after Frei's six-year term. In those intervening years, however, Washington changed, as Lyndon B. Johnson deployed hundreds of thousands of soldiers to Vietnam. In 1968 alone, nearly seventeen thousand American soldiers died there—prompting major protests at home—and a beleaguered Johnson decided not to seek reelection.[55]

Amid this instability, Chile's politics seemed relatively stable. To manipulate Chile's 1965 congressional election, the 303 Committee sanctioned just $175,000. For the 1967 municipal election, it approved no funds at all. America was still directing overt aid into Chile, but money for covert electoral interference had dried up just as conditions in Chile were deteriorating.[56] The CIA reported in a series of memoranda that Frei was enduring an "upsurge of strikes for higher wages," "serious inflation," "economic stagnation," and political isolation.[57] Frei had moved to "Chileanize," or partially control, copper mines, but many voters remained unsatisfied, and most of his other reforms had failed. In March 1968, the CIA warned that Chile's struggling economy could catapult leftist parties into power.[58]

Even still, the CIA spent just $200,000 interfering in Chile's 1969 congressional election. For this operation, the agency worked to undermine the left rather than promote a specific party. After Frei's victory in 1964, Mann, the assistant secretary of state, had told CIA representatives that America was not in the business of helping one "non-Marxist" group defeat another, because *that* would amount to intervention. The CIA abided by this line. In 1969, its officers supported candidates of varying party affiliations competing against members of Allende's coalition in swing districts. "The basic concept is to undertake a district by district analysis of the voting patterns and electoral trends in each district so that we can determine where covert leverage can be most effectively applied," explained William Broe, a senior CIA official, prior to the election. Of 180 races, the CIA identified just twelve candidates worth backing. Even for such a limited effort, the CIA noted internally, "the risk of exposure is always present in an election operation."[59]

Ultimately, ten of the twelve U.S.-backed candidates won. But Richard Helms, the CIA director, was not feeling celebratory; Frei now predicted that Allende would make a "very strong bid" in the upcoming presidential election, scheduled for September 1970. Helms urged advance planning. "CIA has learned through experience that an election operation will not be effective unless an early enough start is made," he told the 303 Committee in April 1969. "A great deal of preliminary work is necessary." Helms's argument fell on deaf ears, as the newly inaugurated Richard Nixon and his national security adviser, Henry Kissinger, focused on other issues.[60] In January 1970, a Popular Unity coalition chose Allende as its nominee for the election, to compete against Radomiro Tomic of the increasingly unpopular Christian Democratic Party and Jorge Alessandri, a right-wing candidate and former president.[61]

Unlike in 1964, little momentum existed in Washington for covert electoral interference. Neither of Allende's competitors held obvious appeal. Tomic was "running a distant third," the CIA reported, while Alessandri was of "advanced age" and boasted an "undistinguished record."[62] Washington had also evolved: New personalities held positions of power. Many were reluctant to act. At an interagency meeting, John Crimmins, a senior State Department official, said he was skeptical that the United States should involve itself in the election at all. Edward Korry, the U.S. ambassador to Chile, said that he, too, "would not be unhappy if we decided to do nothing," although he did worry about the political risks of inaction, since an Allende victory would reflect poorly on the Nixon administration.[63]

Perhaps seeking to protect themselves, the officials settled on a half measure: an operation to undermine Allende's candidacy. The 40 Committee (the 303 Committee, renamed) approved this plan. The budget: a mere $125,000. "If Allende is the threat the paper posits, should we not do more than we propose to insure his defeat?" Viron Vaky, an adviser to Kissinger, asked in response.[64]

—

For its operation, the CIA adopted familiar tactics: disseminating black propaganda, spreading posters and leaflets, and planting articles in outlets like the influential *El Mercurio* newspaper. "The difference with *El Mercurio* was it was not a rag," said Jack Devine, who was stationed in Chile as a CIA officer from 1971 to 1974. But the agency was working with limited funds and had abandoned several key tools: polling, grassroots organizing, and direct support for a specific candidate.[65] The CIA had also become a "potent . . . political target" in Chile, according to *The New York Times,* as Allende's allies alleged that Frei had won the presidency with the agency's help. This fraught environment, the CIA cautioned internally, was "not conducive to the mounting of a large-scale election operation."[66]

The CIA's restrained mandate made some of Nixon's advisers nervous. In June, Helms told Kissinger that the agency was in "a quandary as to what action" to take in Chile. That same month, the 40 Committee approved an additional $300,000 for the CIA's operation, largely at Kissinger's urging. "I don't see why we need to stand by and watch a country go communist due to the irresponsibility of its own people," he told his colleagues. Vaky, still skeptical of the plan, had told Kissinger that "there is no guarantee it would have any real effect."[67] The $425,000 that the 40 Committee had approved was far less than the $3 million spent in 1964, and no money was going directly to Allende's opponents. "If the funds approved in March were much too little, those reluctantly voted at the end of June were far too late. (They were also too little)," Kissinger later wrote.[68] (Kissinger, through a representative, declined to be interviewed for this book.)

Washington was bringing a butter knife to a gunfight. Allende had his own benefactors. Cuba had transferred roughly $350,000 into his campaign, and the Soviets were supporting him as well.[69] In early 1970, the KGB sent Kuznetsov, Allende's contact, back to Chile. "He was tasked with establishing a business relationship with Allende, receiving political information and conducting active operations to benefit Popular Unity," according to the KGB's archives.[70] In addition to a $400,000 annual subsidy for the Chilean Communist Party, the KGB delivered $50,000 to Allende personally and paid a lawmaker $18,000 to remain in his coalition. In July, the Soviet Politburo sanctioned even more funds for Chile's Communists.[71] The KGB also tried to strengthen its hold over Allende. "KGB focused on deepening Allende's anti-American sentiments," the agency's archives read, through a "serious and focused" effort to provide Allende with "information gathered by the KGB residency in Chile about the actions of American agents."[72] For years, the CIA had been manipulating Chilean politics. The KGB now turned this hidden history to its advantage.

While the KGB assisted Allende, the White House hesitated. In July, Kissinger requested a report on how the United States should react to an Allende victory.[73] National Security Study Memorandum 97 (NSSM 97), submitted in response on August 18, had a two-pronged argument. On the one hand, Allende would seek to establish an "authoritarian Marxist state," and his victory "would undoubtedly provide Marxists everywhere with an enormous boost in morale and in propaganda." But on the other, Chile mattered little in the broad sweep of American foreign policy. In 1964, Washington had judged Allende a major threat. But at this critical moment, NSSM 97 concluded that "the U.S. has no vital national interests within Chile."[74]

Allende was, evidently, not such a threat after all. And regardless, the CIA believed that he would lose. In the president's daily briefings, Allende was portrayed as overexposed and faltering, while Alessandri was said to have a "slight lead."[75]

But Allende actually won the election, receiving 36.6 percent of the vote, next to Alessandri's 35.3 percent and Tomic's 28.1 percent.[76] The scenario that Johnson's administration had worked so hard to prevent in 1964 had come to fruition six years later. The CIA, changing its tune, described Allende's victory as a "political watershed" but did not reflect upon the failure of its operation.[77] David Robarge said the agency now assesses that it came up short because of a dearth of resources and preparation, as well as the decision not to assist a specific campaign. "They didn't bite the bullet on it," commented Jack Devine, the former CIA officer. "What they authorized was stupid, a denigration campaign against the Socialists, but not support for either candidate."[78]

It is, of course, possible that Allende would have triumphed even if the CIA had acted more aggressively. But his margin of victory was just thirty-nine thousand votes, and the CIA's operation was, as the Senate put it, "much smaller" than it had been in 1964. Kissinger, for his part, was filled with regret. "Had I believed in the spring and summer of 1970 that there was a significant likelihood of an Allende victory," he wrote in his memoirs, "I would have had an obligation to the President to give him an opportunity to consider a covert program of 1964 proportions, including the backing of a single candidate."[79]

—

The Nixon administration had forgotten a key lesson of Italy: Covert electoral interference succeeds when it is sustained. The 1964 operation, as extensive as it was, only helped to delay Allende's victory. While Frei's election marked a triumph from the perspective of the CIA, the 1970 election marked an unforced error.

And in its aftermath, the White House entered into crisis.

—

Richard Nixon now faced a question that Harry Truman and Lyndon B. Johnson had avoided: what to do when covert electoral interference fails. Because Allende had achieved only a plurality of support, the Chilean Congress would vote on whether to elect him or Alessandri, the second-place finisher. If Nixon hoped to prevent an Allende presidency, he had to act before October 24, when this vote would take place. The choice was stark: further subvert Chile's democracy, or allow Allende—whom American analysts had so recently deemed an inconsequential threat—to take office.

For Nixon, it was not much of a dilemma at all. Ahead of October 24, the CIA assaulted Chile's political system to an extraordinary degree, all to keep Allende out of power.[80]

One of the CIA's tactics involved rigging the congressional vote through a concentrated operation of covert electoral interference. Back in August, Kissinger had authorized planning for vote buying, in case Allende won a plurality.[81] Altering ballots was the backup option for a reason. "The buying of congressional votes is a far more sensitive operation than a propaganda campaign, and would have penalties for disclosure far more heavy and wide-ranging," warned Charles Meyer, an assistant secretary of state.[82] But manipulating the masses had failed. The contingency plan was to purchase a congressional majority for Alessandri, who could then resign and call for a new election. The result would, in effect, be an electoral do-over. At least one step in this sequence of events actually happened.

On September 9, Alessandri announced that he would step down if he won the vote, triggering a second election. And on September 14, the 40 Committee authorized $250,000 for vote buying.[83]

But interfering in the congressional vote quickly proved impractical. Given Allende's sizable coalition in Chile's two-hundred-person Congress, the CIA estimated that he needed the support of just eighteen additional lawmakers to secure a majority, and that its officers would have to persuade not one, not two, but several dozen representatives to back Alessandri.[84] Although the $250,000 was still approved, none of it was spent. The likelihood of exposure was too high, as was the number of votes to be purchased. And Frei, plagued by electoral insecurity, would not participate in the scheme.[85] As Helms had warned, when it comes to covert electoral interference, planning is paramount. The CIA was a day late and a dollar short.

Working with limited options, Kissinger had also requested a "cold-blooded assessment," according to the 40 Committee's meeting minutes, of the "pros and cons and problems and prospects involved should a Chilean military coup be organized now with U.S. assistance."[86] By this point, the White House had authorized two types of electoral interference: influencing minds and altering votes. Neither had succeeded, so the CIA turned to other ideas. "It is reasonably clear, in exploring avenues to prevent an Allende government from exercising power, that (a) the political/constitutional route in any form is a non-starter," the CIA cabled its Santiago station. As a result, the cable continued, "the only prospect with any chance of success whatsoever is a military [coup]."[87]

In Italy, officials like William Colby had argued, and genuinely believed, that their actions were democratic at heart. No such sentiment existed here. "We don't want a big story leaking out that we are trying to overthrow the Govt," Nixon told Kissinger on September 12.[88] In a phone call two days later, Secretary of State William Rogers conveyed a similar message to Kissinger:

> R: My feeling—and I think it coincides with the President's—is that we ought to encourage a different result . . . but should do so discreetly so that it doesn't backfire.
> K: The only question is how one defines "backfire."

R: Getting caught doing something. After all we've said about elections, if the first time a Communist wins the U.S. tries to prevent the constitutional process from coming into play we will look very bad.

K: The President's view is to do the maximum possible to prevent an Allende takeover, but through Chilean sources and with a low posture.[89]

Debates about the threat posed by Allende persisted in these hectic weeks. On September 14, Viron Vaky, Kissinger's adviser, described a coup as "impossible" to execute and ill-advised. "What we propose is patently a violation of our own principles and policy tenets," he wrote of further intervention in Chile. "If these principles have any meaning, we normally depart from them only to meet the gravest threat to us, e.g., to our survival. Is Allende a mortal threat to the US? It is hard to argue this."[90]

But only Nixon's opinion mattered, and he wanted to thwart Allende. On September 15, the president ordered Helms to foment a coup d'état in Chile, which set off a chain of events that has been detailed in other works but is briefly examined here, for insights into what can follow an unsuccessful covert electoral interference operation.[91]

"1 in 10 chance perhaps, but save Chile!" Nixon instructed Helms, per the CIA director's handwritten notes. "Not concerned risks involved . . . no involvement of embassy . . . $10,000,000 available, more if necessary . . . full-time job—best men we have . . . make the economy scream."[92] The next day, Helms briefed his team on Nixon's directive, to which neither the Defense and State Departments nor Ambassador Korry was alerted. A cable from CIA headquarters to its Santiago station relayed that "it is firm and continuing policy that Allende be overthrown by a coup" and that it would be "much preferable to have this transpire prior to 24 October but efforts in this regard will continue vigorously beyond this date."[93]

And so the CIA sought to topple a democratically elected government. As part of this effort, the agency engaged with two groups of Chilean military officials planning to kidnap General René Schneider, the head of the Chilean Armed Forces who had pledged to accept Allende's government. The CIA has itself explained, "Schneider was a strong supporter of the Chilean Constitution and a major stumbling block for military officers seeking to carry out a coup to prevent Allende from being inaugurated."[94] At 2:00 a.m. on October 22, the CIA delivered submachine guns to one group of Chileans. A few hours later, the other group ambushed Schneider and shot him to death. (Later, the CIA provided a member of this cohort with $35,000 to "keep the[ir] prior contact secret.")[95]

Schneider's death prompted a moment of national unity inside Chile, at a time when America's aim was to sow division. Thousands attended his funeral, after which Frei and Allende together led pallbearers out of a Santiago cathedral. Rumors of CIA involvement in the murder immediately circulated. "All of these people have been trained by the CIA," Chilean senator Aniceto Rodríguez alleged at the time.[96]

Allende, meanwhile, adeptly removed the roadblocks to his confirmation. On October 24, he won the congressional vote. A few days later, he announced that three Communist Party members would serve in his fifteen-person cabinet. And on November 3, he was sworn in as president.[97]

Over the next three years, the CIA spent millions of dollars seeking to destabilize Allende's government.[98] Jack Devine, who took part in these operations, had hoped that the White House would learn from Alessandri's defeat in 1970 and authorize "big-time political action" in future elections. But, he continued, Chile "never got there." On September 10, 1973, the young Devine, tipped off by sources inside Chile, cabled Washington: A COUP ATTEMPT WILL BE INITIATED ON 11 SEPTEMBER.[99] Indeed, on September 11, the Chilean military overthrew Allende's government; Allende himself committed suicide before he could be taken into custody. Afterward, Augusto Pinochet, a Chilean general, established a repressive military dictatorship.[100] Chilean democracy had died with Allende. (It was not until December 1989 that Chile again held a competitive election, after which Patricio Aylwin, the victor, succeeded Pinochet as the country's leader.)

The road to Allende's downfall had begun a decade earlier, when the United States first targeted Chile's elections, as part of a global strategy of covert electoral interference. When Allende won the presidency, in 1970, Nixon was unwilling to accept this outcome. He cared more about destroying Allende than maintaining a foreign democracy. One form of covert action—electoral interference—gave way to another: coup plotting. Although the CIA was not directly involved in Allende's eventual overthrow, historian Peter Kornbluh concludes that the Nixon administration "sought, supported, and embraced the coup."[101]

"Our objective was not to preserve a free democratic election process in Chile," Morton Halperin, an adviser to Kissinger in 1969 and 1970, testified a few years later, after the CIA's covert action programs there had been outed publicly. "Our objective was very simple. It was to keep Salvador Allende from coming to power," including by "intervening in elections," "creating false propaganda," and pushing the military toward "overthrowing the constitution."[102]

Chapter 4

THE STASI CHANGES HISTORY

Half a world away, a spectacle was unfolding in West Germany. On April 27, 1972, its citizens gathered around radios and televisions; journalists prepared to file breaking news stories; and in the White House, Richard Nixon and Henry Kissinger awaited updates. Willy Brandt, the West German chancellor, would learn his fate in just a few minutes.

Rainer Barzel, the conservative opposition leader, had called for a vote of no confidence within the Bundestag, the West German parliament. If successful, the motion would result in Brandt's removal. It would also mark the end of his conciliatory foreign policy, Ostpolitik, designed to renew ties with the Soviet Union and its Eastern bloc.[1] Barzel needed the support of a majority of lawmakers to take power. This concentrated electoral process could redirect West Germany at a pivotal moment in the Cold War. Since becoming chancellor in 1969, Brandt, the head of the Social Democratic Party, had negotiated reconciliation agreements with the Soviet Union and Poland. If he fell, these agreements would fall with him.

One by one, lawmakers entered a booth and marked their voting cards with a "yes" or "no," or, to abstain, left the card blank.[2] All ballots were anonymous. Brandt watched, stone-faced, as his colleagues determined his future.

For the Soviet Union, however, the stakes were too high to do nothing. Behind the scenes, the East German Stasi, on orders from Moscow, worked to succeed in West Germany where the CIA had failed in Chile: to rig a parliamentary vote of succession. "We were a very good team and could count on each other and did what was necessary," Horst Kopp, a former Stasi officer who participated in this covert operation, told me in Berlin, forty-five years later.[3]

After lawmakers cast their ballots, the president of the Bundestag motioned for silence, results in hand. West German citizens held their breath. So did Soviet and East German officials, who would soon learn whether their plan had worked.

—

Covert electoral interference operations often reflect the character of the states that execute them. In America, presidential elections occur every four years, so CIA officers instinctively knew how to export traditional campaign techniques to faraway places. William Colby's work in Italy, and the 1964 operation in Chile, benefited from this familiarity with competitive campaigning.

The Soviet Union and its Eastern European satellites had a far different domestic experience. Competitive elections were not held, and secret police terrorized citizens. The KGB and its peer agencies like the Stasi, East Germany's security service, proved most adept at exporting the tool kit of a surveillance state: bribery, blackmail, and psychological warfare. At opportune moments, Eastern operatives could use these weapons to manipulate foreign electoral processes. Such was the case in April 1972.

The road to the Stasi's operation had begun years earlier, when its intelligence officers set their sights on two men: Julius Steiner and Leo Wagner. Both were conservative members of the Bundestag who drank heavily, chased women, and amassed debts. Both were thus ripe for recruitment. "Irresponsible habits are all classic signals that someone can be recruited, and money was always the go-to tool for people in debt," said Donald Gregg, a CIA operations officer for almost the entirety of the Cold War.[4]

Steiner, the first lawmaker, was a junior member of Barzel's conservative bloc, made up of the Christian Democratic Union (CDU) and Christian Social Union (CSU). He needed money to support his lavish lifestyle. "He was a drinker, seeking women, in debt," recalled Kopp, who worked for the Stasi from 1960 to 1985 as a member of Department X, a branch of its foreign intelligence division. In exchange for cash, Steiner began feeding information to

East German officers as early as 1970.[5] The intelligence he provided was documented carefully in the Stasi's files:

> SA7301219: Foreign policy measures of the CDU.
> SA7301725: The current situation and the process of differentiation in the CDU/CSU resulting from the disputes over the basic contract.
> SE7301717: Efforts by CDU politicians to reach an agreement with the FDP.
> SE7301719: Proceedings within the CDU and CDU/CSU factions regarding the struggle for leadership positions.[6]

The second target, Wagner, was a high-ranking member of Barzel's conservative bloc. The Stasi studied him closely, recording his home address and birthday, political activities, and family details: "Catholic, married, two children."[7] In 1961, Wagner was elected to the Bundestag; he quickly became a rising star. Wagner was a friend and "close confidant" to Franz Josef Strauss, the longtime head of the CSU. By 1971, he was one of the conservative bloc's parliamentary managing directors.[8]

In public, Wagner appeared confident and ambitious. He even had a nickname: Handsome Leo. In private, however, he was near financial and personal ruin. While campaigning for the Bundestag, he frequently took out loans that he then struggled to repay. He was a regular at high-end clubs like Chez Nous, where he spent up to 4,000 deutschemarks (roughly $7,800 in 2020 values) each night on champagne and caviar. A married man, Wagner carried out several affairs at once. "Leo Wagner, for us he was the mysterious Leo," Hans Korneli, a former bartender at Chez Nous, recalled in a documentary about Wagner produced by his grandson. "He was a real VIP guest and a very reserved person." Wagner's longtime driver, Wolfgang Jankowiak, described him as a "politician by day, and by night, in these bars, a totally different person."[9]

Wagner's reckless behavior tore his family apart. "I basically buried him long before his death," Ruth Schwarzer, his daughter, said in the documentary. Wagner spent most of his time in the West German capital, Bonn, away from his wife and children, who lived in his home district. His Bonn apartment had a back entrance, so visitors—including mistresses—could visit without detection. On one occasion, Elfriede, Wagner's wife, called without warning; another woman answered the phone. "You whore," Elfriede yelled, before hanging up. She pleaded for a divorce, but Wagner, ever mindful of his reputation, refused. "You'll never get a divorce. It's out of the question," he screamed, based on Ruth's recollection. Elfriede, trapped in a loveless marriage, descended into alcoholism and depression. She soon died of cancer. A distraught Ruth then attempted suicide by drinking ant poison. She fell into a weeks-long coma but ultimately survived.[10]

The instability of Wagner's personal life made him vulnerable. "We tried to recruit Leo Wagner because he was so open to attack, especially for financial reasons," Kopp explained. Wagner tried to hide his indiscretions. He succeeded at least partially: His colleagues did not notice his self-destructive behavior. For the Stasi, this disconnect presented an opportunity.

The recruitment of Wagner was a complex affair. It began when he met Georg Fleissman, a Bavarian journalist employed by the Stasi, toward the end of the 1960s. As Kopp told me, "You can hardly understand this story without the shining person Georg Fleissman." Fleissman targeted Wagner on behalf of the Stasi, working meticulously to master Wagner as an individual. "Fleissman had Leo Wagner completely under his control," Kopp continued. "He was completely aware of his financial and family situation up to the tiniest detail."[11]

Beginning in 1970, Wagner provided intelligence to Fleissman, who claimed to represent private corporations desiring access to Eastern markets. The Stasi crafted Fleissman's cover story. "It was developed by experts here," Kopp said. "We had faked documents for the trade interest groups with proper names, addresses, and letterheads," all to convince Wagner that Fleissman worked for lobbyists aligned with American rather than Soviet interests. In exchange for Wagner's reports, Fleissman provided cash and insider information about Brandt's coalition, which he claimed to have obtained through his work as a journalist. But Fleissman's actual source was the Stasi.[12]

Over time, Wagner came to depend on these secret payments. He often sent Wolfgang Jankowiak, his driver, to back alleys, where anonymous couriers waited with packages. "It had always been a brown envelope," Jankowiak said in the documentary, "filled with quite some bills." Jankowiak did not know who was providing the money.[13] It is possible that Wagner did not, either, because he worked through Fleissman, a middleman. Sometimes, with covert operations, interfering actors prefer to keep key players in the dark. Whether Wagner knew it or not, this arrangement lent him plausible deniability. "Wagner just wanted to receive the money," Kopp said. "He was deep in debt, and he fully relied on Fleissman [to live] a lifestyle like somebody great without having the means for such a lifestyle."[14] Wagner did not care for whom Fleissman worked; what mattered was what Fleissman could give him.

———

While the Stasi targeted Steiner and Wagner, Moscow was seeking an economic lifeline in high politics. By the end of 1968, Leonid Brezhnev, the Soviet leader, had become insecure about the stability of his sphere of influence, which was rotten from the start. The Soviet Union had established control over Eastern Europe through a liberation turned occupation and then through aggressive electoral interference operations. Lacking access to the ballot box, Eastern Europeans instead expressed discontent through revolt. Between 1953 and 1956, East Germans, Poles, and Hungarians all staged popular uprisings. And in 1968, Czechoslovakia seemed to follow suit by pursuing a series of liberal reforms that Alexander Dubček, the country's leader, called "socialism with a human face."

The Czechoslovak movement, known as the Prague Spring, alarmed Moscow. The events of 1968 "brought upheavals whose effects were long-lasting," Brandt later wrote, even though "the traces of change seemed to vanish swiftly." That August, Soviet and allied forces invaded Czechoslovakia, some twenty years after Communists had seized control of the country. Worried that other states in the Eastern bloc would imitate Czechoslovakia, Brezhnev announced what became known as the Brezhnev Doctrine: A threat to socialism in one country, he said, would be treated as the "common problem" of "all socialist countries." Externally, this pronouncement signaled resolve; internally, it was a bluff that Soviet leaders hoped would deter further dissent. Brezhnev, a lifelong Communist Party member, was a "cautious, reactive, formulaic, and technocratic" figure intent on maintaining a fragile sphere of influence.[15]

What Brezhnev needed was stability, which he hoped to achieve through détente, or deepened cooperation, with the United States and its allies. Engaging with the West could jump-start Eastern economies, which had begun to stagnate. In August 1970, while meeting with Brandt, Brezhnev emphasized that "the Soviet Union is ready to join in wide-ranging economic ventures." Joseph Wippl, a CIA officer stationed in West Germany in the mid-1970s, concluded that the Soviet Union's and East Germany's "real policy was based on just one thing: money, hard currency. They desperately need[ed] it."[16] Beyond economics, a superpower rapprochement would also position the Soviet Union to secure international recognition of Europe's postwar borders, which occurred at Helsinki in 1975, and to demonstrate its continued leadership of the world Communist movement, despite a break with China.[17]

But Brezhnev had a problem: Before achieving a period of détente, the Soviet Union had to mend relations with West Germany, the dividing line between East and West. Tensions over Germany's future had spawned some of the Cold War's most dangerous episodes, including the Berlin airlift of 1948 and 1949, the Berlin crisis of 1961, and the Cuban missile crisis of 1962 (when Washington was convinced that Moscow's *real* plan was to seize all of Berlin).[18] Reconciling with West Germany was the required first step in reaching across the Iron Curtain.

And this is why Moscow so valued Brandt. Before 1969, a conservative coalition had governed West Germany without interruption. Each of Brandt's predecessors had abided by the Hallstein Doctrine, which called for the nonrecognition of East Germany and any state that recognized East Germany (excluding the Soviet Union). Conservative lawmakers also resented that as part of the postwar settlement, Poland had received German lands east of the Oder and Neisse Rivers.[19] Under the Hallstein Doctrine, Kopp said,

East Germany was a "non-state [and] isolated in trade relations, culturally, and politically." But, he continued, Brandt "broke the pattern."[20]

After the 1969 election, Brandt secured a majority coalition and became chancellor. He was determined to be "the advocate of our own interests vis-à-vis the governments of Eastern Europe," and to build new connections with the Soviet Union and its satellites.[21] His objectives aligned with Brezhnev's: to remove Berlin as a Cold War flash point and open West Germany to trade. It was in this context that Moscow sought to preserve Brandt's government.

—

Covert electoral interference is always motivated by security-based concerns, real or imagined. The United States believed that containing leftist candidates would minimize threats to its welfare, identity, and even survival; next came CIA operations in countries like Italy, Chile, and Japan.[22] The Soviet Union had manipulated elections to establish a security buffer across Eastern Europe. The KGB then backed like-minded politicians around the world who, if elected, would provide Moscow with friends abroad and talking points at home that Communism was an appealing ideology. The CIA's and KGB's interference operations varied in their objectives—some were meant to preserve regimes, while others were meant to install new ones—but they all reflected the threats and opportunities of the moment.

The vote of no confidence came at a pivotal historical moment, in which Brandt was center stage. As chancellor, he pursued his conciliatory Ostpolitik, which coincided with Moscow's interest in détente. Brandt first negotiated a treaty with the Soviet Union. In May 1970, Bonn and Moscow reached a preliminary reconciliation agreement.[23] That same month, cracks within Brandt's coalition emerged. He had been updating his cabinet on negotiations, but lawmakers still complained about a lack of transparency. Rumors circulated that members of his coalition might switch sides. During a cabinet meeting, however, Brandt allayed the concerns of his wary allies—for the time being.[24]

The foreign ministers of the Soviet Union and West Germany

finalized their agreement in August 1970, in what *The New York Times* described at the time as "an almost jovial atmosphere."[25] The signatories not only confirmed the boundaries of Europe but also pledged to "improve and extend cooperation between [their two countries], including [in] economic relations." With the agreement complete, Brandt traveled to Moscow, a gesture to which he believed the Soviets would attach "major importance." A visibly thrilled Brezhnev invited Brandt into his office, where they talked for four hours. Then, in a television address, Brandt advertised the merits of what was called the Moscow Treaty, declaring that it was "time to rebuild our relations with the East."[26]

Next, in December, West Germany and Poland agreed to the Treaty of Warsaw. The agreement normalized relations between the two countries and, as in the Moscow Treaty, confirmed their postwar border along the Oder-Neisse line, infuriating conservative lawmakers.[27] While in Warsaw, Brandt, in a scene captured by television crews, fell to his knees after laying a wreath at the memorial to the Warsaw Ghetto Uprising of 1943, when German soldiers had slaughtered Jewish resistance fighters. Brandt, humbly and intentionally, was attempting to reestablish trust with the nations Hitler had terrorized.[28] A transit accord between East and West Germany, signed in 1971, advanced Ostpolitik still further.[29]

Brandt's treaties won him global acclaim, including a Nobel Peace Prize in October 1971. They also made him enemies in parliament. The conservative bloc derided his accolades as premature: The Bundestag had not even debated the accords. While meeting with Brandt toward the end of 1971, Brezhnev, preoccupied with his economic interests, asked, "just between ourselves," whether the Moscow Treaty would be ratified. The answer was anyone's guess. When the Bundestag finally opened debate on Brandt's agreements in February 1972, the conservatives remained fiercely opposed. As Kenneth Rush, the U.S. ambassador to West Germany, warned Richard Nixon, "[The conservatives] oppose détente. They're Catholic and feel you can't deal with the devil."[30]

Admired abroad, Brandt had become an increasingly divisive figure at home. He had failed to anticipate the domestic uproar his foreign policy would generate. He put it best: "The battle over the treaties had become a struggle to overthrow my government."[31] Empowered by a series of defections, Barzel pursued a vote of no confidence. Neither the Soviet Union nor East Germany could stop him from trying to unseat Brandt. An electoral mechanism in the West German constitution, Article 67, permitted a constructive vote of no confidence in the chancellor. "It was really important [whether] to pass those treaties," recalled Joseph Wippl, the former CIA officer. "I must say I give Barzel credit for rolling the dice on the no-confidence vote."[32]

Barzel aimed to reverse, by ballot and at the eleventh hour, the policies of Ostpolitik.

—

Interference in the vote of no confidence had little to do with ideology—Brandt was no Communist—but much to do with the interests of the Soviet Union. "Many in Moscow saw in Chancellor Willy Brandt and his coalition partners for their policies," Barzel, the opposition leader, later wrote.[33]

Moscow worked through Markus Wolf, the Stasi's feared and elusive spymaster. "I knew Wolf personally," said Oleg Kalugin, the former KGB general. "West Germany was totally infiltrated by the East Germans, and Markus Wolf in that sense was their number one man." Wolf led the Stasi's foreign intelligence directorate for more than three decades. In his memoirs, published in 1997, Wolf detailed how he manipulated his targets—most famously, by planting so-called Romeo Spies inside West Germany, who then seduced women with access to state secrets. "The link between romance and espionage is no invention of mine," he wrote. "But if I go down in espionage history, it may well be for perfecting the use of sex in spying." Wolf was comfortable crossing boundaries to achieve his objectives. And, like many in East Germany, he valued Brandt, whom he described as an "engaging, intelligent, [and] morally upright man."[34]

In early 1972, as Brandt's domestic standing faltered, Wolf and other Eastern leaders lent a helping hand. Brezhnev announced that he would consider recognizing the European Economic Community, a precursor to the European Union—a tactical move meant to bolster support for the Moscow Treaty, détente, and Brandt. In February, the East German Politburo temporarily implemented its transit accord with West Germany; more than a million residents of West Berlin then visited the other side of the Iron Curtain. Such maneuvers, all meant to showcase the benefits of Brandt's policies, intensified after Barzel told his colleagues, on April 19, that he would call for a vote of no confidence. Wolf referred to the subsequent week as the "Protect Brandt Week." On April 25, the East German Politburo offered concessions in ongoing treaty discussions to enhance Brandt's reputation as a negotiator. Barzel, by this point, had cried foul. "As Barzel complains, the numerous steps taken by the Soviets or East Germans in the last several weeks have cumulatively had effects on German opinion," a U.S. embassy official in West Germany reported.[35]

Washington watched closely. "This is the first time in the whole postwar history that anyone has attempted a vote of no confidence. It shows how weak [Brandt's] government is," Kissinger, still the national security adviser, told Nixon.[36] Just a year and a half earlier, these two men had attempted to interfere in another parliamentary electoral process, in Chile, to prevent Salvador Allende's confirmation. But on this occasion, America's puppeteers were reduced to spectators.

The Soviet Union, though, was at the center of this saga. Brandt believed that Brezhnev had "staked his entire reputation" on the treaties, while Kissinger predicted that "Brezhnev will be finished if the treaties don't get ratified." For Moscow, the stakes were indeed high—too high, in fact, to manipulate minds and hope for the best. Ballots had to be bought. "Everyone was buying votes," Wolf said in 1996, with a touch of exaggeration and self-exoneration.[37]

The KGB had tried to interfere directly in the vote. In a closed-door meeting, a Soviet representative had asked Egon Bahr, Brandt's adviser, why he was not "buying parliamentarians," and then signaled that Moscow could provide any needed funds. Bahr learned later that the KGB was ready to deliver a "suitcase full of money" for buying votes.[38] Presumably for a host of reasons—both ethical and practical—Bahr refused the advance.

Moscow, desperate to protect Brandt, also activated the Stasi.

"We received a directive from Moscow . . . to do everything we could to keep Brandt in power," Kopp explained, an account confirmed by Wolf and KGB archives.[39] The Soviet Union, lacking the relationships to approach conservative lawmakers directly, had to work through Bahr, a middleman. The Stasi, by contrast, had spent decades penetrating West German society. "The Stasi was everywhere," said Bobby Inman, the former CIA deputy director. Porter Goss "feared the Stasi" while stationed in Europe as a CIA officer in the 1960s. "I would not have put anything past them," he said. "They were thugs with files on everybody."[40]

Because Barzel called the motion just days before it was held, the Stasi had to move quickly. Manipulating an electoral process was not the norm for the Stasi, which focused on information gathering abroad and mass surveillance at home.[41] Rigging the vote presented major risks, including detection. But to protect Brandt, East German officials could not just watch—they had to act.

The Stasi had two aces up its sleeve: Steiner and Wagner, the corrupted lawmakers.

—

As the vote approached, Horst Kopp and his colleagues concocted a plan: to offer both Steiner and Wagner 50,000 deutschemarks (roughly $97,000 in 2020 values) to abstain from the vote of no confidence. The final tally would be close, and robbing Barzel of two votes—Steiner and Wagner belonged to his coalition—could prove pivotal. Kopp, though, was worried about exposing Wagner. "I was partly against using Wagner because I did not want to burn him," he said. But ultimately, he and his colleagues felt they had no choice. Moscow had issued an order, and sustaining Brandt's government was "a question between war and peace," Kopp told himself, because "if the Eastern contracts didn't get ratified, then [Ostpolitik] is finished."[42]

The Stasi next moved to secure Steiner's and Wagner's cooperation. Both men had, by this point, already compromised their integrity, increasing the likelihood that they would accept the bribes. Steiner agreed almost immediately. When pressed by Fleissman, Wagner did as well. "His debts, his position, everything was on the line" in the vote, Kopp said, because "without the money from us, he would have already been bankrupted." The pressure took a toll on Wagner. Ahead of the vote, he took "strong stimulants" to help him remain "above water," according to Benedikt Schwarzer, his grandson.[43]

The day of the vote, Wagner and Steiner joined their colleagues in the Bundestag. By all accounts, Brandt was prepared for his government to collapse. Later, he wrote that he had "accepted the possibility of defeat."[44] But unbeknownst to him, when Wagner and Steiner cast their anonymous ballots, they abstained in service of a foreign power.

Once lawmakers had taken their seats, the president of the Bundestag announced the results: "Dr. Barzel, proposed by the conservatives, has not achieved the majority of the votes." The motion had failed. Only 247 lawmakers had cast their ballots against Brandt—2 short of the 249 required. Members of Brandt's coalition embraced. A few even attempted to hoist him into the air. Barzel, meanwhile, shook his head in disbelief. "Brandt Defeats Move to Oust Him," read the front page of *The New York Times*.[45]

Wagner's and Steiner's betrayals had cost Barzel the chancellorship. Covert electoral interference, sometimes used to generate change, had in this instance prevented change from taking place. While Brandt celebrated, so did the Stasi. "We were all very happy and proud," recalled Kopp, who received a medal for his efforts. High-ranking politicians alluded to the operation privately. Just before the vote of no confidence, East Germany's leader, Erich Honecker, had told Egon Bahr that Brandt would persist "not least with our support and thanks to our measures."[46] Then, in May 1972, Honecker wrote to Nicolae Ceaușescu, the head of Romania, about the effectiveness of his government's methods:

> We took several measures to support the Brandt government shortly before the vote of no confidence that had been presented to the Bundestag by the CDU/CSU. . . . We proceeded because this government is obviously more convenient for all of us than a government under the leadership of Barzel and Strauss.[47]

For Moscow, maintaining Brandt's government came with immediate benefits. Three weeks after the vote failed, the Bundestag ratified the treaties with Warsaw and Moscow. Confidence in Barzel's leadership plummeted. A year later, he resigned as the leader of the conservative bloc. "His stock dropped dramatically when he forced a no-confidence vote against Mr. Brandt in April 1972 and lost by two votes," explained a *New York Times* feature titled "Exit Mr. Barzel."[48]

Brandt, meanwhile, rose to new heights. In the November 1972 election, his coalition secured 272 seats, compared with just 224 for the conservatives, giving Brandt a "firm mandate," according to one press report, "to continue [his] bold Eastern policy of normalizing relations with the Communist states of Europe."[49] The opportunity to reverse Ostpolitik had come and gone. "That second election confirmed the legitimacy of the former vote," Joseph Wippl, the former CIA officer, said. "It re-stabilized the government, and it showed that the majority of Germans were on Brandt's wavelength regarding Ostpolitik."[50]

Relatively simple covert electoral interference operations can alter the course of nations. Consider what would have happened had the Stasi done nothing. In the immediate term, Brandt would have fallen from power, and his treaties with Moscow and Warsaw would not have been ratified. Ostpolitik would have collapsed as a failed and radical foreign policy gambit. As time progressed, Barzel's government would have isolated East Germany anew. The two superpowers, without the groundwork of Ostpolitik, would have struggled to achieve a period of détente. Brezhnev, as Kissinger predicted, might have been ousted as the Soviet leader. And in the long term, the reunification of Germany, precipitated by deepened ties between East and West Germany, would have unfolded entirely differently, as would the trajectory of Soviet history. The very arc of the Cold War, therefore, might have been transformed—if not for covert action.

Today, Brandt is rightly remembered as one of the Cold War's pivotal leaders. "In Willy Brandt," writes historian Timothy Garton Ash, "Germany has a historical figure at least touched with greatness."[51] And yet Brandt owes his legacy, at least in part, to a foreign intelligence service. Despite his talents as a diplomat, he needed the Stasi's help to preserve his chancellorship and, ultimately, to change the world.

—

Nearly everyone had expected Brandt to be ousted. When he wasn't, suspicions immediately arose that someone had paid members of the opposition to abstain. "One or more Christian Democrats . . . obviously voted against Dr. Barzel," read an article the morning after the vote of no confidence.[52] Joseph Wippl encountered ceaseless speculation about interference in the contest. "I knew that a couple of people were bribed in the vote," he recalled. "But I didn't know where the money came from."[53]

The losing side, lacking evidence of foreign interference, was left paranoid and bitter. Franz Josef Strauss, a conservative leader, called the vote's failure "one of the biggest scandals in the history of [West Germany]." In his memoirs, Barzel lamented that "vote buying and national treason were in the game when it got to the stalemate between Brandt and me in the German Bundestag on April 27, 1972. This is how politics was done. Without this illegality, German history, and also my personal life, would have taken a different course." Even Brandt, who benefited from the Stasi's operation, suspected foul play. "Since the ballot was secret, it will never be known how the voting went," he wrote in 1976. "My conjecture that 'corruption' had been at work during the run-up to the vote could not be definitely substantiated, but the whole affair left an unpleasant aftertaste."[54]

Brandt, critically, knew nothing of the Stasi's operation. A foreign power can—and often does—affect electoral processes without coordinating with the beneficiary. It would have been self-defeating to involve Brandt in the scheme. Had his participation been uncovered, his electoral legitimacy would have collapsed—the exact outcome that Moscow hoped to avoid. In 1972 at least, it was in Moscow's interests to preserve the ignorance of its preferred candidate.

A weakness of the Stasi's operation, then, was that its officers could not ensure the silence of Wagner and Steiner, whose self-destructive behavior made them useful before the vote but potential liabilities in its aftermath.

If the Stasi's operation had a fall guy, it was Steiner, whose treasonous behavior was nearly uncovered a year after the vote of no confidence. What is now known as the Steiner Affair was sparked, rather predictably, by Steiner's own indiscretion. During a May 1973 interview with *Der Spiegel,* he said that Barzel had been unfit to serve as chancellor—a scandalous statement from a member of Barzel's coalition. Steiner then claimed that he had abstained from the vote of no confidence as a matter of conscience.[55]

One of the two abstainers had unmasked himself. Days later, reports emerged that Steiner had actually been paid to abstain from the vote; right-wing papers like *Rheinischer Merkur, Bild,* and *Die Welt* proclaimed a "Watergate in Bonn." *Der Spiegel* reported, "Once again, corruption seemed to be involved, this time in the coalition. A member of parliament who only a few insiders knew weeks ago had caused doubts and excitement, accusations and denials."[56]

Steiner covered up his lies with more lies. Abandoning his initial story, he next claimed that Karl Wienand, a lawmaker in Brandt's Social Democratic Party, had given him 50,000 deutschemarks to abstain. *Der Spiegel* confirmed that the day after the vote of no confidence, Steiner had, in fact, deposited 50,000 deutschemarks into his personal bank account. In a June interview, Steiner insisted that he had received the bribe in Wienand's office and that he regretted accepting it.[57]

By this point, the Stasi had no more use for Steiner. His every move was now under scrutiny, his reputation tainted by scandal. Politicians who betray their country lack security; in the blink of an eye, Steiner was left to fend for himself. For the Stasi, his downfall amounted to perhaps the only cost of its interference operation. It was an acceptable loss. Wolf later called Steiner a "mediocre source of information." Kopp, too, dismissed Steiner's value: "No one cared for him anymore, in the West nor in the East."[58]

Of more serious concern for East Germany was whether the Steiner Affair would expose its broader operation. As the press scrutinized Steiner, the Stasi watched closely. The agency's files include press reports alleging that Steiner was one of the two defectors from Barzel's camp, as well as step-by-step coverage of the ensuing scandal.[59] On June 15, 1973, the Bundestag launched a formal inquiry into Steiner. This bipartisan committee aimed to determine "who bribed whom and by what means before Barzel's vote of no confidence in Chancellor Brandt." The Stasi noted in its files that the committee would investigate, in part, whether "foreign intelligence services played a role during the vote and before Steiner's abstention."[60]

But the work of the committee soon stalled. Over the summer, its members struggled to make sense of conflicting witness accounts. "At no point has Mr. Steiner received any money from me," Wienand said in July. Wienand's colleagues came to his defense, testifying that he did not enter his office after the vote, as Steiner claimed. "First round of examination goes to Wienand," reported the *Frankfurter Rundschau* newspaper.[61] The committee presented its final report in March 1974. Its members had reached no firm conclusions. The Stasi's file on Steiner notes specifically that the inquiry had "not determined whether there [were] any connections" between him and the Stasi.[62]

Even with the powers of a special committee, the Bundestag failed to discover the hand of the Stasi, which had used untraceable tools like cash and in-person meetings. By blaming Wienand, Steiner had misdirected the investigation, which devolved into a partisan squabble. Brandt's allies charged that the *real* agenda of the inquiry was to tarnish the chancellor's electoral legitimacy. "The aim of the Steiner affair is to try to drag the Chancellor into it," Horst Ehmke, one of Brandt's advisers, said in September 1973.[63] In hindsight, the committee's existence was more than justified—the vote had indeed been sabotaged—but when the prospect of electoral interference is raised, the parties that might have benefited naturally fear that investigating a vote's legitimacy means risking their own.

—

It can take decades, not years, to uncover the full extent of a covert electoral interference operation. And sometimes, key participants in such operations face no consequences.

Wagner's relationship with the Stasi persisted after the vote of no confidence. In 1975, when reports of his disastrous finances finally emerged, he stepped down as parliamentary managing director. He left the Bundestag late the next year.[64] Sometime before then, Wagner had approached Fleissman in search of money, and the relationship between the two men resumed. Between late 1975 and 1983, Wagner continued to work as an informant, leveraging his enduring access to conservative circles. The Stasi's files, which list Kopp as Wagner's handler, contain forty-one entries summarizing the materials Wagner provided in this period.[65]

The information sharing between Wagner and Fleissman, unlike the 1972 operation, fit the Stasi mold. East German intelligence was uniquely positioned to penetrate West German society because of the two countries' shared culture, language, and history. In the 1950s, Wolf had planted spies throughout West Germany, including one who advised Brandt closely and whose unmasking led to the chancellor's resignation in 1974.[66] Because of his network and status, Wagner proved useful to the Stasi. "He delivered great information, information nobody else had about the developments within the party," Kopp said. "He was an exceptional, top source."[67] As Wagner's supervisor, Kopp is not without bias, but it is indisputable that Wagner was a high-ranking and influential conservative lawmaker.

In 1980, Wagner appeared in court on fraud charges; prosecutors subsequently uncovered that he had received 50,000 deutschemarks from an unknown source in 1972, just around the time of the vote of no confidence.[68] Then the Berlin Wall fell, Germany reunified, and former intelligence officers started talking. In 1993, Markus Wolf revealed that his men had purchased Steiner's vote. KGB archives likewise document that Steiner abstained from the vote "on instruction" from the Stasi.[69] In 1995, Fleissman was found guilty of spying for East Germany. He died soon after. And in 1996, Wolf disclosed that in addition to Steiner, the Stasi had bribed a second lawmaker.[70]

Then came the biggest revelation of all: In 2000, *Der Spiegel* reported that Germany's Office of the Federal Prosecutor believed Wagner was the other abstainer. By then eighty-one years old,

Wagner announced that he would relinquish his remaining affiliations with the CSU. "I do not want the party to be burdened by these allegations," he told the press. He denied the accusations until his death a few years later.[71]

—

Since then, German officials have concluded that the Stasi used Wagner to rig the vote of no confidence. A government report from 2013 found that Wolf's team knew of Wagner's financial troubles early and, through Fleissman, paid him to abstain. By bribing Wagner and Steiner, the report concludes, the Stasi caused the motion against Brandt to fail.[72]

Few people ever knew the real Wagner, who kept his subversive activities secret until well after the Cold War had ended. His life underscores the range of characters who can participate in foreign interference operations. A leading conservative, Wagner was willing to betray his own party, even when the stakes were as high as deciding the leader of West Germany. In countries like Italy and Chile, the CIA had manipulated the masses. The Stasi, by contrast, studied and manipulated two parliamentary voters. Kopp's life, meanwhile, illuminates what drove Eastern intelligence officers. He had one overriding motive: "to achieve something meaningful."[73]

Kopp called the 1972 operation, especially his oversight of Wagner, the greatest accomplishment of his life.

Chapter 5

THE KGB TARGETS AMERICA

From vote buying and letter writing to scare campaigns and secret subsidies, the Soviet Union and the United States manipulated foreign elections for much of the twentieth century. Before this book moves to the twenty-first, one piece is still missing: What was happening *within* the United States during the Cold War?

As the CIA interfered in elections abroad, its leaders thought that no foreign intelligence service would or could interfere in America's elections. "No, no," said Bobby Inman, when I asked if the prospect of a foreign actor manipulating an American election crossed his mind between 1977 and 1982. During those years, he served as the director of the National Security Agency (NSA) and then as the CIA's deputy director, at a time when Congress was newly regulating the CIA's covert action programs. "There was the worry way, way back about the Comintern and its effort to influence countries throughout the world," Inman explained, "but that premise dissipated."[1]

Oleg Kalugin, the former KGB general, had a different story to tell. While stationed in the United States from 1958 to 1970, he worked tirelessly to interfere in American elections, including by spreading disinformation, finding and releasing damaging information about presidential aspirants, and attempting not just to coordinate directly with candidates but to develop influence over them. "That was part of the job," he said, "to promote those who would make less damage to the Soviet Union in the election." Then as now, Moscow's objectives were threefold: to sow discord within the United States, undermine hostile candidates, and promote friendlier ones.

For Moscow, interfering in U.S. elections was a high-risk, high-reward proposition. If the KGB were caught, superpower relations would deteriorate, and the United States could deploy economic, diplomatic, or covert countermeasures. "There was always a sense of potential feedback, that [the United States] could strike back, and it may be worse for the initiator," Kalugin said.[2] But the potential upside often proved irresistible: an opportunity to influence American voters as they determined the direction of their country. The operations that followed were motivated not by ideology—no Communist ever gained traction in American politics—but by the security interests and personal grudges of Soviet leaders.

So in a series of American elections between 1960 and 1984, Moscow identified threatening presidential candidates and worked to destroy them.

—

The first target would be Richard Nixon.

"I want to show you this kitchen. It is like those of our houses in California," then vice president Nixon had told Nikita Khrushchev, the head of the Soviet Union, in July 1959. The two men were in Moscow, touring an exhibit of a so-called typical American home. Nixon pointed at a pristine dishwasher as evidence that capitalism trumps Communism.

Khrushchev took the bait. "In Russia, all you have to do to get a house is to be born in the Soviet Union," he retorted. "You are entitled to housing."

In this famous back-and-forth, known as the kitchen debate, the ideological became personal.

"You do all the talking and don't let anyone else talk," Nixon countered. "You never concede anything. . . . You must not be afraid of ideas."

Khrushchev, bristling, said, "We're saying it is you who must not be afraid of ideas. We're not afraid of anything." Nixon remarked that Khrushchev "do[es]n't know everything," infuriating the Soviet leader further. "If I don't know everything, then you know absolutely nothing about Communism, except for fear!"[3]

Khrushchev left the exchange bitter. So in 1960, as Nixon glided toward the Republican nomination for president, he watched closely. "[Nixon's] aggressiveness toward the USSR, the anti-Communism that he preached, and his former ties with the reactionary and obscurantist Senator Joseph McCarthy promised nothing good," Khrushchev wrote in his memoirs.[4] His views trickled down to the KGB's foot soldiers. "Moscow was afraid of Nixon," recalled Kalugin, who was based in New York in 1960. "Nixon represented the right-wing Republicans, and the Russians were just fearful: He comes to power, and [U.S.-Soviet relations] may become totally different, and the Cold War could be turned into a real war."[5]

Republican Party officials suspected that Khrushchev might seek to undermine Nixon's campaign. In February 1960, Henry Cabot Lodge Jr., the U.S. ambassador to the United Nations and Nixon's eventual running mate, spoke with Khrushchev in person. Lodge offered both reassurance and counsel. He told Khrushchev that contrary to expectations, Nixon hoped to bolster ties between America and the Soviet Union. So, he continued, the Soviets should not seek to influence the upcoming election. "Your intervention in support of one or another candidate is not something we need. . . . [I]t would be harmful," Lodge said, based on Khrushchev's telling. "Our request is that you maintain strict neutrality. Don't interfere in our internal affairs during the presidential elections." Khrushchev understood the logic behind Lodge's ask. "In general," the Soviet leader wrote, noninterference in U.S. elections was "the sensible line to take," given the risks involved.[6]

But Khrushchev was never one to avoid risks. His life had been one great gamble. A child of peasants, he had improbably penetrated Stalin's inner circle and assumed power after Stalin died in 1953.[7] As the leader of the Soviet Union, Khrushchev acted unpredictably and often erratically: denouncing Stalin's cult of personality, bluffing about Moscow's long-range missile capabilities, igniting a superpower standoff in Berlin, and installing missiles in Cuba. Khrushchev pursued the objectives he wanted, when he wanted.

In 1960, Khrushchev wanted Nixon to lose. Unbeknownst to Lodge, just before their meeting Khrushchev had made his first move. The intended beneficiary was Adlai Stevenson, the Democratic nominee for president in the previous two elections. Khrushchev viewed Stevenson as a "man who thought realistically" and desired a "rapprochement with the [Soviet Union]."[8] The problem was that Stevenson had opted against running for president again. Khrushchev hoped to change his mind.

One afternoon in January 1960, Stevenson went to the Soviet embassy in Washington to meet with Mikhail Menshikov, Moscow's ambassador to the United States. After they enjoyed caviar, fruits, and drinks, courtesy of Moscow, Menshikov reached into his pocket and removed a message from Khrushchev, which he then read out loud.

"We are concerned with the future, and that America has the right president," Khrushchev wrote, based on Stevenson's account. "All countries are concerned with the American election. It is impossible for us not to be concerned about our future and the American Presidency which is so important to everybody everywhere." Of "all the possible candidates" for the 1960 election, Khrushchev explained in his letter, he preferred Stevenson. "Because we know the ideas of Mr. Stevenson, we in our hearts all favor him."

Khrushchev then offered to help Stevenson win the presidency:

Could the Soviet press assist Mr. Stevenson's personal success? How? Should the press praise him, and, if so, for what? Should it criticize him, and, if so, for what? (We can always find many things to criticize Mr. Stevenson for because he has said many harsh and critical things about the Soviet Union and Communism!) Mr. Stevenson will know best what would help him.

After finishing the letter, Menshikov asked Stevenson to keep its contents confidential. Moscow, it seemed, was attempting to draw Stevenson into an electoral conspiracy. Stevenson refused. After relaying his thanks for Khrushchev's "confidence" and "proffer of aid," he reminded Menshikov that he was not running for president. But more important, he emphasized his "grave misgivings about the propriety or wisdom of any interference, direct or indirect, in the American election." Stevenson found Khrushchev's advance not just inappropriate but reckless. "I said to him that even if I was a candidate I could not accept the assistance proffered," Stevenson recounted. "I believe I made it clear to him that I considered the offer of such assistance highly improper, indiscreet and dangerous to all concerned."

A few days later, Stevenson, apparently unable to get this meeting out of his mind, penned a letter of his own. In a private message to Menshikov, he reiterated that he did not intend to run for president but that even if he did, "I would have to decline to take advantage in any way of the confidence and good will I am happy to enjoy among your compatriots."[9]

Khrushchev's first attempt to interfere in the 1960 election had failed, but he kept trying. Nixon and Senator John F. Kennedy eventually became the nominees of the two major parties. Khrushchev, in his memoirs, said there were "more hopes for improvement in [U.S.-Soviet] relations" were Kennedy elected. "Kennedy was viewed as far more liberal," Kalugin explained, so Moscow sought to help him. Alexander Feklisov, then the KGB's Washington station chief, received instructions to "inform the Center periodically about the development of the electoral campaign, and to propose measures, diplomatic, propagandist, or [any] other, to encourage Kennedy's victory."[10] Not much is known about the KGB's subsequent operation, in which Kalugin claimed to have been an active participant. The KGB spread "all sorts of propaganda" during the campaign, he went on, while acknowledging that he lacked evidence. "A lot of things happened. This area of active measures is so wide, it's really a matter of imagination. It could be forgeries, it could be special publications, books, magazines, radio broadcasts, television . . . and, of course, anonymous letters."[11]

Khrushchev didn't just use the KGB to influence American voters; he also turned international events to his advantage. In May 1960, when an American U-2 spy plane was downed in Soviet airspace, Moscow took its pilot, Francis Gary Powers, into custody. Then, in July, the Soviet Union shot down an American RB-47 reconnaissance plane and captured its two surviving airmen. At the United Nations, Lodge called their imprisonment "illegal" and urged the Soviet Union to release them.[12]

Khrushchev refused. "If we release the prisoners now, that will be to Nixon's advantage," he told the Politburo, the Soviet Union's chief decision-making body. "Even the slightest shift that might tip the scales in his favor would not be good for us." Nixon and Lodge, the Republican ticket, were also members of the outgoing administration, which Khrushchev, by stonewalling, hoped to portray as feckless to voters. In September, Llewellyn Thompson, America's ambassador to the Soviet Union, again asked Khrushchev to free the RB-47 captives, but he was rebuffed. The Soviet leader remained convinced that "the timing of their release and return home had a certain political significance."[13]

—

On Election Day, Kennedy defeated Nixon by roughly 100,000 votes and a 303–219 split in the Electoral College. Khrushchev "beamed with satisfaction," according to his son, after learning that Kennedy had won.[14] Five days after Kennedy's inauguration, Khrushchev relented in hostage negotiations. Kennedy then announced that the two RB-47 airmen were coming home. "This action of the Soviet government removes a serious obstacle to improvement of Soviet-American relations," Kennedy said. In 1962, Powers was released as well.[15]

There is no way to know whether Moscow's efforts changed the minds of many Americans. (As compared with, say, Nixon profusely sweating during a televised debate, a twist not even Moscow could have dreamed up.) Once Kennedy was in office, though, the KGB's operations continued. The New York station sought to gather information on Kennedy's private life, Kalugin further claimed, so that Moscow could "take advantage of that knowledge and play some games of sorts, so-called active measures." This directive fit the KGB's playbook: to collect facts, Kalugin continued, and "put on top of the fact your own inventions, and then present to the general public some fictional material, in fact, though, based on something real."[16]

While the KGB worked in the shadows, Khrushchev attempted to win favor with the new administration. He had intentionally assisted Kennedy's campaign, and he wanted the president to know it. In his memoirs, Khrushchev recounted the following exchange at a June 1961 summit in Vienna:

> At one point I asked him: "Mr. Kennedy, do you know that we voted for you?"
>
> He looked at me quizzically: "How so? How is that to be understood?"
>
> I informed him about the appeal from Washington to Moscow just before the end of the election campaign, giving the exact date, and said that if we had returned Powers and the others at that point, it would have been considered an accomplishment of Nixon's.
>
> He began to laugh and when he had collected himself he replied: "You've drawn the right conclusion. I agree that, just at that time, even the slightest shift in the balance could have been decisive. So I grant your point that you took part in the elections and voted in my favor."
>
> This joking reflected reality. I should say that I have no regrets about the position we took.[17]

Khrushchev's primary objective had been to secure Kennedy's victory. His secondary objective was to establish influence over Kennedy. By telling the president that Moscow had "voted for" him, Khrushchev was suggesting that Kennedy owed his power, at least in part, to the Soviet Union. This tactic, while common, proves effective when the benefiting party knows about an interference operation as it is ongoing, as was the case with Eduardo Frei and Alcide De Gasperi, and as would have been the case with Stevenson, had he accepted Khrushchev's offer. But prior to his election, Kennedy had not realized that Moscow was working to advantage his campaign, so he had no reason to feel insecure about his electoral legitimacy or psychologically indebted to Khrushchev once in office.

—

As Kennedy celebrated his victory, controversy erupted in the United States. In November 1960, UN delegates from Asian and African countries received a threatening letter signed by the Ku Klux Klan. "Racist Hate Note Sent to U.N. Aides," reported *The New York Times*.[18] The scandal worsened when Ambassador Jaja Wachuku of Nigeria read the letter, in its entirety, before the UN General Assembly. "This came to my office and I think it is necessary that we should put it on record," Wachuku said. "It is headed: 'White America rejects a bastardized United Nations.'" Wachuku then read the message:

> The black races of Africa and yellow races of Asia . . . have invaded the United Nations. It is enough to make every white Protestant American vomit. These sub-humans have come down from the trees and out of the swamps to lord it over the white race. . . . These monkeys should have been tanned and feathered.[19]

It was a humiliating and humbling moment for the United States. In response, U.S. senator Wayne Morse, a delegate at the session, called the letter "an affront to the American people" that "in no way bespeaks the point of view of any responsible citizens of the United States." If the letter were, in fact, written by "an American crackpot," Morse continued, then "it is only fitting and proper" for the United States "to express to the General Assembly our apologies that anyone in our country would see fit to spread such vicious bigotry."[20] Before the world, the United States, a democratic superpower, had apologized for its internal racism and division.

But the Ku Klux Klan had not written the letter. It was a forgery, produced by Soviet intelligence officers stationed in the United States. KGB archives reveal that "a leaflet in the name of the Ku Klux Klan was prepared and circulated among UN delegations" and that the leaflet's "content and form were borrowed from racist literature." The KGB had studied similar writings so that its letter would appear authentic. The plan worked. "The issue of racism in the USA was raised at the General Assembly," the archives read, when Wachuku recited the "complete text of the disinformation leaflet," prompting American officials to apologize and the United Nations to add its contents to the official record.[21]

The purpose of Moscow's operation against Nixon was straightforward: to damage the candidate less aligned with Soviet interests. In parallel, the KGB pursued another objective: to foment discord within the United States and, in the process, undermine its rival at home and abroad. Those objectives can coexist, as they did in 1960 and, later, in 2016. "We tried to take advantage of all these differences and to sow more anti-black movements," recalled Kalugin, who was directly involved with the Ku Klux Klan operation. The KGB's aim, its archives explain, was "to present the American way of life in an unfavorable light in the eyes of the rest of the world— especially Asian and African countries—by publicizing expressions of racism and chauvinism."[22] To Moscow, America's diversity was its greatest vulnerability. In 2016, when Russians spread racist content online, Kalugin saw more of the same. "That's an old Soviet tactic," he said, "adjusted to the realities of political life today."[23]

The KGB's disinformation operations focused on two minority groups: black and Jewish Americans. The success of these schemes depended largely on the media, which, in the pre-digital era, operated as a gatekeeper in determining what information reached the public. To attract the attention of reporters, the KGB mailed anonymous anti-Semitic letters to Jewish leaders, arranged for swastikas to be painted onto synagogues, and paid assets to desecrate Jewish cemeteries. "We spread anti-Semitic, anti-Negro [materials] inside the United States," Kalugin recalled, "just to show that America is behind it all, not Russia, oh no, on the contrary: America is not as it tries to present itself to the world. It's anti-Semitic; it's militaristic; it's the devil."[24] The goal was to persuade regular people, Americans and non-Americans alike, to hold the United States in lower regard. If a staged hate crime made its way into a major newspaper, Moscow considered it an operational success.

At least one subset of reporters always covered these stunts: KGB officers posing in the United States as foreign correspondents. Their readership was primarily Russian. In this sense, the KGB's games had as much to do with the Soviet Union as with the United States. Its disinformation operations could be used to demonstrate to Soviet citizens that the United States, despite its inclusive rhetoric, was actually a hotbed of hate. "We wanted to show that America is not a God-blessed country; it's just full of anti-Semitism and neo-fascism," Kalugin recalled. "That was part of the official Soviet propaganda, and KGB would use special methods to make this propaganda more effective."[25]

———

Fostering division and influencing elections were core aspects of the KGB's playbook in America. For each of its operations, Moscow had to decide how much risk to assume. In 1960, Khrushchev had not utilized, it seems, the KGB's most simple weapon: cash. Around the world, the Soviet Union was financing its preferred parties. But bankrolling one of America's major parties could prove self-defeating. If American investigators uncovered a secret funding scheme, an uproar would ensue that, at the height of the Cold War, would undermine the intended beneficiary along with U.S.-Soviet relations.

In 1968, Moscow again aimed to undermine Nixon, who had secured the Republican nomination a second time. Much had changed in eight years. Nixon was running against Hubert Humphrey, the sitting vice president, who was associated with the unpopular Vietnam War. By 1968, as we have seen, Leonid Brezhnev, Khrushchev's successor, hoped to forge new ties abroad to achieve stability at home. All Nixon seemed to offer was hostility. Humphrey was the "better choice," recalled Kalugin, because "he was more liberal and easier to deal with."[26]

Fear and desperation are powerful motivators, especially when it comes to covert electoral interference. Brezhnev was filled with both. So "the top Soviet leaders took an extraordinary step," recalled Anatoly Dobrynin, then the Soviet ambassador to the U.S., "by secretly offering Humphrey any conceivable help in his election campaign—including financial aid." Andrei Gromyko, the Soviet foreign minister, told Dobrynin in a "top-secret instruction" to lend Humphrey whatever assistance he needed.[27]

Dobrynin hesitated to carry out Gromyko's order. He feared this "dangerous venture," if discovered, would destroy Humphrey and undermine Soviet interests, so he urged Moscow to reconsider. Unmoved, Gromyko replied, "There is a decision, you carry it out."[28]

Not long after that, Humphrey hosted Dobrynin in his home for breakfast. The ambassador arrived ready to propose a conspiracy at the highest levels of the American and Soviet governments. While eating, as a segue, Dobrynin asked Humphrey about his campaign's financial state. A direct offer of support was on the tip of Dobrynin's tongue. But Humphrey caught on. "He knew at once what was going on," Dobrynin wrote, and said "it was more than enough for him to have Moscow's good wishes."

Moscow had tried and failed to fund a major U.S. presidential campaign. Once Humphrey rebuffed this advance, the plan was over. "The matter was thus settled to our mutual relief, never to be discussed again," Dobrynin concluded.[29] Directly conspiring with an American presidential candidate requires a willing partner. In Stevenson and then in Humphrey, Moscow found only rejection. Nixon went on to win the 1968 election by a razor-thin margin, which Humphrey perhaps could have overcome with foreign funding.

The great irony of the 1960 and 1968 campaigns is just how poorly Moscow had assessed Nixon, who spent much of his presidency working toward détente. His realist outlook also empowered Willy Brandt to reach out to the East without somehow betraying the West.[30] Any covert electoral interference operation is based on imperfect information and forecasting. Sometimes, the candidate who appears friendly turns out to be hostile. And sometimes, the candidate who appears threatening turns out to be far more complex.

—

On electoral matters, America's domestic experience differed dramatically from the Soviet Union's. Not only was the United States the only superpower that held competitive elections, but the CIA, which itself interfered in elections overseas, was also part of a democratic society, complete with a free press and a legislative branch able to conduct oversight. The CIA's covert action programs, unlike the KGB's, could thus be outed, investigated, and regulated.

In its early years, the CIA nevertheless operated with minimal accountability. When Salvador Allende died by suicide in 1973, the only thing standing between the agency and public scrutiny was that so few people knew about its covert action programs. "I don't think members of Congress were even aware that there was much going on at the agency," said Porter Goss, the 1960s-era CIA officer and, later, director. "The amount of operations going on were very closely guarded, hardly ever discussed; people just did not dream about talking about these things—not at the A-list parties, not anywhere." John McLaughlin, another Cold War–era CIA officer who went on to lead the agency, described congressional oversight of the CIA as initially amounting to informal conversations with key senators, who typically said, "Just do what you have to do, I don't need to know, and it's not even a good thing for me to know some of this."[31]

That all changed in September 1974, when the reporter Seymour Hersh exposed the CIA's work in Chile. These revelations, combined with reports of secret operations in Southeast Asia, caused Congress to pass the Hughes-Ryan Amendment, which mandated that key lawmakers be alerted to all covert action operations and that the president provide those lawmakers with a "finding" justifying each one.[32] Harold Hughes, the senator who sponsored the amendment, described it as "only the beginning" of regulating "cloak-and-dagger operations." Some American policy makers feared these reforms would cripple the CIA. Henry Kissinger, by then the secretary of state, complained that "something on file which the president has signed" robbed him of plausible deniability and that "you simply cannot brief 50 congressmen on a covert activity and expect it to be kept covert."[33]

Hersh's most explosive reporting, though, did not involve elections. "Huge C.I.A. Operation Reported in U.S. Against Antiwar Forces, Other Dissidents in Nixon Years," *The New York Times* revealed on December 22, 1974. The CIA had surveilled thousands of American citizens opposed to the Vietnam War while separately conducting wiretaps, break-ins, and mail reviews of suspected foreign agents. These activities violated the CIA's charter, which barred the agency from carrying out "internal security functions."[34] Congress had to act. In early 1975, the Senate and House of Representatives each established select committees that would investigate the U.S. intelligence community. "Between the fall of 1974 and the start of 1976, the CIA became the leading political issue before the nation," writes historian Rhodri Jeffreys-Jones.[35]

The Church and Pike Committees, as they were called, brought many of the CIA's activities into the light, including certain details of its work in Italy. Politicians like Jimmy Carter, then a presidential candidate, turned their backs on the decades-old scheme, long a point of pride within the CIA. "I would certainly hate to see Italy go Communist," Carter said in November 1975, but "I don't think we ought to intervene militarily or by any sort of covert means. . . . I don't think that would be right."[36] The following month, Cyrus Vance, a former deputy secretary of defense, urged Congress to pass "legislation prohibiting interference with the electoral processes in other countries." His recommendation was ignored.[37]

Other aspects of the CIA's covert operations generated more blowback, including a government report on overseas assassination plots. In February 1976, President Gerald Ford issued an executive order establishing that "no employee of the United States Government shall engage in, or conspire to engage in, political assassination."[38] That year and the next, the Senate and House established Permanent Select Committees on Intelligence.

The CIA's leaders suddenly felt pressure to defend their work publicly. In 1976, William Colby, the just-retired CIA director, sat down for an interview with Oriana Fallaci, an Italian journalist. It was an explosive pairing. Colby had subverted Italy's democratic processes; Fallaci was a fierce defender of Italy's sovereignty. When Fallaci pointed out that the Chilean people had elected Allende, Colby retorted, "Didn't Mussolini win elections? Didn't Hitler become the chancellor of Germany in an election?"[39] Regarding Italy, Fallaci demanded "the names of those bastards who took CIA money in my country." Colby refused, insisting that the CIA had to keep the identities of its assets secret. An era of oversight did not mean total transparency; much of the agency's operational records remained classified.

Colby then laid out the rationale for covert electoral interference. He insisted that manipulating foreign elections is "an activity that is necessary in the world we live in because a little help in some countries to some friends can avoid a serious crisis later." As a matter of proportionality, he continued, the United States had to counter the KGB. "Why don't you ask the Soviet government for the names of the Communists who take Moscow's money in Italy?" Most of all, the ends justified the means. "American assistance in Italy helped it from becoming an authoritarian [country] for 30 years," Colby said. "You live better today than you would have lived if you had had a Communist government in 1948 . . . so the American policies have not been a mistake in Italy. We did a good job."[40]

In Italy, debate raged about the impact of foreign electoral interference. The CIA had released almost no details about its decades-long operation, other than its existence, which gave rise to much speculation and paranoia. Italy's Communist leaders, eager to distract from their own missteps, blamed the CIA for their many defeats. In this environment, everyday Italians came to resent and fear the CIA. "If you're in Italy, the importance of America, of the ambassador, of the CIA is enormous; it seems as though the CIA has magical powers," recalled Jack Devine, who, as a senior CIA officer, was stationed in Italy toward the end of the Cold War. "I used to hate movies like James Bond, which I thought trivialized the business," he said. "Then I realized, 'If the world thinks that is how we are, it is in our interests for them to think we're omnipotent.' "[41]

—

While the CIA adjusted to an era of oversight, the KGB continued to target American elections without any such limitations. Congressional investigations into the CIA, which spanned most of 1975, coincided with the Republican and Democratic presidential primaries. In both contests, the Soviet Union sought to undermine its perceived rivals.

The KGB's first target was Ronald Reagan, who was competing against Gerald Ford for the 1976 Republican nomination. Much of what differentiated Reagan was his anti-Soviet posture. The historian John Lewis Gaddis describes Reagan as one of America's "sharpest grand strategists ever," largely because he could distill the complex to the simple. "What [Reagan] saw," Gaddis writes, "was simply this: that because détente perpetuated—and had been meant to perpetuate—the Cold War, only killing détente could end the

Cold War."[42] Reagan was an ardent and outspoken critic of détente, on which Nixon, Ford, Brezhnev, and Brandt had all staked so much. He instead advocated power, strength, and national resolve. "Peace does not come from weakness or from retreat," Reagan declared in March 1976. "It comes from the restoration of American military superiority."[43]

Nearly everything about Reagan alarmed Moscow. "[We] were afraid of him," said Kalugin, then the KGB's chief of counterintelligence.[44] Yuri Andropov, the head of the KGB, personally issued a directive against Reagan. "Andropov confirmed the 26 May 1976 supplementary plan for [active measures] against Reagan, in addition to the existing and already sanctioned plan regarding the US presidential elections," the KGB's files reveal.[45] This sentence contains two key points: The KGB was already executing an operation to interfere in the 1976 election, and Andropov had expanded that operation (by planting anti-Reagan articles in foreign news outlets). Not much is known about how else the KGB sought to disadvantage Reagan, who ultimately lost the nomination to Ford.[46]

Sometimes, covert electoral interference only helps to delay rather than prevent outcomes. Nixon won in 1968 after losing in 1960. Allende won in 1970 after losing in 1964. And Reagan won in 1980 after losing in 1976.

In his first term, Reagan's hawkish rhetoric infuriated Moscow—and prompted more electoral interference. In 1982, Andropov ordered his overseas officers to undermine Reagan's reelection bid. Early the next year, Moscow instructed its U.S. stations to establish contact with presidential campaign staffers and to propose steps to tarnish Reagan's candidacy. The KGB circulated specific lines of attack against the president: He was corrupt, racist, and militaristic. Nevertheless, Reagan won the 1984 election in a landslide.[47]

The KGB worked against Nixon and Reagan not because they were Republicans but because they seemed to threaten Soviet security. The same can be said for Henry "Scoop" Jackson, a Democratic senator and known anti-Soviet hawk.

In February 1975, Jackson announced his candidacy for president, just as Reagan prepared to do the same and as Congress investigated the CIA. Anticipating Jackson's run, the KGB had been studying him closely. Its files noted that he married a woman only at the age of forty-nine and kept his personal life strictly private, which "may mean some compromising material exists that could be used against Jackson and members of his family."[48] One KGB station chief cabled Moscow that one of Jackson's core strengths was his squeaky-clean reputation, a trait that had become "exceptionally important" after the Watergate scandal.[49]

For the Soviet Union, there was value in using state resources to discover a politician's secrets. Salacious revelations about a presidential aspirant could sink his campaign. So the KGB sought to "find dark spots in [Jackson's] biography and conduct active measures to compromise him," according to its files, as well as to "discuss with our American friends (communists) the best ways to counter Jackson's intention of becoming U.S. president." For insider information, the KGB turned to preexisting connections. "Make full use of confidential contacts," Moscow instructed, with "figures hostile to Jackson for unofficial exchanges of views about ways to undermine Jackson's efforts."[50]

The KGB hoped above all that Jackson was a closeted homosexual. Its officers investigated his sex life, including whether he was romantically involved with John Salter, a longtime friend and adviser. "The station in the capital was tasked with finding out when Jackson had moved to Washington, the year and month, the address of his apartment, where he had lived in 1940–41, [and] whether John Salter had lived with him then," per the KGB's files, while all "stations were asked to collect information about any prosecutions of homosexuals" in this period, in the hopes that Jackson's name turned up.[51] For Moscow, Kalugin explained, labeling a politician a homosexual served to "discredit the leadership of a country, and show to the world that this country cannot be trusted, because its people were not the right ones for leadership."[52] The Soviet Union aimed to destroy Jackson, a public figure, by outing his private life—a totalitarian tactic, exported to the United States. As Hannah Arendt wrote, the promise of totalitarianism is to abolish "the separation between private and public life" so all things become the business of the state.[53]

In June 1975, as the KGB searched for a basis for blackmail,

Dobrynin, still the ambassador, had breakfast with Jackson. Taking a page from its 1968 playbook, the Kremlin had instructed Dobrynin to "confidentially warn" Jackson not to alienate Soviet leadership "before he even reaches the White House." At their meeting, Jackson said that he actually hoped to work with Moscow and asked that Brezhnev be informed of his intentions. Dobrynin replied that "a departure . . . from [your] anti-Soviet line would not go unnoticed in Moscow, if [you] really intended to do it."[54]

The breakfast had gone well, but Moscow was unmoved. The KGB still pursued its plan, code-named Operation Vice, to sink Jackson's campaign. As part of this effort, the KGB worked to "find weak spots in the relationship between the Jewish community in the USA and Jackson" and to "encourage the Arab countries to counter Jackson's pro-Israel Jewish line."[55] But mostly, Operation Vice revolved around a single goal: "to denounce Jackson as being a homosexual."[56] The KGB had one problem: It could find no evidence that Jackson was gay. So the KGB created the evidence. "We could make up any sorts of documents," Kalugin recalled, with a laugh. "Our disinformation service was one of the best in the world."[57]

In early 1976, a forged FBI document arrived in the mailboxes of the *Chicago Tribune,* the *Los Angeles Times,* and Jimmy Carter's campaign headquarters. Dated June 20, 1940, the memorandum claimed that Jackson was secretly gay.[58] The tactic was a familiar one: Years earlier, the KGB had disseminated forgeries alleging that J. Edgar Hoover, the FBI director, was a homosexual who had turned the bureau into a "den of queers."[59] Attempting to "develop and drag out the homosexual idea," Soviet officers mailed another set of documents—again, alleging that Jackson was a closeted homosexual—to Carter, Senator Frank Church, *Playboy* magazine, *Penthouse* magazine, and Senator Edward Kennedy, whom the KGB believed "personally dislike[d] Jackson."[60]

For Operation Vice to work, recipients had to believe in the authenticity of the files and then publicize them. The forged KKK letter had proven effective because UN delegates thought it was genuine and broadcast its contents. But in this case, the fake FBI file was never published, so Operation Vice failed. In a world without the internet, Moscow could not upload disinformation directly into

America's information ecosystem. Instead, the KGB had to rely on third parties: major campaigns, popular magazines, mainstream news outlets, and prominent political figures. These gatekeepers could stop Moscow's schemes in their tracks, and, in 1976, they did. Although Jackson eventually dropped out of the Democratic primary, the KGB's dirty tricks did not contribute to his defeat.

Taken together, Moscow attempted to interfere in various U.S. presidential elections during the Cold War. But none of it mattered much. A gap existed between the intent of Soviet leaders—to disrupt and direct America's process of succession—and their actual capabilities. In the pre-digital age, the Kremlin lacked the means to shape public discourse, target voters on a personal basis, or reach the American population at scale.

—

Alongside its largely ineffective electoral operations, the Soviet Union kept trying to divide Americans. The KGB's schemes ranged from disseminating disinformation to murdering U.S. citizens. In July 1971, in what was known as Operation Pandora, the KGB station in New York was instructed to plant explosives in "the Negro section of New York"—ideally, "one of the Negro colleges"—and then to blame the attack on the Jewish Defense League.[61] The KGB hoped to turn black and Jewish Americans against one another, through a deadly operation that, ultimately, never came to fruition.

On rare occasions, the KGB was exposed. In 1984, while the Soviets targeted Reagan, they also attempted to embarrass the United States through a letter-writing campaign similar to that of 1960. But this time, the United States caught on. That August, Attorney General William French Smith and the FBI director, William Webster, announced that the KGB had sent fake letters to athletic officials from roughly twenty Asian and African countries, in advance of the 1984 Summer Olympics in Los Angeles.[62] The racist messages—again, purportedly from the KKK—warned,

THE OLYMPICS—FOR THE WHITES ONLY! African monkeys! A grand reception awaits you in Los Angeles! We are preparing for the Olympic games by shooting at black moving targets. In Los Angeles our own Olympic flames are ready to incinerate you. The highest award for a true American patriot would be the lynching of an African monkey. Blacks, Welcome to the Olympic games in Los Angeles! We'll give you a reception you'll never forget![63]

Using "linguistic and forensic techniques," Attorney General Smith explained, Washington had detected the KGB's operation almost immediately.[64] A war of words ensued. Smith had publicly attributed the letters to the Soviet Union in order to reduce their effectiveness. Moscow then denied the charges, claiming instead that Smith was trying to divert attention from America's racism. The Soviet Union's state-run news agency, TASS, insisted that the hate mail merely "expressed in an extremely base manner what the architects of American policy have in their mind" and that Smith was peddling "delirious myths."[65] A difficulty in combating disinformation is that even when it is outed, convincing the public that a forgery is, in fact, a forgery can prove challenging.

—

To foment division in America, the KGB also funded the Communist Party of the United States of America (CPUSA). Gus Hall, the party's leader, ran for president four times between 1972 and 1984 but never received more than 0.07 percent of popular support. By 1988, the CPUSA had fewer than twenty thousand members. Still, the Soviet Union bankrolled its activities: Funding increased from $1 million annually in the late 1960s to $2 million in the late 1970s, to $3 million in 1988, after Hall wrote Moscow in 1987, pleading for even more money."[66] The KGB's support for the CPUSA had nothing to do with its electoral prospects and everything to do with its existence, which promoted paranoia inside the United States and thus furthered one of Moscow's key objectives: to turn Americans against Americans. "We had to maintain [the party]," Kalugin said, to foster distrust in the United States. Through the end of the Cold War, the FBI worked to penetrate the party's ranks, famously recruiting Morris Childs, one of its leaders, as well as his wife and brother as double agents.[67]

As the FBI spied on the CPUSA, the KGB spied on well-known figures in the United States. Kalugin recalled that, toward the end of the Cold War, the KGB set its sights on Donald J. Trump, a famous real estate developer. In July 1987, Trump visited Moscow to explore building and operating a hotel there. "He was well received in those days, and he had some friends in Russia," said Kalugin, then a KGB general stationed in Moscow. Kalugin later heard from his colleagues that they had collected intelligence on Trump during his trip. "Trump left some of his presence in Russia, and the Russians know something about him," Kalugin continued, citing only his memory. Did this have anything to do with "extracurricular activities"? "Yes, let's call it that," Kalugin responded, laughing. (Trump has historically denied any such allegations.)[68] Kalugin never anticipated, however, that Trump, a generation later, would sow more discord within the United States than any letter-writing campaign ever did.[69]

———

As the Cold War neared its end, the KGB continued to target elections around the world. In the 1980s, Moscow spent more than $200 million funding political parties in eighty countries.[70] The CIA moved in the opposite direction, as a result of congressional reforms and public revelations. The post-Italy consensus about the value of covert electoral interference had vanished after Chile. In its place was a set of drawbacks: most important, the prospects of accountability and detection. The finding process had robbed the president of plausible deniability. And the outing of operations in Chile and elsewhere had demonstrated that covert action could always be made public.

But the CIA could and did still interfere in elections. In "specific instances" since the mid-1970s, David Robarge told me, the "agency would get the call to go directly into an election and engage with it." In El Salvador in the early 1980s, and in Nicaragua in 1990, the CIA delivered money and support to specific candidates.[71] "From the standpoint of the Reagan period, we were in favor of democratic governance," said George Shultz, the secretary of state from 1982 to 1989, when asked about Italy-style covert action programs. "If people wanted to do that themselves, we would be helpful."[72]

If the CIA provided help, its leaders had to be ready to answer for it. Investigative journalists now wanted to know where and how the American government was manipulating elections. In July 1982, the CIA director, William Casey, publicly denied that the agency had "meddled" in El Salvador's election.[73] Two years later, when America's preferred candidate—José Napoleón Duarte—won the El Salvadoran presidency, reports emerged that the CIA had funneled $2.1 million into the election.[74] "We were concerned to see El Salvador become a good economy with a good political system," explained Shultz, who rejected the notion that the Reagan administration had secured Duarte's victory. "Duarte was a very fine figure. . . . He was like a saint to people. They loved him. So it wasn't us that elected him; he elected himself."[75]

Newfound scrutiny, above all, forced U.S. officials to grapple with an uncomfortable question: Was the practice of covert electoral interference defensible, let alone worthwhile? Or, as Porter Goss, the former CIA director, put it to me: "What is tolerable? What is tolerable in our values system?"[76]

For Bobby Inman, these tensions reached their peak at the start of the Reagan administration. After directing the NSA from 1977 to 1981, Inman served as the CIA's deputy director until 1982. In this role, he appeared before the newly formed Senate Select Committee on Intelligence. During one session, CIA representatives raised a potential covert electoral interference operation against Mauritius, a small island nation. Daniel Patrick Moynihan—the committee's vice chairman and a CIA critic—pushed back. "He said, 'You don't know what the hell you're doing, you don't know anything about elections, how do you know who will be a good candidate, not a good candidate, do they actually have the capacity to win or not win, this is just outrageous,'" Inman recalled. "Moynihan got up and walked out of the hearing," Inman continued, to confer with Senator Barry Goldwater, the chairman of the committee. "They came back, and the two of them, instant agreement: 'You ought not to be in this business. You don't know what you're doing other than wasting money.'"[77]

Divided internally, the CIA was still engaging in covert electoral interference, but with less pride and frequency than it once had.

American policy makers now worried that manipulating elections would produce unintended outcomes. And sooner or later, any covert action program could be revealed, exposing the CIA to criticism. As the Cold War neared its end, CIA-led electoral interference—a crucial weapon from Italy to Chile—had faded in importance.

Chapter 6

DEMOCRACY PROMOTION

n June 1992, Boris Yeltsin, the first president of the Russian Federation, visited Washington. He received a hero's welcome. With "reason begin[ning] to triumph over madness," Yeltsin declared before a joint session of Congress, the United States and Russia must no longer view each other "through gunsights, ready to pull the trigger at any time." American lawmakers chanted, "Boris, Boris, Boris," and gave him thirteen standing ovations. But Yeltsin wasn't just there for the fanfare; he also had a request: for Congress to "take measures now to support Russia."[1]

A few years earlier, in 1989, popular revolutions had transformed Eastern Europe. Competitive elections took place in countries where Joseph Stalin had, a generation earlier, rigged them. Mikhail Gorbachev, the last Soviet leader, broke from his predecessors and exercised restraint; the Eastern bloc promptly and peacefully unraveled.[2] In 1990, Germany reunified.[3] And soon after, in December 1991, the Soviet Union itself ceased to exist.[4]

Washington moved quickly to fill the power vacuum that the Soviet Union left behind. Congress passed the Support for East European Democracy Act of 1989, which directed hundreds of millions of dollars toward Poland and Hungary; one U.S. senator dubbed the bill a "wager" on an "experiment with democracy." And just before Yeltsin's visit, President George H. W. Bush had proposed the Freedom for Russia and Emerging Eurasian Democracies and Open Markets (FREEDOM) Support Act, which would provide $410 million in direct aid to Russia and other former Soviet republics, as well as $12 billion to the International Monetary Fund

(IMF).[5] Joseph Biden, then a U.S. senator, said the FREEDOM Act would help "secure democracy in Russia," while Secretary of State James Baker warned that without it "if democracy collapses and authoritarianism returns . . . we will all lose." All four living former U.S. presidents—Nixon, Ford, Carter, and Reagan—issued a joint statement in support of the bill, which they said was needed to "guarantee a peaceful transition to democracy" in formerly Communist countries.[6]

After Yeltsin's speech, the FREEDOM Act passed and was signed into law. The bill authorized funding for reforms in areas associated with democratic governance, such as banking, education, and an independent media. In a presidential debate that fall, Bush said he was working to make the former Soviet republics "totally democratic" as part of an evolving foreign policy mission. "The new world order, to me," Bush explained, "means freedom and democracy."[7]

For decades, Washington's central aim abroad had been to contain Communism. The CIA had interfered in elections across the world in support of this objective. Now Washington could pivot from containing Communism to expanding democracy. No other superpower was left standing. What had been a competition between capitalism and Communism had become a competition between liberal democracy and . . . nothing at all. Whereas Lenin had once hoped to establish a global Communist order, it now appeared inevitable that the United States would establish a democratic one. The end of history, thinkers like Francis Fukuyama proclaimed, had arrived.[8] "There was a tremendous sense of possibility," said James Steinberg, a senior White House and State Department official in the 1990s. "People were very optimistic and excited by this positive agenda of molding a peaceful, prosperous, democratic world."[9]

With no ideological competitor, Washington promoted democracy as an end in itself. The first step was guiding the countries of Eastern Europe and the former Soviet republics. A provision of the FREEDOM Act stipulated that in determining where to dole out assistance, the United States would account for whether a state was establishing "a democratic system based on principles of the rule of law, individual freedoms, and representative government determined

by free and fair elections."[10] What followed was an explosion of
pro-democracy initiatives managed by the State Department, the
U.S. Agency for International Development (USAID), and the
National Endowment for Democracy (NED), a private nonprofit
funded almost entirely by the U.S. government. By 1994, NED's
annual budget had more than doubled to $35 million.[11] Bill Clinton,
Bush's successor and the first fully post–Cold War president, labeled
the promotion of democracy one of the three pillars of his national
security strategy.[12]

—

The heart of a democracy is its elections. In promoting democracy,
the United States had to decide how to engage with foreign elections in the post-Soviet period. Washington's objective had shifted
from defeating leftist candidates to helping countries conduct stable,
fair, and competitive elections. A new type of electoral operation
followed: overt, regulated efforts to help "democratic" candidates.
For the most part, two U.S.-funded NGOs carried out these operations: the International Republican Institute (IRI) and the National
Democratic Institute (NDI).[13] Between 1989 and 1999, IRI and NDI
went to work in dozens of countries. They offered political parties
training sessions—run by both American and foreign officials—on
campaign strategy, message development, volunteer recruitment,
fundraising, candidate selection, door-to-door canvassing, policy
planning, and get-out-the-vote efforts. "Most IRI and NDI programs," the U.S. government found in 1999, "have focused on helping parties mount successful election campaigns."[14]

Federal laws stipulated that foreign assistance programs could
not influence election outcomes. NED's charter, too, specified that
its grants could not go directly to campaigns. In interviews, most
U.S. government officials emphasized that IRI and NDI were inclusive and nonpartisan: They did not buy votes or bankroll candidates,
and they offered support to a range of parties.[15]

But IRI and NDI were never entirely neutral. Their purpose
was to promote democracy, and as such they assisted parties that
advanced the democratic cause. Sometimes, this meant backing
opposition forces in an effort to "level the playing field" against a

dominant ruling party. Other times, it meant withholding support from "non-democratic" parties that espoused violent, nationalistic, or intolerant views, as well as Communist Parties that still seemed, well, too Communist.[16] "With NDI and IRI, we will train any party that wants it, other than the extreme fringes, such as parties advocating authoritarianism, violence, or antidemocratic practices," said Victoria Nuland, who began working for the State Department in 1985 and departed in 2017 with the rank of career ambassador. Kenneth Wollack, who, in 2018, retired as NDI's longtime president, said that, in rare cases, his organization offered aid only to select parties. "Outside assistance in those situations I would argue helped," Wollack said, "but they were by no means the only reason why those forces won."[17]

In the 1990s, IRI and NDI backed specific parties in countries like Poland, South Africa, Croatia, and Bulgaria. "IRI's assistance to Bulgarian democratic parties helped take them from near oblivion in 1995 to winning the presidency in 1996," the IRI boasted in its annual report. IRI had even flown Bulgarian opposition leaders to the United States so they could study the New Hampshire presidential primary.[18] "Throughout the '90s," Nuland continued, "we generally would do more mentoring behind the scenes of reformist candidates." According to the U.S. government, this type of work contributed to "electoral victories" and "stronger than expected showings" by democratic parties in various cases, from NDI's program in Bosnia and Herzegovina to IRI's programs in Mongolia, Romania, and Slovakia.[19]

—

The most biased case of U.S. democracy promotion came in 2000, when Slobodan Milošević, the Yugoslav president, was competing for reelection in Serbia.[20] Milošević was many things: a Moscow-aligned Communist, a Serbian nationalist, and a grave abuser of human rights. In the mid-1990s, he had enabled a campaign of ethnic cleansing in Bosnia and Herzegovina. A few years later, he did the same in Kosovo as his soldiers systemically terrorized, murdered, and expelled ethnic Albanians. The severity of these atrocities prompted NATO, in 1999, to launch an air campaign against

Milošević's forces, and an international court to indict him as a war criminal.[21] In Washington, Milošević had earned enemies on both sides of the aisle. "My view on Milošević was he was a problem to deal with," said Porter Goss, then the Republican chairman of the House Intelligence Committee. Leon Panetta, Clinton's chief of staff from 1994 to 1997, added, "Milošević was viewed as a bad guy and influence and somebody that was going to turn that part of the world upside down if there weren't steps taken to go after him."[22]

The 2000 election presented such an opportunity. "I don't know that we publicly said that our goal was regime change," said James O'Brien, then Clinton's special envoy for the Balkans, but "we did not see Milošević being able to lead a normal country."[23] Secretary of State Madeleine Albright had set her sights on the election. "She wanted him gone," William Montgomery, then the U.S. ambassador to Croatia, said in 2000. "Seldom has so much fire, energy, enthusiasm, money—everything—gone into anything as into Serbia in the months before Milošević went."[24] (Albright and Montgomery both declined to be interviewed for this book.) By supporting the opposition, James O'Brien explained, the United States aimed to level the playing field in an election that Milošević was poised to manipulate. "Milošević had the benefit of an entire state apparatus," O'Brien said, including "state media, everything, and had the opposition been provided any of that, there would have been very little need for our involvement."[25]

What followed was an aggressive effort to help Milošević's opponents influence voters' minds. From mid-1999 to late 2000, public and private U.S. organizations together spent roughly $40 million on Serbian programs, supporting not just the opposition but also the independent media, civic organizations, and initiatives meant to encourage citizens to turn out to the polls and to ensure their votes would be tallied fairly.[26] In nearly all aspects of the campaign, Americans were involved. In October 1999, Kenneth Wollack hosted opposition leaders at a Budapest hotel to plot campaign strategy, informed by a poll NDI had paid a U.S. firm to conduct. "[That] poll showed the Serbians that if they united, there was a possibility that they could succeed," said Wollack, whose organization, in this instance, only offered to assist the opposition. USAID, through a third party, produced millions of anti-Milošević stickers with a simple message: "He's finished." And critically, U.S. funds and training went toward Otpor, a vibrant youth resistance group. "We had a lot of financial help from Western nongovernmental organizations. And also, some Western governmental organizations," one of Otpor's leaders said at the time, including from USAID's Office of Transition Initiatives. IRI and NED directed $1.8 million and $3 million, respectively, into Serbia before the election, focusing on Otpor, while still supporting other initiatives, such as a get-out-the-vote campaign.[27]

Back in the United States, Bill Clinton remained pessimistic. "These elections are going to be important, but they probably won't be fair," Clinton told Vladimir Putin, the new Russian president, while meeting in New York two and a half weeks before the vote. "Milošević is running behind in the polls, so he'll probably steal it. It would be preferable for him to lose, but he'll probably arrange not to." (Putin, in response, complained about NATO's intervention the previous year. "We weren't consulted in the decision to bomb Yugoslavia," he said. "That's not fair.")[28]

U.S. officials and U.S.-backed NGOs, sharing Clinton's concerns, sought to ensure that Milošević could not falsify the vote count. IRI trained more than fifteen thousand activists to monitor polling places.[29] On Election Day, opposition members tallied ballots alongside government officials. "The parallel vote count: This was again training, training the trainers, there were thousands of polling stations, and our aim was to have three people at each one," said O'Brien, the special envoy.[30] The government's vote count suggested that Milošević had a narrow lead. The parallel count, however, revealed the truth: He had lost overwhelmingly. Major protests erupted. Milošević, unable to quell a popular revolution, was forced to resign.[31]

The United States had worked to oust a foreign leader at the ballot box. The levers of U.S. democracy promotion had helped the opposition reach voters and prevent Milošević from altering ballots. Should this effort be considered overt? O'Brien called it "discreet."[32] On the one hand, most Serbs had no idea that the United States had guided the opposition's strategy and bankrolled items like the anti-Milošević stickers. On the other, it wasn't exactly a secret. After the election, news outlets published reports about NDI, IRI, and the State Department's campaign against Milošević.

This type of electoral support is not equivalent to CIA- or KGB-led electoral interference, which operated in the shadows, financed campaigns, presented foreign voices as domestic ones, and misdirected and misinformed citizens. NDI and IRI published public reports. They did not spread disinformation or mask their identities. And their primary objective was to foster competitive elections.

What is also true, though, is that the United States was influencing elections through IRI and NDI. Since the federal government worked through these NGOs, foreign citizens were unlikely to realize where the support was coming from. This new form of electoral influence—visible but privatized—was more tenable for U.S. presidents than CIA-led covert action. "I really preferred the NDI approach" to the CIA, Bill Clinton told me, because "NDI was open, aboveboard, sanctioned by Congress, public in its activities, and in any genuinely democratic election offered technical support and advice to competing parties."[33] That which was public could not be dramatically outed, and the tactics of IRI and NDI, even when favoring specific parties, were less explosive than, say, waging a non-attributable scare campaign. For Washington, overt democracy promotion, rather than covert electoral interference, had become the rule.

—

To defeat Milošević, however, the United States departed from this emerging pattern. In 2000, as NDI, IRI, and the State Department worked overtly, the CIA covertly supported Milošević's opposition, according to former U.S. officials with direct knowledge of the operation. John Sipher said that between 1991 and 2014, when he was serving as a CIA operations officer, he knew of just one "successful" operation to interfere in an election: in Serbia in 2000. "There was a covert effort to try to support the opposition to Milošević," Sipher said, recalling that after Clinton notified select members of Congress, the CIA went to work "supporting and funding and providing help to specific opposition candidates—that was the main thing."

Sipher, who became the CIA's station chief in Serbia just after the election, explained that the agency funneled "certainly millions of dollars" into the anti-Milošević campaign, mostly by meeting with key aides to Serbian opposition leaders outside their country's borders and "providing them with cash" on the spot.[34]

Clinton confirmed in our interview that he authorized the CIA to interfere in the 2000 election in favor of Milošević's opponents. "I didn't have a problem with it," he said of the CIA's covert action program, because Milošević "was a stone-cold killer and had caused the deaths of hundreds of thousands of people." In this instance, the CIA's focus was on influencing minds rather than altering ballots. "We did not rig the vote nor knowingly lie to the voters to get them to support the people we hoped to win," Clinton said. Instead, the CIA provided money and other types of assistance to the opposition. Congressional leaders knew about and backed this secret plan. Trent Lott, the Senate majority leader, recalled that when he was briefed on the CIA's operation, he supported it wholeheartedly. "[Milošević] was totally out of control," Lott said. "We weren't gonna invade, but it was a mess, and we had to do something." Lott judged that the CIA's work had a "positive" impact on the final outcome. "Innocent people were being killed and it was a violent place," he said, so interfering in the election "had to be done to help bring a solution into place and, hallelujah, it did work."[35]

Douglas Wise and Steven Hall, two former CIA station chiefs, were both based in the Balkans in 2000 as senior operations officers. They declined to explicitly acknowledge that Clinton sanctioned a covert action program against Milošević, but they nevertheless provided details about the CIA's engagement with the election. "Everybody who was in the Balkans at that time was all focused on Serbia and the Milošević regime," Hall said.[36] Milošević was a "genocidal maniac," Wise added, and so "the intelligence community was engaged as part of a whole-of-government engagement on that particular issue of Milošević." The U.S. intelligence community's involvement in the election was "substantial," Wise continued, as Washington used "all the instruments of our national power to create an outcome that was pleasing for the United States." When asked whether American intelligence supported the protests that culminated with Milošević's resignation, Wise said only: "It was a broad-spectrum involvement."[37]

These former CIA officers exuded unexplained confidence that the agency's work proved pivotal in defeating Milošević. John Sipher commented on the "success" of the CIA's operation. Douglas Wise said that America made "a big difference," and that "a combination of both" covert and overt tactics "produced an outcome that was from the perspective of the United States a positive outcome." As in Italy in 1948 and Chile in 1964, however, the CIA could not assess its precise impact in 2000. "Measuring it is hard," Sipher recognized. But, he noted, Serbian government officials did credit the CIA for their victory against Milošević when speaking behind closed doors. "Many of the key players who became senior figures in the follow-on government continued to meet with us and continued to tell us that it was our efforts that led to their success," Sipher said, "in terms of helping them with everything, from advertising to financing to how they did things" during the campaign.[38]

NDI and IRI, meanwhile, were left in the dark. "I'll tell you the truth, honest to God, I never knew it, I never saw evidence of it," Kenneth Wollack said, regarding CIA interference in the election. CIA officers, unlike NDI officials, could operate undercover. "Because of the nature of the way we do business," Douglas Wise explained, "Serbia was a lot more penetrable than it was for people who were much more overt, shall we say."[39]

In interviews, senior government officials grew uncomfortable at any mention of the CIA and Milošević's defeat. "I know stuff about that, but I'm not able to talk about it," said John McLaughlin, who was the CIA's deputy director in 2000. When asked about the CIA's operation, James O'Brien, Clinton's special envoy, responded carefully: "There was a U.S. government–wide, well-considered policy of supporting the opposition, and this was because the opposition was organic and well-rooted and felt more than likely to win a fair competition."[40] Others expressed frustration that former CIA officers were discussing the election at all. "I can't talk about what we did or didn't do. I'm just not going to talk about it," said a high-ranking White House official serving in 2000. "They may not take their oaths and legal obligations seriously, but I do."

This discomfort made sense: CIA interference in the 2000 election was not representative of the agency's post–Cold War operations. How often, after all, can a war criminal be ousted by ballot? "It seemed to be a holy thing to do by that point," John Sipher said. "I don't remember any resistance in the State Department or anywhere else." Steven Hall said it was "accurate" that there was minimal internal pushback to CIA involvement in the election. "There seemed to be a higher comfort level not just in the intelligence part of the world but really just policy writ large that something had to be done in the Balkans," he said. For Washington, "electoral manipulation" has become "a tool of last resort," Douglas Wise said, and the Serbian case was "the complete exception," in part because of Milošević's atrocities and in part because of the "receptive," "credible," and "attractive" nature of the opposition. For such cases, Wise argued generally, "The ends justify the means . . . The risk is you maybe do something that is unAmerican in the eyes of some," but the result is "the genocidal maniac is no longer in power."[41]

When I asked Clinton why covert action was merited in Serbia, he said simply, "There's a death threshold, and Milošević crossed it."[42]

———

How, then, had the role of the CIA changed in the post–Cold War era? Even as NDI and IRI promoted democracy overtly, only the CIA could influence elections directly and covertly. In 2004, President George W. Bush was on the verge of authorizing another such operation. This story unfolded in the White House Situation Room, where, in the summer and fall, America's national security officials weighed a familiar proposal: for the CIA to engage in covert electoral interference. This time, the target would be Iraq.

In March 2003, the United States had invaded Iraq to remove Saddam Hussein, the country's longtime dictator, and seize weapons of mass destruction that he allegedly possessed. Hussein's government fell within weeks, but no such weapons were found. By the end of the year, hundreds of American soldiers and thousands of Iraqis had died.[43] Struggling to justify this war, Bush renewed his promise to transform the essence of Iraq. In late 2003, he declared that "Iraqi democracy will succeed" and that its establishment would serve as "a watershed event in the global democratic revolution."[44] Bush had weaponized the pro-democracy rhetoric of previous administrations. Titans of American foreign policy resented him for it. "We were clearly on the side of democratic governance and willing to be helpful," said George Shultz, Ronald Reagan's long-time secretary of state. "But we were not crusading as later the Bush administration was, and I think we were more effective."[45]

Bush had proclaimed that in Iraq, democracy would replace tyranny, and citizens would enjoy popular representation. "For [the U.S. government] at that time it was extremely important to have free and fair elections because that's actually justifying the invasion," said Arturo Muñoz, then a senior CIA operations officer. "As long as we didn't find weapons of mass destruction, we were kind of desperate by then to justify ourselves, so at least we can create democracy in this place."[46] American democracy-promotion organizations poured resources into Iraq. IRI and NDI, in particular, launched massive programs there, helping to produce voter-education materials, train party officials, and facilitate political debates and get-out-the-vote efforts.[47]

The central purpose of elections, though, is for voters to determine the direction of their state. In this sense, Bush had a problem: Intelligence reports indicated that his preferred candidate, Ayad Allawi, would lose in Iraq's first-ever parliamentary election, scheduled for January 2005.

The U.S. intelligence community believed that Iran, a regional foe, was manipulating the election in favor of Allawi's opposition. "Of course, Iran was involved," said John McLaughlin, who served as the CIA's deputy director in 2004. "Why wouldn't they be? They're right next door, they have the capability, and they were close to some of the leadership." Douglas Wise was based in Iraq ahead of the election as an operations officer and, a few years later, became the CIA's station chief there. He described Iranian interference in the Iraqi election as wide-ranging: "We're talking money, activists, threats, extortion, a paramilitary presence."[48]

Bush and his advisers weighed whether to respond with covert action. John Negroponte, then the U.S. ambassador to Iraq, regularly participated in interagency teleconferences from Baghdad with a sole agenda item: CIA-led electoral interference. "We really thought about it hard," said Negroponte, who told me that he had been "open to the possibility" during discussions with other senior administration officials, including McLaughlin and Secretary of State Colin Powell. (Powell, in an email, said he was "not involved" in any such talks, and then, in a second email, clarified that he had "no recollection of the details" of the conversations Negroponte referenced, but did not elaborate further.)[49]

Deliberations reached a serious enough stage that the White House briefed congressional leadership on its planning. "[The] top line was that there's an opportunity here to engage in a way that could provide much more of a guaranteed outcome," recounted Tom Daschle, then the Senate minority leader. The officials I interviewed could not recall, or were unwilling to share, the operational details of the CIA's plan, although Daschle said it included "a lot of activities that we thought were just untoward and inadvisable."[50] George W. Bush, Vice President Dick Cheney, National Security Adviser Condoleezza Rice, and Deputy National Security Adviser Stephen Hadley all declined, through representatives, to be interviewed for this book.

For the CIA, interfering in Iraq's election would be the latest rendition of an age-old operation. And by the summer, the agency was moving toward action. Allawi had come to expect covert help. "The initial attitude of the U.S. was to support moderate forces, financially and in the media," he said in 2007. Then, unexpectedly, this assistance "was brought to a halt," Allawi said, "under the pretext that the U.S. does not want to interfere."[51]

Within the CIA, the White House, and Congress, an unlikely alliance of officials had united *against* covert electoral interference. The CIA's representatives, Negroponte recalled, "least wanted to be involved" with this operation, since it could expose the agency to criticism if detected. McLaughlin, laughing, said in an interview that he "wouldn't disagree" with Negroponte's recollection. "We had, after all, invaded a country to make it democratic," he said. "How hypocritical would it be then to subvert their election?" Speaking generally, Muñoz said, "If you're going to ruin the elections, and it becomes known, and things frequently leak," then once "word gets out that so-and-so won because the CIA did X, Y, and Z, then you've just wrecked the whole foreign policy adventure that you've embarked on."[52]

Congressional leaders also objected to the plan. For Daschle, the arguments against covert action were twofold. The first was a matter of optics: how "terrible it would look" if exposed. The second was normative. "It was no longer the Cold War," he said. "Doing what we had been doing even twenty years earlier was just not appropriate; it wasn't keeping with what our country should be all about." Daschle recalled that Nancy Pelosi, his counterpart in the House, was "very vocal" in opposing the plan.[53] Pelosi reportedly found an ally in Rice, the national security adviser.[54] "As I heard the debate go on," Negroponte said, "I realized, 'It is just not worth it, and people do not want to do it,' and we rejected it."[55]

President Bush, in attempting to build a democracy, was unwilling to intervene in that democracy's elections covertly. "You wanted to be pretty much clean and free when it came to interference in their electoral processes," McLaughlin said. "I was involved in a lot of covert action planning and decisions, and you always have to ask yourself, 'What are the unintended consequences of what we are proposing to do or thinking about doing?'"[56]

The CIA's plan was shelved. And come January 2005, Allawi's coalition lost resoundingly, in a contest marred by instability and terrorist attacks. A governing coalition with close ties to Tehran then took power.[57]

—

The Russian president, Vladimir Putin, has claimed that America still manipulates elections globally. He is not the only one who believes this. "The CIA hasn't stopped; they will never stop," said Oleg Kalugin, the former KGB general.[58] From Kyiv, to Brussels, to London, government officials told me that *of course* the CIA still interferes in elections. This perception is understandable: For decades, it was true.

But times have changed. Outside suspicions do not align with internal realities, as demonstrated by the decision not to interfere in

Iraq and, as former U.S. officials put it, the "extraordinary" nature of the decision to do so in Serbia. Based on my interviews with eight former CIA directors and acting directors, as well as former CIA deputy directors and directors of national intelligence, the United States has all but abandoned the use of covert electoral interference.

—

These former spies, in discussing the CIA's covert action programs, fell into two groups. The first claimed that the CIA has turned the page entirely. "The U.S. did historically intervene in elections, but that ended," said Michael Morell, a former CIA acting and deputy director who worked for the agency from 1980 to 2013. Former CIA deputy director David Cohen similarly said "it is not true" that the agency still interferes in elections as Russia does, and David Petraeus, who led the CIA in 2011 and 2012, said he is "not aware . . . in more recent times" of such operations. John Brennan, the CIA's director from 2013 to 2017, offered a more blanket assurance: "With President Obama and President Bush 43, there was never an effort to try to influence the outcome of a democratic election. We believed it was antithetical to the democratic process to do that." The CIA once targeted foreign elections, he continued, "but over the course of the last eighteen years or so, that has not been the case."[59]

The second group of officials did not speak in absolutes. They suggested that the CIA has moved away from, but not necessarily stopped, influencing elections overseas. "There wasn't much of it. This is not something that intelligence does with anything like the sense of flexibility and freedom that it might have had in the early Cold War," said John McLaughlin, who, as the CIA's number two in 2000, would have been involved with the Milošević case. Since then, such operations have, at the very least, been raised at the highest levels. The Bush administration debated the Iraq scheme; the Obama administration weighed similar proposals. "It's not like these ideas don't resurface, but at least in [the Obama] administration they would get rejected," said Tony Blinken, who served in senior national security positions from 2009 to 2017. Avril Haines, the CIA's deputy director from 2013 to 2015, offered one guarantee.

"The United States has made clear in modern history that it is not acceptable to tamper with votes in an election," she said while declining to comment on how the CIA may still seek to influence voters' minds. "It's all a question of degree," added James Clapper, the director of national intelligence from 2010 to 2017, when asked whether the United States still influences elections behind the scenes.[60] He would not elaborate further.

Of this second group, Leon Panetta, the director of the CIA from 2009 to 2011, was the most forthcoming. He said he never "got into" altering votes directly or spreading disinformation. But on rare occasions, his CIA did influence foreign media outlets ahead of key elections, in order to "change attitudes within the country." The CIA's method, Panetta went on, was to "acquire media within a country or within a region that could very well be used for being able to deliver" specific messages, or working to "influence those that may own elements of the media to be able to cooperate, work with you in delivering that message." Panetta declined to specify further, but Arturo Muñoz, a CIA officer from 1980 to 2009, said that historically the agency's approach toward foreign media has been straightforward: "You just pay for it; you just pay people to put stuff in newspapers." In such cases, America's hand remained hidden. "It usually always is a covert operation," Panetta said. "I can't recall anything that was not covert, because people usually protected that process."[61]

These efforts to influence minds mirrored past practices. As in Italy or Serbia, the programs that Panetta described complemented overt propaganda campaigns. "Even though we were operating on a covert basis," he said, "you had to make sure that the overt methods that were being used at least delivered the same message." As ever, he could not prove that the CIA made a difference. "To be frank, you could not really measure whether or not any of that was having a real impact or not," he said, although "Congress was always asking that question." Even this type of covert operation presented risks. "There is no question it's a gamble," Panetta continued, which is why it was an option of last resort and why more aggressive tactics had been sidelined.[62]

Every interview pointed to the same conclusion: For the CIA, covert electoral interference has become the exception rather than the rule. Either the agency no longer seeks to influence election outcomes, as Morell and Brennan asserted, or it does so in rare cases when, as with Milošević, a tyrant can be ousted by ballot. The exact truth is unknown. But this general shift marks a dramatic departure from the Cold War, when, as David Robarge, the CIA's internal historian, put it, the agency was interfering in the elections of "many, many" countries. In modern times, the costs of such operations have come to outweigh the benefits. "Frankly, political action of that kind is really part of the past. Iraq convinced me of that. It was just zero appetite for [electoral] intervention," said John Negroponte, who, in the Bush administration, also served as the director of national intelligence.[63]

Skeptics will insist that America's intelligence chiefs are lying. But considering present-day realities, the skeptics may be the ones defying logic. It would be self-defeating for the CIA to manipulate foreign elections in all but the most exceptional of circumstances. One reason why concerns the end of the Cold War, which robbed the CIA of its long-running purpose: to counter the Soviet Union. Milošević, for one, was a relic of a previous era. Generally, with peace seemingly at hand, the CIA was left adrift. "What kinds of covert action are we doing in the '90s? The answer is not much," said Porter Goss, the former CIA director. "I could count on less than two hands the number that I think would be qualified as covert action." With the Soviet Union gone, Arturo Muñoz explained, the thinking inside the agency became, "if you're not afraid anymore, if you don't view these guys as a huge threat, then why dick around with elections anymore, who cares?"[64] In September 2001, the CIA found a new focus in counterterrorism, which called for drone strikes and paramilitary operations, not electoral interference.

America's post–Cold War leaders declared an era of liberal democracy, defined by free and fair elections. This transition, from containing Communism to promoting democracy, made covert electoral interference a riskier proposition: If the CIA was caught, American hypocrisy would be broadcast before the world. "You can't stand up and be for free and fair elections and then turn around and intervene in them covertly. So we don't do it anymore.

[Russia] does; we don't," said Michael Morell, the former CIA acting director. Michael Hayden, a former CIA director, similarly explained, "Meddling in an electoral process cuts across the grain of our own fundamental beliefs. You might want to do it to level the playing field, you might want to do it because of just the demands of national security, but it doesn't feel right." John McLaughlin, another former CIA acting director, best captured America's evolving outlook: "If you are interfering in an election and are exposed as doing so, you are a lot more hypocritical than you would have appeared in the Cold War, when that sort of thing tended to be excused as part of the cost of doing business."[65]

Hypocrisy, however, had not stopped the CIA before. And in recent years, as great-power competition has reemerged, the United States has had a stake in many foreign elections. Changes in high politics, then, only partly explain this shift in CIA activity.

The rest of this story has to do with the spread of the internet, a momentous technological disruption that has made it harder to maintain the secrecy of operations to manipulate an electorate. "It's very difficult to keep that kind of activity from ultimately getting out," said David Petraeus, the former CIA director. And for America, getting caught matters. "If the United States were identified as having promoted disinformation or tampering with votes in an election, it would undermine our credibility and our policy efforts, given how inconsistent such actions would be with the values we promote, which are at the heart of our soft power," Avril Haines said. "The same is not true for Russia."[66]

None of this is to say that the CIA cannot keep a covert electoral interference operation secret. It certainly could. But in the digital age, the risk of detection is greater. And were such an effort revealed, it would become a piece of propaganda for America's enemies. John McLaughlin said that when considering covert operations targeting elections, "it only makes sense that the bar for admission has to be much higher than it used to be, given the high likelihood of exposure."[67]

The digital age, as detailed later, has also exposed American elections. Officials in Washington are reluctant to authorize the type of operation to which their country has become so vulnerable. "If you're in a glass house, don't throw stones," David Petraeus said, "and we're the biggest glass house when it comes to internet connectivity."[68]

Adjusting for these new dynamics, the United States has been influencing foreign elections overtly and with less brazen methods. "The terms changed. The expectations changed. What might have been termed a covert action, people say, 'Why bother to hide this?' " Goss said. One option is public endorsements. America does "all sorts of perfectly overt messaging about our preferences in foreign elections," explained David Cohen, the former CIA deputy director. In 2016, for example, President Barack Obama endorsed the Remain campaign in the United Kingdom. "In the Brexit scenario, how can you say that we were not trying to influence the outcome of the vote? That is ridiculous," said Avril Haines, the deputy national security adviser at the time.[69]

The other option is democracy promotion, a procedural and budgeted alternative. "We intervene in countries' politics overtly, through pro-democracy NGOs; this is the U.S. government, the State Department doing this, but doing it openly," Morell said. Between fiscal year 2007 and fiscal year 2017, the United States directed, on average, more than $2.5 billion annually toward democracy promotion initiatives, including several hundred million dollars each year for "political competition." IRI and NDI are still operating in dozens of countries. Separately, there is the NED: By 2010, its annual budget had increased to $118 million and, by 2020, to $300 million. Hayden said these "aboveboard NGOs [are] trying to spread what we think is a successful formula for self-governance." Sometimes, though, these initiatives show bias. "The State Department does do some things where it prefers not to be seen as doing it. My view is that that is inappropriate," Morell said. But, he continued, the CIA is removed from such operations. "From a covert action perspective," he said of his time in CIA leadership, "there was really nothing that touched on elections."[70]

Democracy promotion persists, but the hopeful days of the 1990s are gone. U.S.-Russian relations have deteriorated. Great-power competition is back. And democracy is on the retreat as authoritarian-minded leaders rise globally. Freedom House found that, in 2019, sixty-four countries experienced declines in political rights and civil liberties, while just thirty-seven countries experienced gains, marking the fourteenth straight year of net losses.[71] Behind this trend are a range of economic, social, and political factors.[72] But the most pertinent is that the United States, in the post–Cold War period, no longer stands alone in seeking to influence states around the world. As Washington moved away from covert electoral interference, Moscow rediscovered and enhanced this weapon. It has done so under the leadership of one man: Vladimir Putin.

Chapter 7

FROM YELTSIN TO PUTIN

On April 21, 1996, Bill Clinton and Boris Yeltsin huddled inside the Kremlin. Pleasantries were exchanged. Then Yeltsin raised the topic that had become his obsession: how the United States could help him win Russia's first-ever presidential election, scheduled for that summer. He urged Clinton "not to embrace" his Communist opponent. "You don't have to worry about that," Clinton replied. "We spent fifty years working for the other result." Yeltsin pressed further: "You know, Bill, in this Russian campaign you are a factor." Clinton wanted Yeltsin to win, to be sure, but he worried that overt interference would backfire; when an outside actor makes an appeal to voters, he told Yeltsin, they tend to do the opposite. "I'm trying to figure out a way to do this that will give you all the benefits and none of the disadvantages," Clinton said—by expressing support "in the most appropriate way" and without "say[ing] something that could be used against you."[1]

Clinton had been walking this tightrope for nearly a year. Back in May 1995, Yeltsin, polling in the single digits, had complained to Clinton that his electoral prospects were "not exactly brilliant."[2] So began Yeltsin's campaign to get an American president to interfere in a Russian election. "He was always like that: 'Help us, Bill!'" Strobe Talbott, then Clinton's deputy secretary of state, told me. Leon Panetta, Clinton's chief of staff in 1996, explained that Yeltsin and Clinton had a "very strong" and "very frank" relationship, so much so that, ahead of the election, "Yeltsin pretty much told Clinton what kind of help he needed" and that "the decision was to basically try to boost him"—within reason. James Steinberg, the

State Department's director of policy planning, recalled his "great discomfort" whenever Yeltsin invited Clinton to influence the election. "He's clearly making these asks, no doubt that he wanted it, but we really didn't think it was good for him to do this, and so it was worrisome." Yeltsin believed in democracy, Steinberg insisted, but did not understand that soliciting campaign assistance from a foreign power actually undermined Russia's democracy. "There were things Yeltsin was asking which we were not going to do, because they were not the right things to do, even if we thought it would help him in his election," Steinberg said. "Part of what Clinton was trying to do was help Yeltsin learn what it meant to be a small-*d* democrat."[3]

Yeltsin's foremost focus, however, was on maintaining his power. First on his agenda was NATO, the military alliance that Clinton had been working to enlarge.[4] "Let's postpone NATO expansion for a year and a half or two years," Yeltsin suggested in May 1995. "There's no need to rile the situation up before the elections." Clinton responded carefully, explaining that on this issue a win-win was possible. "I've made it clear I'll do nothing to accelerate NATO," he said. "I'm trying to give you now, in this conversation, the reassurance you need. But we need to be careful that neither of us appears to capitulate." Clinton promised to "take some heat" for Yeltsin, because he did not "want to see [him] get hurt."[5]

Yeltsin, in that same meeting, had another request: for Clinton to "follow through on including us in the G-8." The United States was a member of the Group of Seven (G7), an international organization of seven democracies that Yeltsin wanted to join (hence, "G8"). "This will help me on the eve of the elections here," Yeltsin said. In another meeting, Yeltsin told Clinton that joining the G7 before its summit in Lyon, France, "would add 10 percent to my vote."[6] Clinton promised to try but, in early 1996, came back with discouraging news. "All of us want to help you," he told Yeltsin. "But the truth is that we cannot go to a G8 at Lyons." Clinton pledged to still "make Lyons a big success for you," in that there would be no "negative stories coming out of Lyons, only positive stories for you right before the election runoff. . . . It has to be a hundred percent win for you."[7]

Yeltsin pressed Clinton for financial assistance, too. He had phoned in January about a multibillion-dollar loan that the International Monetary Fund (IMF) was issuing Russia. Yeltsin complained that the IMF had "delayed their payments to us and obligation of credits of $9 billion," and asked Clinton to "help and push them a little to make the payment." Clinton said he would do his best.[8] The next month, Yeltsin urged Clinton "to use [his] influence" with the IMF "to perhaps add a little, from nine to 13 billion dollars—to deal with social problems in this very important pre-election situation."[9] Clinton again said he would try, but Yeltsin was unsatisfied. "Then there is the matter of finances, which is not proceeding very well," Yeltsin said in early May, before dropping all pretenses and urging Clinton to interfere in the contest directly. "Bill, for my election campaign, I urgently need for Russia a loan of $2.5 billion." Clinton suggested a subtler approach: getting the IMF, a third-party institution, to quicken its payments to Russia. "I'll check on this with the IMF and with some of our friends and see what can be done," he said. "I think this is the only way it can be done."[10]

Carlos Pascual, then the director for Russian affairs at the White House, said that he and his colleagues held an "extensive internal discussion" about Yeltsin's request for a direct loan. "They wanted cash," he said, so Clinton's team debated whether to provide it—overtly, covertly, or not at all. The decision was a near unanimous no. "It obviously was not what the Russian side wanted to hear," Pascual said, but "that kind of direct support for an individual candidate" would have marked "an inappropriate intervention in the Russian political process." Pascual said that Clinton instead instructed Larry Summers, the deputy Treasury secretary, to continue working with Moscow in enacting market reforms that would expedite investment from the IMF.[11] When asked about this period, Summers said, "I don't think I ever thought of myself as trying to manipulate the Russian election." He continued, "It was a priority for the United States to support the reform movement in Russia and to try to make negotiations between the IMF and Russia work as effectively as possible, and so that was what my colleagues and I tried to do."[12]

In these months, Clinton rebuffed many of Yeltsin's pleas but still lent support. A few months before the election, the United States helped Russia finalize the multibillion-dollar IMF loan, in what *The New York Times* described at the time as "a major election-year boost" for Yeltsin.[13] "I want this guy to win so bad," Clinton told Talbott, "it hurts."[14] Behind the scenes, private American consultants (with marginal influence) advised Yeltsin's campaign and provided regular updates to one of Clinton's political advisers, who in turn updated the president.[15] The levers of U.S. democracy promotion also operated overtly. "Throughout Russia's various local, regional, and national campaigns were IRI-trained Russian political activists," IRI's 1996 annual report said, "working on behalf of democratic candidates."[16] Based on all available evidence, though, the CIA did not assist Yeltsin's campaign. "We didn't sneak around about it," Clinton told me, of the methods he used to support Yeltsin. "I thought it was okay for me to make my policy preferences clear in ways that everybody knew, and my preference for Yeltsin—everybody knew that." Panetta, Clinton's chief of staff, further explained that the risks of covert action were too high. "There would have been a concern that if whatever the CIA was trying to do was discovered, that it could have a negative impact on what was happening there," Panetta said, so it was "more cautionary than anything else not to have them play a big role."[17]

For Clinton, the first round of Russia's 1996 election was nerve-racking. As voting unfolded on June 16, he phoned Talbott to discuss the contest. Clinton said that he had "seen a CIA poll on Thursday or Friday that showed [Yeltsin] comfortably ahead of [his opponent], 40% to 28%," but that he was "concerned about the narrowing of the gap" between the two candidates. Talbott and Clinton then discussed the upcoming G7 summit, where "the name of the game" would be to "steady Yeltsin out." Clinton remained preoccupied with Yeltsin's prospects. "I've never been as much into one of these things unless I was running myself," he told Talbott. "I gotta tell you, I feel in my gut he's going to win in part because he really wants to—this guy is all-out; he's determined."[18]

That July, Yeltsin won the second round of the election by more than thirteen percentage points, amid widespread reports of voter fraud. Talbott said it was a "credible worry" and "probably a credible fact" that the vote was corrupted.[19] Still, the outcome thrilled

Clinton, who called Yeltsin to say, repeatedly, how "proud" he was of his friend. "You came back from a low standing in the opinion polls," Clinton said, comparing Yeltsin's victory to his own. "They called me the 'come back kid.' Now I have to hand the title over to you, Boris." Yeltsin was overjoyed—and grateful. "I appreciate that throughout the campaign up to the last day, you said the right things and never sent the wrong signals," he told Clinton. "Rest assured, I will do the same for your campaign. There will be no interference in your internal affairs. But I know deep in my heart who I support and who I hope will win."[20] That November, Clinton secured a second term. "Because of your election [and] my election," Clinton then told Yeltsin, "we have an historic opportunity to secure a free and peaceful future for our countries and all the world."[21]

What matters most about Russia's 1996 election is not what the United States did for Yeltsin—Clinton generally exercised restraint—but the dynamic that had developed between these two leaders. Yeltsin, competing in an open election, was desperate for Clinton to help him win. Clinton, therefore, held all the cards. The United States led the international institutions—the G7, the IMF, NATO—on which Yeltsin believed he had staked his political future. Organizations like IRI and NDI, meanwhile, were continuously shaping Russia from within. "We supported reform in Russia, and we did it quite openly," said Tom Donilon, then the State Department chief of staff.[22] To many Russians, Moscow's reliance on Washington was an embarrassment. Democracy, it seemed, meant subservience to the West. "There was a kind of patronizing quality" emanating from the United States "that Russians deeply resented," said Steven Erlanger, who reported from Moscow for *The New York Times* from 1991 to 1995.[23]

Clinton's chief advisers tend to recognize that their policy toward Russia, though well intentioned, had certain negative consequences. Talbott noted a backlash to U.S. democracy promotion among "a whole lot" of Russians who "hated what had happened" to their country. Larry Summers, who went on to serve as Clinton's Treasury secretary, said that America perhaps inadvertently "treat[ed] Russia as a charity case" through aid programs that were "insufficiently respecting of the dignity of a people who had thought of themselves

a very short time before as one of the world's great superpowers."
Summers now believes that NATO expansion and U.S. action in
Serbia might have "manifest[ed] disrespect in a way that made
it easy for Russian pride to be mobilized by revanchist elements
unsympathetic to markets, capitalism, and the United States."[24]

One especially resentful Russian was Vladimir Putin, who became acting president on December 31, 1999, after Yeltsin resigned
unexpectedly.[25] In private, Yeltsin assured Clinton that Putin, his
handpicked successor, was "a democrat" who "has the energy and
the brains to succeed," "knows the West," and has a "big soul." The
day after assuming the presidency, Putin spoke with Clinton. "We
thank you personally," Putin told him, "because you have done a lot
to develop Russian-American relations."[26]

What to expect of Putin? The answer, at first, was not at all
clear. "He's very smart," Clinton had told Yeltsin.[27] Putin, a former
KGB officer, certainly knew how to deceive through flattery. Talbott
later learned that when he visited the Kremlin in early 2000, his
counterpart in the Russian government informed Putin, "Strobe is
here. He's a friend of ours." Squinting, Putin shot back, "We have
no friends there."[28] When speaking with U.S. officials, however,
Putin was effusive. He called Talbott "an excellent diplomat" from
whom he had "learned a great deal," and praised Clinton for his
"very open-minded and constructive attitude toward my country."[29]
He even complimented Clinton's wife on her promising political
future. "I want to pass on my congratulations to Hillary for her
victory in the New York Senate race," Putin told the president in
November 2000.[30]

Putin's actions had nonetheless signaled his cleverness, stubborn-
ness, and grand ambition. Just before Yeltsin resigned, Clinton had
urged Putin, then Russia's prime minister, to exercise restraint in
bombing Chechnya. "You understand that we cannot sit back and
wait," Putin snapped. "There will be no massive bombing campaign,
no carpet-bombing. We have a sound military operation going. Lis-
ten to what the CIA tells you."[31] In September 2000, Putin criticized
NATO's mission against Milošević. And in December, he reminded
Clinton, offhandedly, that Russia was still "a big power."[32] Clinton
left these meetings both impressed and concerned. Putin was clearly

"disciplined," "tough," and "very able," Clinton told me, and "never pretended to be something he wasn't privately—and I liked that." The trouble was that Putin seemed neither to "care much" about Russian democracy nor to approve of Yeltsin's chumminess with Western leaders. Clinton concluded, over time, that "Putin thought I had played Yeltsin a little bit to increase America's power in the post–Cold War world."[33]

Putin was no Yeltsin. He had his own worldview, skill set, and paranoid tendencies. While Russia's first president had drawn power from the United States, Putin was determined to be the source of his own power.

—

Born in 1952 to a working-class family, Putin grew up in Saint Petersburg—then known as Leningrad—during the height of the Cold War. He was not particularly close to his parents, whom he later lamented "never told me anything about themselves," and who only reluctantly permitted him to train in boxing, Sambo (a Soviet martial art), and then Judo. As a teenager, Putin dreamed of joining the KGB. "Even before I graduated from school, I wanted to work in intelligence," he said in 2000.[34]

The KGB's covert operations intrigued Putin. So did its power. "What amazed me most of all," he marveled, "was how one man's effort could achieve what whole armies could not. One spy could decide the fate of thousands of people."[35]

In 1975, Putin fulfilled his ambition and became a member of the KGB; for years, he shuttled between domestic assignments and official training courses. A decade into his career, Putin was assigned to Dresden, East Germany, where his work revolved around studying and manipulating unsuspecting minds—skills central to covert electoral interference. "Recruitment of sources, procurement of information, and assessment and analysis were big parts of the job," Putin said. "It was important to know who was doing what and how." In East Germany, Putin learned to analyze foreign governments: "I looked for information about political parties, the tendencies inside these parties, their leaders."[36]

Then came the popular revolutions of 1989, when the Berlin

Wall collapsed, and the Eastern bloc unraveled.[37] Still stationed in Dresden, Putin found it "upsetting" to watch protesters storm the Stasi's office and ransack the agency (which had, just seventeen years earlier, covertly preserved Willy Brandt's government). Demonstrators also gathered around the KGB's district office, where Putin worked.

"Those crowds were a serious threat," he thought, and yet "nobody lifted a finger to protect us." When Putin's team sought assistance, the reply was clear: "We cannot do anything without orders from Moscow. And Moscow is silent." Putin's experience was representative of the Kremlin's posture generally. "It is simply stunning to observe how easily the Iron Curtain fell in 1989," writes historian Vladislav Zubok, "and how complacently the central Soviet leadership reacted, in contrast to the alarmist and warning signals from Soviet representatives in Central European countries." Putin and his colleagues were left to hurriedly burn the KGB's files. Eventually, the crowd around their office disbanded.[38]

By the time Putin left Dresden in 1990, he had been shaped in important ways. He had worked for the KGB for fifteen years. In that period, he had learned to exist in the world as an intelligence officer: to manipulate and lie, to subvert, and to see conspiracy everywhere. The KGB, competing with the CIA, had long manipulated elections across the world. Putin did not participate in those operations, but he did study the tradecraft of the agency that executed them, including how to mold minds and achieve large ends with limited means. His natural foe was the United States—in particular, the CIA. And by chance, he saw firsthand how popular demonstrations could topple closed societies.

The fall of the Eastern bloc scarred Putin, who so intimately connected his self-worth with the standing of his country. "We would have avoided a lot of problems if the Soviets had not made such a hasty exit from Eastern Europe," he later said. "I wanted something different to rise in its place. And nothing different was proposed. That's what hurt. They just dropped everything and went away."[39] Putin had come up in a conservative corner of Russian society. The KGB's leaders had opposed Mikhail Gorbachev's domestic reforms and, in August 1991, attempted a coup d'état, which Yeltsin played a pivotal role in thwarting. Four months later, the Soviet Union dissolved, and Yeltsin became the first president of the newly independent Russian Federation.[40]

Putin returned to Saint Petersburg, where he worked as a local politician before moving to Moscow. He then ascended rapidly. In 1998, he became the director of the Federal Security Service (FSB), the main successor to the KGB. About a year later, he was appointed prime minister.[41] All the while, Yeltsin stewarded the future of the state that Putin would soon inherit.

—

Under Yeltsin, Russia's security service had a new name but the same hardline ethos. John Sipher was based in Moscow for much of the 1990s as a CIA operations officer. The FSB bugged his home with video and audio surveillance, followed him at all hours, and interviewed whomever he talked to. His station had to go to "incredible lengths" to meet with its "handful of strategic [Russian] assets" every few months. "We were followed and harassed as much as anyone was even during the Cold War," Sipher said. "Yeltsin may [have] mean[t] well, but the services [were] still as aggressive and [saw] us as the enemy. There was no corresponding change in the way they treated us on the ground." Leon Fuerth, the national security adviser to Vice President Al Gore, said the White House was well aware of "growing resistance" inside Russia's intelligence agencies to Yeltsin's push for transparency and democratization.[42]

The United States nevertheless worked to push Russia toward market economics and democratic governance. "I don't think there was any illusion at that time that the United States could simply on its own totally redirect the course of Russian history," Fuerth said. "On the other hand, the collapse of the Soviet Union essentially created a blank slate—maybe not as blank as we thought—but under Yeltsin there was a certain willingness to become what they called a 'normal state.' "[43]

—

Clinton recognized the enormity of this ambition. Russia, with its history of tsarism and Communism, had no history of democracy.

To usher Russia into the family of Western nations, the thinking went, the West would have to provide a helping hand. The United States, the G7, and the IMF channeled billions of dollars into Russia, primarily to enhance its economic development.[44] International institutions were "tools that we could leverage in getting Russia to adopt the economic reforms that we wanted," said James Steinberg, the deputy national security adviser during Clinton's second term. In 1996, after winning reelection, Yeltsin told Clinton he was "counting on your support and leadership" in urging U.S. businesses "to invest in Russia on a massive scale."[45]

By August 1998, however, Russia's economy had entered into crisis. Clinton faulted himself for not doing more. "What the IMF and the banks have done for Russia is chickenshit when you look at the size of the problem and the size of the stakes," Clinton complained to his advisers during a flight to Moscow that month. "We're giving them a big, tough reform message, but there ain't no dessert—hell, I'm not sure they can even see the main course."[46] Russia's future remained uncomfortably uncertain. "You can't underestimate the impact of this thing on our own national security and on the global economy if Russia goes south," Clinton continued. "If we can get them to do the right thing and keep the money in the country and doing some good, then we need to do more and faster—much more and much faster." Talbott asked the president if his vision amounted to a Marshall Plan for Russia. "You bet. It's that big a deal," Clinton replied. "I'm all for Marshall Plans but they've got to make it possible for money to help."[47]

The problem was that Yeltsin never did make it possible. In the 1990s, greed, theft, and fraud crippled Russia's political institutions and, according to James Steinberg, became a "major constraint" as Clinton pushed for more economic aid. There was no telling where the money would go. Larry Summers explained, "We were not going to accomplish anything by getting money to the Russians that was going to get lost in some Swiss bank account or funneled into some oligarch's business."[48]

Yeltsin had developed a hollow democracy, featuring weak courts, pervasive corruption, and an oligarchic class. He sold state assets to moneyed elites, partly to fund his reelection campaign.

Rumors circulated that the 1996 election was rigged in his favor. The FSB retained the same basic structure, attitude, and power as the KGB.[49] Yeltsin's alcoholism, meanwhile, made him an unreliable partner. "CIA doctor told me just before I came out to get on this plane that [Yeltsin's] not taking his blood pressure medicine but taking booze, because someone told him that's good for blood pressure," Talbott informed Clinton in August 1998. He went on to describe Yeltsin as "stubborn, resilient, defiant, tough—and not a quitter," but also as a "sick, weak, erratic jerk," to which Clinton replied, "But he's *our* sick, weak, erratic jerk, right?"[50] More than twenty years later, Leon Panetta reflected, "Look, nobody is kidding anybody: Yeltsin had his problems; he drank a lot and was somewhat unpredictable in his behavior. But at the same time, he was someone who, I think everybody felt, represented kind of a new Russia."[51]

When Yeltsin resigned, he left Russia in a precarious position. John McLaughlin, the CIA's deputy director in 2000, said Russian democracy was by then a "mess" and had "pretty much gone to hell." Others were more generous. "You had a form of democracy. It was chaotic, it was shallow rooted, but it was really there," Fuerth said. Regardless, Putin inherited a moldable state. "There were already problems on the horizon [in Moscow]," Clinton told me, as a result of Russia's "old Communists on the left," "ultranationalists on the right," "unreliable" banking system, and lack of "institutionalized democratic forces." But, Clinton continued, "I was hoping we could work through them, and I tried, and I used to tell people that whatever Yeltsin's limitations were, he was still by a good long distance the best available person who could actually get elected in Russia, and I still believe that."[52]

Several of Clinton's top advisers now say they were naïve in their attempts to shape Russia's future. Larry Summers, in particular, judged that he and his colleagues "tended to overstate our capacity to have efficacy in changing what was going to happen" in Moscow. He added, "Given the degree of challenge after seventy years of Communism, given the absence of any kind of democratic or market tradition in Russia, I think the situation was substantially more difficult than we appreciated, and that we were substantially too optimistic about our ability to influence events. What happened in Russia would largely be determined by what the Russian government and its people wanted, not by our calibration of flows of money."[53]

———

By 2001, Yeltsin and Clinton were out of office. Putin, a career intelligence officer, would now chart the future of a former superpower. Once in power, he methodically dismantled the fragile democratic structures of the Yeltsin years. He first moved to systematically manipulate the minds of his people. State authorities seized Russia's television stations, the heart of its information space, which the Kremlin then used to spread disinformation, subdue the masses, and broadcast a manufactured reality. "TV is the only force that can unify and rule and bind this country," writes Peter Pomerantsev, a former Russian television producer. Putin was also operating during an economic boom: From 1999 to 2008, real wages in Russia increased by an average of 10.5 percent annually, bolstering Putin's domestic standing, and thus his ability to roll back Russian democracy without provoking a popular backlash.[54] "Putin is a typical product of the Soviet KGB, not the Stalinist time, of later years," said Oleg Kalugin, the former KGB general. "His role is to tighten the screws and keep an eye on everyone."[55]

While distracting the public, Putin consolidated his power and enriched himself. In 2005, a Moscow-based research organization found that Russian businesses were paying more than $300 billion in bribes annually—a tenfold increase in just four years.[56] By 2014, the wealth share of the top 1 percent was a remarkable 66.2 percent. Of the world's major economies, Russia's had become the most unequal.[57] Putin and his inner circle reaped the benefits. Russians like Sergei Roldugin, a cellist and confidant of Putin's, hid billions of dollars in offshore accounts (a detail revealed by the so-called Panama Papers, a set of leaked documents that emerged in early 2016 and that Putin interpreted as a U.S.-backed conspiracy against him).[58] Karen Dawisha, a leading expert on Russia, has aptly described Putin's governing structure as kleptocratic authoritarianism. Putin sought to strengthen Russia "not by breaking up the oligarchic system" developed under Yeltsin, Dawisha writes, "but by transforming an oligarchy independent of and more powerful than the state into a corporatist structure in which oligarchs served at the pleasure of state officials."[59]

Amid this corruption, Putin has lived in fear of his own 1989 moment: the day when protesters will storm the Kremlin and overthrow his government. Whether Putin actually should worry about a full-blown revolution is debatable. On the one hand, his domestic approval ratings have been remarkably resilient and high. But on the other, as of 2016, just 14 percent of Russians thought their economy was improving. Of all policy issues, voters most fault Putin for failing to address wealth inequality.[60] In this context, Putin believes that a popular uprising could topple his regime. And ever the conspirator, he has long suspected that the United States would support such a movement.[61]

Putin's paranoia can be traced, at least in part, to the Yeltsin era. John Sipher, the former CIA officer, said there is a "strong, strong" view inside Russia that Clinton unduly influenced the 1996 election in favor of Yeltsin. Steven Hall, who worked as a CIA officer in Russia in the 1990s and, later, as station chief there, said Yeltsin's reliance on Clinton disturbed Putin, who concluded that "flirting with so-called democracy was nothing more than the United States and other western countries trying to weaken great Russia." When Putin became president at the turn of the century, he remained "very close to the intelligence services," which bore "their own grudges from the Yeltsin period," recalled John McLaughlin, the former CIA chief.[62]

Putin then watched, as president, as the United States supported grassroots movements against strongmen. Slobodan Milošević's downfall in 2000 caught the Kremlin off guard. Douglas Wise, the former CIA officer, said Russia's security services "were asleep" and "weren't paying attention" to the election in Serbia. "The Russians weren't involved and they were not in it," he said, in part because Moscow "would not have been able to know" about the CIA's involvement in the contest; otherwise, Putin would have "gone after" the agency's efforts. "The Russians would have applied the Russian antibiotic to our infection," Wise said, with a laugh. Steven

Hall, then based in the Balkans as a station chief, likewise said that Putin and his advisers would have outed the CIA's work "if they could have convincingly done so," but they struggled to "even understand it themselves."[63]

Six days after the Serbian election, Clinton called Putin. The opposition had clearly won, Clinton explained, but Milošević was calling for a second round of voting. "I think the best thing to do is to try to get Milošević to leave, but I think you're the only person who can do that," Clinton said, because Milošević was relying on Russia's support. Putin ducked and dodged, before saying that a second round of voting seemed inevitable. Clinton grew impatient. "I want to ask you another question," he said. "How are we going to get him out of there?" Putin was confused, or at least acted like it. "You mean remove him?" he asked. "Yeah," Clinton replied, "is he afraid to leave office?"[64]

In the coming days, as protests against Milošević swelled, Putin held out. He issued a statement saying that he was "watching . . . the tragic development of the situation in friendly Yugoslavia." Only on October 6, the day Milošević resigned, did Putin recognize the outcome of the election. Madeleine Albright, then the secretary of state, was furious. "[The Russians] did not play the role they needed to at the right time," she said.[65] In Moscow, lawmakers howled about a Western plot of regime change. When Milošević fell, Steven Hall said, Putin surely looked at the United States and concluded, "You guys screwed us over."[66]

Putin resented that the United States seemed to be molding nations in its image. "Indeed, in recent years it is as if people are saying to us: we are waiting for you, we want to welcome you into our family, into our civilized western family," Putin said in 2007. "But, first of all, why have you decided that your civilization is the best?"[67]

One of America's tools for unseating authoritarians was military intervention. In 2003, a U.S.-led coalition invaded Iraq and ousted Saddam Hussein, the longtime dictator. "It seems easy to 'crush' such a small country," Putin complained. "But the ramifications, the 'splashes,' are such that even today we don't know what to do."[68] Then, in 2011, NATO forces helped depose yet another dictator,

Libya's Muammar el-Qaddafi, who died at the hands of rebel soldiers who beat, sodomized, and shot him.[69] Putin called NATO's mission "a medieval call for a crusade" and questioned whether all the world's "crooked regimes" would soon come under attack.[70] "The United States actively contributed to the destruction of these state institutions," Putin said. "Do you understand what this leads to?"[71] The answer, to him, was coups d'état and chaos.

For Putin, the most threatening form of U.S. intervention did not involve air raids or armed invasion. Not even he believed that the American military would bomb a nuclear-armed Russia. But he certainly thought that the United States could target his regime by igniting mass protests. Ukraine's 2004 election seemed to provide the proof. While Putin backed his preferred Ukrainian candidate, the United States poured millions of dollars into the country, supporting not just voter education and party training but also a pivotal exit poll. This secondary vote count revealed massive fraud and sparked what is known as the Orange Revolution, which secured the presidency for Viktor Yushchenko, a pro-Western politician. "[Putin's] paranoia was reinforced by the Orange Revolution in Ukraine in 2004," writes the historian Anne Applebaum. "The Libyan revolution showed an even more frightening prospect: street mobs, supported by the West, chasing out and then murdering a dictator who only months earlier had seemed to be in total control."[72]

Putin saw threats all around him. His country could not compete with America's economy, military, or vast network of alliances. But he didn't have to match the Americans; he just had to disrupt and weaken them. And in the digital age, he found a means to do it.

—

Before systematically interfering in Western elections, Putin tested his digital tool kit on his neighbors. In 2007, Estonia removed a World War II memorial honoring slain Soviet soldiers. An incensed Russia responded with a weeks-long cyberattack, shutting down Estonia's government web pages, news sites, and bank portals. The following year, Russia invaded Georgia, another former Soviet republic, with a mix of conventional and cyber tactics.[73] Even then, most American policy makers presumed that Putin merely sought to preserve his influence over nearby states. The cases of Estonia and Georgia marked "the first time [Russia had] used cyberattacks to help paralyze or confuse an opponent," writes journalist David Sanger, but an "absence of imagination" in Washington inhibited planning for attacks of a similar nature.[74] In 2008, a term-limited Putin transitioned to the post of prime minister and behind-the-scenes power broker.

A turning point came in late 2011, when Putin announced that he would once again stand for the presidency. Any lingering delusions of Russian democracy evaporated. Putin, in robbing his country of a process of succession, now sought to direct attention toward an external enemy: the United States.[75]

Tensions came to a head on December 4, 2011, when Russia held a parliamentary election. The United States had distributed millions of dollars ahead of the contest to a range of civil society groups, including Golos, Russia's only independent election monitor.[76] The purpose of Golos was not to determine who citizens elected; it was to stop Putin from electing himself.

For an authoritarian like Putin, electoral monitoring *is* electoral interference, because it exposes efforts to rig votes. As December 4 neared, Golos reported thousands of electoral violations. Putin complained that "so-called grant recipients" were manipulating Russian affairs, while state prosecutors launched an investigation into Golos. On Election Day, poll monitors documented rampant voter fraud in favor of Putin's United Russia party. Thousands of Russians took to the streets, chanting, "Putin is a thief." Hundreds were arrested.[77] Steven Hall, the CIA's station chief in Moscow, walked outside and spoke with protesters, even though embassy officials had cautioned that Putin would accuse the CIA of orchestrating the emerging movement against him. "Well, they're going to say that regardless," Hall replied.[78]

To Putin, an American plot was unfolding against him. Golos had helped spark the demonstrations. Then Hillary Clinton, the secretary of state, fanned the flames. Clinton was one of the most well-known figures in American politics. A former first lady and senator, she had nearly won the Democratic nomination for president in 2008. At the State Department, she supported the White

House's pursuit of a so-called reset in relations with Russia while simultaneously lambasting aspects of the Kremlin's policy making, especially toward Georgia. "We continue to object to and criticize actions by Russia which we believe are wrong," she told a Georgian audience in 2010. "And at the top of the list is the invasion and occupation of Georgia. We say it, we mean it, we support actions to try to give you the backing that you need in order to stand up to the threat that you believe comes from Russia."[79]

Clinton and Putin had never gotten along. "When I would see Putin, he was just always bristly, would do what they call mansplaining, in the way he would sit and talk to me," she told me, behavior she attributed both to her being "a skeptic about Russia" and to Putin's "sexist view of the world." Clinton had also advocated military intervention against the forces of Muammar el-Qaddafi, whose death in October 2011 had so disturbed Putin.[80]

In December 2011, Clinton received reports that Russia's parliamentary election had been "blatantly rigged," so she decided to speak out. "Russian voters deserve a full investigation of all credible reports of electoral fraud and manipulation," she said on December 5, because citizens deserve to have "their votes counted" in "free, fair, transparent elections" with "leaders who are accountable to them."[81]

For Putin, this was political warfare: Clinton was inciting demonstrations against him. She "set the tone for some actors" in Russia and "gave them a signal," Putin alleged on December 8, and protesters then "heard the signal and with the support of the U.S. State Department began active work."[82] He had seized the opportunity to assail Clinton—and to make her the foreign scapegoat for domestic discontent. Clinton assumed that Putin was using her to distract from his own woes. "I don't think I had very much, if anything, to do with the outpouring in the streets that happened, so when he started attacking me, I thought it was theater," she told me. "But they were huge demonstrations, and that scared Putin."[83]

On December 10, tens of thousands of Russians participated in the largest demonstration in the country's post–Cold War history.[84] These protests had "really got Putin's attention," said Michael Morell, then the CIA's deputy director, because he had long been "scared to death" of a popular revolution and was convinced that this movement was "originating in the United States." Of Putin's thinking, the CIA took a somewhat different view than Clinton. Its analysts assessed that in this moment she epitomized all that he feared and loathed about the United States. What Putin saw, Steven Hall said, was "a powerful person in the United States who he honestly believed was trying to start a color revolution in the streets of Moscow, and that's something that he takes very personally."[85]

Relations between Clinton and Putin deteriorated further in the months ahead. During their next encounter, Clinton scolded Putin for blaming the protests on her. "I said to him, 'That wasn't me, Mr. President, that was your people.'" Putin was dismissive. Then, in June 2012, at the G20 Summit in Mexico, Putin was forty-five minutes late to a meeting with Obama and Clinton. "I told Obama that I would have just canceled it. I would not have waited on Putin," Clinton said. Even after Putin arrived, she recalled, "it was a most unsatisfactory meeting." Later that year, at a conference at Vladivostok, Putin refused to see Clinton altogether. "He wouldn't talk to me," she said. (In the end, they met briefly, just before a dinner where they had to sit next to each other.) When I asked Clinton whether she, in hindsight, would have handled her relationship with Putin any differently, she expressed no regret. "I suppose I could have said nothing [during the protests], but I wasn't about to do that."[86]

—

Putin, while jousting with Clinton abroad, retained control at home. After reassuming the presidency in May 2012, he moved, as he had in 2000, to get his house in order. "What remained of U.S. democracy promotion disappeared upon Putin's return to power very quickly," said Ellen Barry, then the *New York Times* Moscow bureau chief, because "there was absolutely no ambiguity in the Russian view of this: It was money sent to undermine the Kremlin's control over its own people."[87] In September, Sergey Lavrov, the Russian foreign minister, informed Clinton that the Kremlin was expelling USAID, which had been spending $50 million annually in Russia, in part on democracy and human rights work. Senator John McCain called the decision "an insult to the United States." By

December, IRI and NDI, both funded largely by USAID, had been forced out of Russia. Putin also targeted online platforms, where many protesters had organized, by signing a law empowering federal authorities to block websites unilaterally.[88]

The shadow war unfolding in Putin's mind worsened in late 2013, when another grassroots uprising emerged. The location was Ukraine; the target: Viktor Yanukovych, a pro-Russian politician who had succeeded Yushchenko as president (and whom Putin had supported back in 2004). A series of protests and government crackdowns caused the movement against Yanukovych to balloon into a full-blown revolution. Putin saw only conspiracy. American aid had been flowing into Ukraine since the end of the Cold War.[89] And as these protests escalated, American officials like Victoria Nuland, an assistant secretary of state, toured opposition camps in Kyiv and met with their leaders, as well as with Yanukovych. Sergei Glazyev, an adviser to Putin, lambasted the United States for "unilaterally and crudely interfering in Ukraine's internal affairs." In early February 2014, Russian intelligence, through an online cutout, released a phone intercept of Nuland discussing the future shape of the Ukrainian government. It was an aggressive and unexpected move. "I knew they were listening," Nuland told me. "But that they would consider me so dangerous that they would try to destroy me, take me off the board as a player, it was a badge of honor and also a serious ramp-up of their tradecraft."[90]

Russia's hack and release, while a sign of things to come, did not stop Ukrainians from calling for change. The protests persisted. Then, between February 18 and 20, Ukrainian security forces fired upon demonstrators; dozens were killed. Yanukovych's remaining authority collapsed. The next day, he fled Kyiv, while citizens stormed his residence. "What is happening today, mostly, it is vandalism, banditism, and a coup d'état," Yanukovych said from eastern Ukraine. Putin deployed special forces to bring Yanukovych to Russia, where he has remained.[91]

—

Putin was alarmed that protesters in Ukraine, as in Russia, had organized online. "When he was forced to think about the internet during the protests," a Russian journalist said in 2014, Putin became "very suspicious" and moved "to put this thing under control."[92] After Yanukovych fled Ukraine, Putin called the internet a "CIA project." In April 2014, the CEO of VKontakte, Russia's most popular social media platform, announced that he had been ousted and that Kremlin loyalists had taken "full control" of the company. In May, Putin signed a law mandating that blogs with more than three thousand daily viewers register with the government and not post anonymously. Lawmakers also approved a bill requiring that online platforms store data about Russian users on servers inside Russia.[93] Government operatives, meanwhile, flooded websites with disinformation designed to confuse and subdue the masses.[94] The Kremlin was waging a coordinated assault against the minds of its own people.

—

The events of 2011 and 2014 left Putin vengeful. The United States had backed a popular movement inside Russia, he thought, and then sparked a revolution next door. "Why did you encourage the government coup in Ukraine?" he asked Megyn Kelly, an American journalist. "Why did you do that? The U.S. directly acknowledged spending billions of dollars to this end." Putin loathed the status quo: Washington influencing nations as it liked, while Moscow toed the line. "That you can interfere anywhere because you bring democracy, but we cannot, is what causes conflicts," he continued. "You have to show your partners respect, and they will respect you."[95]

Putin was at a crossroads. He did not want to repeat the mistake his predecessors made in 1989, when, as he put it, "nothing different was proposed," the Eastern bloc collapsed, and, soon after, the Soviet state collapsed too. The United States was, from his perspective, manipulating nations everywhere: ousting leaders like Yanukovych and Milošević, attacking countries like Iraq and Libya, and promoting democracy in places like Ukraine and Russia. "He always gave us more credit than we deserved for careful conspiracies, but that was his worldview," said William J. Burns, the U.S. deputy secretary of state from 2011 to 2014.[96] To Putin, all of America's activities abroad revolved around a single objective: to gain influence at Russia's expense. His world is zero-sum. When Washington wins, Moscow loses.[97] Russia could win only by hitting back.

It is important to understand what Putin considers a win. He does not share Lenin's ambitions for a global revolution based on an ideology. He believes he is locked in a power struggle—not an ideological struggle—with the United States. Principles do not matter; only influence does. Analysts who argue that Putin aims to re-create the Soviet Union are mistaken. He cannot re-create a superpower with control over half of Europe. Unable to surpass America by strengthening Russia, Putin's remaining option is to reduce America's global influence by manipulating its allies and tearing apart its electorate. "Their principal goal is to create instability, particularly in democratic countries that they feel are competitors to Russia," Leon Panetta said.[98]

Putin wants the United States and its allies to abandon internationalism for nationalism, open for closed, and inclusion for exclusion. The logical way to accomplish this mission is to support authoritarian-minded candidates in foreign democracies and to sow discord within those democracies. For Putin, this strategy offers many benefits. At home, it demonstrates to the Russian people that the democratic model is dysfunctional and unenviable, just as the KGB's staged hate crimes once did. In the United States, it undermines societal cohesion and Washington's ability to lead. And globally, it spawns new opportunities for influence. Well-functioning democracies tend to align with America. It is a shared liberal vision that has maintained international institutions like the European Union and NATO, which enhance American power in the world and prevent Russia from bullying isolated European states. By subverting democracies, Putin can undermine U.S.-led institutions, counter U.S. democracy promotion, and, in the process, bolster Moscow's relative power at Washington's expense.

So Putin resolved that Moscow would again target the democracies of the world. "If you see yourself in a life-and-death struggle, which he does, with the United States, you are going to use the assets you have," Michael Morell said.[99] Only, Putin possessed few assets: He lacked the economic resources or alliance network to fund illiberal activities in the light. He also lacked the ability to use his nuclear weapons and, with rare exceptions, his military. What was left, then, was a single resource: his highly capable intelligence services, for which he had once worked. The FSB and the GRU, Russia's military intelligence agency, also possessed a new tool in the internet. "In many ways, Putin resorts to the old Soviet techniques, in trying to influence the minds, the moods of other nations, and of course the elections," Oleg Kalugin said.[100]

Here enters covert electoral interference, adjusted for the digital age. Putin, a trained KGB officer, turned to the KGB's successors to undermine the United States and other democracies. He would use the internet to enhance age-old tactics. As Vladislav Surkov, one of Putin's closest advisers, wrote in February 2019, Russia launched "an information counteroffensive against the West" after the "ruinous" 1990s. "Foreign politicians accuse Russia of interfering in elections and referenda around the world," Surkov continued. "In reality, things are even more serious: Russia is interfering in their brains, and they don't know what to do about their own altered consciousness."[101]

Distracted by the war on terror, Washington did not anticipate Putin's aggression or ingenuity. "We took the eye off the Russia ball," said Michael Hayden, director of the NSA from 1999 to 2005 and of the CIA from 2006 to 2009. "We were consumed with counterterrorism, counter-proliferation. I went to more than fifty countries as director and not one of them was Russia . . . if I have any sin to confess of my directorship at CIA, it is that I didn't pay any attention to Putin."[102]

Putin, however, had kept his eyes on the United States. And now he would use the means at his disposal to disrupt the democratic world. "This is about breaking the unity of Western countries," said Liubov Tsybulska, an adviser to the chief of the general staff of Ukraine's armed forces, during our interview in Kyiv. "It is much easier for Russia to win over a country if this country doesn't have any allies or supporters. And when societies are divided, it's much easier to defeat them."[103]

Chapter 8

A NEW AGE

One night in February 2014, as revolution unfolded in Ukraine, Vladimir Putin convened his security chiefs. They plotted through the morning how to counter what they deemed a Western-backed coup d'état. "We must start working on returning Crimea to Russia," Putin instructed his lieutenants.[1] In 1954, the Soviet Union had transferred the Crimean Peninsula to Ukraine, then one of its republics; now Putin wanted it for Russia. He ordered his forces to seize Crimea and invade parts of eastern Ukraine, initiating a years-long assault on Ukraine's democratic and territorial integrity.[2]

Russia's attack prompted international outrage. Putin responded not with contrition but anger. In a March 18 speech, he complained that without a superpower counterweight to the United States, "we no longer have stability," as Washington and its allies have "lied to us many times" and "made decisions behind our backs." America acts based not on international law, he continued, but on its own interests. "They have come to believe in their exclusivity and exceptionalism, that they can decide the destinies of the world, that only they can ever be right." Citing Yugoslavia, Afghanistan, Iraq, and Libya, Putin declared that "with Ukraine, our western partners have crossed the line."[3] A crucial benefit of his aggression abroad was a surge in his popularity at home.[4]

Two months later, on May 25, Ukraine held a presidential election. Amid Russia's territorial offensive, President Barack Obama warned Putin not to interfere in the contest. "If, in fact, we see the disruptions and the destabilization continuing so severely that it impedes elections," Obama said at a press conference, "we will not have a choice but to move forward with additional, more severe sanctions."[5]

Putin was not swayed. A few days before the election, a pro-Kremlin hacking group known to U.S. intelligence as a "front for Russian state-sponsored cyber activity" sabotaged the systems of Ukraine's Central Election Commission, raising the specter of foreign operatives disrupting the actual voting process. Ukrainian officials frantically repaired the damage so votes could be tallied and reported on Election Day. "This was a serious, preplanned attack," said Valeriy Striganov, the commission's head of IT, in 2015. The hackers then leaked personal emails and photos stolen from the commission's network. The KGB's totalitarian idea—publicizing people's private lives—had returned in the digital age. The day of the election, the Ukrainian government only just detected a virus that would have caused the commission to display an inaccurate vote count (which Russian state media published, anyway).[6]

The goal of this covert electoral interference operation was to sow chaos and confusion in an already unstable country. In addition to targeting election systems, Russia's digital operatives also targeted the minds of Ukrainian voters. "In 2014, Russia was trying to test all these approaches with fake news," explained Yevhen Fedchenko, the co-founder of StopFake, an organization based in Kyiv that aims to detect and debunk Russian disinformation in real time. In the United States, journalists focused on the physical annexation of Crimea rather than this digital assault upon Ukraine, although the latter proved more foreshadowing. "It's what Russia is trying to push on the global scale," Fedchenko said, "and you cannot stop it in one particular place, it's like a disease, like a viral disease, where you can directly look at what Russia was using for elections in Ukraine and you can very easily substitute Ukraine with any other nation."[7]

—

Ukraine is just one of the more than two dozen countries in which Russia has interfered in recent years.[8] "It's important to keep in context that Russia's 2016 operation was part of a pattern of Russian activities in Europe and elsewhere over the past ten years," said Nadia Schadlow, Donald Trump's former deputy national security adviser for strategy.[9]

For Putin and his advisers, the digital age has made covert electoral interference an increasingly appealing policy option. In a 2013 article, Valery Gerasimov, a top Russian general, described a strategy of hybrid warfare that would employ the "broad use of political, economic, informational, humanitarian, and other non-military measures"—actions that fall within the gray zone between war and peace.[10] Using digital tools, Russia can weaken democracies without declaring war, putting soldiers at risk, or spending much money. It is a practice as well suited to Russia's strengths as it is to democracies' vulnerabilities. Open societies, unable to censor the internet, are asymmetrically vulnerable to this type of assault. "Enemies will exploit a free, democratic, open society," said Porter Goss, the former CIA director. "Elections are an easy target. Innocent people are an easy target. Gossip is an easy target. Uninformed people are an easy target." A Spanish envoy to the European Union told me that Spain has been detecting "constant attempts by the Russians" to manipulate its elections. Arild Heiestad, a Norwegian representative to NATO, described Russian operations to influence elections as unrelenting. "If you look around the Baltics," he said, "it's their everyday life."[11]

The active measures that Russia has been deploying against elections mark a natural extension of past practices. The most basic consistency is cash. Just as the Communist International, the KGB, and the CIA bankrolled their preferred parties, Russians have more recently funded political movements like Marine Le Pen's far-right National Rally in France in the lead up to electoral contests.[12] But other parallels exist:

> Just as the Soviets and their collaborators altered actual votes in postwar Poland and Hungary, Russia uses the internet to target voting systems and voter registration databases.
> Just as the KGB and the CIA spread propaganda through third-party cutouts, such as radio programs and newspapers, Russia uses the internet to work through third parties

like WikiLeaks, anonymous social media accounts, and unsuspecting foreigners.

Just as the KGB circulated forged FBI files about politicians, Russia uses the internet to hack and release emails that reveal the personal lives of public figures.

Just as the CIA waged scare campaigns, Russia uses the internet to spread propaganda meant to provoke fear.

Just as the KGB sowed discord by staging racist and anti-Semitic hate crimes, Russia uses the internet to disseminate divisive content designed to pit citizens against each other.

Just as the CIA worked to turn out certain voters in countries like Italy and Chile, Russia uses digital advertisements and propaganda to motivate some citizens to vote and persuade others not to.

Just as democracies struggled to defend their electoral processes during the Cold War, so, too, are democracies struggling to secure their elections today.

The new variable is the internet, which provides Putin with previously unattainable flexibility and reach. While the CIA and the KGB spent years laying the groundwork for covert electoral interference, Russia can now manipulate elections with little warning, as it did in Ukraine in 2014. These operations have become cheaper, more accessible, and more far-reaching. The CIA and the KGB spent billions of dollars, adjusted for inflation, manipulating elections during the Cold War. Today, Putin can reach many millions of voters with far fewer resources. Democracies are unable to detect the full scope of such interference in real time. Putin, all the while, deploys active measures abroad without suffering any consequences at home. As William J. Burns, the former deputy secretary of state, said of Putin, "He's smart enough as a trained professional to understand that the biggest intelligence successes oftentimes are taking advantage of your opponent's weakness rather than asserting your strength."[13]

—

In October 2016, Russia carried out yet another interference operation—this time, against Montenegro's parliamentary election. Milo Đukanović, the country's prime minister, and his Democratic Party of Socialists were running on a platform to join NATO, which Putin had complained was "moving closer to our borders: one step, then another one."[14] As the election approached, Russian state entities financed the parties challenging Đukanović. "I can tell you with certainty, tens of millions," Đukanović said.[15] According to the Montenegrin government, Russia also spread disinformation on social media—including allegations of voter fraud—and brought down government and news websites. For the night of the election, members of an elite GRU unit, charged with destabilizing European countries, had planned a violent coup d'état, which would have culminated in Đukanović's assassination and the installment of a pro-Russia government. Montenegrin authorities said they thwarted the operation the night before, and Đukanović's party then won the election.[16]

Two years after the foiled coup, I sat down with Đukanović, now the president of Montenegro. Escorted by an entourage of bodyguards, Đukanović, at six feet six, had a commanding presence. He spoke calmly for a head of state describing a foreign plot to kill him, though he did occasionally talk over his translator in impassioned bursts. He was certain that Russia would keep targeting his country's elections. "It is high time that we organize ourselves to defend and preserve our values," he said.[17]

The Kremlin has denied interfering in Montenegro's 2016 election, and Đukanović's opponents have dismissed any such charges as political fiction. But there is no doubt within the U.S. intelligence community that Russia was behind the plot. Douglas Wise, then the deputy director of the Defense Intelligence Agency, was "certainly well aware" of Russia's coup plotting. "We knew they had a whole hit team there," added Victoria Nuland, then an assistant secretary of state. The United States had tried to help Đukanović before the election; according to Celeste Wallander, then a senior White House adviser, Washington sought to "make sure the Montenegrins knew what was going on."[18] Afterward, American lawmakers were united in their outrage. Senator John McCain called the scheme against

Đukanović the most "disturbing indication of how far Vladimir Putin is willing to go to advance his dark and dangerous view of the world."[19] When I asked Đukanović if he was certain that the Russian state was behind this operation, he leaned forward and replied, "Undoubtedly."

—

Democracies like Montenegro, Latvia, and Estonia—all targeted by Russia in recent years, and all populated by fewer than two million people—are especially susceptible to digital forms of covert electoral interference. "The smaller we are, the more vulnerable we are," Đukanović said.[20] Lacking formidable intelligence services, these countries struggle to detect, let alone respond to, assaults on their electoral sovereignty.

This threat spans the globe. In the summer of 2018, Juan Manuel Santos, then the Colombian president, personally provided Enrique Peña Nieto, his Mexican counterpart, with an urgent warning: He possessed intelligence indicating that Russia would interfere in *both* of their countries' upcoming elections. (Santos and Peña Nieto, both term limited, were ineligible for reelection.) "We received a lot of warnings that this was going to happen," Santos told me. "I took tremendous care and gave pertinent orders to investigate . . . and even had some foreign intelligence services help us."

Santos never received concrete evidence of Russian interference in Colombia's election, which a right-wing populist won, or in Mexico's election, in which a left-wing, similarly antiestablishment candidate triumphed. "Again, the Mexicans could not prove it," he said. But Santos, whose term expired in August 2018, left office unsettled. The politics of both victors aligned with Putin's strategic objectives. Santos recognized that Russian meddling could have gone undetected, and he has wondered whether he left Colombia equipped to defend its electoral sovereignty. "I hope I did," he said. "But I can't control that, because technology advances so fast."[21]

Confusion and frustration have enveloped even the world's oldest democracies. In June 2016, the United Kingdom narrowly voted to exit the European Union, in a sharp repudiation of international-ism, immigration, and establishment politics.[22] Evidence has since accumulated that Russia covertly assisted the Leave movement. In late 2017, researchers discovered that more than 150,000 Russian-language Twitter accounts had spread pro-Leave content, in English, just before the referendum. And in late 2018, Twitter disclosed that Russia-connected accounts had posted thousands of pro-Leave messages the day of the contest. All of these accounts targeted the minds of British voters; many of them would later direct pro–Donald Trump content at American voters.[23]

Robert Hannigan, the director of Britain's equivalent to the NSA from 2014 to 2017, entirely overlooked the threat of Russian interference across social media. "We thought that Russia wanted Brexit, no question, because it weakened Europe and sowed disruption, that was clear," Hannigan told me of his time with GCHQ. "But we had no sense that they might be systematically using social media to influence the campaign, partly because we were not really looking."[24] Russia's information warfare across social media was definitionally covert, because its accounts presented foreign voices as domestic ones.[25]

Putin's reasons for assisting the Leave movement were straight-forward: to sow discord within the United Kingdom and to subvert the European Union. "What a great opportunity to drive a wedge between the U.K. and Europe, and us, then trying to influence the Brexit vote," said James Clapper, the U.S. director of national intelligence from 2010 to 2017.[26] Perhaps even more so than the *outcome* of Brexit, the *process* of Brexit furthered Putin's aims. For Britain, exiting the European Union proved extraordinarily complex and divisive, much to Putin's glee. "Brexit passed, and no one wants to implement it. They're not accepting the results of elections. Democratic procedures are being weakened; they're being destroyed," he said more than two years after the referendum.[27] Only in December 2019, after three and a half years and two general elections, did the British Parliament approve a plan for Brexit.[28]

Having left GCHQ, Hannigan is filled with regret. Russian intelligence had been a step ahead of him before the referendum. "We thought Putin wanted Brexit, so someone should have sat down and said how might he affect that, and no one did that, and that was a failure," Hannigan acknowledged. "Whether Russia made the difference at the margins, who knows—personally, I doubt it—but they saw an opportunity and amplified it."[29]

—

Much of the ill preparedness of countries like the United Kingdom can be explained by timing. The Brexit referendum took place prior to July 2016, when Russian intelligence, working through WikiLeaks, released emails stolen from the Democratic National Committee (DNC). In the history of covert electoral interference, this moment was a watershed. Before then, few intelligence professionals grasped Putin's emerging strategy. "Quite frankly, nobody paid a lick of attention to the Russian involvement in Brexit," Douglas Wise said.[30] Foreign correspondents were no exception. "Frankly, the Brexit thing was before the American election," said Steven Erlanger, the London bureau chief for *The New York Times* in 2016, who, years later, would still "like to know a lot more about how thoroughly the bots were going during the referendum campaign." Back then, however, this question eluded Erlanger and his colleagues. "Maybe we all failed, but I just don't remember any serious look at it at the time . . . to be honest, I just don't think it even occurred to me," he said. "But it would have been a hell of a good story."[31] It did not help matters that, for years, American newspapers had been slashing their foreign staffs, which had traditionally provided citizens with eyes and ears across the globe.[32]

All the while, a pattern was emerging. "We've seen Russian interference in Europe for the past ten years. We saw identical techniques—stolen information, misinformation, all of that—in a variety of countries," said David Cohen, the CIA's deputy director from 2015 to 2017. Yet America's security chiefs still viewed covert electoral interference as a distant threat—the type of weapon that the CIA had once deployed *over there,* in faraway places. "You would think previously: 'Oh, this only happens in third world countries,'" said Jeh Johnson, the homeland security secretary from 2013 to 2017. It seemed implausible that Putin, despite targeting foreign democracies, would target the world's most powerful democracy.

In Washington, few sensed the coming storm. "One of the things we did not do as well as we should have was sound the alarm,"

Cohen continued. "We didn't do a good enough job of better pre-paring ourselves, of saying, 'The Russians did that there, so there is no reason to think they're not going to do the same thing here.'" Inside the CIA, Steven Hall, who was, in 2015, the division chief with oversight over Russia, never would have predicted or believed that Putin would launch a covert operation against a U.S. election: "There was no sense" of that, he said.[33] Because the KGB had struggled to interfere in American elections, Washington had no history of defending its electoral sovereignty, despite its own his-tory of targeting elections overseas. America's Cold War experience blinded its policy makers. "We were wrong and naive [in that] we were very focused on Russian meddling in one kind or another but we were not at all focused on Russian meddling here," said Tony Blinken, the deputy secretary of state from 2015 to 2017. "That was not something that we thought was part of the game plan, and I think we thought ourselves much too resilient to anyone trying to pull that in the United States. We were wrong."[34]

Years later, Russia's operation against America's 2016 election may seem inevitable. But this revisionism overlooks the factors that Putin had to weigh in real time. Officials like Cohen, Johnson, Hall, and Blinken felt secure for a reason. For one, Moscow had never meaningfully disrupted an American election. For another, targeting the United States, under any circumstance, was a riskier proposition than targeting a country like Ukraine, which bordered Russia and lacked sufficient means to retaliate. If provoked, the United States— with its massive military, intelligence apparatus, and economy— could impose significant costs on Russia.

Putin had to decide whether to attempt to succeed where the KGB had failed: to disrupt, direct, and determine the outcome of a U.S. presidential election.

—

As Russia set its sights on America's election, personalities mat-tered, as they always have with covert electoral interference. They mattered in 1960, when Nikita Khrushchev, offended by Richard Nixon, worked to thwart his political ambitions; in 1976, when Leo-nid Brezhnev, fearful of Ronald Reagan, deployed active measures against his candidacy; and in 2016, when Vladimir Putin, resentful of Hillary Clinton, sought to damage her campaign and sow discord within the United States. "There was no question about [his] animus for Hillary Clinton," said James Clapper, the former director of national intelligence.[35]

Obama's other intelligence chiefs reached the same conclusion: Putin resented nearly everything about Clinton. He resented that she was a woman who challenged him publicly and, he believed, helped facilitate the release of the Panama Papers.[36] He resented that her husband, Bill Clinton, had expanded NATO and invested in U.S. democracy promotion. And he resented that she had voiced support for protesters in Moscow in 2011 and advocated military action against Iraq and Libya.

Tensions between the two persisted after Clinton left the State Department in 2013. Her domestic approval ratings were approaching 70 percent, and most political analysts anticipated that she would run for president. To any clear-eyed observer, the Democratic nomination was Clinton's to lose. Her views on Russia therefore still carried weight. In one of her final acts as secretary of state, Clinton had submitted a classified memorandum urging Obama to adopt a harder line against Putin.[37] More publicly, in 2014, as the crisis in Ukraine unfolded, she compared Putin's favor for ethnic Russians to "what Hitler did back in the '30s." Once again, a popular revolution had shaken the Kremlin; once again, Clinton had called out Putin; and once again, the Russian leader was left seething. "It's better not to argue with women, but Ms. Clinton has never been too graceful in her statements," Putin shot back, when asked about her comments. "Maybe weakness is not the worst quality for a woman."[38]

What was going through Putin's mind, we now know, was whether to target Clinton's impending campaign. The choice was his alone. "He's really the single decision-maker in Russia," Steven Hall said.[39] For Putin, deciding to interfere in an American election was not necessarily obvious. On the one hand, such an operation would enable him to undermine his rival and, as the KGB did, foster division inside the United States. But on the other, what Khrushchev had articulated about America's 1960 election remained true decades later: Targeting an American election could backfire. If Moscow were caught, Washington could hit back—hard. And in the age of the internet, detection was all but guaranteed, as the Bush administration had concluded in 2004.

Putin, an intelligence professional, knew that at least some aspects of his operation would be attributed to Moscow almost immediately. The question was how Barack Obama, the U.S. president, would respond. In this sense, whether Russia would interfere in the 2016 election rested partially on Putin's analysis of Obama, another personality central to this story.[40]

—

Obama's ascent to the White House had been swift. In 2002, as a state senator, he had opposed the invasion of Iraq, warning that the Bush administration was pursuing a "dumb" and "rash" war. In 2007, while serving as a U.S. senator, Obama announced that he was running for president; his charisma, calls for change, and early stand against the Iraq War inspired voters. After defeating Clinton in the primary, Obama won the 2008 election and nominated her to serve in his cabinet. He then pledged in his inaugural address to tackle an ongoing economic recession at home and to wind down America's forever wars abroad.[41]

In Russia, Obama saw a declining power with which the United States could, and should, forge new ties and that lacked the means to cause him much trouble. At the start of his administration, Obama attempted a so-called reset in relations with Moscow. As late as October 2012, just after Putin expelled USAID, Obama mocked Mitt Romney, his general election opponent, for his adversarial posture toward Russia. "A few months ago, when you were asked what's the biggest geopolitical threat facing America, you said Russia, not al-Qaeda, you said Russia," Obama said, during a televised presidential debate. "The 1980s are now calling to ask for their foreign policy back because, you know, the Cold War's been over for 20 years."[42] Obama much preferred to talk about al-Qaeda—he had recently authorized a daring and successful raid to kill its founder, Osama bin Laden—than about Russia.

A comprehensive analysis of Obama's foreign policy is a subject for another book, but Putin's perception of Obama is critical.

Vladimir Lenin had a favorite saying: "Probe with a bayonet; if you meet steel, stop! If you meet mush, then push."[43] Putin aimed to push as far as he could without provoking much pushback. And in Obama, he saw a leader elected to wind down wars, not start them, wary of stumbling into great-power conflict, and largely dismissive of Russia. "This was a cautious administration in general," said David Petraeus, the CIA director in 2011 and 2012, citing Obama's decision not to strike Syria in August 2013, after its president, Bashar al-Assad, disregarded a "redline" Obama had set and used chemical weapons to kill more than a thousand civilians. Petraeus continued, "It was an administration that had a redline that was crossed, and they didn't act, that said Bashar al-Assad must go, but then did nothing really to make him go, that repeatedly issued fairly ringing rhetorical statements and policies and did not always back them up."[44]

Inside the White House, many of Obama's advisers had urged him to take military action against Syria. But some, including Chief of Staff Denis McDonough, cautioned restraint, since the use of force could set off an unpredictable escalatory cycle.[45] Obama, wary of foreign entanglements, demurred and, in doing so, ceded *escalation dominance*: he decided not to retaliate against an adversary precisely because that adversary might then escalate its destructive behavior.[46] According to Victoria Nuland, an assistant secretary of state under Obama, the president often opted against offensive action for fear of making a bad situation worse. "That was a favored Obama refrain when he was cautious about getting involved," she said. "He was always worried about escalation. He was not a natural practitioner of deterrence."[47]

Obama demonstrated this same tendency in Ukraine. After America and the EU sanctioned Russia for annexing Crimea and invading eastern Ukraine, Putin showed no sign of backing down. A bipartisan coalition of lawmakers urged Obama to go further and send lethal arms to the Ukrainian government. Secretary of Defense Ashton Carter and Martin Dempsey, the chairman of the Joint Chiefs of Staff, publicly indicated their support for such a step. But Obama, wary of provoking Russia, refused.[48] Michael Morell, who twice served as the CIA's acting director under Obama, directly connected the president's restraint in Ukraine with Putin's calculus ahead of America's 2016 election. "I bet that part of his calculation was 'I got away with Ukraine, I got away with the first land grab in Europe since World War II, and I am getting away every day with interfering in Ukraine, and I am paying very little cost for it,'" Morell said. "I bet you any amount of money that was part of his calculation, whereas if the United States had pushed back harder on Crimea and on eastern Ukraine, then this might never have happened."[49]

Leon Panetta, who served as Obama's first CIA director and then as his secretary of defense, likewise said that the president's restraint in key foreign hot spots emboldened Putin to target America's election. Obama had taken risks early on, Panetta said, such as the bin Laden raid, but had grown warier in his decision-making over time. "The more cautious [Obama] became, the more he sent a signal to adversaries that they could do things to take advantage of him," Panetta said, pointing to Syria as a turning point. "Unfortunately, I think that when Obama failed to back up the redline in Syria, it sent a message not just to Syria, but sent a message to the world that there was some question as to whether we would stand by our word," Panetta said. "That was a message of weakness, and I think Putin read it as weakness, and read it as an opportunity to be able to not only do Crimea, but to go into Syria without having anyone stop him from doing that, and thirdly then going after our election institutions as well. I think he felt that he would be able to do it and to get away with it."[50]

Panetta, Petraeus, and Morell—each of whom directed the CIA while Obama was president—all believe that Obama signaled to Putin that he could interfere in an American election without suffering significant consequences. Petraeus explained, "There were moments, the most glaring of course was the redline, but others, too, that just indicated a degree of reluctance, perhaps understandably given the experience in Iraq and Afghanistan, but a reluctance to take action for fear that it might escalate, and where does it go from here."[51]

Even so, what Obama signaled abroad did not provide Putin with any guarantees. Unlike his more hawkish national security team, Obama had been elected by the American people, who were increasingly skeptical of overseas commitments. In 2014, 41 percent of U.S. adults said their country should "stay out of world affairs," the highest-ever proportion recorded by one survey group across its four decades of polling.[52] In this environment, Obama had exercised caution in Ukraine and Syria. Whether he would do the same in his own house, in response to an attack on the heart of American democracy, was not preordained. "If you put yourself in [Putin's] shoes, this was a huge step for him," Morell said of the decision to interfere in an American election. "This must have been a big-time decision on his part to do this."[53] For Putin, the benefits of such an operation proved irresistible: to undermine Clinton, divide the United States, and advertise the democratic model's vulnerabilities to his own people and the world.

—

In 2014, Putin did not presumably know how far he would go in interfering with America's election, but he did initiate the operation. By May, the Internet Research Agency (IRA), an information warfare center based in Saint Petersburg, had begun manipulating Americans across social media. The goal: to "spread distrust towards the candidates and the political system in general," according to communication intercepts later released by the U.S. government.[54] Also in 2014, the Russian government began directing "extensive activity" against America's electoral systems.[55] By July 2015, Russian intelligence had gained access to the networks of the Democratic National Committee.[56]

None of this had anything to do with Donald Trump, who did not launch his initially long-shot presidential campaign until the summer of 2015. In targeting America's election, Russia initially had two goals: "to hurt Clinton," the then CIA director, John Brennan, explained, and to "stir up these political fissures here in U.S. society."[57] Russians like Alexander Dugin, a fascist and theorist with Putin's ear, had long argued that Moscow should destabilize "the political processes within America" and introduce "geopolitical chaos within the American daily experience by encouraging all manner of separatism, ethnic diversity, social and racial conflict."[58]

Through covert electoral interference, Putin could at least accomplish this objective. What is unknowable is whether Putin would have proceeded as aggressively had the Republican Party nominated a more conventional candidate like, say, Senator Marco Rubio, whose views on Russia more mirrored Clinton's.

The Republican primary put America on a different path as two developments progressed in parallel. Russian actors spread propaganda across social media, targeted voting systems, and penetrated Democratic Party networks. And Trump, surging in the polls, deepened his ties with Russia publicly and privately. By November 2015, he had secretly signed a letter of intent for a real estate project in Moscow.[59] An odd dynamic was also unfolding before the world: Trump and Putin appeared to like each other. "There is no doubt that [Trump] is a very colorful and talented man," Putin said in December 2015. "He is an absolute leader of the presidential race." Putin also made sure to add that Russia would "never meddle" in America's election, which was "up to the U.S. voters."[60] It was a Putinist lie, both mocking and misleading.

These two developments—Putin's ongoing operation and Trump's improbable rise—quickly fused. Russia began promoting Trump's candidacy for two reasons: his friendly posture toward Moscow and his rhetoric around race, religion, and gender. For Putin, whose aim was, in part, to divide the United States, Trump's divisiveness was an asset in itself. In February 2016, members of the IRA received explicit instructions: "Main idea: Use any opportunity to criticize Hillary and the rest (except Sanders and Trump—we support them)."[61] In March, Clinton and Trump dominated a pivotal set of state primaries; a face-off between the two candidates now seemed inevitable.[62] Russia promptly turbocharged its covert operation. Between March 10 and April 7, the GRU, Russia's military intelligence agency, targeted the email accounts of more than a hundred members of Clinton's campaign, including Clinton herself, and stole the emails of John Podesta, her campaign chairman. Also in April, the GRU newly breached the networks of the DNC and the Democratic Congressional Campaign Committee.[63]

By May 2016, the stage was set. Trump had secured his party's nomination; Clinton soon did the same.[64] One was Putin's friend;

the other, his foe. Russia had first targeted America's election years earlier, when it seemed certain that both major-party nominees would be similarly hawkish toward Moscow. But Putin had struck gold: Republican voters had coalesced around Trump, whose relations with Moscow stretched back decades. "[Americans] wanted change, and in that sense Trump represented it," said Oleg Kalugin, who was a KGB general when Trump visited Moscow in 1987. "They never thought that he may have been influenced or even did have some sort of connections with the Soviets or the Russians. And that is what happened." Regardless of what else, if anything, actually took place in 1987, it is a fact that in early 2016 Trump was pursuing a business deal with Moscow privately while praising Putin publicly.[65]

Trump's nomination added a third objective—along with new urgency—to Russia's ongoing covert electoral interference operation. David Cohen, the CIA's deputy director, put it best: "They wanted Donald Trump to win, they wanted Hillary to lose, but most of all they just wanted to fuck with us."[66]

Part Two

2016

A my Pope, President Obama's deputy homeland security adviser in 2016, has since moved to London, where she is a partner at an elite crisis management firm. She does for private clients what she once did for the White House: put out fires quickly, discreetly, and strategically. In the summer of 2016, Pope and her colleagues grappled with an explosive crisis: covert electoral interference, aimed at a U.S. presidential election. The minds of American voters were under attack. So, too, was America's electoral infrastructure, or "the equipment, processes, and systems related to voting, tabulating, reporting, and registration."[1]

What Russia was able to achieve—and how far Russia could have gone—in influencing America's election was classified then, and has remained closely guarded information since. "I wouldn't say that the full story is out there," Pope told me in June 2019. "You're talking about a foreign adversary interfering in the United States electoral system—nobody is going to tell you the full story."[2]

Each of the individuals interviewed for this book provided a piece of this puzzle. Obama's former foreign policy advisers told me what it was like to defend against covert electoral interference. The heads of the Trump and Clinton campaigns described what it was like to vie for the presidency while Russia's operation was under way. Leading U.S. journalists and technology experts reflected on how their industries furthered Putin's aims. Across these conversations was a central question: What does 2016 reveal about the evolving nature of covert electoral interference?

The United States has only recently fallen victim to the types of operations it once executed elsewhere. Whether in 1919 or today, covert electoral interference has always involved changing actual votes and changing minds. Only in the twenty-first century, however, have these operations gone from local to transnational. Foreign intelligence services formerly manipulated elections with physical tactics, like stuffing ballot boxes, distributing bags of money, and disseminating leaflets. Establishing a material presence in a targeted democracy was a necessity. Then the internet spread, and America's electoral systems and information ecosystem were digitized. In 2005, just 7 percent of U.S. adults were on social media; by 2015, that number had increased to 65 percent. Nearly nine in every ten U.S. adults were using the internet in some way.[3] The digitization of the United States lent Putin what his Soviet predecessors had lacked: the means to influence a U.S. election at scale. His hackers could suddenly penetrate voting booths and voters' minds from thousands of miles away, on computers in Russia, precisely and powerfully.

Chapter 9

DELAYING OFFENSE

I n 2015 and early 2016, foreboding pieces of intelligence trickled into President Barack Obama's daily briefing. Some concerned probes of America's electoral infrastructure; others mentioned attempts to hack Democratic Party networks.[1] James Clapper, the director of national intelligence, was unsurprised and unconcerned. "We accepted the fact that there seemed to be a certain ambient level of Russian activity in every election," he said during our interview. Clapper, a retired three-star general, worked for the U.S. government from 1963 to 2017, with a few brief interruptions. He came up during the Cold War, when the United States interfered in elections overseas but was largely immune to such interference at home. He assumed, at first, that Russia's covert activities would again prove insignificant. "They're going to be collecting, reconnoitering, lots of countries do that."[2]

Moscow was fixated on Washington, its longtime competitor, but the feeling was no longer mutual. Steven Hall, the CIA's division chief with oversight over Russia in 2015, said the agency had conducted a "massive shift" in resources away from Russia following the attacks of September 11, 2001. John McLaughlin, the CIA's deputy director at the time, agreed that "9/11 did take us away from Russia in the sense that it reduced our focus on almost everything other than terrorism." Michael Morell, the CIA's acting director in 2013, said the legacy of this reorientation lingered. "Russia was one of the places where those resources came from," he said. "As a consequence of that we were not as good on Russia as we should have been."[3] The American people had also stopped worrying about Moscow. In 2014, only 9 percent of U.S. adults said Russia was America's greatest enemy. The new flash point of U.S.-Russian relations, in Ukraine, had barely registered. In 2015, a total of 60 percent of U.S. adults said they had heard either little or nothing about tensions between Russia and Ukraine; just 16 percent could locate Ukraine on a map.[4]

America's disengagement presented an opportunity for Russia. The early warning signs of its interference operation—unremarkable in a vacuum—were alarming only in context. Russia's international posture in 2015 was far more adversarial than it had been even a few years earlier, before America's previous presidential election. In that period, Putin had accused the United States of plotting regime change in Russia and Ukraine, used digital means to wreak havoc upon Ukraine, and begun manipulating the information spaces of countries across Europe. None of this was unknown to high-ranking officials like James Clapper, but none of it was top of mind, either.

The exception was the Obama administration's Russia experts. Two of those officials were Victoria Nuland, the assistant secretary of state for European and Eurasian affairs, and Celeste Wallander, the senior director for Russia and Eurasia on the National Security Council. In 2014, Russia had leaked a recording of Nuland saying "fuck the EU" to the U.S. ambassador to Ukraine.[5] Her tough reputation, already well-known inside Washington, became a matter of public record. She and Wallander, a like-minded policy maker, shared a deep distrust of Putin. Their job was to track his foreign policy, and they feared that initial reports of Russian meddling foreshadowed something more. "We were the first to start sounding alarm bells as early as March and April of 2016 that the Russians were messing with our elections," Nuland said. Initially, Nuland believed that rather than favor a specific candidate, Putin would simply try to make the election "look messy and illegitimate as payback for Ukraine and as a way to say to their citizens, 'See, everyone's elections suck.'" Obama's intelligence chiefs remained unconvinced. "They said it was just the Russia team being paranoid again," Nuland said.[6]

—

That summer, the Russian threat became undeniable. On June 14, 2016, *The Washington Post* reported that CrowdStrike, a cyber-security firm, had concluded that two state-sponsored Russian hacking groups had penetrated the DNC's network—one back in 2015, and another in April 2016.[7] The possibility persisted that Russia was merely conducting espionage. But then something unexpected happened: On June 15, an anonymous persona called Guccifer 2.0 began uploading stolen DNC materials onto the internet. At that moment, the idea that Russia was targeting the 2016 election, said Lisa Monaco, Obama's homeland security and counterterrorism adviser, "crystallized" inside the White House. Monaco was used to combating terrorist threats and disease epidemics; now her focus shifted to defending America's electoral sovereignty.[8]

The DNC email release came at a critical moment in the presidential campaign. In early June, Clinton had clinched the Democratic nomination. Bernie Sanders, her major primary opponent, had spent months contrasting his grassroots energy with her establishment ties. "You're not going to have a government that represents all of us, so long as you have candidates like Secretary Clinton being dependent on big money interests," Sanders had said in April. These tensions endured even after Clinton became the presumptive nominee. When Sanders endorsed her at a rally on July 12, some of his supporters brought "Won't Vote Hillary" signs.[9] The Democratic National Convention, set to begin on July 25, now had a dual purpose: to unite the Democratic Party and to kick off Clinton's general election campaign.

Just before the convention, Russia struck. The GRU, struggling to gain traction on social media, had sent stolen DNC materials to WikiLeaks, an international organization that specializes in uploading files online as a third-party cutout. On July 22, WikiLeaks published a trove of DNC emails. Their contents revealed an internal bias among Democratic Party officials for Clinton over Sanders.[10] National reporters feverishly covered the contents of the emails, which were accurate, accessible, and dramatic. "The principal bias of the news media is toward profit," said Fareed Zakaria, a foreign policy host on CNN, in explaining coverage of the emails. "When you have highly sensational material that has some news value, it's difficult for me to understand what would be the circumstances, given the competitive dynamic of network news, of television news, and now digital news, to not bring that up."[11]

The DNC emails were certainly sensational. Outlets like ABC and *The Washington Post* published articles about the "most damaging" WikiLeaks revelations. Clinton's advisers shouted that Russia was behind the release, but the Obama administration offered no confirmation, and the substance of the emails attracted far more attention than their alleged source.[12] Russia had executed this move before. Ahead of the 2014 election in Ukraine, its hackers had stolen emails belonging to the election commissioner and posted them online. Nonetheless, American news organizations treated the DNC release as a domestic story and neglected its international angle: Russia was applying its global playbook to a U.S. election.[13]

The fallout was swift. Sanders complained that the emails were "outrageous" but "not a great shock." His supporters heckled pro-Clinton speakers. On July 24, Debbie Wasserman Schultz, a Florida congresswoman, announced that she would resign as DNC chairwoman. And on July 25, the DNC issued a statement offering "a deep and sincere apology to Senator Sanders, his supporters, and the entire Democratic party for inexcusable remarks made over email." The convention, intended to unify a divided party, had proven chaotic and divisive, thanks to Putin's hidden hand.[14] Clinton told me that at the time she was "caught off guard" and "dumbfounded" by the audacity and effectiveness of Russia's attack. Putin, for his part, was thrilled. "It doesn't really matter who hacked this data from Mrs. Clinton's campaign headquarters," he said after the convention, while denying that it was Russia. "The important thing is the content was given to the public."[15]

Democratic Party officials had fallen victim to a form of digital totalitarianism. The Russian tradition of espionage is to exploit personal vulnerabilities, as the KGB had attempted in 1976, when its officers searched for private information on Senator Henry Jackson that could be publicized. At the Democratic convention, Russian intelligence executed this same idea with digital means.

—

Inside the United States, the significance of the DNC email release was a matter of perspective. For citizens, what mattered was the actual messages. Few cared how WikiLeaks had acquired the emails. Maybe Russia was involved; maybe not. For Republican Party officials, the document dump provided a boost. Rick Gates, Trump's deputy campaign manager, later told federal investigators that he and his colleagues were "very happy about the release," according to notes of his testimony.[16] And for Democratic Party officials, it was obvious that Russia was seeking to undermine Clinton, but they lacked the evidence that the Obama administration possessed. "We knew it was the Russians; we knew that right away" when WikiLeaks uploaded the emails, recalled Douglas Wise, then the deputy director of the Defense Intelligence Agency. Inside the White House, Obama's advisers reached the same conclusion, even as the U.S. intelligence community pursued an official consensus on the matter. "We had technical attribution very early on and knew that it was Russian actors almost from the moment that we became aware of it," said Michael Daniel, then the White House cybersecurity coordinator, of the theft and release of the DNC emails.[17]

Only select officials in the federal government had access to top secret intelligence and, therefore, the bigger picture. From the outside, the DNC email release seemed like an isolated event. But Obama's team also knew that Russian hackers were scanning and probing America's electoral infrastructure. And, as Jeh Johnson put it to me, "If you could scan it, if you could probe it, you could alter it." This second facet of activity gave the DNC incident graver meaning: Russia was executing a multipart operation to influence the outcome of the election. "The minute the Debbie Wasserman Schultz emails started coming out in July," Nuland said, "it became clear they were going to put their finger on the scale for one side."[18]

Still, it was unclear what, exactly, Russia had planned for the months between July and Election Day. Obama's advisers were most alarmed about the probes of voting systems and voter registration databases. "That was cause for grave concern," Johnson continued, "because I didn't know where it was going to lead, and I know enough about politics to know that you can alter the outcome of a national election, given our Electoral College, and given that there are only certain swing states, by targeting a couple of key precincts in key states." In early July, as the DNC email release unfolded, Michael Daniel convened an interagency committee charged with assessing the vulnerabilities of America's electoral infrastructure. And later that month, a top secret unit of CIA, NSA, and FBI officials began analyzing Russian interference in the election.[19]

By this point, the White House knew that Russia had released the DNC emails and targeted America's electoral infrastructure. But critically, the third element of Russia's operation—information warfare across social media—remained "very poorly understood" through Election Day, explained Susan Rice, then the national security adviser. Nine of Obama's other foreign policy advisers agreed with this assessment. "When it comes to the way the platforms themselves were being manipulated, we didn't understand it in real time," said Tony Blinken, the deputy secretary of state. "We just didn't understand it."[20]

This two-part and incomplete picture of Russia's operation—encompassing the electoral intrusions and email dumps, but not the social media manipulation—is significant because it formed the basis for Obama's decision-making. Even after the DNC email release, many in the White House were skeptical that such dirty tricks would matter much to voters. The other known part of Russia's operation, however, had provoked panic. "The mounting evidence in the summer of 2016 of how many voting systems they had intruded into—and not done anything with, just intruded—was really scaring people, if what they intended to do was to bring down the electoral infrastructure," Celeste Wallander said.[21]

In late June, the FBI had notified Arizona that Russian actors had penetrated its voter registration database. State officials took the system off-line between June 28 and July 8.[22] Then, on July 12, Illinois election officials noticed an unusually high volume of outbound activity in their statewide voter registration database. By the end of the month, the FBI had contacted Illinois election officials and launched an investigation into the breach.[23] These agents would discover that a unit of the GRU, Russia's military intelligence agency, had penetrated Illinois's registration database, accessed the personal records of millions of voters, and exfiltrated those of up to 500,000, including their birth dates, names, addresses, and partial Social Security numbers.[24] The hackers could have gone further. "Russian cyber actors were in a position to delete or change voter data," the U.S. Senate has since revealed.[25]

Rather than actually manipulate voter data, the GRU had shown that it *could* manipulate voter data. Of the Illinois breach, Lisa Monaco, Obama's homeland security adviser, said, "I remember that being one of the most pressing concerns from the panoply of states." Through the summer, the White House received ceaseless reports of Russian probes and intrusions into electoral systems. "Every single day, we were getting reports that this system had been scanned, this system had been penetrated," said Michael Daniel, the White House cybersecurity coordinator. Amy Pope, Monaco's deputy, became convinced that Putin was sending Obama a message: "We want you to know that you are vulnerable."[26]

—

Obama found himself in an unprecedented position. Moscow had targeted American elections in the past, but never before had such an operation been detected as it was happening. Putin was charging forward with his digital bayonet. Obama had to decide when and how to push back. "The bottom line is we were going to punish Russia," Susan Rice said. "The only question was whether it was more or less advantageous to do so before or after the election."[27] This question ignited fierce debate.

One camp of officials wanted Obama to punish Putin that summer, to show that the United States would tolerate no further interference in the election. Celeste Wallander and Michael Daniel evaluated what this approach might entail. In July, they convened an interagency committee that developed countermeasures that could be deployed against Russia. A core member of this group was Victoria Nuland, who was characteristically adamant that America impose costs on Russia quickly. "We wanted to do light deniable countermeasures early, in July," Nuland said. "All of my Soviet and Russia training told me we had to deter with a strong set of measures up front and have them calculate the costs of continuing to attack us, particularly with a player like Putin."[28]

This committee prepared a series of retaliatory options: "sanctions, information revelations, quiet private messages, louder public messages, disruption operations, all kinds of things," Wallander rattled off. In late July, Nuland briefed Secretary of State John Kerry on these steps, including a "very reciprocal" measure that would have been "embarrassing" to Putin. "It would have looked exactly like what he does, been relatively deniable, and been completely painful," she said. "What we were suggesting were deterrent measures, to raise the costs on Putin personally." (Nuland declined to specify further, but several of her colleagues said that Obama considered releasing information about Putin's secret wealth, private dealings, and murky associations.) Nuland recalled that Kerry had told her to "work up countermeasures [and] I will take them to the White House."[29]

But Kerry returned with a clear reply: to stand down. "By August, we were told keep working on the countermeasures and we will come back to it after the election," Nuland said.[30] (Kerry's representatives did not respond to interview requests for this book.)

Wallander sensed that there was "no appetite" for her committee's work, not least because offensive action could jeopardize cooperation with Russia in other policy areas. So instead, on her own authority, she wrote a "frank, higher-level security clearance memo" outlining ways to retaliate against Putin—immediately. Daniel, the cybersecurity coordinator, helped craft the countermeasures included in the memorandum. "I have not been reticent to say that I am one of those that believed that we needed to be forceful with the Russians, and that I advocated for being more active," Daniel said. In late August, Wallander submitted her memorandum, which made clear which retaliatory option she believed would be most effective: to expose the hidden "activities," "associates," and "vacations" of Putin and his inner circle. Wallander declined to say to whom she sent her cable, other than that it went to "my leadership." She received the same reply as Nuland: "The sense I got back was, 'We got this,' " she said.[31]

Wallander's superiors at the time were Susan Rice, the national security adviser, and Avril Haines, Rice's deputy. Both Rice and Haines declined to comment on Wallander's memorandum, although Haines did say that for key national security threats, interagency committees formulate policy options for more senior administration members to consider.[32]

Haines chaired what was known as the Deputies Committee, which included the deputy heads of key government agencies, like Tony Blinken at the State Department and David Cohen at the CIA. Susan Rice, Haines's direct boss, chaired the Principals Committee, a cabinet-level decision-making body that included James Clapper, John Brennan, Denis McDonough, Lisa Monaco, and Jeh Johnson. Together, these forums deliberated whether the benefits of offensive action outweighed the costs. "Just the intensity and frequency of meetings we had was a measure of how much activity it generated," Clapper said.[33]

Only one option was discarded from the outset. "The idea of spreading disinformation was rejected almost immediately," Tony Blinken said. John Brennan was a staunch opponent of the kind of disinformation the agency had once spread in countries like Italy and Chile. "The truth is more powerful," Brennan insisted. "I always felt there was a lot of stuff you can highlight that would make your point, because if we were to fabricate something and it was exposed, it would totally undermine [us]."[34]

Other ideas were more seriously considered. One was leaking details about Putin's secret wealth and corruption. "There was skepticism about how effective that could be," Tony Blinken said, "but it was something that was certainly part of the mix." Jeh Johnson thought there was "a good case to be made that we should take action before the election," and that "whatever we did should be cyber related and correlate to what they're doing to us." But competing with Russia digitally presented major drawbacks. The United States would likely "end up on the losing end" of a "tit-for-tat escalatory cycle with Russia in the cyber domain," Blinken argued, where Russia could "do more harm to us than we could do to them." Few believed that diplomatic expulsions, another option, would much bother Putin.[35]

Obama's advisers concluded that major economic counter-measures were most likely to make Putin think twice about his next move. "I was pleasantly surprised by how forthcoming Treasury was on being willing to support very severe economic responses that we would normally not have gone with," Blinken said, because they "amounted to economic warfare."[36] The case for offensive action was straightforward: Imposing costs on Putin ahead of the election would deter him from further interfering in the contest. But some officials held the opposite opinion: The risks of offensive action were too high, and Obama should wait to retaliate until Election Day had passed.

—

Obama had offensive options available to him, ready to deploy. But, as with Syria and Ukraine, he carefully weighed the risk of escalation. He did not feel as though he was operating from a position of strength: By August, the U.S. intelligence community had reported that Russian hackers could edit actual vote tallies, according to four of Obama's senior advisers. This revelation was a game changer. America's electoral infrastructure was penetrable. Tony Blinken said that in the early summer the foremost concern internally was that "the Russians were actually going to literally try to manipulate the election results by interfering in ballot boxes one way or another. That was the initial preoccupation, and tremendous focus was put on that."[37]

—

At the Democratic convention, Russia showed that it was willing to interfere in the U.S. election. The next step, it seemed, was to subvert the actual voting process. Voter registration databases were especially vulnerable. States are required by law to maintain a centralized voter registration list to "serve as the single system for storing and managing the official list of registered voters throughout the state."[38] Some of these lists were unencrypted and insecure.[39] By September, Blinken said, the U.S. intelligence community had concluded that Russia could not alter enough votes to swing the election. But according to officials like John Brennan, hackers could still manipulate voter databases and, at select locations, actual tallies. The damage would be severe. "If they could get people to question whether the election was valid," Blinken said, "that would be perhaps just as good as actually manipulating the outcome, and so that was the intense focus of our concern."[40]

Within Obama's inner circle, the threat of vote alterations strengthened every argument for delaying offense. "We were all concerned about the escalatory piece," Lisa Monaco said. "We were very worried that the wrong action by us could then tip the balance to actual disruption of the ability to actually vote." If Obama punished Putin, the Russian leader could respond by altering actual votes—the exact outcome Obama hoped to avoid. In this sense, acting prior to Election Day could backfire. "There was consideration given to a number of options that we could have exercised, including rattling the Russians' cyber cage, but if we did that, it could have had very unknown consequences, in terms of whether or not Russia would have doubled or tripled down during the campaign," John Brennan said. "Throughout the course of the summer of 2016, we knew the types of things the Russians *could do;* we didn't know what they were *going to do*. They could have done a lot more than what we saw."[41]

A series of additional and related risks weighed on Obama. There was the concern that in retaliating too soon, Obama would be exposing America's sources precisely when he needed insights into Putin's intentions. The U.S. intelligence community, James Clapper emphasized, had "spent literally billions of dollars acquiring" eyes and ears inside Russia.[42] Going on the offensive could jeopardize those sources. Obama's team would have to justify a retaliatory strike to congressional lawmakers and perhaps the public. Russian intelligence would do all they could to learn what Obama knew and how he knew it. Perhaps internal intelligence assessments would leak. Or perhaps Russian hackers would steal them. The result would be the same: America's sources and methods would be jeopardized, and Russia would take new precautions to evade detection.

Then there was Donald Trump, who seemed intent on

destabilizing the election at an already volatile moment in American politics.[43] On July 27, just after the DNC email release, Trump asked Russia to target Clinton. "Russia, if you're listening, I hope you're able to find the 30,000 emails that are missing," he said. "I think you will probably be rewarded mightily by our press."[44] (Of these comments, Steve Bannon told me, "That's just Trump. Remember it's theater to him. It's part of the show.") A few hours later, Russian hackers, for the first time, tried to breach Clinton's personal office.[45] Trump also began to warn his supporters that "the election's going to be rigged," a claim he repeated during interviews, campaign events, and the presidential debates.[46]

Talk of a rigged election troubled the White House, not least because Russia might actually make the election appear rigged. One frequently discussed scenario was that the GRU would edit voter data in key precincts so that registered voters would be unable to cast their ballots. Trump could use this chaos to substantiate his conspiratorial charges. "He would call into question the entire system," Amy Pope said, by telling his supporters: " 'You can't trust it. It's all fake.' "[47]

This worst-case scenario rested on a near-universal assumption: Clinton would win the election. Putin had "backed the wrong horse," Obama told his advisers in September, confident that his former secretary of state would succeed him.[48]

Anticipating that Trump would shout rigged in defeat, Obama wanted the election to appear as un-rigged as possible. "The president was very clear," said Michael Daniel. "We did not want to do the Russians' job for them and undermine Americans' confidence in the integrity of the electoral process."[49] For that reason, punishing Russia prior to November could backfire in another way. Not only would Obama be accused of using national security to favor Clinton, but he would be signaling publicly that he was concerned about Russia's operation. Voters would be left unsure whether the election would proceed fairly. "Protecting the elections also means protecting people's confidence in the electoral process," said Denis McDonough, Obama's chief of staff. "If handled incorrectly, or handled in what appeared to be a partisan way, I believe[d] there [was] a real risk, especially in light of the fact that the candidate of the Republican Party was making the case that the election itself was rigged, that people would conclude that in fact the election was rigged."[50]

—

With Clinton poised to win, restraint seemed prudent, while offense seemed self-defeating. "A lot of the Russia hawks thought we should just lean a lot harder, that election politics were less important than the national security issues," Amy Pope said, but "there was just so much concern that [Clinton] was already so far ahead," so there was "no good reason" to assume the risks of retaliating. Jon Finer, too, said that Clinton's political strength prompted complacency. "Plenty of people in our administration," he said, believed that Obama could "win both ways: He could win in the sense of Trump not winning the election, and he could win in the sense of having clean hands and staying above the fray."[51] In August, public polling showed Clinton far ahead of Trump—in some cases, by double digits.[52]

This polling did not factor into Situation Room debates explicitly, but it was on the minds of Obama's chief advisers. "Part of the thinking, though it was unsaid, were the polls," Jeh Johnson said. James Clapper recognized that politics influenced decision-making at the highest levels. "There was a feeling that in the end the electorate would do the right thing, and I think that implicitly moderated a more aggressive reaction," he said. When asked to define what he meant by "the right thing," Clapper clarified, "It was obviously a bias I suppose for Clinton against Trump." The notion that Donald Trump, a reality TV star, would succeed Obama as president did not seem possible to many Americans, especially Democrats, and especially Washington insiders. "In some circles there was a sense of inevitability to a Clinton win in the election," said Sarah Bloom Raskin, then the deputy Treasury secretary.[53]

The political winds seemed preordained: Clinton would win the presidency, and then Trump would incite unrest. In this environment, Obama administration officials feared that punishing Russia could prompt escalation. There was a "reluctance to do anything" inside the White House, Celeste Wallander said, because of a sense that the status quo "isn't good, but it's not bad enough, and it could be worse." The DNC hack and release seemed insignificant compared with the threat of actual vote alterations. "There was excessive focus on the vote machines," Wallander went on. "Of all the things to be worried about, why *that* was so important, and why *that* was the priority, and as long as the Russians weren't going in and manually changing the vote count, then it was all okay, to this day I don't understand that."[54]

In interviews, Obama's inner circle of Haines, Rice, McDonough, and Monaco defended their approach. "I believe we made the best decision based on the information we had at the time and what our focus was, which was profoundly to make sure the actual conduct and the integrity of the election was stable," Monaco said. "Imposing some costs could have sparked some escalation again on the state systems." The White House had prepared "a series of very significant responses," Haines explained, that could be deployed if Russia engaged in vote tampering. In the Situation Room, this distinction—between changing votes and changing minds—instructed policy making. Haines continued, "People viewed affecting actual votes, including preventing people from voting, as a redline of sorts, to use an overused term, or at least as materially different from an information campaign that would require a different kind of response." Obama had developed another redline. He did not want to provoke Putin into crossing it. "Our overriding objective was to prevent Russia from doing more and worse than they had already done when we discovered it[s]" operation, Rice said.[55]

At this pivotal juncture, Obama, unsure where offense might lead, exercised restraint. So long as Russian hackers did not manipulate electoral systems, retaliation could wait until after the election, by which point Obama could punish Putin alongside a president-elect Clinton. Permitting one form of electoral interference to prevent another, Obama had settled for a policy of managed interference. Intentionally or not, by showing what he might do next, Putin had established escalation dominance in Obama's house.

Chapter 10

PLAYING DEFENSE

While debating and delaying offense, Obama and his advisers simultaneously played defense. The focus was America's voting systems. "We prioritized our focus on the [electoral] infrastructure," said Denis McDonough, then the White House chief of staff. "We were concerned overwhelmingly about one thing: the sanctity of the election, whether the election would happen, that it happen, and that people have confidence in the outcome, that the vote they cast was recorded as such, and that the outcome itself was not in doubt. We structured all of our policy interventions around that." Lisa Monaco said that Obama's directive was clear: "Priority one: Can we make sure people can cast their votes on Election Day?"[1]

At the center of this effort was Jeh Johnson, the homeland security secretary. By 2016, Johnson was a fixture in Washington, having spent decades shuttling between corporate law and the federal government. After Obama left office, Johnson returned to private practice at the law firm Paul, Weiss. When we met in the summer of 2019, he was friendly but careful. "I don't speculate. I make conclusions based on what I know," he said.[2] And he knew quite a bit. Our interview, scheduled for thirty minutes, lasted several hours.

As early as July 2016, Johnson's Department of Homeland Security (DHS) was working to secure America's electoral infrastructure. But he lacked the authority to make systemic and sweeping changes. The United States contains approximately nine thousand electoral jurisdictions and more than one hundred thousand polling places. State and local governments administer voting, purchase election equipment, and secure that equipment. Voting systems vary by county; voter registration databases vary by state. DHS can suggest— but not mandate—security standards.[3] This decentralized dynamic befuddles officials abroad but is central to the federalist ethos of the United States, where states have always engaged in a push and pull with the federal government for certain key authorities.

—

Before 2016, few national security professionals cared who oversaw American elections. DHS, the FBI, and the CIA had other priorities. But suddenly electoral security had become *the* priority. Matters of foreign and domestic policy had become inextricably linked. As Russia probed America's electoral systems, Johnson had to rely on states to detect and report breaches. They might; they might not. "DHS cannot know what [states] don't volunteer," he said. "We don't have surveillance tools to surveil what is happening with voter registration and election infrastructure unless the state offers up what they have and opens their closet for us."[4]

This decentralization of authority, established before the digital age, had become a major liability. As Russian intelligence scanned voting systems, the federal government could not mandate a nationwide response. White House advisers like Michael Daniel regretted that states "very jealously guard[ed]" their authority over election administration. The federal officials suddenly charged with defending America's electoral landscape felt unfamiliar with its basic structure. "There are hundreds of different municipalities, hundreds of different precincts and ways of doing business," said Amy Pope, the deputy homeland security adviser. "Putting the federal government's arm around all that, especially when it was so politically sensitive, could not have been accomplished in six months."[5] Obama's team hoped to protect America's electoral infrastructure without aggravating an already tense political atmosphere. Much had changed since the height of the Cold War. In 1964, 77 percent of U.S. adults said they trusted the federal government; by 2015, just 19 percent did.[6]

In this charged environment, Johnson pressed his staff on how to shore up America's electoral systems. One of his advisers suggested designating electoral infrastructure as "critical infrastructure"—a classification that would mandate nothing but would enable better information sharing with states and prioritize federal resources for electoral security. It would also send a signal to Putin that the United States was taking the threat of vote alterations seriously. Johnson welcomed the idea. "I wanted to make a formal designation, and make a thing of it," he said.[7] At an event on August 3, Johnson told reporters that he was "carefully consider[ing]" whether to issue a critical infrastructure designation, given the "vital national interest in our election process."[8]

Then, on August 15, Johnson held a conference call with election officials from all fifty states in which he reiterated that he was considering a critical infrastructure designation. Several participants accused Johnson of plotting a federal takeover of America's elections. "I explained probably ten times on the call it's voluntary," Johnson said, but "the state officials had a bad reaction to it, at least the ones who spoke up." Johnson did not raise the Russia threat. "When I started beating this drum, I was not in a position to," he said, as internal intelligence was sensitive and evolving, and the White House was determined not to induce widespread panic about America's vulnerabilities.[9] In the official summary of the August 15 call, DHS said it was "not aware of any specific or credible cyber-security threats relating to the upcoming general election systems."[10] State officials could not unite against a covert operation they did not know existed.

The measured tone of Johnson's conference call belied the intensity of debates in the White House. Soon after the call, Johnson, Rice, McDonough, and other senior officials huddled to discuss Russia's ongoing operation. Johnson sensed "new urgency" among his colleagues. Rice, the national security adviser, turned to him and said, "You know that critical infrastructure thing you were talking about doing, can you do that, like, yesterday?"[11] Rice, in an interview, said she had wanted to issue the designation "sooner rather than later" but that state officials had "reacted extremely negatively" and hampered progress. "What we were dealing with," she said, "was fifty states who were running their own systems and who were unanswerable to the federal government and didn't want to be answerable to the federal government."[12]

McDonough promised Johnson a briefing on what was driving the administration's growing alarm. John Brennan, the CIA director, then met with Johnson in a Sensitive Compartmented Information Facility (SCIF), where top secret information can be shared. "Brennan came up to my headquarters on Nebraska Avenue, no subject, no plus ones," Johnson said, "and in my SCIF he went through in extraordinary detail what we knew about what the Russians were doing and how we knew it."[13] Johnson declined to detail the substance of this briefing, but Brennan presumably relayed what he had told Obama earlier that month: Putin was personally directing a covert operation against America's election, in order to help Trump, hurt Clinton, and sow discord within the United States.[14]

Federal officials knew about Russia's operation, but they also knew they lacked a full understanding of its breadth. They looked to the states for more information. On August 18, the FBI issued a warning to states about two recent breaches into voting registration databases and listed eight IP addresses associated with those attacks. (Media outlets soon reported that the affected states were Illinois and Arizona.) Twenty more states then reported that their networks had made contact with at least one of those IP addresses.[15] By the end of August, Michael Daniel had concluded that Russia was targeting all fifty states.[16] The FBI's warning did not mention Russia, which, again, meant that states lacked insight into Washington's intentions.

The states that responded to the warning did so voluntarily. "We didn't know what we didn't know. We are relying on the states to tell us what is happening in their systems," Lisa Monaco said. Election officials could, hypothetically, run IP addresses, identify matches, and then not report them, as a result of paranoia and partisan distrust. In an article published toward the end of the summer titled "Elections Security: Federal Help or Power Grab?," Brian Kemp, then Georgia's secretary of state, questioned whether the Obama administration would use an exaggerated security threat to seize control of elections. (Georgia was one of the states to decline offers of DHS security assistance.)[17] Johnson did not want to play into this narrative. "The last thing we wanted was to make this a political issue," he said, so by the end of August he had shelved the critical infrastructure idea. "It was better to encourage the states one by one to seek our assistance." Rice, deferring to Johnson's judgment, said that DHS sought to "use more honey than vinegar and try to coax the states into cooperation and sharing," which was not "our preferred course" but was, given the circumstances, "likely to be the most effective course."[18]

Initially a promising idea, a critical infrastructure designation now seemed self-defeating. Obama needed state election officials to cooperate. But it had become obvious that many of those officials were suspicious of Washington. "It was a lack of trust," Pope said, which led states to say, "These are our systems, this is our territory, we don't want you looking over our shoulder, we don't actually trust what your end goals are."[19] Johnson could have issued the designation at the start of August. Instead, he consulted states, and did so without alerting them to the Russia threat. His outreach prompted pushback and, eventually, restraint on the part of the federal government.

—

To get state officials to accept DHS assistance, Obama considered how to earn their trust. He did not want to issue a presidential statement about the importance of accepting DHS assistance, believing that in the middle of a contentious campaign, red states would perceive his voice as a partisan one. So he requested help from the four leaders of Congress: the Republicans Paul Ryan and Mitch McConnell and the Democrats Nancy Pelosi and Harry Reid.

The idea was a traditional one. "Look, there was a time when you really could go to the leadership in Congress on an issue of national security interest and you would get their support," said Leon Panetta, the former chief of staff, CIA director, and defense secretary. His one-time boss, Bill Clinton, had spent much of his presidency working alongside Trent Lott, then the Republican Senate leader, who said in an interview that he preferred to support Clinton on foreign policy matters. "In those days, unlike these days,

I tried to find a way to support the president when I could, because he was the president, and he and I had a pretty good relationship," Lott said, pointing out that after he left Congress, Clinton spoke at the unveiling of his Senate portrait. "He showed up," Lott said. "[It was] very generous, very magnanimous, very gracious"—and a symbol of a bygone era. In Washington today, lawmakers "don't communicate, and the most important leadership tool is your ears—nobody listens anymore," Lott said. "Secondly, there's no chemistry, they don't know each other, they don't like each other, they're mean to each other, they use bad language, it's just totally out of control, but the biggest problem in Washington now is of leadership: There ain't none."[20]

The bipartisan atmosphere that Lott described was dead. Obama and Senate leader McConnell had an ice-cold relationship. "The single most important thing we want to achieve is for President Obama to be a one-term president," McConnell said in October 2010.[21] Even after Obama won reelection, McConnell preferred to obstruct rather than work with him. In February 2016, when the Supreme Court justice Antonin Scalia died, McConnell refused to consider Obama's nominee for the vacant seat, since a presidential election was months away. It was an unprecedented move, which McConnell followed up in May when he published a biting memoir. "He's like the kid in your class who exerts a hell of a lot of effort making sure everyone thinks he's the smartest one in the room," McConnell wrote of Obama. "He talks down to people."[22] Later that year, Obama remarked that McConnell thought that compromise conveyed weakness. "There were times that I would meet with Mitch McConnell and he would say to me very bluntly, 'Look, I'm doing you a favor if I do any deal with you, so it should be entirely on my terms because it hurts me just being seen photographed with you.'"[23] (McConnell's representatives did not respond to repeated interview requests for this book.)

This dynamic extended into the summer of 2016 as Obama weighed how to defend America's electoral infrastructure. Between August 11 and September 6, John Brennan gave congressional leadership one-on-one briefings on Russia's ongoing operation. Brennan recalled that House Speaker Paul Ryan took their conversation "very seriously." But, he continued, McConnell "was not interested in learning the truth."[24] During his briefing in early September, McConnell "challenged the integrity of the intelligence" about Russian interference in the election, Brennan said, and insinuated that the CIA was working to "prevent Mr. Trump from becoming president." Brennan bristled at what he felt was an attack on his character. "I pushed back very hard, and basically said not how dare you, but I basically came across that way," Brennan said. "He knew that I was angered by it."[25] McConnell had fired a warning shot: He would treat covert electoral interference as a political issue, and he would prioritize domestic politics over America's national security.

Democratic lawmakers faced no such choice: With their candidate under attack, their political interests aligned with America's national security interests. After his briefing, Senator Harry Reid concluded that Russia's operation was so alarming that U.S. voters should be alerted to it.[26] On August 27, he wrote FBI Director Jim Comey a letter that was then widely reported on, in which he asked Comey to investigate and publicize how Russia was influencing the election. "I have recently become concerned that the threat of the Russian government tampering in our presidential election is more extensive than widely known and may include the intent to falsify official election results," he wrote, raising Obama's foremost concern without citing the CIA as his source. Reid also urged Comey to examine ties between the Trump campaign and the Russian government. Comey declined to be interviewed for this book, but the FBI had, by this point, already opened a counterintelligence investigation with this very mission.[27]

Reid, in his letter, had fired his own warning shot: He would not remain silent while Russia executed its operation, regardless of Obama's position. "I wasn't asking for permission to write the letters," he said. "I don't work for the White House. I work with them. We're a separate branch of government."[28] Reid had at least one outside voice in his ear: that of John Podesta, the chairman of the Clinton campaign. "I was pushing particularly Reid," Podesta told me, to press the White House to disclose details of Russia's operation.[29]

With these battle lines drawn, Obama invited Pelosi, Ryan,

McConnell, and Reid into the Oval Office at the start of September. His request was straightforward: for the four leaders to issue a statement about the Russia threat and the value of DHS security assistance. Ryan responded positively. Avril Haines's impression was that "Ryan would have signed on to a bipartisan statement that condemned Russian interference in the election if McConnell had supported doing so."[30] (Ryan, through a representative, declined to be interviewed for this book.) But McConnell would not budge. "This is a state issue and the federal government should stay out of it," he told Obama, based on Reid's recollection. A visibly frustrated Obama retorted that covert electoral interference "should not be a partisan issue" and that he did not want to "appear to be favoring one side or another" with a statement of his own. The appeal didn't work. McConnell acted as though "the administration was exaggerating the concern of Russian interference in the election for partisan political reasons," Haines recalled. "I thought, 'You have had decades to watch what goes on with the Russians, how can you possibly think we are making this up?' "[31]

After the meeting, Ryan circulated a draft statement that specifically cited Russia. "The two Democrats said, 'Great, let's go, we're signed on,' " Denis McDonough said, but "for weeks Senator McConnell refused, in fact, struck any reference to the country of Russia from the statement drafted by the speaker."[32] McConnell also insisted on adding a sentence that said the federal government would not establish "any degree of control" over elections through a critical infrastructure designation. Speaking in McDonough's office with Pelosi, Johnson argued that the sentence was inconsequential, because a critical infrastructure designation, by definition, would provide the federal government with no new authority. "The sentence is harmless" and "doesn't make any sense," Johnson told them, so "let's just get them to sign it and get it out."[33]

The final version, issued on September 28, did not mention Russia, but it did encourage states to shore up their electoral defenses. Few media outlets covered its release. The statement had become "so watered down," Reid explained, that it effectively had no impact.[34] Obama's advisers have since blamed McConnell for undermining their efforts. It is true that McConnell, in the Oval Office meeting, worked against Obama. But it is also true that Obama had invited McConnell into the White House and, in the process, empowered his detractor to obstruct progress. "In retrospect they put themselves in a terrible position in September by in essence giving McConnell a veto for a lengthy period of time on the story," Podesta said. Panetta, another former White House chief of staff, said that Obama's approach was ill-fitted for modern political realities. "Congress is not going to simply support you because the partisanship has made it largely dysfunctional," he said. "What that means is that presidents, in order to make clear that they are strong and that they're not to be taken advantage of, have to take executive actions as commander and chief."[35]

Paul Ryan, though, seemed willing to cooperate. So what was stopping the president from issuing a statement sans McConnell? When I asked Denis McDonough, he grew visibly tense. "McConnell has a long history on election infrastructure," he responded, in reference to the senator's legislative record. "So him being on the outside of it would have sent a very negative signal if your preeminent goal is to protect the fucking elections."[36]

Outreach had proven costly. Johnson had conferred with state election officials, met resistance, and then abandoned the critical infrastructure idea. Obama had similarly opted to involve congressional leaders. McConnell, using his newfound leverage, delayed and then neutered the requested statement. Haines called McConnell's position "one of the clearest examples of partisan politics hampering our national security."[37]

—

Another component of Obama's defensive strategy unfolded abroad. One way to prevent an Election Day cyberattack was to bolster the security of voting systems; another was to urge Russia to stand down. On August 4, the CIA director, John Brennan, spoke by phone with Alexander Bortnikov, his counterpart in the Russian government. Toward the end of their conversation, Brennan issued a warning similar to the one that Lodge had given Khrushchev in 1960: Interfering with a U.S. election would backfire, in that it would tarnish U.S.-Russian relations and unite Americans in outrage. Bortnikov, after offering standard denials, said he would relay the message to Putin.[38] But in the ensuing weeks, the White House became even more concerned that Putin would order his hackers to alter votes or voter data.

Another debate emerged inside the Obama administration: how to engage Putin in person, on September 4 and 5, when both he and Obama would be attending a summit in China. Obama pressed his advisers on "what to say, when to say it, what to do, when to do it, should we tell Putin what we know, all those considerations," according to Jeh Johnson. These questions alone warranted extensive debate. Ahead of the summit, Tony Blinken recalled, there were "multiple, multiple" meetings of the Deputies Committee, the Principals Committee, and the full National Security Council.[39]

The White House hosted a series of interagency discussions about Putin's psychology and how to get inside his head. The consensus was that Obama should issue a private, in-person warning to the Russian leader. Haines said that while a warning would not address what Russia had already done to influence the election, it seemed to be "the most effective way to deter and stop the Russians from proceeding to affect the vote or otherwise continuing to lean into their interference in our elections."[40] Obama accepted the recommendation.

On September 5, the two leaders met face-to-face, at a precarious and historic moment in U.S.-Russian relations. Just twenty years earlier, Bill Clinton and Boris Yeltsin had won reelection and pledged to collaborate further. Now Obama was struggling to protect the United States from a massive covert operation that Yeltsin's successor was overseeing. In China, Obama huddled with Putin, looked him in the eye, and threatened: "You fuck with us and we'll take you down," as one of his senior advisers put it. (Obama, recounting the exchange in December, said he told Putin to "cut it out" or face "serious consequences.")[41] The thrust of Obama's warning had little to do with Russia's efforts to manipulate minds and everything to do with the threat of direct vote alterations. "We delivered the message to Putin and others in response to what we were seeing in the state systems," Monaco explained. "That was our focus."[42]

Years later, Obama's closest aides say his warning signaled

strength. "The president of the United States doesn't go to the president of the Russian Federation with a very robust threat based on restraint," said McDonough, who argued that Obama's "decisive action" and "clear messaging" did deter Putin. Other former advisers to Obama disagree. "I don't think they mattered at all," Celeste Wallander said of both Obama's and Brennan's warnings. Michael Morell, Obama's former CIA chief, was similarly dismissive. "That is absolutely silly if anybody believed either one of those would be effective," he said. "That's not imposing costs or denying objectives. There is no deterrent effect whatsoever with either one of those. I just don't see how anybody thought those could be helpful besides the PR benefit of being able to say you did it."[43]

Initially, it appeared as though Obama, facing roadblocks at home, had deterred Putin overseas. Just after the summit, the U.S. intelligence community reported that Russia's covert reconnaissance of voting systems had abated. "We thought, 'Message received,'" Tony Blinken said. Within weeks, however, the White House was receiving new intelligence about Russia targeting America's electoral infrastructure, according to four senior administration officials. "It was a steady state," said Lisa Monaco, the homeland security adviser, of the frequency of Russia's covert probes through October. "We did not see a spike. We didn't see an escalation."[44]

Whether one was forthcoming remained unknown.

—

Meanwhile, it was becoming harder to keep Russia's operation from the American people. Back in early September, Jim Comey had offered to publish an op-ed about Russia's theft and release of the DNC emails, as well as its probes of voter databases. But the White House had demurred. "The Obama team's deliberations were, as usual, extensive, thoughtful, and very slow," Comey writes in his memoirs.[45] As September progressed, the case for going public grew stronger. Unconfirmed media reports about Russia's operation were confusing voters. Clinton's campaign team was shouting that Putin was trying to derail her candidacy. And inside the Obama administration, there was now "sufficient confidence and coordination among the relevant components of the intelligence community,"

Avril Haines said, "to make a statement about Russian interference in the election."[46]

In the Situation Room, Jeh Johnson clashed with Jim Comey. "I forcefully urged that we make a public disclosure," Johnson said, but "there were others around the table, specifically Jim Comey, who believed that simply by making that public declaration, you're playing into the Russians' hands, by sowing the seeds of doubt about the integrity of our democracy."[47] Despite offering to run an op-ed, Comey argued that a public statement might "accidentally accomplish the Russians' goal of undermining confidence in our election system." Johnson retorted that American voters, akin to shareholders of a stock, deserved to know about market manipulators and that remaining silent was akin to political suicide. "Think about if we say nothing and [Trump] wins," Johnson told his colleagues, "and it comes out that we knew what we knew and didn't say anything, that would be unforgivable, it would be a scandal." This argument eventually won over the room.[48]

But what should be said, and who should say it? Much of what Brennan had told congressional leaders would remain classified, including Putin's personal involvement and preference for Trump. And Obama, as the head of the Democratic Party, opted not to issue the statement himself. "[Obama] had a clear favorite in the outcome of the election," David Cohen said. "That played into how we publicized the issue." In one meeting, Obama's advisers went "around and around" debating, Johnson said, until he and James Clapper agreed to issue a statement together. Their nonpartisan positions lent them credibility. "We tried to have the least politicized parts of our government make the statement so it would be perceived as more credible and nonpartisan," Haines said.[49]

In their announcement, Johnson and Clapper made two disclosures: first, that senior members of the Russian government had ordered the DNC hack and release and, second, that states had been experiencing scans and probes of their electoral infrastructure. Both of these revelations withheld key details. "At one point the draft said Vladimir Putin" had orchestrated the DNC release, Johnson recalled, but Putin's name was subsequently removed. When asked about this change, Clapper grew irritated. There were "good reasons" at the time not to single out Putin, he insisted, and interagency debate and time constraints had hampered the editing process. "People parse the wording of a statement, amazing," he told me in early 2019. "Look, you can go back and do coulda, woulda, shoulda's all day long, two years later, okay?"[50]

The part of the statement about America's electoral infrastructure was purposefully vague. The statement did not attribute the scans to the Russian government, although readers could draw that conclusion. "We were not in a position to publicly say, 'We know it is the Russian government screwing around with the electoral infrastructure,'" Johnson said, as the White House sought to "warn people about the threat" without making it seem as though the vote would be "all manipulated [and] all screwed up." The statement also stressed that it would be near impossible for hackers to change the outcome of the election, since America's electoral apparatus was so decentralized. This point struck Johnson as misleading. "It's a bit awkward because we say there are thousands of jurisdictions, it would be hard to alter, which in reality is not really true, because all you'd have to do is go to key precincts in key states," he said.[51]

The statement was scheduled for release on October 7, which proved to be one of the most surreal and chaotic days in the history of American politics. That morning, Johnson briefed Clinton and Trump, separately, about an ongoing hurricane-relief effort. During his briefing, Trump invited Johnson to have lunch with him at Trump Tower after Obama left office. "Well, you know you might win," Johnson replied, to which Trump said, dismissively, "Oh yeah, I might win." Johnson was not "authorized" to tell either candidate about his impending statement. "When I hung up with Trump," he recalled, "I said to myself, 'Gee, I just told them about [the relief effort], and they have no idea about this statement that we're about to issue.'"[52]

Johnson and Clapper released their statement at 3:00 p.m., anticipating that it would receive wall-to-wall coverage. But just after 4:00 p.m., *The Washington Post* published a recording from 2005 of Trump boasting to Billy Bush of *Access Hollywood* that he could grab women "by the pussy." Then, at 4:32 p.m., WikiLeaks began uploading the personal emails of Clinton's campaign chairman,

John Podesta.[53] Journalists immediately started sifting through the stolen emails, which were released on a daily basis through the election. "There were probably some instances where we covered the emails too much," said Philip Rucker, the White House bureau chief for *The Washington Post*. "And I absolutely worry about being used as a tool of a foreign interference operation. But Russia understood the news media in the United States, Twitter, competitive pressures that news organizations face, and they knew what they were doing with those emails, dripping them out day by day, because every new piece of information the media would jump on."[54]

Johnson and Clapper's statement barely registered, in part because of the next phase of Russia's operation—the WikiLeaks dump—and in part because of the *Access Hollywood* tape. "Our message got completely emasculated," Clapper said. Johnson regretted that the statement was "below-the-fold news," as reporters "ran off to chase after sex, lust, and greed."[55] Members of the Trump campaign paid the statement little mind. "It might have been different had *Access Hollywood* not come out; maybe [the statement] would have gotten more attention," Steve Bannon said. "The Billy Bush tape was so overwhelming that I don't even remember the Podesta emails coming out that day."[56]

A week and a half later, at the final presidential debate, the moderator Chris Wallace asked Clinton about comments she had made about "open borders" during a paid speech about which "we've learned from the WikiLeaks." Clinton quickly cited Johnson and Clapper's statement and emphasized what Wallace had omitted: that Russia, not WikiLeaks, was behind the release. But Wallace's focus was on the contents of the messages, not their source. Trump pounced. "That was a great pivot off the fact that she wants open borders. Okay? How did we get on to Putin?" he shot back, before casting doubt on the veracity of the October 7 statement. "She has no idea whether it's Russia, China, or anybody else."[57] Trump's obfuscation helped to divert attention from Russia until after the election. "It was in December, after the election, when the mainstream presses said, 'Oh my God, the Russians interfered,'" Johnson complained. "We told you that two months ago."[58]

But the Obama administration, too, made choices that limited the impact of the statement. The first was what was *not* disclosed. It was not until after the election that the U.S. intelligence community revealed that Putin was overseeing a complex interference operation to sow discord, hurt Clinton, and help Trump. "My instinct would have been to publicize and act earlier and just tell the American people this is what we discovered and this is what we're doing against it," said Dennis Blair, Obama's first director of national intelligence. "The strange thing on all of this is that our enemies know and yet our own people don't know. Who the hell are we keeping the secrets from?" asked Blair, who said it would have been "better for the country" had the White House disclosed more about Russia's operation sooner. "We needed to impose penalties and I think we needed to give a lot more information to people as to what's going on, and it was derelict not to."[59]

The key revelation of the statement—that the Kremlin was behind the DNC release—had already been widely covered in the media. "The administration's October statement was at best a marginal addition to the public's knowledge," Comey later wrote.[60] Obama had also waited until October to disclose what his team had known for months. "We were wrestling with an unprecedented situation," Johnson said, in defense of the timing of the statement. "The considerations as to whether to disclose were serious considerations. Are we compromising sources and methods? Are we playing into Trump's hands, his talking points? Are we playing into the Russian government's hands? I'm just glad we made the statement when we did and not on November 7."[61]

Obama also chose not to issue the October statement himself. He delegated the task to Johnson and Clapper, as he had with Reid, Pelosi, McConnell, and Ryan. On this point, Obama's closest aides are especially defensive. "I've heard the argument that had the president said it, and not the director of national intelligence and the secretary of homeland security, that more reporters would have covered it," Denis McDonough said. "I think that's bullshit. Reporters report. That's what they do."[62]

Obama, in grappling with an unfamiliar threat, had met resistance at every turn. The October 7 statement had received little play. McConnell had diluted the congressional statement. And some election officials remained wary of Washington's intentions. By reaching out to states directly, DHS made some headway. Before Election Day, thirty-three state election offices and thirty-six local election offices let DHS assess the security of their voting systems.[63] But this progress, while positive, was insufficient. Various states were still refusing to cooperate. "Ahead of elections, states reject federal help to combat hackers," CBS reported on October 28, listing nearly a dozen states that had yet to accept DHS assistance, from New Hampshire to Georgia to Michigan.[64]

And despite Obama's warning, Putin did not seem to be relenting. Russia's targeting of electoral infrastructure, Celeste Wallander said, remained "active" through October. In early November, GRU officers sent malicious emails to more than 120 Florida county election officials, in an attempt to gain access to their computers. The FBI later concluded that the GRU successfully penetrated the networks of at least two Florida counties, exposing voter registration data.[65] Just before the election, Michael Daniel, in a final ploy, used a cybersecurity hotline to warn Moscow to "cease and desist" its "scanning of and penetrations of the voter registration databases." Within forty-eight hours, his counterpart in the Russian government had replied. It was "the normal Russian response," Daniel said, "which was: 'Received, send us more information.'"[66]

On Election Day, the U.S. intelligence community still believed that Russian hackers could, if authorized, alter voter data and even the actual vote count.[67]

It was up to Putin whether to pull the trigger.

Chapter 11

ELECTION DAY

When Jeh Johnson woke up on November 8, 2016, his mind was on Russia. He had already ordered DHS to establish a crisis response center, in case Russian intelligence disrupted the voting process. "That was my decision," he explained, when asked who formed this secret team, which was prepared to offer "quick cyber assistance" to states, were a "cyber intrusion [to] manifest itself on Election Day such that people who show up to vote can't vote, or there is a problem in the reporting of the votes." For months, Johnson had tried to shore up America's defenses. These efforts had borne some fruit but ultimately failed; electoral systems remained vulnerable. Johnson's focus had thus transitioned from preventing a cyberattack to managing one.[1]

In secret, the Obama administration awaited an Election Day cyberattack. Emergency plans were in motion. "Everybody was prepared for the worst-case scenario," Amy Pope said, including by establishing "a whole crisis team, a whole team, a pretty big team, ready to respond" to a Russian strike. "It was very high alert," she said. "People were taking it very, very, very seriously."[2]

At the center of this emergency apparatus was the White House. "We did, in fact, have an entire crisis team set up in the White House," Michael Daniel said, as did the "usual national security agencies." Daniel lacked direct evidence that Russian intelligence was still inside voter registration databases, but it seemed likely, given the intrusions that had been detected since the summer, as well as Washington's limited insight into the security of state electoral systems. As voting progressed, Daniel updated Susan Rice and Lisa

197

Monaco, who, in turn, updated Obama. "We were monitoring very carefully, not just on Election Day, but in the run-up to the election, whether there was any evidence of Russia mechanically distorting the vote, whether that was by manipulating or falsifying voter rolls, before or on Election Day itself," Rice said, when asked about these crisis teams. "That was obvious to do and necessary to do."[3]

Putin had signaled elsewhere that he would cause chaos as the election unfolded. The U.S. intelligence community was well aware that in Ukraine, Russian hackers had sabotaged electoral systems, and that in Montenegro, Russian intelligence had plotted an election night coup d'état.[4] It seemed entirely feasible that Putin would escalate his operation against the United States the day of the election.

America was vulnerable, and Obama's security chiefs knew it. "[Russia] could have done things as far as voter registration rolls; they could have done things as far as tallies," John Brennan said. The White House considered it "very possible," Amy Pope explained, that there would be "actual interference with the voting record and voting systems" on Election Day. For Jeh Johnson, the nightmare scenario involved "data being manipulated in a handful of key precincts in Miami-Dade, in Dayton, Ohio, in a key precinct in Michigan, a key precinct in Wisconsin, a key precinct in Pennsylvania."[5]

The White House was most concerned that Russian hackers would manipulate voter registration databases. After arriving at polling places, voters would find that their addresses were inaccurate or that their names were missing altogether. "If that happened at scale, you could have a real problem. You would have chaos in the actual conduct of the vote," Lisa Monaco said of this specific threat. As Americans struggled to cast their ballots, mass confusion would erupt, as would news reports of electoral tampering. Cyber experts might say Russia was responsible, but it wouldn't matter, because Trump would say otherwise. "What did seem very plausible," Avril Haines said, "was that [Russia] could affect the votes of a small percentage of the population by, for example, changing the addresses of registrants to make it more challenging for them to vote and thereby undermine faith in the election process."[6]

Public polling pointed to Trump's defeat. On Election Day, six forecasts tracked by *The New York Times* assessed that Clinton had a 71 percent, 85 percent, 89 percent, 92 percent, 98 percent, and greater than 99 percent chance of victory.[7] Trump had signaled that he would not concede quietly. At the third presidential debate, he questioned the integrity of voter registration databases. "If you look at your voter rolls, you will see millions of people that are registered to vote . . . that shouldn't be registered," he said, before declining to say whether he would concede on Election Day, were Clinton to win. "I will tell you at the time. I'll keep you in suspense."[8]

It seemed obvious to Obama's team that Trump, after losing, would label the election illegitimate. A cyberattack on electoral systems would strengthen his case. In this chaotic atmosphere, "law enforcement [was] planning for a contingency outcome," Denis McDonough said, involving "instability [and] violence."[9] A separate strain of crisis planning focused on this scenario. "The working hypothesis was that Clinton was going to win, and that [Trump] was then going to go and incite people to violence by claiming that the system was rigged," Pope said, so there was "planning around riots and all of that." Pope went on, "The expectation was this was a guy who was not playing by the rules and if it served his personal strategy, he would very happily push a narrative that the electoral process was rigged against him."[10]

The U.S. intelligence community was also tracking the looming uncertainty of what Russia intended for *after* the election. Covert electoral interference rarely ends with a specific vote. "The Russians already had shift[ed] gears," Clapper said. "They were already anticipating [Clinton] winning the election, and were bent then on what they could do to undermine the legitimacy of her presidency."[11]

The next phase of Russia's operation, internal intelligence indicated, would begin just after Election Day. First, Moscow would reveal that voter data had been altered, legitimizing Trump's claims of a rigged election. Next, Russia would leak information damaging to Clinton that the CIA knew the Kremlin possessed but had not yet released. "They fully expected Hillary Clinton to become president, and they wanted to have bullets they could use during her presidential term," Brennan said, in explaining why Moscow held on to these materials. "It's one thing to bloody a candidate, and it's something else to be able to continue to wound a president of the

United States, maybe on the eve of certain meetings," he continued, "so there's a clear rationale why you don't want to shoot your entire wad prior to an election." Brennan declined to elaborate further. Clinton said in an interview that she didn't know of these withheld materials and did not believe they existed.[12]

Russia had "lots more stuff that they stole that they never released," Celeste Wallander added, including from "people who might serve in a Clinton administration," as well as "lots of stuff that they stole from Republicans that is compromising material that they could use if they wanted to."[13]

But none of these uncertainties came to fruition. No cyberattack caused chaos at polling places. No files stolen from these unnamed individuals appeared online. The one thing taken for granted inside the White House—the outcome of the election—turned out to be wrong, too. Although Trump lost the popular vote by nearly three million votes, he won three pivotal swing states by a margin of fewer than eighty thousand votes and, therefore, won the Electoral College.[14] Obama's chief advisers, many of whom said Clinton's lead had influenced their decision-making, were stunned. "It was kind of a shock to me personally how disconnected I was from flyover America," Clapper said.[15]

In making sense of Trump's victory, Harry Reid, the Senate minority leader in 2016, insists that the full scope of Russia's operation remains unknown. With the CIA, the KGB, and the Stasi, the extent of their Cold War–era covert operations became clear only decades after they took place. The GRU archives have not been opened, and Putin's closest advisers have not started talking. Once they do, Reid is convinced that the United States will learn that an Election Day cyberattack did take place. There is "no question," Reid said, that Russian hackers covertly altered the vote count. "I think one reason the elections weren't what they should have been was because the Russians manipulated the votes. It's that simple," Reid advanced, his only evidence being the concerns expressed by Jeh Johnson and others prior to the election about the exposure of America's voting systems. "It doesn't take a math expert to understand that by just changing a few votes, the outcome will be different. So, I have no doubt."[16]

Obama's leading advisers dismissed Reid's theory, with a catch: They could not rule it out. "We saw no evidence of interference in voter tallying, not to say that there wasn't, we just didn't see any evidence," James Clapper said. Susan Rice said that she had not seen any indication that Russia had "successfully altered votes or electoral databases." And Denis McDonough said that "as of right now, our best information says that the person who was elected was freely elected."[17] Perhaps Reid will eventually be proven correct, or perhaps it is the straightforward and alarming notion of direct vote alterations that has continued to captivate him, as it did Obama.

After the election, Obama was left in a surreal position. The Election Day cyberattack he had envisioned had not manifested itself, but the candidate that Putin preferred had won. In an interview just before leaving office, he acknowledged that he had not grasped how the internet had so exposed Americans to foreign influence. "I underestimated the degree," Obama said, "to which, in this new information age, it is possible for misinformation, for cyber hacking and so forth, to have an impact on our open societies, our open systems, to insinuate themselves into our democratic practices in ways that I think are accelerating."[18]

—

The exposure of America's electoral infrastructure was so glaring that it had dominated Obama's decision-making process. One vector of Russia's operation—intrusions into state voting systems—distracted from the other two: email releases and social media manipulation. "That is what they were focused on," Victoria Nuland said, in explaining how the specter of vote alterations distracted Obama's inner circle. "They were not focused at all on what we knew had been very effective elsewhere: the influence campaign, changing public opinion."[19]

Obama had tried to deter a knockout punch on Election Day, but he had not at all deterred Putin from manipulating voters. Celeste Wallander said that leading administration officials showed "complacency" in their presumption that tactics like the email releases "wouldn't have an effect" on the outcome of the election. To "get people to take this seriously—as being really important—was really hard," she said. Jim Comey similarly sensed that Obama did not believe Russia's attempts to influence voters would end up mattering much. "Why risk undermining faith in our electoral process, [Obama] seemed to conclude, when the Russian efforts were making no difference?" he writes in his memoirs. Some of the president's key advisers accept the thrust of this analysis. "Without question," Avril Haines said, "we did not have as clear a picture as we do now of what the Russians were doing and of the potential impact of their influence campaign."[20]

The United States, which had long manipulated elections abroad, had forgotten a key lesson of this history: Covert electoral interference rarely involves changing votes directly but almost always involves changing minds. It's a lesson that a previous generation of American policy makers would have known from experience. In 1948, the CIA arranged for Italian Americans to send millions of letters to loved ones in Italy, urging them to vote against the Communist Party. In 1964, no White House adviser would have said the only way to interfere in an election was to target the actual voting process. The CIA had, after all, just orchestrated a massive propaganda campaign against Salvador Allende of Chile. Letters, posters, pamphlets, articles, rallies—all were designed to influence opinion; so, too, were tweets and hacked emails in 2016. "There is no question," Rice said, "that the advent of the internet has created new avenues of attack, not just for the Russians, but for everybody."[21]

Whether Putin intended it or not, the threat of one type of interference—altering votes—had distracted Obama. "Why they decided not to do it? Maybe they never planned to," Brennan said, of the cyberattack against electoral systems that never came, while maintaining that Russia was "prepared" to be "much more aggressive" in interfering in the election but "chose not to" escalate its operation. "I'm not sure how much we deterred, if we deterred anything, if we deterred a lot with the messages we sent." John Podesta, a former counselor to Obama, said the president and many of his top advisers "misperceived the problem" in focusing on vote alterations, which he described as a "very narrow view" of Russia's operation. "That's where all their energy went and that's where their warnings went to the Russians," Podesta said. "They went to the direct interference rather than this indirect interference. I think that was a mistake."[22]

One of the threats Obama underestimated was personal to Podesta: the hack and release of emails. This vector of Russia's operation leveraged a core democratic attribute—the free press—by leaking documents that journalists would want to cover. "It's really easy to blame reporters," said Zeke Miller, then the White House correspondent for *Time,* but "undoubtedly those emails were newsworthy," not least because "they provided a window into the functioning of a major party presidential campaign that was at times enigmatic to say the least, into the psychology of the candidate and the people around her . . . and their unvarnished thoughts on what was going on." Philip Rucker of *The Washington Post* likewise said that the Podesta and DNC emails merited coverage because they were accurate and provided insights into powerful institutions. "If we did it all over again, we would still cover the emails," Rucker said. "The coverage probably would have been a little less breathless," he continued, but "we would not have kept information from the public if it were newsworthy."[23]

What is inarguable is that the media aggressively covered the hacked emails, which reached voters' minds at critical moments in the campaign. The emails "infected press coverage," writes communications expert Kathleen Hall Jamieson, "add[ing] arguments to Trump's rhetorical arsenal" and "foster[ing] an anti-Clinton agenda and frame in news."[24] *The New York Times,* for instance, ran at least nine stories on the contents of Podesta's emails, with headlines like "Highlights from the Clinton Campaign Emails: How to Deal with Sanders and Biden." None of those headlines mentioned Russia, in part because the Obama administration had not yet attributed the Podesta release to Moscow, and in part because insider details were more attention grabbing.[25] "Our human nature is such that we're going to focus on the truth rather than the medium, on the message rather than the medium," said Paul Sonne, then a national security reporter for *The Wall Street Journal,* of the emails.[26] Foreign policy professionals were left seething. "*The New York Times* ended up being a useful idiot of a Russian operation," Celeste Wallander said. "They were an instrument of the Kremlin's strategy.

They let themselves be used."[27] In a December 2016 feature, three veteran *New York Times* reporters acknowledged, "Every major publication, including *The Times,* published multiple stories citing the D.N.C. and Podesta emails posted by WikiLeaks, becoming a de facto instrument of Russian intelligence."[28]

John Podesta and Steve Bannon, regarded as the masterminds behind the Clinton and Trump campaigns, respectively, agree on at least one thing: Podesta's emails received more media attention than they deserved. Journalists "treated news gathering and democracy the way *BuzzFeed* treats clickbait," Podesta said, in their "some-what obsess[ive]" coverage of his emails. "They pumped shit up, that if somebody had walked on a street corner and said it, it was like nothing." Bannon found the contents of the emails insignificant. "When the emails came out, they were inner-office emails with some snarky shit in there. Does anyone even remember what the Podesta emails said today?" he said in September 2019. And yet, Bannon continued, reporters covered the emails "like it was the end of days."[29]

———

For Russia, the email dumps proved spectacularly successful. The cost was negligible, and the benefits were immense. The first WikiLeaks dump, in July, sowed chaos and division within the Democratic Party; the second, in October and early November, revealed the contents of Clinton's paid speeches to banks, received sustained coverage, and distracted her inner circle.

"It was the worst month of my life in the context of the worst two years of my life," said Teddy Goff, Clinton's chief digital strategist, of the period between October 7 and November 7, when WikiLeaks released thirty-three batches of stolen emails. "The psychologi-cal impact of that cannot be overstated. At a senior staffer level, [WikiLeaks] deliberately did it with a drop every day and twice some days. In addition to everything else going on, it's like, 'What am I going to find out tomorrow about my colleagues and what we've all been saying about each other?' "[30] For Podesta, the month of October felt like "the fog of war," as his private inbox became public fodder. "There's yet another effect, which is personally the most painful and the most difficult," he continued, which is that his correspondence spawned "a whole world of completely fake news which claims to be evidenced and proven by the emails even though it's all fucking made up."[31]

Russia's hack and release of emails built on past practices. In 1976, the KGB sent U.S. newspapers a forged FBI file—a single document—about Senator Henry "Scoop" Jackson's personal life. Reporters, playing the role of gatekeeper, opted not to run it, so the operation failed. In 2016, rather than create a single fake document, Russian intelligence stole tens of thousands of accurate documents. And rather than send those files to newspapers, Russian intelligence posted them online. "In today's media world, we're no longer the filter we once were," said Peter Baker, the chief White House correspondent for *The New York Times*.

The Soviet Union's totalitarian idea—nothing is private, and everything is the business of the state—had taken hold in the United States. "This was a window into something inherently private and secret," Philip Rucker said. "In the case of John Podesta, it was exploiting his privacy and his personal space to be reading all of those emails, but once it becomes public, as it did on WikiLeaks, that's not a reason to hide them from the public if it's newsworthy."[32]

—

And then there was social media. Emails aside, the U.S. intelligence community committed a major oversight: failing to detect Russia's systemic manipulation of platforms like Facebook and Twitter. "We only scratched the surface of the depth and the pervasiveness of what the Russians were doing on social media," James Clapper said. "I didn't fully comprehend at that time the magnitude of what they were doing."[33] The rare journalists tracking Russia's covert operations abroad anticipated what the U.S. government did not. In July 2016, Anne Applebaum wrote that a "host of fake websites and Twitter accounts with Russian origins" were "actively support[ing] Trump and are contributing to some of the hysteria on the Internet."[34] Washington's attention, however, was elsewhere. Michael Daniel, now the head of the Cyber Threat Alliance, said that, despite certain warning signs, America's national security apparatus "focused very little" on "understanding the scope and scale" of Russian interference across social media. In October 2016, the FBI's Counterintelligence Division had a contractor examine Russian propaganda on Twitter rather than devote internal manpower to the task.[35]

It was not just the FBI that overlooked this threat. During parts of our interview, David Cohen, the CIA's deputy director in 2016, stared at the ceiling of his law office, reflecting on the decisions he and his colleagues made ahead of the election. The U.S. intelligence community, he recognized, had not sensed the bigger picture. "We probably should have anticipated that what we were seeing, as is often the case in intelligence, was the tip of the iceberg," he said. John Brennan, Cohen's boss, said that, when Special Counsel Robert Mueller indicted a Russian entity for manipulating America's social media environment, he was "unaware" of much of what Mueller's team found. "I was aware of things that were happening but not a lot of specifics," he said. "I do not know the full extent of what [Russia] did."[36]

With the intelligence provided to him, Obama had responded to Russia's operation based on its email dumps and probes of voting systems, without realizing that Russia was also covertly manipulating millions of Americans across social media. Michael Morell called this oversight "an intelligence failure"—and has said as much to his colleagues who were still in government in 2016. "There were Russians in Russia doing this," he has told them, "and you didn't see that, you didn't have an asset, a human spy, or a technical penetration of the Kremlin, or of these organizations that were doing this, so that you could have told the president here is what they're doing." Douglas Wise, the deputy director of the Defense Intelligence Agency in 2016, agreed with Morell. "It was an institutional failure on the part of [the intelligence community] in our failure to anticipate that the Russians were adopting the use of these very powerful social media tools," he said. "That certainly was on my part an individual failure." Leon Panetta, a former CIA director, said the U.S. intelligence community had demonstrated "a real misjudgment of the capability" of Russia, not only with respect to social media, but with respect to its intentions generally. "Nobody anticipated the kind of bold effort that was involved" in 2016, he said, "and that is without question a real miss in terms of what our intelligence agencies are supposed to be able to protect us from."[37]

Only in December 2016, when Obama ordered an interagency review of Russia's operation, did his team begin to grasp what they had missed. "During the excavation in December," Victoria Nuland said, "we found more than even Celeste and I, who had been considered paranoid lunatics in the summer, had expected."[38] The U.S. intelligence community then released a classified assessment of Russia's operation to federal officials, as well as an unclassified version to the public. Its top-line conclusions, Brennan said, were the same as those he had shared with congressional leaders in August. Putin had directed a covert electoral interference operation to help Trump, hurt Clinton, and divide the United States.[39]

At the end of December, Obama, as planned, announced diplomatic and economic countermeasures against Russia.[40] But many of his advisers now say those retaliatory steps were overdue and insufficient. "I don't think anything we did deterred future action," Wallander said. "We haven't begun to raise the costs on the Kremlin for this kind of interference." Morell said "what Obama did fell far, far, far short" and that "if I were Putin, I would have seen it as a slap on the wrist." Even Haines said the president, near the end of his term, was reluctant to sanction Russia more aggressively, partially because Trump could undo such action once in office. "One issue, among many, that was raised," she said, was that "if we enacted heavy sanctions, it would give the next administration, which seemed obviously less inclined to seriously counter Russian aggression, the excuse to roll those sanctions back upon coming into office."[41]

Obama's team had unearthed additional details about Russia's operation, but much remained hidden. "We only scratched the surface of what the Russians were doing," James Clapper said, "and a lot of that has come out since then." As new information has emerged, many of Obama's former advisers have concluded that the United States should have retaliated against Russia in the summer of 2016, after all. Clapper would have "preferred" that Obama announce the December countermeasures prior to the election.

Tony Blinken added, "Knowing then what we know now, yeah, we should, absolutely should, have done more, faster, harder." Sarah Bloom Raskin, the deputy Treasury secretary in 2016, said that, looking back, the sanctions that Obama announced in December amounted to a "light package," relative to the severity of Russia's actions. "From one perspective, the time to have protected all of this was before the elections," she added, especially had the scope of Russia's social media operation been better understood internally. "That was the point at which, possibly, you could have escalated the use of the [sanctions] tools to make Putin's manipulation more costly," she said. Other officials regretted that politics had influenced policy making. The "outcome of an election" is "too unknowable and too uncertain to predicate your policy on," said Jon Finer, the State Department's chief of staff, who "would have done more sanctions sooner." He went on: "I would have just done what was in the interests of the country and in the interests of national security, and that cut very strongly in favor of telling people what had happened in a very clear and direct way and imposing very real and onerous consequences on Russia. We eventually got there. We got there slowly."[42]

Obama, meanwhile, prepared to leave the White House. But first, he issued warnings about the threat he had underestimated months earlier: that foreign actors could manipulate American voters in new and powerful ways across the internet. In private, he urged Mark Zuckerberg, the head of Facebook, to combat fake news.[43] And in an interview with ABC, he cautioned, "If we're not vigilant, foreign countries can have an impact on the political debate in the United States in ways that might not have been true ten, twenty, thirty years ago."[44] The White House had spent months defending America's electoral infrastructure. Now Obama recognized the need to defend America's information space. But it was too late. Russian propaganda had already reached tens of millions of U.S. voters. The damage, as we will see, was already done.

Chapter 12

SOCIAL MEDIA

In June 2014, two Russian citizens, Aleksandra Krylova and Anna Bogacheva, arrived in the United States. Carrying drop phones, evacuation plans, and cameras, the pair spent twenty-two days traversing at least nine states, from Texas to California to New York. Then they returned to Russia and filed a detailed intelligence report about their trip. Krylova and Bogacheva were not mere tourists. They went to the United States with a mission: to lay the groundwork for a covert operation against America's upcoming election.[1]

Krylova and Bogacheva worked for the Internet Research Agency, an information warfare center based in Saint Petersburg. Funded by a Russian oligarch with close ties to Putin, the group's purpose was to spread propaganda on social media. Just before Krylova and Bogacheva's trip, the IRA launched the "translator project," which focused on targeting American audiences. Its "specialists" created Facebook pages, Twitter accounts, Instagram handles—entire lives that appeared to belong to real Americans. By the fall of 2016, the IRA's monthly budget exceeded $1.25 million and the translator project had more than eighty full-time employees.[2] The Kremlin had developed an off-the-books U.S. campaign, directed from inside Russia.

The U.S. intelligence community overlooked the work of the IRA. So, too, did Facebook. Alex Stamos, a computer scientist, became Facebook's chief security officer in 2015. He left the company three years later, filled with regret. "I'll be completely honest: Facebook fucked up. I fucked up," he told me. Ahead of the 2016 election, Stamos's team neglected to investigate the activities of the

IRA. "We didn't have the IRA stuff in 2016," he said. "Nobody had a full grasp of it. Nobody did."[3]

The clues were there. In 2014 and 2015, a handful of reporters published exposés about the IRA's inner workings. These select journalists painted an alarming portrait: Inside a secretive factory, hundreds of people had assumed fictitious online identities and were spreading propaganda designed to influence public opinion in Russia, Ukraine, and America.[4] Stamos's team "went and shut a bunch of stuff down" in response to these articles. But, he continued, the investigation stopped there. "There was never an attempt to put together a dedicated team to follow up on that, and we should have." Reporters moved onto other subjects.[5] Inside the CIA, Steven Hall, the division chief overseeing Russia through 2015, said the IRA's existence was such a poorly kept secret that he assumed its work was insignificant. "The fact that we were discussing this in a public venue would indicate to me that there was probably not a whole lot there," Hall said. "But it turns out that the Russians were just being much more aggressive than we anticipated and cared apparently a lot less about being found out."[6]

As 2016 progressed, Stamos felt good. His team, he recalled, was on top of GRU-run accounts probing the personal Facebook accounts of Democratic Party officials.[7] "A known GRU account going and doing some reconnaissance—that was a Tuesday. Every week we handled three or four incidents like that," Stamos said. "We reported that to the FBI," he continued, but "got nothing back from them."[8] Disclosing the GRU's activities publicly was out of the question; the potential blowback seemed too significant. "Everybody thought Hillary was going to win, and I think there was a huge fear, just as there was obviously in the Obama White House, inside of Facebook of looking like we were putting our thumb on the scale," Stamos said. Just as Obama wanted Clinton to win, so did most of Facebook's leaders. "Almost every member of the executive team, other than a couple of really important exceptions, was a Hillary Clinton donor or a donor to the Democratic Party," Stamos explained, citing rumors that Sheryl Sandberg, Facebook's chief operating officer, was in the running to be Clinton's Treasury secretary. "The company was so kind of tied to the Democratic

Party," he continued, that "nobody wanted to be looking to help her win." When asked about Stamos's comments, Nathaniel Gleicher, Facebook's head of cybersecurity since 2018, confirmed that the company detected "more traditional" targeting of specific accounts prior to the election, and that the standard "practice" at the time was to alert those targets and the FBI. "That's why we didn't make a public announcement," he said. "Not because of rumors."[9]

Election Day came and went. Trump became the president-elect. This third vector of Russia's operation, executed by the IRA, remained unappreciated. "It was nobody's job to track professional propagandists, especially with our elections," Stamos said. "It was nobody's job in the government; it was nobody's job at the companies." The IRA had been infesting social media platforms with content aligned with Putin's objectives: to sow discord, help Trump, and denigrate Clinton.[10] Only in 2017, during an internal probe, did Facebook officials grasp what they had overlooked. Concerns about the appearance of partisanship persisted internally. "The company just didn't want to take the blame for Trump winning," Stamos explained.[11] Facebook went into damage control mode. "I can't talk about it," Sheryl Sandberg told me, when asked in June 2018 how Facebook was responding to Russia's operation. "But we're working hard on it."[12]

Available figures on the IRA's achievements, while incomplete, are stunning. On Facebook alone, the IRA reached an estimated 126 million Americans and generated 76.5 million engagements. On Twitter, the IRA generated 72 million engagements. On Instagram, the IRA reached 20 million Americans and generated 187 million engagements.[13] On YouTube, the IRA posted roughly eleven hundred videos across seventeen channels.[14] And, on Tumblr, the IRA reached 11.7 million Americans. Other platforms that the IRA targeted include Reddit, Pinterest, Medium, and LinkedIn.[15] (The GRU also sought to influence American voters on social media, but its posts generated comparatively negligible engagement.)[16]

The work of the IRA can feel disorienting—so much propaganda, across so many platforms, with so many meanings. This chapter, in elucidating the work and significance of the IRA, advances two arguments. The first is that Russia, by transforming social media into a weapon of covert electoral interference, manipulated American voters more broadly and effectively than the KGB ever did. The second is that this achievement, while innovative, built upon decades-old ideas, which can be used to anticipate what Russia will do next. The novelty of the IRA is an illusion. Almost everything about its work marked a continuation of past practices, enhanced by new technology. "There is nothing new here," said Porter Goss, the former CIA director. "What has changed is the platform—the devices, the means, the IT world."[17]

There were three major consistencies between the IRA's work and like-minded operations of the Cold War: the idea of molding minds across a penetrable news source, the objectives to sow division and advantage a specific candidate, and the methods used to attain these objectives.

THE IDEA

To mold minds, interfering actors identify and then manipulate conduits for information. This is what the KGB and the CIA did during the Cold War, when they corrupted newspapers, radio programs, and television stations. And this is what the IRA did in 2016, when its employees corrupted social media platforms. The cost of the operation was low, the accessibility was high, and the potential reach was vast. Any Russian with a computer could study and influence American voters. "It's the new cheap warfare," Nikki Haley told me while serving as UN ambassador. "Countries regardless of their wealth can now use this power to fight and infiltrate a country."[18]

Social media had become a dominant part of America's information ecosystem remarkably quickly. In 2003, neither Facebook nor Twitter existed. By 2016, many millions of Americans had plugged into these platforms and others, from Instagram to Pinterest to Snapchat.[19] While surging in popularity, these companies systemically collected the personal data of their users. "It really amuses me about how people get all exercised" about government-run "'mass surveillance,'" James Clapper said. "The government pales compared to the social media platforms, and the insight they have on individuals and personal information that people give up."[20]

(Cambridge Analytica, a political analytics firm retained by the Trump campaign, used improperly harvested Facebook data to amass psychographic profiles of millions of American voters.)[21]

With these platforms came the ability to influence user behavior on an individual basis. Facebook understood this power early. In 2010, the company showed roughly 60 million Americans a post encouraging them to vote; researchers found that an additional 340,000 people cast ballots as a result of this intervention.[22] American campaigns caught on. Political spending on digital advertisements in 2016 totaled $1.4 billion—a 789 percent increase from the previous cycle.[23] "I'm not a believer in television [advertisements]—not with all the social media options around," Steve Bannon said. Discourse on social media, research has shown, spreads to other information channels, such as cable news and fringe websites. Teddy Goff, the Clinton campaign's chief digital strategist, described social media as an essential tool in modern campaigning. "These platforms are highly sophisticated attention-sucking systems," he said. "That's their whole business model."[24]

Russia launched its own digital campaign that played by its own set of rules. With nearly two-thirds of U.S. adults getting at least some of their news from social media, Russia seized the opportunity to manipulate an election by manipulating minds.[25] Putin's strategists have since gloated about their ingenuity. "When the internet was being hailed everywhere as an inviolate space of unrestricted freedom, a place where everything was open to everyone and where all were equal, it was from Russia that hoodwinked humanity heard the sobering question: 'So who are we in the worldwide web—the spiders, or the flies?'" wrote Vladislav Surkov, one of Putin's closest advisers, in February 2019. "And today everyone's rushing to disentangle the Net, including even the most freedom-loving bureaucracies, and to denounce Facebook for facilitating foreign interference."[26]

THE OBJECTIVES

What the Internet Research Agency sought to achieve was entirely unoriginal. Its primary objective, to sow division, was central to

Soviet operations inside the United States. During the Cold War, KGB officers divided Americans by staging hate crimes and spreading disinformation. "They have long tried to cause chaos and diminish democratic institutions," said Bobby Inman, the CIA's deputy director in 1981 and 1982. "But social media has made it so much easier, and you can do it directly." Nor was America the only victim of Russia's digital subversion. Juan Manuel Santos, Colombia's president from 2010 to 2018, struggled to counter Russian attempts to "encourage and strengthen polarization" by interfering in his country's social media environment. "Russia is more interested in maintaining the disorder than anything else," he said.[27]

By May 2014, the IRA had incorporated this longtime aim into its U.S. operations. Intercepted and since released communications reveal that the IRA resolved to "spread distrust towards the candidates and the political system in general," including by fomenting "political intensity through supporting radical groups, users dissatisfied with [the] social and economic situation and oppositional social movements."[28] Putin, ever the KGB officer, sought to weaken the United States and prove to the world—and especially to his own people—that the democratic model was flawed and penetrable.

To achieve Putin's desired end, the IRA exploited preexisting fissures in American society. As Stamos put it, "They were looking to radicalize people that are already a little radical. You like Black Lives Matter, we're going to try to make you hate cops. Do you dislike immigrants? We're going to try to make you a super-villain, horrible, anti-immigrant racist."[29] Many of these posts intentionally contained lies, designed to mislead readers and go viral. On social media, disinformation thrives; MIT researchers have found that on Twitter false news stories spread far more quickly and widely than accurate ones.[30] It is the ideal platform on which to spread hate. "What is most alarming," H. R. McMaster, Trump's former national security adviser, told me, "is the degree to which Russia was able to take advantage of divisions within our own polity and exacerbate those divisions in a way that pit communities against each other while diminishing confidence in our democratic principles, institutions, and processes."[31]

—

The secondary objective of the IRA was also familiar: to advantage one presidential candidate and damage another, just as the CIA and the KGB had in elections around the world, and just as Moscow had attempted in America's 1960, 1968, 1976, and 1984 elections. A few weeks after Trump launched his campaign, in July 2015, IRA-run accounts began posting pro-Trump content and attacking his Republican rivals, including Senators Ted Cruz, Lindsey Graham, and Marco Rubio—the Henry Jacksons and Ronald Reagans of 2016. The IRA developed an impressive following among right-wing voters: Content on its "Being Patriotic" Facebook page generated 6.3 million likes; on its "Stop All Invaders" page, 773,305 comments; and on its "Heart of Texas" page, 4.8 million shares.[32]

The other half of the equation was Hillary Clinton, Putin's foe. In September 2016, an IRA supervisor criticized an employee for uploading a "low number of posts dedicated to criticizing Hillary Clinton" on the IRA's "Secured Borders" page. "It is imperative to intensify criticizing Hillary Clinton," the supervisor instructed.[33] IRA specialists heeded this directive, spreading disinformation about Clinton's personal email server, family foundation, and tenure as secretary of state. They especially derided her character. One IRA-run Facebook post displayed a picture of Clinton alongside the text "Hillary Is Our Enemy"; another showed Clinton and instructed users, "Like if You Agree: Hillary Clinton Is a Serial Liar"; while another warned, "Hillary Clinton Will Eliminate the Free Speech Rights of Anyone Who Gets in Her Way."[34] The IRA—along with Russia's state-sponsored media outlets, Russia Today (RT) and Sputnik—frequently posted about the GRU-orchestrated email dumps. "There was a synergistic relationship," writes Kathleen Hall Jamieson, "between the WikiLeaks releases and Moscow-backed social media content." As has often been the case across history, overt mechanisms—in this case, RT and Sputnik—enhanced the covert components of Russia's operation.[35]

IRA-run accounts also pushed veterans, evangelicals, and other traditionally conservative communities to vote while prodding traditionally left-wing communities to stay home or to support Jill Stein, a third-party candidate. This voter suppression effort especially targeted black Americans, who predominantly supported Clinton.[36] In October 2016, the IRA-run "Woke Blacks" Instagram account posted, "[A] particular hype and hatred for Trump is misleading the people and forcing Blacks to vote Killary. We cannot resort to the lesser of two devils. Then we'd surely be better off without voting AT ALL." The IRA targeted other minority groups. In early November, "United Muslims of America," another IRA creation, posted, "American Muslims [are] boycotting elections today, most of the American Muslim voters refuse to vote for Hillary Clinton because she wants to continue the war on Muslims in the middle east and voted yes for invading Iraq."[37]

The IRA further attempted to disadvantage Clinton by sowing confusion among left-wing audiences, including and especially Bernie Sanders supporters. Just before the election, an IRA-run Twitter account warned, "Heads Up: If you voted for Bernie in the Primaries, the Election Board will NOT let you vote for Hillary on Nov 8."[38] Even the most discerning voters had no way to know these misleading posts were produced outside the United States.

THE METHODS

Reaching voters is a prerequisite of manipulating them.

During the Cold War, the KGB and the CIA went to great lengths to influence as many voters as possible: funding news outlets, recruiting reporters, spreading physical propaganda, and orchestrating voter registration drives. Yet the "limited circulation" of certain pieces of KGB propaganda in the United States, its archives explain, meant they "were very unlikely to get any real resonance."[39] Social media offered new opportunities to influence the masses. To do so, the IRA had to attract an audience.

The first step was making it seem as though IRA accounts belonged to actual Americans. Foreign operatives do not enter the public square—or log on to Twitter—and declare their identities and intentions. Covert electoral interference necessarily involves cutouts, or middlemen, designed to hide the hand of the interfering actor. In East Germany, Georg Fleissman, the journalist, hid the Stasi's hand from Leo Wagner. In Chile, corrupted reporters hid the CIA's hand from the general populace. And in the United States, the IRA hid Russia's hand from voters. "The thing that is powering this [operation] is their ability to lie about who they are," Stamos said.[40] For interfering actors, cutouts are essential. Without them, the covert becomes overt, and foreign machinations are exposed as such.

IRA employees lived inside these digital creations. Specialists focusing on Facebook had to manage six fake personalities at once. The all-consuming nature of this work took a toll. "Of course, if every day you are feeding on hate, it eats away at your soul," a former IRA employee said in 2015. "You start really believing in it. You have to be strong to stay clean when you spend your whole day submerged in dirt." Marat Mindiyarov, another former member of the IRA, described the organization's disorienting nature. "Your first feeling, when you ended up there," Mindiyarov told a reporter in 2018, "was that you were in some kind of factory that turned lying, telling untruths, into an industrial assembly line."[41]

Like KGB officers, IRA specialists studied U.S. discourse before mimicking it. Supervisors offered feedback on whether posts "appeared authentic."[42] Proficiency in English was a prized asset. In December 2014, Mindiyarov, then an IRA employee, applied to join the U.S.-focused translator project, which paid handsomely. His entrance exam entailed writing a paper about Hillary Clinton. "I failed the test because you had to know English perfectly," he later explained. "The reader must not have the feeling that you are a foreigner. The language demands were in fact very high."[43]

IRA specialists, posting in English, sought to persuade Americans to engage with their accounts. One tactic was advertisements: The IRA purchased 3,393 online ads that reached more than eleven million Americans, at a cost of just $100,000.[44] But more important, the IRA attracted followers through regular posts—tons of them, across multiple platforms. On Facebook, the IRA issued 61,500 posts across 81 unique pages; on Twitter, 10.4 million posts across 3,841 accounts; and on Instagram, 116,000 posts across

133 accounts.[45] "This is an information ecosystem problem. This is not limited to one platform," said Renée DiResta, an information warfare expert.[46]

IRA specialists tracked which elements of their content engaged the most people. They assembled detailed metrics reports and tailored their messaging to the news of the day.[47] On September 11, 2016, when Hillary Clinton physically stumbled in public, IRA-run Twitter accounts quickly promoted hashtags like #ClintonCollapse, #ZombieHillary, and #SickHillary. Oxford researchers have found that IRA accounts entered into overdrive at other key moments in the campaign, such as the primary and general election debates.[48] Posts about topical issues could generate significant activity. "When there were black people rioting in the United States we had to write that US policy on the black community had failed," a former IRA employee explained in 2015.[49] IRA-run accounts also frequently linked to polarizing local news stories, perhaps because U.S. adults tend to trust local outlets more than national ones.[50]

By 2016, IRA-run pages boasted hundreds of thousands of followers—akin to major regional newspapers.[51] On Twitter, 118 IRA-run accounts had more than 10,000 followers, and 6 had more than 100,000 followers. On Instagram, 10 IRA-run accounts had more than 109,000 followers, including @Blackstagram (over 300,000 followers), @american.veterans (215,680 followers), and @sincerely_black (196,754 followers). And on Facebook, the IRA's pages attracted an estimated 3.3 million followers.[52]

—

The size of these audiences lent the IRA's accounts credibility. Just as newspapers unwittingly picked up the KGB's propaganda, online influencers unwittingly picked up the IRA's. On Election Day, Donald Trump Jr. retweeted the IRA-run @TEN_GOP account: "This vet passed away last month before he could vote for Trump. Here he is in his #MAGA hat. #voted #ElectionDay." The IRA had worked hard to develop accounts like @TEN_GOP into "leader[s] of public opinion," according to intercepted communications, so their posts would attract the attention of famous personalities. Eric Trump, Sean Hannity, Michael Flynn, Kellyanne Conway, and other conservative figures also unintentionally engaged with IRA-produced content.[53] Their many followers were thus exposed to disguised Russian messaging.

The IRA used its digital cutouts not only to spread propaganda but to get people to do real things in real life. In May 2016, the IRA concocted and advertised competing demonstrations outside a Houston Islamic center. The dueling events generated mainstream media coverage—the ultimate aim of KGB operations a generation earlier, and the GRU's focus ahead of the election.[54] Then, in the summer and fall of 2016, the IRA planned pro-Trump rallies in New York, Florida, and Pennsylvania. Some of these events gained minimal traction; others attracted hundreds of Americans. One pro-Trump rally in Miami caught the attention of Trump campaign officials, who then posted about it on the candidate's Facebook page.[55] Digitally masked Russians persuaded Americans to help plan these events, from a Trump campaign volunteer who provided rally materials to another American citizen who was paid to dress up as Hillary Clinton in a prison uniform. These unwitting recruits had to be managed: The IRA kept an internal spreadsheet tracking the more than a hundred U.S. citizens its specialists had contacted.[56]

—

The gold standard of covert electoral interference is targeting voters based on their individual views and biases. In 1972, the Stasi weaponized the vulnerabilities of two lawmakers—Leo Wagner and Julius Steiner—to change history. More precise than any news article, this type of interference long proved difficult to execute at scale. Then came social media, which, by design, profiles each of its users. All Americans on Facebook relinquish information about themselves. Their locations, their interests, their backgrounds—all of it is recorded online.

Basic functions of social media platforms reveal the personalities of users. When an American joins a page like "Secured Borders," he does so because of a personal investment in immigration issues. "People self-organize into these homogeneous hyperactive ideological echo chambers, as is intended by the platforms," said Jonathon Morgan, the CEO of Yonder, an information integrity company.

The IRA also used advertisements to reach specific types of voters: One thousand eight hundred and fifty-two of its ads incorporated interest-based targeting. "The thing that's really special about advertising is it's the only function on Facebook that allows you to put content in front of somebody who had no desire to see it," Stamos said.[57]

The IRA also targeted voters by location, another long-running tactic of interfering actors. In Chile, the CIA only aided congressional candidates competing in swing districts. The IRA similarly focused on swing states. In June 2016, an IRA employee, under an alias, messaged a Texas-based organizer who explained the importance of "purple states like Colorado, Virginia & Florida." From then on, the IRA "commonly referred to targeting 'purple states' in directing their efforts," according to U.S. investigators.[58] The IRA also incorporated geographic filters into about eight hundred of its advertisements. One IRA-run ad, issued in the fall of 2016, targeted voters aged eighteen to sixty-five within specific regions of Pennsylvania, a swing state, and with these specific interests: "Donald Trump for President, Job title: Coal Miner."[59]

The IRA focused on fomenting tensions around the same racial and religious groups as the KGB once did—namely, black and Jewish Americans. "We tried to take advantage of all these differences," Oleg Kalugin recalled, "to fan discord."[60] The IRA actively spread anti-Semitic content. One IRA-run Twitter account, for example, warned real-life Jewish reporters that Trump was "warming up an oven" for them.[61] But above all, the IRA targeted black Americans. "By far, race and related issues were the preferred target of the information warfare campaign designed to divide the country in 2016," the Senate has since concluded.[62] On some pages, the IRA spread racist propaganda; on others, it attracted black Americans as followers. The IRA-run "Blacktivist" Facebook page generated 11.2 million engagements. The vast majority of the IRA's 1,107 YouTube videos concerned race and police brutality. Five of the IRA's ten most popular Instagram accounts focused on issues related to black Americans. And on Tumblr, the IRA appealed to black users on accounts like "blacknproud" and "black-to-the-bones."[63]

Through these accounts, the IRA had two objectives: to suppress black voters, and to exacerbate racial tensions. "That's an old Soviet tactic," Kalugin said, "adjusted to the realities of political life today."[64] Russia's current leaders, like the KGB's, believe that America's diversity is one of its greatest vulnerabilities. The IRA was seeking to exploit fissures already ingrained in American society. Some had to do with race and religion; others had to do with national unity. After Britain voted to exit the European Union in June 2016, the IRA cited this vote—in which its specialists had covertly interfered—in urging Texans to secede from the United States. "If Brexit," one IRA-run post asked, "why not Texit?"[65] The IRA, whatever its shortcomings, was certainly not lacking in ambition.

—

Across its accounts, the IRA weaponized fear—again, more of the same. The thrust of the CIA's information warfare operation in Italy, according to David Robarge, the CIA's chief internal historian, was to "scare the Italians into not voting for the Communists."[66] The IRA's pages for left-wing audiences, right-wing audiences, and black audiences—all of them sought to scare voters. Conspiracy theories flooded online platforms. Some IRA-run accounts posted conspiratorial content about the murder of Seth Rich, who had worked for the DNC. (RT and Sputnik also amplified falsities about Rich's death.) Others spread disinformation about pandemic diseases, vaccines, and even aliens. One IRA-run post went so far as to claim that the Hillary Clinton appearing in public was not actually Hillary Clinton. "Where is a real one?!" the post asked.[67]

The IRA's scare tactics focused, in part, on the sanctity of the 2016 election. Its right-wing accounts alleged that voter rolls and voting machines had been corrupted, and that Clinton would "steal" the election. One account displayed a mug shot of Obama alongside the text "Like if You Agree: Obama Should Be Prosecuted for Enabling Voter Fraud." Another post warned of systemic voter fraud and that "if Killary wins there will be riots nationwide, not seen since the times of Revolutionary war!!" As voting unfolded, the IRA issued posts about rigged election systems and impending violence.[68]

This aspect of the IRA's scare campaign has raised eyebrows among experts. On Election Day, the GRU was in a position to alter voter rolls and the vote count, in order to make the election appear rigged. All the while, the IRA was alleging, in the shadows, that the election would be rigged. Celeste Wallander has become convinced that had Trump lost, Russia intended to use its "intrusions into some voting sites" to erase voter data retroactively, so it would appear as though "all these people voted [for Clinton who] weren't registered" and therefore that Trump had been cheated. "[They'd] make it look like the Clinton people had done it: that there was nefarious activity, not by the Russians, but by Americans, and to cast doubt on the results." Alex Stamos has reached a similar conclusion. "She wins, you've left all of these bread crumbs all over the place, and you create a bunch of new personas who are like, 'I'm a pro-Hillary hacker,'" he said. "You can then have a social media disinformation campaign that is powered by the facts to push the idea and then make half the country feel like [the election] was stolen."[69]

—

Once Trump won, the IRA stopped spreading propaganda about voter fraud delivering the election to Clinton. Putin's preferred candidate was headed for the White House. The specialists who had managed multiple cutout accounts—and spent years manipulating American voters—were left wondering if they had secured Trump's victory. It's a timeless question, with one discernible pattern: An interfering actor whose preferred party triumphs naturally feels all-powerful. In 1948, after Italy's Christian Democrats prevailed, CIA officers assumed their work had made the difference. IRA specialists reached the same conclusion. "On November 9th, 2016, a sleepless night was ahead of us," one IRA employee recalled, in since intercepted communications. "And when around 8 a.m. the most important result of our work arrived, we uncorked a tiny bottle of champagne . . . took one gulp each and looked into each other's eyes . . . we uttered almost in unison: 'We made America great.'"[70]

Whether Russia's operation actually proved decisive is a separate question. Kathleen Hall Jamieson concludes it is "likely" that the IRA's campaign, along with the email dumps, changed the outcome of the election.[71] Intelligence professionals like James Clapper have said the same.[72] Even a former senior national security official in the Trump White House told me that Russia's operation—a "direct assault on our sovereignty"—very well "may have been decisive" in its impact.

Others are not so sure. Yochai Benkler, a professor at Harvard Law School, argues that there is "little evidence" that Russia's operation "actually made a meaningful difference" in tilting the election and that speculation to the contrary, if anything, has generated discord within the United States.[73] H. R. McMaster went further: He disputed that Russia sought to help Trump at all. "Did Russia meddle in the election such that a particular candidate would win? I don't think so," he said. "I think it was just to sow chaos. Of course, because of the disruptive and unconventional nature of the Trump candidacy, that gave them an opportunity to polarize Americans even further."[74]

What must be beyond debate is that the IRA influenced the minds of unsuspecting voters. Its divisive content spread far and wide, reaching more than 100 million Americans. "This content is being shared by thousands and thousands of real people," said Renée DiResta, the information warfare expert, "so the idea that it had some impact, that it influenced or that it amplified the existing biases of the people who saw it, is actually indisputable to me."[75] Whether the IRA therefore flipped the election is unclear—and, if history is any guide, will remain so. What matters now is the perception of Americans and Russians. Inside the United States, this lingering question of decisiveness has divided voters and degraded trust in democratic institutions. Inside Russia, the degree to which Putin believes he succeeded will instruct his policy making. Feelings of triumph after Italy's 1948 election inspired a generation of CIA-led electoral interference. Moscow, emboldened by Trump's victory, may be headed in the same direction. (Indeed, after Trump won, IRA-run accounts entered into overdrive fomenting discord by, for example, advocating protests against the Electoral College.)[76]

—

So much of the IRA's operation is familiar.

As with the KGB, the IRA covertly targeted a U.S. election.
As with the KGB, the IRA identified and weaponized an influential platform for information.
As with the KGB, the IRA aimed to sow discord and advantage one candidate over another.
As with the KGB, the IRA used cutouts to promote fear, secure the help of unwitting Americans, and manipulate voters based on their location, race, and interests.
And once Russia's preferred candidate won, the IRA's employees assumed they had made the difference.

These patterns of behavior provide a foundational understanding of covert electoral interference—past, present, and future.

—

What, then, about the IRA was groundbreaking? The answer has to do with both process and ambition—and everything to do with social media. Platforms like Facebook and Twitter enabled Russia to turbocharge preexisting tactics at little cost. Rather than work through a few human cutouts, the IRA created thousands of digital cutouts. Rather than spread a single line of messaging, the IRA spread many messages—to vote, not to vote, to beware of voter fraud, to be racist, to be outraged by racism—all at the same time and all tailored for specific audiences. In the pre-digital era, interfering actors could target a few voters specifically or reach many voters randomly. Social media empowered Russia to manipulate the masses and to do so in a targeted way. For David Cohen, the CIA's deputy director in 2016, this aspect of Russia's operation was a major break from the past. "I feel it in my bones," he said. "Harnessing this new technology, this new capability, to essentially broadcast to millions of people, and to target those broadcasts to people who you are able to identify as particularly receptive to the message, *that* is different."[77]

The other revolutionary aspect of the IRA was that its specialists so deeply penetrated the world's most powerful democracy. During the Cold War, the KGB and the CIA influenced the masses in far-away countries, but Russia was never able to do so in America. The internet changed what was possible. What was unprecedented about Russia's operation, said Jake Sullivan, a former senior State Department official and policy adviser to Clinton, "was the degree to which the Russians were able to take to scale the weaponization of political discourse."[78] In September 2016 alone, IRA-run accounts reached up to thirty million U.S. citizens.[79] Titans of U.S. national security cannot help but marvel at Russia's ingenuity. "The speed with which they recognized the opportunities that social media presented and the skill with which they have executed on them—pretty dazzling," Bobby Inman said. "To some extent, good on them for figuring out how to do it," added Cohen. Tom Donilon, a former U.S. national security adviser, put it best: Putin saw both "a weakness in the West in terms of internal divisions" and "the power of these social media platforms," and "he sought to and did take advantage of it in a brazen way."[80]

Today, the United States is struggling to address its newfound exposure. "This social media stuff, it's a different world," said Harry Reid, the former Senate leader, who was born in 1939. "To completely understand social media, you have to be less than thirty years old." American officials, many of whom feel personally unfamiliar with social media, also lack authority over these platforms. Just as the White House had to rely on states to report intrusions into voting systems, the federal government must rely on social media companies to provide data related to foreign interference operations. (Lawmakers could regulate these platforms, to be sure, but they cannot censor them or seize their files.) Under immense pressure, Facebook and Twitter have revealed certain details about the IRA's operation, but smaller platforms have not. Much about the IRA's work therefore remains unknown. "We don't know anything about Russian activity on any of these other sites," Stamos said. "But I guarantee they're doing it, because it is a lot easier."[81]

Other democracies are grappling with the consequences of the social media age. In 2019, Germany both restricted Facebook's data-collection practices and fined the company for underreporting instances of hate speech.[82] A challenge for foreign countries is that social media platforms like Facebook and Twitter are based in the United States. "Imagine how much harder it is for a government outside the United States to get information from them," said Robert Hannigan, who led GCHQ, Britain's equivalent to the NSA, from 2014 to 2017. National security officials in London are at a loss. "There is no bit of government that does monitoring on social media to see whether it is being used systematically by a foreign power," Hannigan explained, as surveilling social media could jeopardize civil liberties. "There is something about the cross international nature of social media that just disempowers sovereign parliaments."[83]

Democracies like the United States must maintain their openness while also defending their electoral sovereignty. Leaders like Vladimir Putin and Xi Jinping of China can monitor and censor their digital environments. Open societies cannot. "In this day and age, especially with social media, trying to control or manage the content of what is out there and who puts it out, it is the challenge of our time," said John Brennan, the former CIA director.[84] For now, policy makers are pessimistic. "I don't believe that we can get the social media influence campaigns to near zero, because the openness of our social media ecosystem is a feature, not a bug, of democracy, so that is something we more have to manage," Jake Sullivan said. Alex Stamos predicted that the operations of foreign organizations like the IRA cannot be brought even "close to zero." And Nadia Schadlow, a former deputy national security adviser for strategy to Trump, said that this challenge is not necessarily Washington's to resolve. "The problem in responding to disinformation is that the U.S. government does not have a serious operational capability to respond," she said. "We don't own the internet platforms. So as people get upset, given Russian actions, they have yet to articulate how—operationally, how—the U.S. government should respond on private platforms. The problem is broader than government."[85]

Chapter 13

INACTION

Before 2016, the threat of covert electoral interference was not a part of America's domestic consciousness. The FBI focused on other challenges. Politicians spoke about other issues. Researchers studied other forms of covert action: arms programs, assassinations, and staged coups.[1] Then Vladimir Putin struck, and the vulnerabilities of democracy were laid bare. "The American populace understands now—to a much greater level than the past—what hybrid warfare is, what political warfare is," Nadia Schadlow said. "In a sense, that is a good thing; that is a silver lining to this: We're a bit less naïve."[2]

The specter of covert electoral interference now hangs overhead. John Brennan retired in 2017 having reached two conclusions. "One is how persistent and insidious Russian efforts are going to be, particularly under Putin, to try to manipulate and exploit events outside their border. We have to come to grips with that and we have to realize that. It's in his blood," Brennan said. The second, he continued, is "just how exploitable the digital environment is for nefarious purposes."[3] Leading intelligence and law enforcement officials are bracing for the next digital assault upon America's electoral sovereignty. "It wasn't a single attempt," Special Counsel Robert Mueller said in July 2019, regarding Russian interference in American elections. "They are doing it while we sit here. And they expect to do it during the next campaign." That same month, the FBI director, Christopher Wray, put it even more bluntly: "The Russians are absolutely intent on trying to interfere with our elections."[4]

The call to action is clear. Yet since January 2017, little has been done to address America's exposure. Fiona Hill, the top White House adviser on Russia until the summer of 2019, testified before Congress about this lack of progress. "Right now, Russia's security services and their proxies have geared up to repeat their interference in the 2020 election," she said. "We are running out of time to stop them."[5]

—

The elephant in the room is that President Donald Trump has never shown interest in securing America's elections. Rick Gates, his former deputy campaign chairman, has testified that in July 2016 Trump spoke with an associate by phone and then relayed that "more information would be coming" from WikiLeaks.[6] Trump also asked Russia, openly, to find and release Hillary Clinton's emails. As the election approached, Trump was aware, at the very least, of reports that Russia was helping his campaign. "The [Trump] Campaign expected it would benefit electorally from information stolen and released through Russian efforts," Robert Mueller's team concluded in its final report.[7]

Trump's attitude matters greatly. In 1961, Nikita Khrushchev attempted to establish influence over John F. Kennedy by telling him that Moscow had assisted his candidacy. Because Kennedy had been unaware of the Soviet Union's efforts, he had no debts to repay. Trump was no Kennedy. His posture more closely mirrored that of Alcide De Gasperi of Italy, who knew of the CIA's work on his behalf, and Eduardo Frei of Chile, who hoped that Washington would downplay its support for his campaign so that his domestic standing would not suffer. After winning the presidency, Trump became, in this sense, the newest member of a distinct club: leaders who came to power psychologically indebted to foreign actors and insecure about their electoral legitimacy. "Trump thought the fact that the intelligence community assessed the Russians had interfered in the 2016 election was his Achilles heel," Hope Hicks, Trump's longtime adviser, told federal investigators, based on notes taken during her testimony. "Even if it had no impact on the election,

Trump thought that was what people would think. He thought the assessment took away from what he did."[8]

In this context, Trump has not recognized the threat of covert electoral interference, let alone crafted a response to it. In the second and third presidential debates, he said that Clinton "doesn't know if it's the Russians doing the hacking. Maybe there is no hacking," and that she "has no idea whether it's Russia, China, or anybody else." In November 2016, as president-elect, he said, "I don't believe they interfered," and, "It could be Russia. And it could be China. And it could be some guy in his home in New Jersey." As president, Trump has, at points, acknowledged Russian "meddling" in the election, but usually with qualifications, and almost always backtracking later. In July 2017, he said, "It could very well have been Russia, but I think it could well have been other countries." And, in July 2018, Trump, standing next to Putin at a news conference in Helsinki, said, "I have President Putin; he just said it's not Russia. I will say this: I don't see any reason why it would be."[9]

Many of Trump's security chiefs know that Putin cannot be trusted. "My reaction to President Putin's statement is that he's lying, like he is all the time," H. R. McMaster said, of the Russian leader's denials at Helsinki and elsewhere. "He's crossed the line to what one of my British colleagues calls implausible deniability." (McMaster and Trump reportedly clashed internally over Russia policy, but McMaster declined to comment on any such tensions.)[10] Elaine Duke, Trump's former acting homeland security secretary, was puzzled by Trump's reaction to Putin's denials. "Did Trump really believe him? I don't know. Or did Trump pretend to believe him because it fit his agenda?" she asked. "What is that game they're playing?"[11]

Whatever the game, its result has been to sow confusion among Americans. Just one in three Republicans believes that Russia sought to influence the 2016 election in Trump's favor.[12] "When the president gets out publicly and denies it all, that introduces dissonance in the electorate, and people in the hinterlands don't know what to think," said a former senior NSC adviser to Trump who worked in the White House for more than a year and frequented

Oval Office meetings. "It's powerful, and the Russians know that's powerful." Trump is not the first head of state to deny established but inconvenient facts. Just as Putin implausibly claimed in 2014 that his soldiers were not in eastern Ukraine, Trump has rejected the consensus of the U.S. intelligence community. These denials have had a similar effect: shifting debate away from *how* to respond to a threat to *whether* the threat actually exists. "Is he doing it because he doesn't want to be seen as an illegitimate president? That may well be the case," said the former NSC adviser. "Is he doing it because he's covering for the Russians? I don't know."[13]

Inside the government, officials have tried to ignore Trump's rhetoric and get to work. But for political appointees, acknowledging Russia's operation publicly invites personal risk. In February 2018, while speaking at a conference in Munich, H. R. McMaster said it was "incontrovertible" that Russia had interfered in the 2016 election, just a day after Mueller indicted thirteen Russians for doing so. "There was no plan or anything there. I wanted to be behind the scenes," McMaster said, regarding his mindset at the time. Trump quickly tweeted that McMaster "forgot to say that the results of the 2016 election were not impacted or changed by the Russians" and that a range of actors could have influenced the contest: "It may be Russia, or China or another country or group, or it may be a 400 pound genius sitting in bed and playing with his computer." Within weeks, Trump replaced McMaster. "When I was done, I was done," McMaster said. "I just resolved from the beginning that I was not going to fight to keep my job."[14] McMaster's departure, one of his subordinates said, served as a warning for other administration officials: Don't "speak out strongly on this issue."

Some members of Trump's national security team left the White House having concluded, reluctantly, that the president was impeding efforts to defend America's electoral sovereignty. A former senior official in Trump's White House said it was "perplexing" that the president sought to "minimize what were Putin's activities" in the 2016 election, even as the U.S. intelligence community concluded that "this actually is a big deal." This official, clearly frustrated, continued, "Whoever won, the responsible thing to do would have been to really make this a priority, this is simply unacceptable, and push back hard on Russia, but perhaps because of this president's clear penchant for liking strongmen . . . he's not being as forceful as he should, and that's unfortunate." A former senior NSC adviser to Trump, referenced earlier, said that the West Wing was inhospitable to forward-looking policy making on this issue. "If you say the Russians interfered in our elections," the official said, "what President Trump hears is, 'Okay, you don't think my election was legitimate; you think I cheated my way into the White House,' and so he kind of goes off the reservation." At the highest levels, Trump's team has focused on assuaging his electoral insecurities. "We talked less about the purpose than the not purpose" of Russia's operation, Elaine Duke said, "and what I mean by that is that it didn't change votes." Beyond that, she continued, electoral security "is definitely not consuming a lot of time operationally" within the White House.[15]

Trump has stymied but not stopped efforts to bolster America's electoral defenses. The president is not all-powerful: Federal departments, states, and cities have their own authorities. Many of his agency heads have warned that America is exposed. Joseph Maguire, as Trump's acting director of national intelligence, testified that the "greatest challenge" before the U.S. intelligence community "is to make sure that we maintain the integrity of our election system."[16] Christopher Wray, in an email, told me that responding to foreign operations against U.S. elections is a top priority for him and the FBI.[17] This position is commonplace: Most of Trump's security chiefs have, at the very least, affirmed the U.S. intelligence community's assessment of Russian interference in the 2016 election.[18] "I don't remember any disagreement where people said: 'Did this really happen?'" Elaine Duke said. "When the intel community tells you something, you generally believe it." DHS has continued to respond to state requests for election assistance. The U.S. military has even taken offensive steps against Russia. In November 2018, America's cyber warriors disrupted the networks of the Internet Research Agency.[19] "We did all of that and more," a senior Trump appointee in the Pentagon told me. (McMaster said that inside the Trump administration officials broadly "recogni[zed] that you can't defend yourself effectively if you aren't able to use offensive capabilities" in cyberspace.) And in July 2019, Dan Coats, then the director of national intelligence, established the position of intelligence community election threats executive, charged with coordinating the fight against foreign operations to influence U.S. elections.[20]

—

These steps, while productive, exist without a presidential mandate. "Left to themselves, the cabinet officers would have gone even farther, even stronger, but their recommendations were watered down by the West Wing," said the former senior NSC adviser, who found that, following Russia's attack in 2016, Trump's department and agency heads were "unified in their view of the threat and unified in the view that we ought to take actions to mitigate the threat, but that doesn't seem to be in step or in line with where the president is." Where this dynamic has played out most visibly is with Congress. In 2017, lawmakers overwhelmingly approved new sanctions against Russia in retaliation for its interference operation. Trump signed the bill into law while still lambasting its provisions.[21]

Two different accounts exist as to the president's mentality at the time. Of the bill, McMaster, then the national security adviser, said that there was "no one slowing it down," that there was "alignment between the president and Congress," and that the sanctions "imposed a significant cost" on Russia.[22] Others advising Trump at the time disagree. "The president would have vetoed the additional sanctions legislation in the summer of '17 except that the majority was veto-proof," the senior NSC official said. "If he could have gotten away with a veto, he would have vetoed it."

Since 2016, the United States has been sending Russia conflicting messages. Lawmakers and agency leaders claim the country will tolerate no interference in the 2020 election. Trump, however, not only has failed to acknowledge the threat of Russian interference but also privately invited the president of another country, Ukraine, to investigate one of his 2020 rivals.[23] Three of Trump's former foreign policy advisers said they fear the president wants Russia to assist his reelection campaign. "I don't think the Russians are particularly frightened about what might happen to them if they try this again," the former senior NSC adviser said. Trump, like Boris

Yeltsin, cares more about preserving his power than about preserving the sanctity of an election—only in this instance, Moscow holds all the cards. Inside the Kremlin, the former NSC adviser continued, Putin and his lieutenants have likely concluded, "We don't expect a lot of problems from the American president," so we can "do this again without a risk of a serious consequence."

Putin's meetings with Trump have surely informed his decision-making process, but Trump has kept the details of those conversations secret. At the 2017 G20 Summit in Hamburg, Trump spoke twice with Putin. In the first meeting, his secretary of state and interpreter were present, but, according to *The Washington Post,* Trump subsequently confiscated the interpreter's notes. In the second encounter, the two leaders spoke at length, with only Putin's interpreter joining. At Helsinki, Putin and Trump met for two hours—once again, flanked only by interpreters.[24] "Was there a reason that he didn't want anybody to be overhearing the conversation?" the former senior NSC adviser asked. "It's problematic when the president meets with Putin and there are no notes, no records, no transcripts. . . . It's very hard to know what was discussed, what was agreed, it's almost unprecedented, maybe it is unprecedented." Over time, some White House officials came to suspect that Trump was speaking by phone with Putin—without alerting the NSC—in conversations left off the public record. "I suspect it may have happened," the former senior NSC adviser to Trump continued. "I know there were cases where he spoke with Putin where we were not present or the transcripts were not generated. . . . I can't say with certainty that we were even aware every single time he may have spoken with Putin."

This senior NSC official spent more than a year inside Trump's White House trying to think of an explanation for the president's friendliness toward Putin and apathy toward America's electoral security. "By the end of my time there," the official said, "I reluctantly concluded, as did many of my peers, that Trump was doing Russia's bidding, and that Russia had leverage over him." The official offered only suspicions, based on Trump's posture and policymaking toward Russia, but no evidence in support of this allegation, which Trump has long denied.[25]

For now, there is but one certainty: Trump will not be the president to spearhead a national response to the threat of covert electoral interference.

—

But this challenge is not just about Trump. There will be another president, and his or her administration will face an uphill battle in defending America's electoral sovereignty while helping other democracies do the same. America's vulnerabilities run far deeper than just one person. Trump's neglect aside, he did not expose America's elections. Russia targeted the 2016 election when Barack Obama was president. There are systemic reasons why the United States has not united against this threat.

Russia's 2016 operation was a matter of national security, to be sure, but it also preyed on preexisting divisions. Americans are at odds with one another. Just 17 percent of Republicans and 20 percent of Democrats say their political parties work together, and less than half of both Republicans and Democrats value politicians who seek compromise.[26] Deal-making is out of fashion. "Politicians that are bipartisan are having trouble. It's almost like you're looked down upon if you can make a deal," said Elaine Duke, who regrets that "politicians that are doing hate politics . . . [are] most popular," as lawmakers display a "hate level to match Trump's hate level."[27]

Pillars of American democracy have decayed. Local media is in crisis. Since 2004, nearly two thousand community newspapers have gone out of business or merged; many more have been hollowed out.[28] This trend has critical implications for foreign interference: As America's media environment becomes increasingly national, the news becomes easier to manipulate. Mainstream outlets devote resources to chasing sensational tweets and document dumps, while citizens look to social media, in part, for local news. Meanwhile, public schools offer either limited or no instruction on how to be an informed citizen in a digital democracy. "The critical factor in the Constitution to make this work is an informed electorate. We have a disinformed, misinformed, uninformed electorate these days. An informed electorate: That should be on our tombstone. Where is the informed electorate?" demanded Porter Goss, the former CIA director. David Cohen, the former CIA deputy director, likewise said, "We don't have as well-informed a citizenry as we ought to have, so people are more susceptible, you have less critical-thinking skills, they're just more susceptible to basically buying bullshit."[29]

In this environment, the United States is struggling to unite against any threat, let alone one that its president says does not exist. Turn on MSNBC and Fox News, and it is apparent that two realities have emerged inside the United States. A recent *Wall Street Journal* headline captured the status quo: "Democrats and Republicans Aren't Just Divided. They Live in Different Worlds."[30] The more divided a democracy, the more fragile it becomes, and the less able it is to defend itself. Milan Svolik, a political scientist at Yale, has argued that "deep social cleavages and acute political tensions—polarization, to use a term recently in vogue—undercut the public's ability to curb the illiberal inclinations of elected politicians," as voters prioritize partisan interests over the health of their democracy.[31]

Entrenched polarization *is* a national security threat, especially on matters of covert electoral interference. Foreign actors do not create societal divisions; they inflame them. On this point, H. R. McMaster and Susan Rice, the former national security advisers, agree. "[Russia] didn't create the fissures, but they're taking advantage of the fissures," McMaster said, in order to "polarize our polity, our society, and diminish our confidence in who we are as a people." Rice likewise said, "The thing that makes us most vulnerable is not simply what the Russians are doing. It is that we are ourselves internally divided, and we don't consume information intelligently."[32]

The United States was and remains a ripe target, unable to muster a coherent response to its exposure. Its citizens do not trust each other. Facts are up for debate. Anger is pervasive. Russian leaders have long worked to tear apart the United States from the inside, to show the world that democracy does not work. Americans have, in recent years, been making this mission easier. "So much of this is about getting our own act together," said Jon Finer, the former State Department director of policy planning, and "address[ing] our own democratic deficiencies and failings." In seeking to discredit the democratic model, he continued, Russia need only shine "a fun house mirror" on America's divisions. "They aren't creating racism or corruption in the United States," he said. "We are doing a pretty effective job through our own dysfunction, and Europe as well, at revealing the limitations of a model that we have been waving in everyone's faces as the be-all and end-all."[33]

America's enemies benefit when America is divided. Russia favored Trump, in part, because he is a divisive figure. He was, as Jeb Bush warned in 2015, a "chaos candidate" who would be a "chaos president." Every time Trump defies a norm, provokes a political crisis, or threatens an opponent, American democracy erodes, and Russia celebrates. The examples are numerous. In August 2017, Trump said there were "some very fine people on both sides" of violent protests in Charlottesville, Virginia, involving neo-Nazis and white supremacists, one of whom murdered a counter-protester. In July 2019, Trump told four congresswomen of color to "go back" to their home countries, even though three of them were born in the United States and the fourth was a U.S. citizen who had fled war-torn Somalia as a child. Who needs the IRA when the president is sowing racial discord so openly? And in October 2019, Trump accused the lawmakers Adam Schiff and Nancy Pelosi of "treason"—a crime punishable by death—as they investigated his presidency.[34] It was an authoritarian moment, brought to the United States by the candidate Russia helped elect. Trump "is the quintessential autocrat," John Brennan said. "He is following almost to the letter the playbook of authoritarian leaders: you discredit the media, you control the judiciary, you control the intelligence security services, you delegitimize and discredit anybody who poses a threat to you, you keep harping on it and harping on it, and then it becomes into the bloodstream of the public perception."[35]

The exposure of Russia's 2016 operation, rather than forge a consensus around electoral security, has only split Americans further. The Mueller investigation, probes in the House and Senate, Trump's allegations of a witch hunt—all of it has fostered division. "As long as this remains the issue and we're arguing about it," said Tony Blinken, the former deputy secretary of state, "the Russians don't have to do anything else and it creates some of the doubt that they're trying to sow." Arturo Muñoz, who worked for nearly thirty years as a CIA officer, likewise said, "This is what Putin wants. He wants us to be arguing. He wants us to be afraid of his hackers. And he's achieved it with stunning, stunning success."[36]

—

A challenge in the years to come will be that citizens, depending on their politics, tend to exaggerate or minimize the threat of covert electoral interference. Millions of Republicans do not believe that Russia interfered in the 2016 election. Elaine Duke, Trump's former acting homeland security secretary, argued that "we have to raise the visibility" of this issue and "recognize that it is a threat" rather than "make the American people feel comfortable" to avoid generating alarm. "What we need is some more moderate politicians that will agree on something. In the past we would agree that *Russia* was the enemy," she continued, but today, as Democrats and Republicans clash with one another, "Russia is off scot-free." As Trump minimizes the threat of Russian interference, many Democrats have portrayed Putin as ten feet tall, a characterization that aligns with their party's interests, and, inadvertently, with Russia's. Putin *wants* to seem all-powerful. The Russians "were more than happy to get caught," said Douglas Wise, the deputy director of the Defense Intelligence Agency in 2016. "All eyes go, 'Holy crap, those Russians are ballsy,'" causing other countries to conclude, "'Holy crap, they did that to the U.S.? They'll crush us.'"[37]

Americans themselves are losing faith in democracy. A striking 40 percent of U.S. adults say they favorably view a system of governance in which "experts, not elected officials, make decisions according to what they think is best for the country," while 22 percent say they favorably view a system where "a strong leader can make decisions without interference from parliament or the courts." Just 18 percent of U.S. adults believe their democracy is working "very well"; 61 percent want "significant changes" made to their government's structure and design.[38] Gerrymandering, dark money, gridlock, voter suppression, economic inequality—these phenomena have convinced millions of Americans that the system is already rigged. Who cares, then, if Russia is rigging it too? "There's this notion that the system is corrupted irrespective of what the Russians do," Blinken said. "People think that if you're in with the right crowd, your interests will be protected. If you're not, they won't, and that has nothing to do with Russians or anyone else interfering, it has to do with distortions and imperfections in our own system."[39] If citizens do not believe in democracy, and do not care if their democracy is corrupted further, then the fight for electoral sovereignty is lost.

There was a time when Americans opposed foreign electoral interference. Well over a century ago, in September 1888, an American wrote to Lionel Sackville-West, the British ambassador to the United States, claiming to be a naturalized citizen originally from Britain and seeking advice about whether to support the Democrat, Grover Cleveland, or Benjamin Harrison, his Republican opponent, in the upcoming presidential election. "Any political party which openly favored the mother country at the present moment would lose popularity," Sackville-West replied, but Cleveland seemed "desirous of maintaining friendly relations with Great Britain," ready to "manifest a spirit of conciliation," and, therefore, was London's preferred candidate.

Sackville-West had been played: The American who wrote to him had used a fake name and was, in fact, a staunch Republican. On the eve of the election, Harrison's allies leaked Sackville-West's letter to the press, setting off a national scandal that cast Cleveland as a British puppet. It seemed that London was interfering in the election on Cleveland's behalf. Republicans feverishly pitched Harrison as the candidate whom a foreign rival opposed and therefore Americans should support. "The letter was a political Republican plot," Sackville-West told the British foreign secretary in late October. "The plot was due to the approaching election."[40] On Election Day, Harrison lost the popular vote, but he won the Electoral College and, with it, the White House. Historians have since argued that Americans' outrage over British interference in the election—in this instance, one private letter—likely proved decisive in securing Harrison's victory.[41]

Foreign interference in American elections should offend all voters, regardless of party loyalties. The fight for America's electoral sovereignty can be a force for national unity rather than division.

In 1888, Britain preferred a Democrat. In 2016, Russia backed a Republican. There is no telling who will benefit next. Iranian hackers have already targeted email accounts associated with Trump's 2020 campaign, as other foreign intelligence services follow Russia's lead.[42] China, North Korea, Iran—all have recently breached the networks of U.S. institutions, from Sony Pictures to the Office of Personnel Management. These countries can use digital means to damage campaigns like Trump's. "Chinese intelligence is all over us," Porter Goss said. Non-state actors possess similar capabilities. John Brennan warned that in the future, any government could pay "illegal and illicit" hacking groups to wreak havoc upon U.S. elections.[43]

No matter which campaign benefits, the loser will be American democracy.

Conclusion

BREAKING THE SIEGE

A democracy is "most likely to fall," the historian Tony Judt argued, "to a corrupted version of itself."[1]

Today, American democracy withers from within. Russia is using covert weapons to exacerbate this trend. In 2016, Vladimir Putin didn't just help Donald Trump win the presidency. He also used an age-old idea to tarnish a practice at the heart of American democracy: its elections.

Russia's 2016 operation was only the latest chapter in the history of covert electoral interference. Hidden from view, in the shadows of international relations, states have manipulated foreign elections for more than a century. Vladimir Lenin recognized, at the end of World War I, that he could advance his interests by backing Communist candidates, just as Joseph Stalin did after World War II. Seeking to contain Communism, the CIA interfered in Italy's 1948 election and in many elections thereafter. From Japan and Guyana to Chile and El Salvador, the CIA and the KGB competed in democratic contests around the world. Open elections became a battleground of the superpowers. Some operations, like in West Germany in 1972, directly altered votes; others molded public opinion through letter writing and scare campaigns, disinformation and propaganda initiatives, and the manipulation and recruitment of foreign journalists.

The end of the Cold War brought about a divergence in American and Russian policy making. Since 1991, the United States has promoted democracy overtly and through known third-party organizations. CIA-led electoral interference has become the exception rather than the rule. For the United States, no consistent call to

240

action exists without a Communist adversary. The risk of getting caught in the digital age is considerable, and the consequences of detection would be severe. Recent U.S. presidents have concluded that the benefits of these operations no longer outweigh the costs, as in 2004, when President George W. Bush considered using the CIA to manipulate Iraq's election but opted against it. The status quo is tense: The CIA rarely interferes in elections but has reserved the right to do so.

Russia has shown no such equivocation. The ideological divide of the Cold War is gone, but to Putin the United States is still Russia's major adversary. Moscow's objective has evolved from spreading Communism to tearing down democracy. Putin has used covert electoral interference to support divisive candidates and causes in support of this strategy. When chaos is the goal, ideology does not matter, but relative power certainly does. Insecure elections breed dysfunction; dysfunction, in turn, breeds weakness. By undermining the United States, Putin believes he can strengthen Russia and discredit the democratic model.

Putin's great innovation has been technological. He has used digital means to interfere in elections globally. Russia's current methods can best be understood as enhanced versions of old ideas, such as spreading hateful content and exploiting the personal biases of unsuspecting citizens. The internet has empowered Putin to turbocharge these traditional tactics, reaching more people in more countries and in a more targeted fashion. But as Russia manipulated elections in places like Ukraine, the rest of the world barely noticed.

Then Putin hit the United States, and the game changed. For the first time, *the* subject in foreign affairs became covert electoral interference. The practice, though widespread, had garnered minimal attention during the Cold War, in part because few knew about the CIA's and the KGB's operations, and in part because big countries bullying smaller countries seemed, well, normal. Moscow had attempted to interfere in America's elections before. Nikita Khrushchev favored John F. Kennedy, Soviet ambassadors offered to collude with Adlai Stevenson and Hubert Humphrey, and the KGB worked against Richard Nixon, Henry Jackson, and Ronald Reagan. None of these operations seemed to matter much—until 2016. Using digital tools, Putin succeeded where his Soviet predecessors had failed: to disrupt and direct the world's most powerful democracy.

President Barack Obama struggled to respond. Before Election Day, he tried to prevent one form of interference—vote alterations— but neglected another: efforts to influence voters. Stolen emails dominated America's news cycles, while Russian propaganda flooded social media. By the time Obama retaliated against Putin, in December 2016, the damage was done. Russia had interfered in the contest in "sweeping and systemic fashion," according to Robert Mueller, and achieved two familiar objectives: to sow discord, and to advantage one candidate over another.[2] Since then, Donald Trump, the beneficiary, has rebuffed pleas to recognize the threat of covert electoral interference.

Trump's successor, whether in 2021 or 2025, must step in and defend America's electoral sovereignty. This will be a continuous fight, waged against innovative adversaries, that should be informed by ten historical lessons:

(1) Covert electoral interference has always involved efforts to change actual votes and efforts to change minds. The latter is far more common than the former, and America must address both.

(2) It has never been possible to determine the precise impact of operations to change minds. This unanswerable question of effectiveness should not be used to dismiss the threat of covert electoral interference.

(3) Some politicians have historically embraced foreign interference on their behalf, while others have rejected it outright. Leaders who prioritize their countries' sovereignty fall into the latter category.

(4) Revelations of foreign operations to influence elections once outraged Americans on both sides of the aisle. This should again be the case today.

(5) Moscow has long channeled its strategic priorities into its electoral operations. The Soviet Union backed Communist candidates; Putin will continue to back disruptive ones.

(6) Interfering actors adapt to the information environments of the moment. Cold War–era operations targeted radio and television; modern operations will target social media platforms and whatever conduit for propaganda emerges next.

(7) Preexisting societal divisions present opportunities for interfering actors. The more polarized a democracy, the more vulnerable it is to foreign subversion.

(8) Covert electoral interference is a global phenomenon. The simplest way to anticipate how Russia will interfere in America's next election is to monitor how it is interfering in elections overseas.

(9) No silver bullet will secure America's elections. Lenin and Putin were right: Competitive elections are by nature penetrable. They always have been, and they always will be.

(10) The digital age has universalized the threat of covert electoral interference. In the twentieth century, no external actor could meaningfully manipulate America's elections. The internet has upended this dynamic. The United States is now as vulnerable as any democracy to foreign interference.

The United States should use these lessons to inform its response to the modern authoritarian threat. But first we, as Americans, must recognize the essence of that threat: to corrupt democracies from within, in part by corrupting their elections. This is Russia's mission. The stakes of this fight are immense. If foreigners can choose our leaders, then our state is not sovereign. If foreigners can divide us, then our state is destined for dysfunction. And if foreigners can plunge our politics into chaos, then our state cannot lead abroad.

Democracy has never been the simple option. But since the end of the Cold War, many Americans have taken democracy for granted, looked inward, and grown divided. Past presidents used great challenges abroad to unite Americans at home.[3] But today, the great challenges before the American people are internal. Polarization, economic inequality, gridlock, gerrymandering, alternative facts, abuses of power, politicized courts, dark money—the United States is becoming a corrupted version of itself. Russia will keep using electoral operations to further this process.

The United States now stands at a crossroads. In one direction is the path of least resistance: more decay, corruption, and hate. This is the road that America has been walking, to the delight of its rivals. Authoritarians know from experience what democrats often grasp only when it is too late: Democracies die from within. Consider Yeltsin's Russia, where a hollowed-out democracy enabled Putin's rise and consolidation of power. This was Russia's fate. But it need not be ours.

The next president, together with lawmakers and citizens, must choose the more difficult path: one of renewal.

RENEWAL AT HOME

This process begins at home. Because Russia is seeking to degrade democracy, America's response should be to strengthen its democracy, both by guarding its elections and by confronting its preexisting divisions.

The starting point is to prevent foreign adversaries from changing actual votes. In 2016, Putin's hackers, sitting safely inside Russia, penetrated America's electoral infrastructure. It is understandable why the ballot box was so vulnerable: Russia was breaking new ground. No such excuse holds today, and yet progress has been slow. Since Trump became president, the Senate leader, Mitch McConnell, has sanctioned just $805 million in federal funding for election security—a woefully insufficient figure, experts say.[4] "Is our election system secure? Not enough," said Elaine Duke, the acting homeland security secretary from July to December 2017. "We can only help with the permission of the states. They have to request it."[5]

The crux of this challenge is the balance of power between states and the federal government. The status quo—DHS, the FBI, and lawmakers begging states to accept security assistance—is unsustainable. "States should be held accountable regarding their election security measures, and we should understand why some states had refused assistance from DHS," said Nadia Schadlow, a former deputy national security adviser to Trump. Perhaps it made sense, once upon a time, for Washington to cede control over election administration. In the pre-digital world, the sanctity of elections was not a national security concern. Times have changed, and so, too, must the structure of American governance. "I've learned, as we all have, an enormous amount about our election infrastructure, and it is clear to me that a great deal can and should be done to strengthen election security in the United States," said Avril Haines, the former deputy national security adviser. Jeh Johnson, the former homeland security secretary, said that, ideally, America would establish "an independent federal system of voting, like we have an independent system of federally reporting your taxes."[6]

Reform is urgently needed, but the United States should not throw the baby out with the bathwater. America's thousands of electoral jurisdictions provide a degree of security. A nationally uniform system of election administration would conceivably be vulnerable to a single nationwide hack. The problem with the status quo is not that states oversee election systems; it is that certain states refuse to safeguard those systems. Roy Blunt, a Republican senator, has said "some states frankly haven't used" federal funds allocated for election security.[7] Lawmakers should target those irresponsible actors, whether by passing mandatory security standards or otherwise.[8] This threat can and must be resolved. "Tampering with voter rolls, voting machines, the actual mechanics of voting, we can stop that, mostly by hardening cyber defenses fundamentally," said David Cohen, the CIA's deputy director in 2016.[9] The time to act is now. The dynamics of 2016—when a foreign power could have altered votes or voter data—cannot be repeated. Otherwise, the United States will always be defending its elections from a position of desperation, fearing the worst-case scenario and struggling to address more diffuse challenges.

The minds of American voters are also under siege. For more than a century, foreign intelligence services have been influencing voters ahead of elections. In 2016, Russia pursued this old objective with new tactics: releasing stolen emails and manipulating social media platforms.

The best America can do is manage these threats. The first, anonymous document dumps, will not cease entirely. Political operatives will inevitably fall victim to hacks, stolen materials will flood social media, and the press will decide which revelations to publicize. When I asked political reporters whether they would write about stolen materials released by WikiLeaks in the run-up to future elections, the answer was unanimous: of course. "They would be covered if they're newsworthy," said Philip Rucker, the White House bureau chief for *The Washington Post.*[10]

In a digital democracy, outing the private lives of public figures is uncomfortably easy. There is no telling where hackers will turn next: Instagram accounts, browsing histories, private text messages. But the effectiveness of future operations can still be reduced. Reporters, in 2016, focused on the contents of the Podesta and DNC emails rather than on their alleged source. The reverse would have better reflected what was newsworthy about them. "Given what everyone has been through, there is much more of a sensitivity to where these things are coming from," said Peter Baker, the chief White House correspondent for *The New York Times.* "And that would probably be more of interest in the future than it was in the past."[11] The government can help by confirming, as quickly as possible, the mastermind behind future document dumps; speedy attribution would enable better reporting and empower voters to interpret stolen materials with a more critical eye.

Voters can also choose resilience over gullibility. In France, in 2017, hackers linked to Russian intelligence released a trove of stolen emails from the campaign of Emmanuel Macron, a presidential candidate, who was competing against the far-right politician Marine Le Pen. The files were posted just before a national election but received almost no attention, in part because of a required media blackout before the vote, in part because the Macron campaign alleged that some of the documents were forged, and in part because French politicians, journalists, and citizens had watched America's 2016 election and did not want to be similarly played.[12] "Look at the French," said William J. Burns, a former U.S. ambassador to Russia. "They were actually good at not so much deterring but not being distracted by or becoming vulnerable to Russian active measures."[13] America's media environment is distinct, to be sure, but France's underlying attitude—to treat foreign interference as an affront rather than fodder for gossip—is the right one.

Russia's other psychological weapon, information warfare across social media, is similarly challenging. The Internet Research Agency was only the beginning. In 2019, Facebook shut down more than fifty networks of inauthentic accounts, oftentimes before major elections. Russia has also targeted other social media platforms, testing new messaging strategies on websites like Reddit before introducing them more broadly. These outlets remain under siege as Russia works hard to evade detection.[14] While serving in the White House, H. R. McMaster recalled that as new techniques emerged to track foreign influence campaigns, "the Russians would then know what those were and take countermeasures."[15]

Social media executives cannot completely prevent foreign actors from manipulating their platforms. "The social media propaganda piece we can't get close to zero," said Alex Stamos, Facebook's former security chief. But, as with hack-and-dump operations, progress is still possible. In early 2018, Stamos visited the White House and met with Rob Joyce, Trump's cybersecurity coordinator, ahead of the midterm elections. Soon after, the FBI and DHS dispatched specialized task forces to meet with officials from Facebook and a dozen other technology companies. "Coming out of that [we] established a bunch of norms and threat sharing," Stamos said, "and there has been some takedowns thanks to government tipoffs since then." This type of public-private coordination was entirely missing in 2016 and will be invaluable moving forward. So will transparency. Nathaniel Gleicher, Facebook's current head of cybersecurity, said that he "know[s] Russian actors are still active ahead of the 2020 election," and that his team "is going to publicize" any major foreign operation targeting users "whenever we see [that]."[16] Congress must also regulate social media platforms. Plenty of researchers and politicians, of both parties, have put forward ideas for how to do so.[17] "We figured out ways to regulate other human endeavors," said James Clapper, the director of national intelligence in 2016. "Why is social media so unique? Why is it so special? Why should [Facebook CEO Mark] Zuckerberg have free run of the media?"[18]

Foreign efforts to influence voters will keep evolving. History did not stop in 2016. Maybe a Republican will benefit next, or maybe a Democrat will. What is certain is that new tactics will emerge, designed to take advantage of America's rampant polarization. The best way to protect America preemptively is to confront its preexisting divisions and promote awareness about how they are being exploited.[19]

Policy makers at all levels should work to revitalize what many Americans have lost: a sense of belonging, a shared set of facts, and a stake in their surroundings. Local media, a struggling industry, fosters all three, exemplifying why programs like Report for America, which places young journalists in newsrooms across the country, should be expanded dramatically.[20] Another area worthy of investment and innovation is public education. Americans should learn how to function as informed citizens in a digital democracy: how to read online articles critically and sort fact from fiction. Several states have already passed legislation in support of these objectives.[21] America's intelligence chiefs say this is the most effective way to counter Russia. "In a free democratic society, especially with uneducated people, you have a lot of ability to manipulate, so that is why education is so important," said Porter Goss, a former CIA director. "The defense has to be education. You are not going to stop the manipulation." Michael Hayden, another former CIA director, likewise said that Russia's tactics "are not rocket science," but many voters have become uninformed, isolated, and therefore vulnerable. He went on, "I generally trend to physician, heal thyself: [Electoral interference] does not work unless we're stupid."[22]

—

Other countries have responded to the threat of Russian interference with education initiatives. In Finland, the government has trained citizens to identify disinformation online, and schools have incorporated digital literacy into their curricula. In Sweden, students are similarly taught to spot misleading content on the internet. Just before a national election in September 2018, the Swedish government even mailed a twenty-page leaflet about the threat of disinformation to every household in the nation. "Be on the lookout for false information," the pamphlet urged. "Do not believe in rumors—use more than one reliable source in order to see whether the information is correct." These initiatives seem to be paying off: A recent report found that Finland and Sweden were respectively the first and fourth most resilient European countries to disinformation.[23] The United States should learn from their successes.

Polarization and discord will always exist. But lawmakers should recognize what these aspects of American democracy have become: one of the premier national security threats of our time. Russia is tearing at fissures that already exist. "You have to have trust for democracies to work," said Bobby Inman, a former CIA deputy director. "Look at the absence of dialogue across this partisan divide, and it's an absence of trust."[24] Politicians can strengthen communities—and thus defend their country—by doing their jobs and passing legislation. Whether it's child care, education, infrastructure, or health care, Congress can forge a stronger America. Domestic policy challenges are, in this sense, foreign policy challenges.

America is in a precarious position indeed. Its ballot box is insecure. Its information space is exposed to foreign propaganda. And its citizens live in separate realities. Only one of these challenges, the penetrability of electoral infrastructure, can realistically be resolved. The others will have to be managed. "Our sovereignty will not be absolute, because it can be violated, and it is violated on a daily basis in ways that our physical sovereignty is not, and that's just a reality," said Tony Blinken, the former deputy secretary of state. H. R. McMaster similarly said that America will not be able to "completely squash" interference in its politics, but "we ought to make our goal to render [it] utterly ineffective."[25] Minds cannot be fixed the way machines can. But if America can renew itself at home, step by step, it will also become less susceptible to attack.

RENEWAL ABROAD

While fortifying itself domestically, the United States must also defend itself abroad. The next president can and should deter operations like the one Russia executed in 2016.

In this fight, America need not stand alone. Jim Mattis, in his resignation letter as secretary of defense, wrote that "we are strengthened" by "the solidarity of our alliances." This was a lesson Mattis learned during the Cold War, when the Western world united against the Communist threat.[26] A new authoritarian threat has emerged, but Washington has amassed no coalition against it. The current scene is eerily reminiscent of the 1930s, when strongmen targeted vulnerable democracies in an anarchic environment, with no clear mechanism for collective defense. Institutions like NATO, forged in the middle of the twentieth century, do not reflect twenty-first-century realities. If a Russian tank enters Estonia, the United States goes to war. But if Russia rigs an Estonian election, the United States shrugs. Policy makers in Washington have deterred land war in Europe; now they must also deter digital war.

—

Renewed American leadership can drive this effort, which should include four steps. The first is to unite a coalition of willing democracies against covert electoral interference, which must therefore be defined. Avril Haines said it would "be reasonably easy to achieve broad support for a prohibition against vote tampering." But this definition leaves much out: Russia has also been covertly funding campaigns, attempting assassinations, corrupting social media, and stealing and releasing sensitive files. Another approach would be to adopt a wider definition, encompassing all of these tactics, even if fewer countries join initially. "I don't want to wait . . . until the whole world agrees," said Victoria Nuland, a former U.S. ambassador to NATO. "We should set norms with two countries, four countries, ten countries, twenty countries, and then use that to influence and pressure the ones who won't accept those norms."[27] What matters as well is that America move forward quickly; potential coalition members who drag their feet should be dropped.

With this coalition established, the second step is to define costs. Putin has suffered almost no consequences for interfering in elections. America and its allies must decide how to punish interfering actors. "We can and should be punishing [Russia] much more—raising the costs on what they are doing," Susan Rice said.

"We should make their interference in our democracy as costly as possible." H. R. McMaster likewise said that Russia must be made to see future iterations of its 2016 operation "not only as counterproductive, but resulting in the imposition of costs on them that are well beyond the potential payoff of continuing this kind of interference."[28]

Retaliatory options are many. Jake Sullivan, the former director of policy planning, suggested a proportional mindset. "This is a technology-enabled attack on American democratic infrastructure," he said, "and we should tell the Russians that, from our perspective, we're going to be prepared to respond with technology-enabled attacks on their infrastructure." Michael Morell, a former acting director of the CIA, advocated "Iran-style sanctions" that would involve "sanctioning the entire [Russian] economy in a way that really hurts," in order "to make Putin pay a very high price" for his electoral operations, and then communicating to him privately: "'You stop, we'll stop. Simple proposition.'" Larry Summers, a former Treasury secretary, emphasized that in sanctioning Russia, coalition building is vital. "Unilateral sanctions tend to be shoot-yourself-in-the-foot strategies since the countries can do business with other countries," Summers said. "So a lot of emphasis should go into what we can do multilaterally." And Nuland would remind Putin that he, too, is vulnerable. "Should we help Russians who are interested in exposing the corruption and the stealing of the wealth of the nation for the private gain of a few? And expose the lack of democracy and transparency and citizen accountability in their system? Sure. Why not?"[29] Regardless of the exact countermeasures, their overarching purpose would be to make Putin reconsider the relative benefits of covert electoral interference.

The third step is for the next president to prioritize issues of digital sovereignty with Putin, as well as with any leader who imitates him. Just as, say, arms control was the focus of U.S.-Soviet summits, electoral security should be the focus now. Putin must be told that if he subverts elections, he will be caught, isolated, and punished. Assuming he still tries, the U.S. intelligence community, working with allied intelligence services, should expose such operations as soon as possible. "Sunshine is the best disinfectant with any of this stuff," Nuland said. "If we were doing our jobs, we would have a world-class exposure operation, including teams that would help any candidate, with equal opportunity, to expose disinformation."[30] Outing Russian interference as it unfolds would not only keep voters informed but also enable a hard-hitting policy response.

The final step is for the United States *not* to engage in covert electoral interference—ever. As a new authoritarian threat emerges, so, too, will the question Harry Truman faced in 1947: If Moscow is manipulating foreign elections, should the CIA respond in kind? Some influential voices think so. "I wouldn't want to take it off the table," said John McLaughlin, the CIA's deputy director from 2000 to 2004, especially if America has "very serious" interests at stake and "the Russians are already in there wheeling, dealing, paying, promoting, and helping thugs beat up the people you favor." Harry Reid, a former Senate majority leader, similarly said, "I would not be inclined to give a blanket statement that we should not interfere in elections, because there are times when we should." And Leon Panetta, CIA director from 2009 to 2011, said the United States should "absolutely" consider covertly supporting foreign parties with money, propaganda, and other tools, in order to counter Russia's covert operations directly. "Those are things that clearly ought to be looked at," Panetta said. "That kind of approach needs to be considered today because very frankly we are losing this battle right now."[31]

The next president cannot succumb to this temptation. CIA-led electoral interference is an outdated policy solution, ill-fitted for modern realities. Detection is all but guaranteed. "It's very difficult to keep that kind of activity from ultimately getting out," said David Petraeus, a former CIA director. For the United States, getting caught manipulating a foreign election now matters—a lot. "To essentially do the same thing" as Russia, Jon Finer said, would only "substantiate the norm that this stuff is okay." The challenge before America today is to strengthen democracy, not contain an ideology, so it would be self-defeating to corrupt elections. Jake Sullivan explained, "If you proxy war the hell out of democratic elections, you both get dirty, but at the end of the day, over time, the aggregate result is a weakening of democratic institutions that plays to the Russian advantage as opposed to our advantage."[32] Influencing elections covertly, whatever the short-term gains, is no longer worth the long-term costs.

Even in those rare cases where undemocratic tyrants can be voted out, the United States should use overt tools, like sanctions and party training, to bolster the opposition. The distinction between overt and covert action is essential. The former makes clear who is doing the influencing and why; the latter misleads and manipulates, presents foreign voices as domestic ones, and subverts open debate on behalf of hidden interests. The CIA's leaders who grappled with Putin's recent aggression, as well as America's digital vulnerabilities, left government adamantly opposed to CIA-led electoral interference. "It [is] antithetical to the democratic process," said John Brennan, the CIA director from 2013 to 2017, "to try to influence the outcome of a democratic election." Michael Morell advocated a wholesale rejection of the practice. "That's not appropriate for us to be doing," he said. "We're the ones who live in the glass house here, we're the ones standing up taking a moral position that countries shouldn't do this to each other, so if we really believe that, then we shouldn't be doing it to other countries."[33]

Taken together, these four steps would establish a new international standard against covert electoral interference, spearheaded, honored, and enforced by the United States. Norms are not a panacea. They are violated often, and foreign actors would violate this one. But compared with America's current position, consider this achievable alternative: a coalition of democracies allied against covert electoral interference, committed to their sovereignty, ready and waiting to punish Putin and leaders who execute similar operations. "If you cannot shame them from the standpoint of adhering to those international norms and standards," Brennan said, "you then make sure that they understand that you are dead serious about the costs that will accrue."[34]

Trump has cast aside America's allies; the challenge for his successor will be to correct for this error, renew key relationships abroad, and marshal a global movement in defense of the democratic model. The moment is urgent. Democracy is receding globally as Putin's electoral operations tarnish the credibility of the democratic process of succession. Steven Hall, the CIA's former Moscow station chief, said that Putin has long relished the chance to show his people: "You don't want to be like a democratic country because of the chaos." And Nadia Schadlow, Trump's former adviser, predicted that in the years ahead "reducing confidence in democracies is something that is going to be part of the tool kit of our competitors and adversaries."[35]

The United States is, in this sense, in a moment akin to 1948. A systemic threat to democracy has arisen: a resurgence in authoritarianism, advanced, in part, by covert electoral interference.[36] The Truman administration, so many decades ago, responded with a strategy of containment, of which covert action was a key part. A new strategy is needed for a new moment. "The democrats are in this battle with the autocrats," said Denis McDonough, the former White House chief of staff. "Nothing about this democracy is foretold or guaranteed. We have to keep fighting to protect it, and that's particularly the case now after 2016." Schadlow emphasized that America must confront this emerging authoritarian threat, as Truman once did. "We need to support allies and partners abroad," she said. "In Italy after World War II, the Russians had supported the Communist Party," so "if we had not supported [the Christian Democrats], it would have been a loss. Would it have been a good thing for Italy to be a part of the Warsaw Pact? Why wouldn't we support groups who are pro-American and pro-U.S. interests today?"[37]

Schadlow and McDonough, advisers to very different presidents, both believe America has reached a pivotal juncture. Its people must again decide: What kind of country do they want to live in, and are they willing to lead abroad?

—

The threats before the United States are bound not by ideology but by antipathy for open governance. Authoritarians today seek to tear down democracy. America must therefore renew itself, at home and abroad, and prove that democracies can not only survive the threats presented by the digital era but emerge from them stronger.

In the years ahead, how will all societies, authoritarian and democratic, grapple with continuous technological change? Putin, to his credit, sensed how to weaponize the internet to suit his own ends. China, an ascending power, has already established a form of digital authoritarianism at home and targeted elections in countries like Taiwan and Australia.[38] Covert electoral interference, once a weapon of superpowers, is becoming a weapon of authoritarians. All democracies are vulnerable.

But none of this means that the democratic model is doomed. The arcs underlying this history are timeless: open against closed, freedom against subjugation, inclusion against exclusion. Perhaps Putin and like-minded leaders will maintain control over the coming digital storm, or perhaps a tidal wave will catch them by surprise as citizens develop new ways to use online tools to start protests, organize mass movements, and stage revolutions.

In the age-old competition between autocrats and democrats, Russia won the latest battle, in 2016. What comes next is as yet unwritten. Technological achievements like the radio and television were not necessarily pro-democracy; fascists weaponized the former, and Communists weaponized the latter. The internet is no different. The question before democracies is how to integrate this rapidly evolving domain into their societies.

The story of covert electoral interference tells us many things. America's sovereignty is not as secure as it seemed. Democracy is threatened in ways that many did not realize. But history also provides reassurance. Many countries that fell victim to similar operations a generation ago remain vibrant democracies today. Russia is again attacking open societies and subverting elections. The United States can again defend the democratic experiment, so long as we, as citizens, are willing to do the work.

The choice is ours.

Acknowledgments

This book would not exist if not for Timothy Snyder, my long-time academic adviser. He guided me in college and kept advising me after I graduated. He carefully read over my doctoral work in the fall of 2018 and again in June 2019, at which point he offered to send my findings to his agent, Tina Bennett, who then agreed to represent me. And after Knopf took on this project, Professor Snyder welcomed me back to New Haven, where he met with me every few days and reviewed chapters as I wrote them. His generosity astounds me. I will never be able to thank him enough.

The idea for this book first emerged in the summer of 2017, when I was an intern reporter for the Berlin bureau of *The New York Times*. While there, I interviewed a former Stasi officer about how he and his colleagues secretly manipulated a vote of no confidence in Willy Brandt, the West German chancellor. I spent the next year researching this pivotal operation with the support of Yale's History Department, just as details about Russian interference in America's 2016 election were coming into view. When I moved to the United Kingdom to pursue my doctorate, thanks to the Marshall Scholarship Program, I knew exactly what I wanted to research: the evolution of foreign operations to interfere in electoral processes. The freedom Oxford University lends its students enabled me to study this subject obsessively. I traveled across Europe and America examining archives and interviewing relevant individuals, all of whom I thank for their participation in this project.

Between July and December 2019, I wrote this book, in what amounted to the most challenging and exciting period of my life. I am grateful to the professors and scholars who bettered my work in those hectic months. John Lewis Gaddis, Steven Houser, Daniel Kurtz-Phelan, Marci Shore, Timothy Snyder, and Odd Arne Westad reviewed my manuscript; Elizabeth Bradley, Jeanne Follansbee, Flora Fraser, and Michael McFaul commented on sections; and Martin Conway, Beverly Gage, Gilbert Joseph, Peter Kornbluh, and Jake Sullivan gave chapter-specific feedback. John Witt, a key proponent of this book, made sure the doors of Davenport College were open to me while I wrote it. In Davenport, Jay Gitlin and Paul Kennedy talked through various global issues with me.

I received help from some of my dearest friends, three of whom provided essential edits to this entire text. They are Zachary Cohen, Sarah Donilon, and Tyler Foggatt. Others who offered key comments are Nathan Bermel, Gabriella Borter, Madeleine Carlisle, Sam Koppelman, Isabel Mendia, Erica Pandey, Zeve Sanderson, and Jacob Stern. I also benefited from the assistance of excellent researchers. Kelsey Kudak meticulously fact-checked this book; Caroline Shookhoff and Peter James made stylistic suggestions; Edmund Griffiths, Anastasiia Posnova, and Anna Kolot handled translations; and Matthew Kristoffersen crafted reports for me on a range of subjects.

Two individuals in publishing made this book what it is. Tina Bennett, my agent, always believed in me and my ideas. Andrew Miller, my editor, understood why this book mattered, what it would take to release it quickly, and why we had to do so. I am indebted to them both, as well as to their colleagues Michael Collica, Tyler Comrie, Maris Dyer, Alicia Glekas Everett, Jay Mandel, Maria Massey, Daniel Novack, Jessica Purcell, and Ingrid Steiner.

The interests that underlie this book stretch back years and involve individuals, who, despite their hectic lives, have helped shape mine. John Lewis Gaddis began supervising my research into a separate area of Soviet history when I was in the tenth grade, mentored me through Yale, and supported this project from start to finish. Hillary Rodham Clinton met with me when I was still in high school to discuss my Cold War research and has since lent me her time and advice. Jake Sullivan has inspired and pushed me to sharpen my foreign policy analysis in various settings—as his student, as a summer intern at the Clinton presidential campaign, and as a researcher at the Carnegie Endowment for International Peace. Neil MacFarlane, my doctoral supervisor, has molded my thinking and provided me with an academic home. And Sam Chauncey has long blessed me with his friendship, counsel, and confidence.

Above all, my family has been my rock. My extended relatives offered opinions on hard questions and cheered me on at exhausting moments. My twin brother, Adam, and my sister, Nicole, endured my talking about this book constantly and were my sounding board for all things. My stepfather, Howard, and my late stepmother, Deborah, were unfailingly encouraging. And finally, my mother and father, my two biggest fans, did what they have always done: gave me unconditional love and supported me in any way possible.

I wrote the best book I could. Any shortcomings in its pages are my own.

Notes

INTRODUCTION: DEMOCRACY UNDER SIEGE

1. For this book, the author interviewed twenty-six former advisers to President Obama, including fourteen who were serving in his administration as Russia's operation unfolded.
2. Wallander, interview by author, Washington, D.C., July 17, 2019; Michael Daniel, phone interview by author, July 19, 2019.
3. Nuland, interview by author, Washington, D.C., Feb. 22, 2019.
4. Clapper, interview by author, Fairfax, Va., Jan. 3, 2019.
5. Lisa Monaco, interview by author, New York, Sept. 25, 2019; R. Sam Garrett, *Federal Role in U.S. Campaigns and Elections: An Overview* (Washington, D.C.: U.S. Library of Congress, Congressional Research Service, 2018), fas.org. In "Increasing the Security of the U.S. Election Infrastructure," Herbert Lin, Alex Stamos, Nate Persily, and Andrew Grotto further explain, "In accordance with the Help America Vote Act (HAVA) of 2002, systems for voter registration are centralized at the state level. The administration of voter registration databases entails a number of large-scale tasks, including (1) maintaining the correct status of individuals who are properly registered to vote and their relevant information on voter registration lists, (2) removing individuals who are no longer eligible to vote (e.g., those who have moved out of the jurisdiction) off registration lists, and (3) delivering precinct-by-precinct registration lists to the individual precincts where in-person voting occurs (e.g., creating and delivering paper-based or electronic poll books). By contrast, vote casting systems are decentralized down to the county level. Each county within the same state can use a different electronic voting system, which must include the following: (1) electronic voting systems that record ballots cast by citizens in person at individual precincts, (2) tabulation systems that record absentee ballots via postal mail, and (3) programs that tabulate vote totals at levels higher than the precinct." Herbert Lin et al., "Increasing the Security of the U.S. Election Infrastructure," in *Securing American Elections: Prescriptions for Enhancing the Integrity*

and Independence of the 2020 U.S. Presidential Election and Beyond, ed. Michael McFaul, Stanford University, June 2019, 17, fsi.stanford.edu.

6. Brennan, interview by author, Washington, D.C., July 10, 2018.

7. Johnson, interview by author, New York, July 29, 2019.

8. Carol E. Lee, "Obama, Putin Meet as Syria Deal Stalls," *Wall Street Journal,* Sept. 5, 2016, www.wsj.com.

9. Monaco, interview by author.

10. Haines, interview by author, New York, Feb. 23, 2019; Daniel, interview by author. Of Russia's probes of electoral infrastructure through October and early November, Lisa Monaco told me, "We did not see a spike. We didn't see an escalation. It was a steady state."

11. Nuland, interview by author.

12. David Sanger, "Obama Strikes Back at Russia for Election Hacking," *New York Times,* Dec. 29, 2016, www.nytimes.com.

13. Finer, interview by author, New York, Feb. 20, 2019; Blinken, interview by author, Washington, D.C., Jan. 3, 2019; Clapper, interview by author.

14. Hans Morgenthau, *Politics Among Nations* (New York: Knopf, 1967), 301; Robert Jackson, *Sovereignty: The Evolution of an Idea* (Cambridge, U.K.: Polity, 2007), 10; Stephen D. Krasner, *Sovereignty: Organized Hypocrisy* (Princeton, N.J.: Princeton University Press, 1999), 20.

15. Brennan, interview by author.

16. The digital age, as defined in this book, took hold during the first decade of the twenty-first century, when, David A. L. Levy and Rasmus Kleis Nielsen write, there was a "rapid spread of increasingly sophisticated forms of internet access and use throughout the developed world and in many emerging economies." David A. L. Levy and Rasmus Kleis Nielsen, *The Changing Business of Journalism and Its Implications for Democracy* (Oxford, U.K.: Reuters Institute for the Study of Journalism, 2010), 7. In the year 2004 alone, Facebook was founded, Google launched Gmail, and Amazon announced its first-ever full-year profit. See Harry McCracken, "How Gmail Happened: The Inside Story of Its Launch 10 Years Ago," *Time,* April 1, 2014, time.com; Ellen Rosen, "Student's Start-up Draws Attention and $13 Million," *New York Times,* May 26, 2005, www.nytimes.com; Saul Hansell, "Amazon Reports First Full-Year Profit," *New York Times,* Jan. 28, 2004, www.nytimes.com.

17. Avril Haines, "Trump's 'Ridiculous' Spy Claim," interview by Michael Isikoff and Dan Klaidman, *Skullduggery,* Yahoo News, May 25, 2018, play.acast.com; Haines, interview by author.

18. McMaster, phone interview by author, Oct. 17, 2018.

19. U.S. Congress, Senate, Intelligence Authorization Act for Fiscal Year 2017, S. 133, 115th Cong., www.congress.gov.

20. Timothy Snyder, *The Road to Unfreedom: Russia, Europe, America* (New York: Tim Duggan Books, 2018), 47, 251. A country can hold elections, of course, but not be a democracy, as captured by Nic Cheeseman and Brian Klaas's *How to Rig an Election* (New Haven, Conn.: Yale University Press, 2018). Larry Diamond of Stanford describes the democratic

model as including four basic elements: not just (1) a political system for choosing and replacing the government through free and fair elections, but also (2) the active participation of the people, as citizens, in politics and civic life; (3) protection of the human rights of all citizens; and (4) a rule of law, in which the laws and procedures apply equally to all citizens. See Larry Diamond, "What Is Democracy?" (lecture at Hilla University for Humanistic Studies, Hilla, Iraq, Jan. 21, 2004), diamond-democracy .stanford.edu.

21. Professor Don H. Levin has assembled a universe of cases for U.S.- and Russia-led electoral interference operations. He has found that between 1946 and 2000 the United States interfered in eighty-one foreign elections and the Soviet Union/Russia interfered in thirty-six foreign elections. Levin classifies nearly two-thirds of these interventions as covert. See Don H. Levin, "Partisan Electoral Interventions by the Great Powers: Introducing the PEIG Dataset," *Conflict Management and Peace Science* 36, no. 1 (2016): 94–95.

22. Clinton, phone interview by author, April 4, 2020.

23. By 2016, nearly two-thirds of U.S. adults were getting at least some of their news from social media. See Jeffrey Gottfried and Elisa Shearer, "News Use Across Social Media Platforms 2016," Pew Research Center, May 26, 2016, www.journalism.org.

24. Baker, phone interview by author, Oct. 17, 2018.

25. Stamos, phone interview by author, May 28, 2018.

26. Valery Gerasimov, "The Value of Science Is in the Foresight: New Challenges Demand Rethinking the Forms and Methods of Carrying Out Combat Operations," translated from Russian by Robert Coalson, published originally in *Military-Industrial Kurier,* Feb. 27, 2013.

27. Robert Kagan, "The Strongmen Strike Back," *Washington Post,* March 14, 2019, www.washingtonpost.com. See also Olivia Beavers, "National Security Experts Warn of Rise in Authoritarianism," *Hill,* Feb. 26, 2019, thehill.com.

CHAPTER 1: ENTER LENIN

1. Kalugin, interview by author, Rockville, Md., Aug. 7, 2018. For more on Kalugin's backstory, see Oleg Kalugin, *Spymaster: My Thirty-two Years in Intelligence and Espionage Against the West* (New York: Basic Books, 1994). Technically, the KGB was not named as such until 1954. Christopher Andrew and Vasili Mitrokhin explain, "The term KGB is used both generally to denote the Soviet State Security organisation throughout its history since its foundation as the Cheka in 1917 and, more specifically, to refer to State Security after 1954 when it took its final name." Christopher Andrew and Vasili Mitrokhin, "The Evolution of the KGB, 1917–1991," in *The Sword and the Shield: The Mitrokhin Archive and the Secret History of the KGB* (New York: Basic Books, 1999).

2. Steven Lee Myers, "Russia Convicts a Former K.G.B. General Now Living

in U.S.," *New York Times,* June 27, 2002, www.nytimes.com; Scott Shane, "From Soviet Hero to Traitor," *Baltimore Sun,* June 26, 2002, www.baltimoresun.com.

3. Kalugin, interview by author.

4. Tony Judt, *Postwar: A History of Europe Since 1945* (New York: Penguin Books, 2005), 103. Historian Odd Arne Westad similarly argues that World War I "jump-started the destinies of the two future Cold War Superpowers. It made the United States the global embodiment of capitalism and it made Russia a Soviet Union, a permanent challenge to the capitalist world." Odd Arne Westad, *The Cold War: A World History* (New York: Basic Books, 2017), 26–27.

5. Trevor Barnes, "The Secret Cold War: The C.I.A. and American Foreign Policy in Europe, 1946–1956. Part I," *Historical Journal* 24, no. 2 (1981): 399. Of the interwar period, Westad explains, "How could the Soviet system, based on terror and subjugation, appeal to so many people around the world? The Great Depression provided the opportunity. If it had not been for capitalism doing so very badly, Communism would not have won the affection of large numbers of dedicated and intelligent people everywhere. . . . A massive majority of Americans, 95 percent in 1936, thought that the United States should stay out of any war in Europe." Westad, *Cold War,* 35, 40.

6. John Ridell, *Founding the Communist International: Proceedings and Documents of the First Congress: March 1919* (New York: Pathfinder Press, 1987), 1, 75, 161.

7. "Ruse of Soviet to Stir Revolts Officially Shown," *New York Times,* April 19, 1920, timesmachine.nytimes.com; Kevin McDermott and Jeremy Agnew, *The Comintern: A History of International Communism from Lenin to Stalin* (London: Palgrave, 1996), 17.

8. McDermott and Agnew, *Comintern,* 20–23. Fridrikh Igorevich Firsov, Harvey Klehr, and John Earl Haynes, *Secret Cables of the Comintern, 1933–1943* (New Haven, Conn.: Yale University Press, 2014), 44.

9. McDermott and Agnew, *Comintern,* 21–22. By 1922, the Comintern had an annual budget of $21.5 million (in 2020 dollars) and dispersed between $1.1 and $3.7 million each to the German, American, British, Italian, and Czech Communist Parties. Firsov, Klehr, and Haynes provide these figures in *Secret Cables of the Comintern,* 39. Conversion to 2020 values executed by U.S. Inflation Calculator, www.usinflationcalculator.com.

10. Timothy Snyder, *Sketches from a Secret War: A Polish Artist's Mission to Liberate Soviet Ukraine* (New Haven, Conn.: Yale University Press, 2005), chap. 1.

11. Timothy Snyder, *Bloodlands: Europe Between Hitler and Stalin* (New York: Basic Books, 2012), 60–62.

12. Firsov, Klehr, and Haynes, *Secret Cables of the Comintern,* 30–31, 52–57, which further explains that Spain's Communist Party relied on the Comintern's payments, in part, to fund the *Mundo Obrero,* a left-wing propaganda source.

13. Ibid., 39.
14. McDermott and Agnew, *Comintern,* 122.
15. Westad, *Cold War,* 30, 32. The U.S. government went so far as to establish a "concentration camp for Reds" at Camp Upton in New York, reported *The New York Times,* and to arrest and deport hundreds of allegedly radical leftist immigrants, including 249 "undesirable aliens" who were moved out of the country aboard a U.S. military ship nicknamed the Soviet Ark. See "Begin Procedure to Deport Reds," *New York Times,* Jan. 6, 1920, timesmachine.nytimes.com; " 'Ark' with 300 Reds Sails Early Today for Unnamed Port," *New York Times,* Dec. 21, 1919, timesmachine.nytimes.com; "Soviet Ark Lands Its Reds in Finland," *New York Times,* Jan. 18, 1920, timesmachine.nytimes.com. For further reading on the general paranoia of this period, see Robert Murray, *Red Scare: A Study in National Hysteria, 1919–1920* (New York: McGraw-Hill, 1955); Beverly Gage, *The Day Wall Street Exploded: A Story of America in Its First Age of Terror* (New York: Oxford University Press, 2009), chap. 14.
16. Founded in 1920, the British Communist Party received at least £55,000 from the Comintern to jump-start its activities (£2,476,739 in 2019 values), followed by annual subsidies of varying amounts, from £24,000 in 1921 (£1,183,688 in 2019 values) to £16,000 in 1925 (£980,043 in 2019 values). See McDermott and Agnew, *Comintern,* 22, 56. Conversions to 2019 values executed by the Bank of England's Inflation Calculator, www.bankofengland.co.uk.
17. Gill Bennett, *The Zinoviev Letter: The Conspiracy That Never Dies* (New York: Oxford University Press, 2018), 267–69; "Civil War Plot by Socialists' Masters," *Daily Mail,* Oct. 25, 1920. Of the agreements between Moscow and London, Bennett explains, "By early August, after a brief breakdown in the talks, agreement had been reached on two draft treaties, a general Anglo-Soviet treaty and a commercial treaty, with provision for a third whereby the British government would guarantee a loan to the Soviet Union. . . . Although more than one treaty had been negotiated, for the Soviet government the key treaty was the general Anglo-Soviet treaty whose ratification would pave the way for a loan," in *The Zinoviev Letter,* 26, 284. See also Uri Bar-Joseph, *Intelligence Intervention in the Politics of Democratic States: The United States, Israel, and Britain* (University Park: Pennsylvania State University Press, 1995), 298.
18. Bennett, *Zinoviev Letter,* 66–68.
19. A. J. P. Taylor, *English History, 1914–1945* (Oxford, U.K.: Oxford University Press, 1978), 219, in which Taylor concludes the letter "undoubtedly was" a forgery.
20. Bennett, *Zinoviev Letter,* 1.
21. Franz Borkenau, *World Communism: A History of the Communist International* (New York: W. W. Norton, 1939), 428. Separately, Stalin's purges of the Comintern's ranks had undermined its functionality, as explained by McDermott and Agnew in *Comintern,* 145–55. For further

reading on Stalin and his domestic terror, see Anne Applebaum, *Gulag: A History* (New York: Doubleday, 2003), chaps. 1–23; Golfo Alexopoulos, *Illness and Inhumanity in Stalin's Gulag* (New Haven, Conn.: Yale University Press, 2017); Snyder, *Bloodlands,* chaps. 1 and 3; Stephen Kotkin, *Stalin: Waiting for Hitler, 1929–1941* (New York: Penguin Books, 2017).

22. Firsov, Klehr, and Haynes, *Secret Cables of the Comintern,* 49.

23. Fernando Claudin, *The Communist Movement: From Comintern to Cominform* (New York: Monthly Review Press, 1975), 45.

24. Anne Applebaum, *Iron Curtain: The Crushing of Eastern Europe, 1944–1956* (New York: Doubleday, 2012), chap. 9; Delbert Clark, "Soviet Grip Broken By Berlin Election," *New York Times,* Oct. 22, 1946, times machine.nytimes.com; "Leader of Anti-Reds in Berlin Threatened," *New York Times,* Dec. 10, 1947, timesmachine.nytimes.com; Delbert Clark, "Soviet Forces Out Kaiser, German Opposition Leader," *New York Times,* Dec. 21, 1947, timesmachine.nytimes.com; "Kaiser Ouster Disliked," *New York Times,* Dec. 23, 1947, timesmachine.nytimes.com; "Kaiser Carries On as Exile in Berlin," *New York Times,* Dec. 24, 1947, timesmachine.nytimes.com.

25. Applebaum, *Iron Curtain,* chap. 9; Richard F. Staar, "Elections in Communist Poland," *Midwest Journal of Political Science* 2, no. 2 (1958): 210.

26. Applebaum, *Iron Curtain,* chap. 9; "Hungarian Leader Seized by Russians," *New York Times,* Feb. 27, 1947, timesmachine.nytimes.com; Burnett Bolloten, *The Spanish Civil War: Revolution and Counterrevolution* (Chapel Hill: University of North Carolina Press, 1991), 551.

27. "Excerpts from Communique Adopted by Cominform," *New York Times,* Nov. 30, 1949, timesmachine.nytimes.com. On the formation of the Cominform, see Westad, *Cold War,* 96; Csaba Békés, "Soviet Plans to Establish the COMINFORM in Early 1946: New Evidence from the Hungarian Archives," *Cold War International History Project Bulletin,* no. 10 (March 1998): 135–36. On American policy making toward the countries of Eastern Europe in the immediate postwar period, see Marc Trachtenberg, "The United States and Eastern Europe in 1945: A Reassessment," *Journal of Cold War Studies* 10, no. 4 (2008): 94–132.

28. Judt, *Postwar,* 143. Historian Silvio Pons argues that "the formation of the Cominform was more a sign of retreat than a shift toward the offensive." Silvio Pons, "Stalin, Togliatti, and the Origins of the Cold War in Europe," *Journal of Cold War Studies* 3, no. 2 (2001): 26.

29. The Soviet Union had possessed intelligence services since its inception, known at various times as the Cheka, the OGPU, and the NKVD. Their work reflected the priorities of the top. Lenin and Stalin used these agencies, above all, to crush perceived enemies at home. Andrew and Mitrokhin explain, "To understand Soviet intelligence operations between the wars, it is frequently necessary to enter a world of smoke and mirrors where the target is as much the product of Bolshevik delusions as of real counter-revolutionary conspiracy." Take the Cheka, which brutally

tortured and killed many thousands of people during the Russian Civil War, or the NKVD, which carried out Stalin's Great Terror in the late 1930s. In December 1920, Moscow did establish a foreign intelligence directorate—and it did penetrate the highest levels of the British and American governments—but eventually most of its officers fell victim to Stalin's purges. For most members of this unit, "torture and confession to imaginary crimes were followed by a short walk to an execution chamber and a bullet in the back of the head." See Andrew and Mitrokhin, *The Sword and the Shield,* 22–80.

30. Kalugin, interview by author.

CHAPTER 2: THE CIA IN ITALY

1. For further reading on containment, see John Lewis Gaddis, *Strategies of Containment: A Critical Appraisal of American National Security Policy During the Cold War* (New York: Oxford University Press, 2005); John Lewis Gaddis, *We Now Know: Rethinking Cold War History* (New York: Oxford University Press, 1997). Dean Acheson, the famed secretary of state, details foreign policy making during the Truman years in *Present at the Creation: My Years in the State Department* (New York: W. W. Norton, 1969). See also James Chase, *Acheson: The Secretary of State Who Created the American World* (New York: Simon & Schuster, 1998). For further reading on Truman, see David McCullough, *Truman* (New York: Simon & Schuster, 1992); Alonzo L. Hamby, *Man of the People: A Life of Harry S. Truman* (New York: Oxford University Press, 1995).

2. On the establishment of the CIA, the ultimate successor to the wartime Office of Strategic Services, see Barnes, "The Secret Cold War: The C.I.A. and American Foreign Policy in Europe, 1946–1956. Part I"; Daniel Yergin, *Shattered Peace: The Origins of the Cold War and the National Security State* (Boston: Houghton Mifflin, 1977); David F. Rudgers, *Creating the Secret State: The Origins of the Central Intelligence Agency, 1943–1947* (Lawrence: University Press of Kansas, 2000); Burton Hersch, *The Old Boys: The American Elite and the Origins of the CIA* (New York: Scribner's, 1992); Michael J. Hogan, *A Cross of Iron: Harry S. Truman and the Origins of the National Security State, 1945–1954* (Cambridge, U.K.: Cambridge University Press, 1998).

3. The economic ruin of Europe presented Moscow and Washington with opportunities for influence. Westad explains, "The Cold War between capitalism and Communism, and between the United States and the Soviet Union, fit the European disaster to a T. Not only had the military outcome of the war left the Americans and the Soviets in command of the continent, but Europeans, hungry for a miracle, or just plain hungry, looked to Washington or Moscow for answers. . . . The disasters that had befallen Europe put the prestige of the new masters of the continent—the Americans and the Soviets, or the Superpowers as Europeans had started calling them—into sharp relief." Westad, *Cold War,* 72–73.

4. Huntington Smith, "Unemployment, Overcrowding Seen Bolstering Reds in Southern Italy," *New York Times,* April 17, 1948, timesmachine .nytimes.com.

5. Robert Ventresca, *From Fascism to Democracy: Culture and Politics in the Italian Election of 1948* (Toronto: University of Toronto Press, 2004), 25, 52.

6. John Foot, *The Archipelago: Italy Since 1945* (London: Bloomsbury, 2018), 17, 22, 72; Ventresca, *From Fascism to Democracy,* 49. See also Rosario Forlenza, *On the Edge of Democracy: Italy, 1943–1948* (Oxford, U.K.: Oxford University Press, 2019), chaps. 2 and 4.

   Westad explains that the Communist Parties of Western Europe attracted major followings in the immediate postwar period, not only because they "had a model ready for Europe's transformation," but also because they "were genuinely admired by many for their role in the resistance to German occupation, including by people who regretted their own failure at taking up weapons." He continues, "In the first postwar western European elections, the Communists made inroads everywhere. In Norway they got 12 percent of the vote, in Belgium 13 percent, in Italy 19 percent, in Finland 23.5 percent, and in France almost 29 percent." Westad, *Cold War,* 54, 74.

7. "Crisis in Italy," *New York Times,* Jan. 22, 1947, timesmachine.nytimes .com; Kaeten Mistry, *The United States, Italy, and the Origins of Cold War: Waging Political Warfare, 1945–1950* (Cambridge, U.K.: Cambridge University Press, 2014), 48. See also James E. Miller, "Taking Off the Gloves: The United States and the Italian Elections of 1948," *Diplomatic History* 7, no. 1 (1983): 37.

8. Silvio Pons, "Stalin, Togliatti, and the Origins of the Cold War in Europe," *Journal of Cold War Studies* 3, no. 2 (2001): 3–27. For further reading, see Alessandro Brogi, *Confronting America: The Cold War Between the United States and the Communists in France and Italy* (Chapel Hill: University of North Carolina Press, 2011); Donald Blackmer and Sidney Tarrow, *Communism in Italy and France* (Princeton, N.J.: Princeton University Press, 1975); James E. Miller, *The United States and Italy, 1940–1950: The Politics and Diplomacy of Stabilization* (Chapel Hill: University of North Carolina Press, 1986).

9. James Clement Dunn, "The Ambassador in Italy (Dunn) to the Secretary of State," March 10, 1948, *Foreign Relations of the United States* (hereafter cited as *FRUS*), *1948,* vol. 3, *Western Europe,* doc. 521, history.state .gov.

10. Miller, "Taking Off the Gloves," 37–43; Arnaldo Cortesi, "Communists Widen Riots in Italy," *New York Times,* Nov. 12, 1947, timesmachine .nytimes.com; Carlo Sforza, "Italy, the Marshall Plan, and the 'Third Force,'" *Foreign Affairs,* April 1948, www.foreignaffairs.com; Ventresca, *From Fascism to Democracy,* 62, 75.

11. Arnaldo Cortesi, "Italian Socialists Vote Unity with Communists for Elections," *New York Times,* Jan. 24, 1948, timesmachine.nytimes.com;

Arnaldo Cortesi, "Leftist Campaign Is Begun in Italy," *New York Times,* Feb. 2, 1948, timesmachine.nytimes.com.

12. Arnaldo Cortesi, "Italian Communist Aim Is to Win 1948 Election," *New York Times,* Dec. 14, 1947, timesmachine.nytimes.com; Ventresca, *From Fascism to Democracy,* 6.

13. James Clement Dunn, "The Ambassador in Italy (Dunn) to the Secretary of State," Jan. 21 and Feb. 7, 1948, *FRUS, 1948,* vol. 3, *Western Europe,* docs. 506 and 511, history.state.gov.

14. James Clement Dunn, "The Ambassador in Italy (Dunn) to the Secretary of State," March 1, 1948, *FRUS, 1948,* vol. 3, *Western Europe,* doc. 515, history.state.gov. Dunn had been serving as the U.S. ambassador in Italy since February 1947. A navy veteran and experienced diplomat, he had advised several secretaries of state before arriving in Italy. On his background, see Mistry, *United States, Italy, and the Origins of Cold War,* 53–57.

15. Wyatt, interview by CNN for *Cold War,* Nov. and Dec. 1995, web .archive.org/web/20010831150516/http://www.cnn.com. See also Central Intelligence Agency, "Possible Soviet Moves to Influence Elections," April 12, 1948 (declassified Sept. 2006), www.cia.gov; D. W. Ellwood, "The 1948 Elections in Italy: A Cold War Propaganda Battle," *Historical Journal of Film, Radio, and Television* 13, no. 1 (1993): 19–33.

16. Central Intelligence Agency, "Communist Party Plans All-Out Election Effort," Jan. 28, 1948 (declassified July 2005), www.cia.gov.

17. Central Intelligence Agency, "Consequences of Communist Accession to Power in Italy by Legal Means," March 5, 1948 (declassified Aug. 1993), www.cia.gov.

18. Camille Cianfarra, "Last U.S. Troops Quit Italy; Rome Hails Truman Pledge," *New York Times,* Dec. 15, 1947, timesmachine.nytimes.com; Bertram Hulen, "Truman Promises Watch to Uphold Italian Freedom," *New York Times,* Dec. 14, 1947, timesmachine.nytimes.com.

19. Hulen, "Truman Promises Watch to Uphold Italian Freedom."

20. "NSC 1/1: The Position of the United States with Respect to Italy," Nov. 14, 1947, *FRUS, 1948,* vol. 3, *Western Europe,* doc. 440, history .state.gov.

21. Miller, "Taking Off the Gloves," 43. The U.S. Congress, in 1976, found, "As the elections in 1948 and 1949 in Italy and France approached, the democratic parties were in disarray and the possibility of a Communist takeover was real. Coordinated Communist political unrest in western countries combined with extremist pressure from the Soviet Union, confirmed the fears of many that America faced an expansionist Communist monolith. The United States responded with overt economic aid—the Truman Doctrine and the Marshall Plan—and covert political assistance. This latter task was assigned to the Office of Special Projects, later renamed the Office of Policy Coordination (OPC). The Office was housed in the CIA but was directly responsible to the Departments of State and Defense. Clandestine support from the United States for European

democratic parties was regarded as an essential response to the threat of 'international communism.' OPC became the fastest growing element in the CIA." See U.S. Congress, Senate, Select Committee to Study Governmental Operations with Respect to Intelligence Activities, *Foreign and Military Intelligence,* bk. 1, Final Report, 94th Cong., 2nd sess., 1976, S. Rep. 94-755, 22.

22. Rhodri Jeffreys-Jones, *The CIA and American Democracy* (New Haven, Conn.: Yale University Press, 2003), 50. See also Sarah-Jane Corke, *U.S. Covert Operations and Cold War Strategy: Truman, Secret Warfare, and the CIA, 1945–53* (Abingdon, U.K.: Routledge, 2007), 48; Robin Winks, *Cloak and Gown: Scholars in the Secret War, 1939–1961* (New Haven, Conn.: Yale University Press, 1987), 380.

23. Jeffreys-Jones, *CIA and American Democracy,* 50; John Prados, *Safe for Democracy: The Secret Wars of the CIA* (New York: Ivan R. Dee, 2006), 39; Forlenza, *On the Edge of Democracy,* chap. 3. Winks explains, "On December 19 the National Security Council, by its directive NSC 4/A, ordered the director of Central Intelligence, Admiral Roscoe Hillenkoetter, to do what he could, including the use of covert activities, to prevent a Communist victory. . . . Hillenkoetter assigned the Italian puzzle to the Office of Special Operations. . . . The OSO promptly established a Special Procedures Group, or SPG, and on December 22 it began to shape its plans." Winks, *Cloak and Gown,* 381. See also Robert J. Donovan, *Conflict and Crisis: The Presidency of Harry S Truman, 1945–1948* (New York: W. W. Norton, 1977), chap. 33.

24. Miller, "Taking Off the Gloves," 48.

25. U.S. Congress, Senate, *Foreign and Military Intelligence,* 49.

26. James Clement Dunn, "The Ambassador in Italy (Dunn) to the Secretary of State," Feb. 7, 1948, *FRUS, 1948,* vol. 3, *Western Europe,* doc. 511, history.state.gov.

27. George Marshall, "The Secretary of State to the Embassy in London," March 2, 1948, *FRUS, 1948,* vol. 3, *Western Europe,* doc. 516, history.state.gov.

28. James Clement Dunn, "The Ambassador in Italy (Dunn) to the Secretary of State," Feb. 7 and 21, 1948, *FRUS, 1948,* vol. 3, *Western Europe,* docs. 511 and 513, history.state.gov. Just three days before Marshall's speech, Dunn had reiterated, in a cable marked "urgent," that Front officials were "becloud[ing] this most damaging argument" that U.S. aid would cease, were they to win the election. See James Clement Dunn, "The Ambassador in Italy (Dunn) to the Secretary of State," March 16, 1948, *FRUS, 1948,* vol. 3, *Western Europe,* doc. 525, history.state.gov.

On the Soviet Union and the Marshall Plan, see Westad, *Cold War,* 92–94. On the broader impact of the Marshall Plan on international politics, Charles Maier concludes, "The Marshall Plan, in effect, was the single most important policy in confirming, but not initiating, the division of Europe," in "The Marshall Plan and the Division of Europe," as part of a spirited dialogue between Michael Cox, Caroline Kennedy-Pipe, Marc

Trachtenberg, John Bledsoe Bonds, László Borhi, and Günter Bischof in *Journal of Cold War Studies* 7, no. 1 (2005). For further reading, see Nicolaus Mills, *Winning the Peace: The Marshall Plan and America's Coming of Age as a Superpower* (Hoboken, N.J.: Wiley, 2008); Greg Behrman, *The Most Noble Adventure: The Marshall Plan and the Time When America Helped Save Europe* (New York: Free Press, 2007); Gregory A. Fossedal, *Our Finest Hour: Will Clayton, the Marshall Plan, and the Triumph of Democracy* (Stanford, Calif.: Hoover Institution Press, 1993).

29. George Marshall, "World-Wide Struggle Between Freedom and Tyranny" (speech, University of California, Berkeley, March 19, 1948), *New York Times,* March 20, 1948, timesmachine.nytimes.com. For further reading on Marshall's career and character, see Ed Cray, *General of the Army: George C. Marshall, Soldier and Statesman* (New York: W. W. Norton, 1990); George Marshall, *Memoirs of My Services in the World War, 1917–1918* (Boston: Houghton Mifflin, 1976); Daniel Kurtz-Phelan, *The China Mission: George Marshall's Unfinished War, 1945–1947* (New York: W. W. Norton, 2018).

30. James Clement Dunn, "The Ambassador in Italy (Dunn) to the Secretary of State," March 20 and June 16, 1948, *FRUS, 1948,* vol. 3, *Western Europe,* docs. 528 and 543, history.state.gov.

31. George Marshall, "The Secretary of State to the Embassy in Italy," March 24, 1948, *FRUS, 1948,* vol. 3, *Western Europe,* doc. 531, history .state.gov; Miller, "Taking Off the Gloves," 48–49; "Pleas to Italy Ask Vote Against Reds," *New York Times,* April 8, 1948, timesmachine .nytimes.com; Eric Martone, *Italian Americans: The History and Culture of a People* (Santa Barbara, Calif.: ABC-CLIO, 2016), 41.

    Decades later, Jimmy Carter, the U.S. president from 1977 to 1981, sought to turn the page. Olav Njølstad explains, "Carter took steps to change the policy of not granting visas to Communist Party members, a practice established before the 1948 election to discourage Italian voters with relatives in the United States from voting for the PCI." Olav Njøl-stad, "The Carter Administration and Italy: Keeping the Communists Out of Power Without Interfering," *Journal of Cold War Studies* 4, no. 3 (2002): 65.

32. James Clement Dunn, "The Ambassador in Italy (Dunn) to the Secretary of State," Feb. 7, 1948, *FRUS, 1948,* vol. 3, *Western Europe,* doc. 511, history.state.gov; Samuel A. Tower, "Interim Aid Steps Rushed by Committees in Congress," *New York Times,* March 21, 1948, timesmachine .nytimes.com; Miller, "Taking Off the Gloves," 49. See also Norman Armour, "Memorandum of Conversation, by the Assistant Secretary of State for Political Affairs (Armour)," Feb. 18, 1948, *FRUS, 1948,* vol. 3, *Western Europe,* doc. 512, history.state.gov; Willard Thorp, "Memorandum of Conversation, by the Assistant Secretary for Economic Affairs (Thorp)," April 7, 1948, *FRUS, 1948,* vol. 3, *Western Europe,* doc. 536, history.state.gov; David Ellwood, "The Propaganda of the Marshall Plan

in Italy in a Cold War Context," *Intelligence and National Security* 18, no. 2 (2003): 225–36.

33. George Marshall, "The Secretary of State to the Embassy in Italy," Feb. 4, 1948, *FRUS, 1948,* vol. 3, *Western Europe,* doc. 510, history.state.gov; Arnaldo Cortesi, "De Gasperi Wins a Record Vote After Denying U.S. Rules Italy," *New York Times,* Dec. 19, 1947, timesmachine.nytimes.com. See also "Italy Signs Pact with U.S. on Aid," *New York Times,* Jan. 3, 1948, timesmachine.nytimes.com.

34. Leonard Dinnerstein and David Reimers, *Ethnic Americans: A History of Immigration* (New York: Columbia University Press, 1999), 50.

35. C. Edda Martinez and Edward A Suchman, "Letters from America and the 1948 Elections in Italy," *Public Opinion Quarterly* 14, no. 1 (1950): 112.

36. Ibid., 112–115. About a decade later, Anfuso, by then a congressman, secretly approved of Christian Democrats reselling American aid in order to raise campaign funds. See Leopoldo Nuti, "The United States, Italy, and the Opening to the Left, 1953–1963," *Journal of Cold War Studies* 4, no. 3 (2002): 50.

37. James Clement Dunn, "The Ambassador in Italy (Dunn) to the Secretary of State," April 7, 1948, *FRUS, 1948,* vol. 3, *Western Europe,* doc. 535, history.state.gov; Mistry, *United States, Italy, and the Origins of Cold War,* 142; Ventresca, *From Fascism to Democracy,* 63.

38. Martinez and Suchman, "Letters from America," 111, 119; Ellwood, "1948 Elections in Italy," 21; "Letter Campaign Denounced," *New York Times,* April 9, 1948, timesmachine.nytimes.com.

39. "Pleas to Italy Ask Vote Against Reds"; Mistry, *United States, Italy, and the Origins of Cold War,* 141; Stephen Gundle, "Hollywood Glamour and Mass Consumption in Postwar Italy," *Journal of Cold War Studies* 4, no. 3 (2002): 102; Miller, "Taking Off the Gloves," 49–51, in which he details how the U.S. government rejected a proposed get-out-the-vote tour by Sinatra as too brazen. For further reading on the Italian Communist Party's struggles with modernity, see Stephen Gundle, *Between Hollywood and Moscow: The Italian Communists and the Challenge of Mass Culture, 1943–1991* (Durham, N.C.: Duke University Press, 2000).

40. Arnaldo Cortesi, "Fear of Red Coup Drives Lira Down," *New York Times,* March 6, 1948, timesmachine.nytimes.com. See also Drew Middleton, "Britons Are Fearful That Italy May Be Next Victim of Red Coup," *New York Times,* March 11, 1948, timesmachine.nytimes.com; James Clement Dunn, "The Ambassador (Dunn) to the Secretary of State," March 1, 1948, *FRUS, 1948,* vol. 3, *Western Europe,* doc. 514, history.state.gov.

41. "The Text of President Truman's Address to the Joint Session of Congress," *New York Times,* March 18, 1948, timesmachine.nytimes.com; Miller, "Taking Off the Gloves," 46–48. For elaboration on Western reactions to the Czechoslovak coup, see Peter Svik, "The Czechoslovak Factor

in Western Alliance Building, 1945–1948," *Journal of Cold War Studies* 18, no. 1 (2016): 133–60.

42. Camille Cianfarra, "Clergy Ordered to Vote in Italy," *New York Times*, Feb. 25, 1948, timesmachine.nytimes.com; Camille Cianfarra, "Vatican Will Back Regime in Election," *New York Times*, Feb. 13, 1948, times machine.nytimes.com. See also Ventresca, *From Fascism to Democracy*, chap. 3.

43. James Clement Dunn, "The Ambassador (Dunn) to the Secretary of State," March 10, 1948, *FRUS, 1948*, vol. 3, *Western Europe*, doc. 521, history.state.gov; Camille Cianfarra, "Pope Tells Clergy to Combat Reds," *New York Times*, March 11, 1948, timesmachine.nytimes.com.

44. Cianfarra, "Pope Tells Clergy to Combat Reds"; Arnaldo Cortesi, "Pope Sees World Facing Critical Danger This Year," *New York Times*, March 29, 1948, timesmachine.nytimes.com; "Text of the Easter Address by Pope Pius to Romans," *New York Times*, March 29, 1948, timesmachine .nytimes.com.

45. "Pravda Sees Plots by U.S. and Vatican," *New York Times*, Dec. 25, 1947, timesmachine.nytimes.com; Foot, *Archipelago*, 46.

46. Central Intelligence Agency, "Measures Proposed to Defeat Communism in Italy," Feb. 9, 1948 (declassified Sept. 2006), www.cia.gov. (However, in this memorandum, one of the steps Dunn recommended remains classified.) Central Intelligence Agency, "US Plans Support of Italy," March 8, 1948 (declassified Sept. 2006), www.cia.gov.

47. Wyatt, interview by CNN; Jeffreys-Jones, *CIA and American Democracy*, 51; Corke, *U.S. Covert Operations*, 48. Technically, Hillenkoetter was the director of Central Intelligence, which was the title of the official in charge of the CIA until 2005, when Congress created the position of director of the Central Intelligence Agency. For consistency and in accordance with other texts, this book refers to holders of either role as the CIA's director.

48. U.S. Congress, Senate, Select Committee to Study Governmental Operations with Respect to Intelligence Activities, *Hearings Before the Select Committee to Study Governmental Operations with Respect to Intelligence Activities: Covert Action*, 94th Cong., 1st sess., Dec. 4 and 5, 1975, 66, www.intelligence.senate.gov. Also in 1948, CIA Director Hillenkoetter told lawmakers that some challenges abroad required an immediate operational response. Citing an example, he said, "Any possible action in connection with the Italian election." See U.S. Congress, Senate, *Foreign and Military Intelligence*, 494.

Clifford was a close adviser to Presidents Harry Truman, John F. Kennedy, and Lyndon B. Johnson. For more on the circumstances surrounding his testimony, see chapter 5 of this book, as well as Loch K. Johnson, "Witness Testimony from the Church Committee Hearings on Covert Action, 1975," *Intelligence and National Security* 34, no. 6 (2019): 899–913. For Clifford's personal recollections, see Clark Clifford, *Counsel to the President: A Memoir* (New York: Random House, 1991). For further reading on voter reactions to overt electoral interference—the issue to which Clifford alluded—see Stephen Bloom and Stephen Shulman, "The Legitimacy of Foreign Intervention in Elections: The Ukrainian Response," *Review of International Studies* 38, no. 2 (2012): 445–71; Daniel Corstange and Nikolay Marinov, "Taking Sides in Other People's Elections: The Polarizing Effect of Foreign Intervention," *American Journal of Political Science* 56, no. 3 (2012): 655–70.

49. "NSC 1/3: Position of the United States with Respect to Italy in the Light of the Possibility of Communist Participation in the Government by Legal Means," March 8, 1948, *FRUS, 1948,* vol. III, Western Europe, doc. 475, history.state.gov.

50. Robarge, interview by author, McLean, Va., July 19, 2019.

51. Ibid.; Wyatt, interview by CNN; Gregg, interview by author, Armonk, N.Y., March 17, 2018.

52. Robarge, interview by author; Mistry, *United States, Italy, and the Origins of Cold War,* 135. Conversion to 2020 values executed by U.S. Inflation Calculator, www.usinflationcalculator.com.

53. Robarge, interview by author.

54. Ibid.; Wyatt, interview by CNN.

55. James Clement Dunn, "The Ambassador in Italy (Dunn) to the Secretary of State," June 16, 1948, *FRUS, 1948,* vol. 3, *Western Europe,* doc. 543, history.state.gov.

56. John Lewis Gaddis captures Kennan as a man of "authority," "eloquence," and "grand strategic" instincts in *George F. Kennan: An American Life* (New York: Penguin Press, 2011), 694.

57. George Kennan, "Measures Short of War," George F. Kennan Lectures, National War College, Washington, D.C., Sept. 16, 1946. In February 1946, Kennan had submitted an unusually lengthy cable, known as the Long Telegram, advocating a strategy of containment. Gaddis explains, "If the task at hand was to shift Washington's policy from afar—and Kennan had been trying to do that since the summer of 1944—then . . . the 'long telegram' expressed what Kennan knew, in a form suited for policy makers who needed to know, better than anything else he ever wrote. No other document, whether written by him or anyone else, had the instantaneous influence that this one did." Gaddis, *George F. Kennan,* 222. For further reading on Kennan, see Walter L. Hixson, *George F. Kennan: Cold War Iconoclast* (New York: Columbia University Press, 1989); John Lukacs, *George Kennan: A Study of Character* (New Haven, Conn.: Yale University Press, 2007); Nicholas Thompson, *The Hawk and the Dove: Paul Nitze, George Kennan, and the History of the Cold War* (New York: Henry Holt, 2009).

58. Robarge, interview by author.

59. George Kennan, "The Director of the Policy Planning Staff (Kennan) to the Secretary of State," March 15, 1948, *FRUS, 1948,* vol. 3, *Western*

Europe, doc. 523, history.state.gov. On Kennan's mindset when he sent
this cable, see Gaddis, *George F. Kennan,* 305–7.

60. Kennan, "Director of the Policy Planning Staff (Kennan) to the Secretary
of State," March 15, 1948.

61. Arnaldo Cortesi, "Fear of a Red Coup Rises in Italy; Adriatic Arms Smug-
glers Hunted," *New York Times,* Feb. 5, 1948, timesmachine.nytimes
.com; James Clement Dunn, "The Ambassador (Dunn) to the Secretary
of State," Jan. 12 and 21 and Feb. 7, 1948, *FRUS, 1948,* vol. 3, *Western
Europe,* docs. 505, 506, and 511, history.state.gov.

62. Arnaldo Cortesi, "Rome Denies Plan to Delay Election," *New York
Times,* Feb. 15, 1948, timesmachine.nytimes.com; Central Intelligence
Agency, "Consequences of Communist Accession to Power in Italy by
Legal Means"; Winks, *Cloak and Gown,* 385; "Le mani sull'Italia,"
Panorama, May 2, 1974, in *Dirty Work: The CIA in Western Europe,*
ed. Philip Agee and Louis Wolf (Secaucus, N.J.: L. Stuart, 1978), 171.

63. "Soviet Press Plays Up Italy," *New York Times,* April 18, 1948, times
machine.nytimes.com; Arnaldo Cortesi, "The Great Issue in Italy: Russia
or the U.S.," *New York Times,* April 18, 1948, timesmachine.nytimes
.com; Arnaldo Cortesi, "Millions in Italy at Party Rallies," *New York
Times,* April 12, 1948, timesmachine.nytimes.com; "Italy to Hold Mass
Early on Voting Day," *New York Times,* April 16, 1948, timesmachine
.nytimes.com; Mistry, *United States, Italy, and the Origins of Cold
War,* 150.

64. James Clement Dunn, "The Ambassador in Italy (Dunn) to the Secretary
of State," April 20, 1948, *FRUS, 1948,* vol. 3, *Western Europe,* doc. 541,
history.state.gov; C. L. Sulzberger, "Italian Reds Rule Out Coup; Two
Arms Depots Attacked," *New York Times,* April 19, 1948, timesmachine
.nytimes.com; Arnaldo Cortesi, "Communists Lose in Italy; De Gasperi
Leads by 3 to 2 and May Hold a Majority," *New York Times,* April 20,
1948, timesmachine.nytimes.com.

  In a letter dated March 26, 1948, Vyacheslav Molotov, the Soviet
foreign minister, had instructed the Soviet ambassador in Italy to warn
Togliatti against launching an armed insurrection. Silvio Pons, in his
analysis of this letter, explains, "Stalin had concluded that any significant
involvement by either the Soviet Union or the newly solidified 'socialist
camp' in a conflict in a Western country would be a grave mistake." Pons,
"Stalin, Togliatti, and the Origins of the Cold War in Europe," 20–21.

65. Camille Cianfarra, "Pope Expresses Joy over Vote; 3 Nations Offered
Him a Haven," *New York Times,* April 20, 1948, timesmachine.nytimes
.com; "Truman Hails Outcome of Elections in Italy," *New York Times,*
April 23, 1948, timesmachine.nytimes.com; "First ERP Ship Reaches
Italy," *New York Times,* June 1, 1948, timesmachine.nytimes.com.

  Thomas Dewey, Truman's Republican opponent, also commented on
the outcome of the election, telegraphing De Gasperi that "our hopes
and prayers have been answered by the smashing triumph of free men

over totalitarian communism." See "Dewey Hails Italy's Vote," *New York Times,* April 21, 1948, timesmachine.nytimes.com. For further reading, see Robert A. Divine, *Foreign Policy and U.S. Presidential Elections, 1940–1948* (New York: New Viewpoints, 1974).

66. "Tagliatti Admits Reds Lost 1,000,000 Votes," *New York Times,* May 6, 1948, timesmachine.nytimes.com; "Italian Reds Accuse Clergy on Election," *New York Times,* June 9, 1948, timesmachine.nytimes.com; Ventresca, *From Fascism to Democracy,* 20.

67. "Appeal to Voters in Italy Assailed," *New York Times,* April 15, 1948, timesmachine.nytimes.com. On the penetrability of U.S. elections during the Cold War, see chapter 5 of this book.

68. Wyatt, interview by CNN; Inman, interview by author, Austin, Tex., Nov. 2, 2018; Negroponte, phone interview by author, May 21, 2019.

69. Robarge, interview by author.

70. Wippl, phone interview by author, Nov. 8, 2018.

71. Central Intelligence Agency, "Analysis of the Power of the Communist Parties of France and Italy and of Measures to Counter Them," by Allen Dulles, Sept. 15, 1951 (declassified Dec. 2006), www.cia.gov. In Italy's 1951 local elections, this memorandum records, the Christian Democrats lost their "substantial popular majority." On July 9 of that year, representatives from the CIA, the State Department, and the Defense Department gathered in Harriman's office to discuss, in part, how to covertly weaken Italy's Communist Party. A few weeks later, Dulles held a meeting at the U.S. Embassy in Rome with the same agenda.

For further reading on Harriman, see Rudy Abramson, *Spanning the Century: The Life of W. Averell Harriman, 1891–1986* (New York: William Morrow, 1992); Walter Isaacson and Evan Thomas, *The Wise Men: Six Friends and the World They Made* (New York: Simon & Schuster, 1986). For further reading on Dulles, see Peter Grose, *Gentleman Spy: The Life of Allen Dulles* (Boston: Houghton Mifflin, 1994); Stephen Kinzer, *The Brothers: John Foster Dulles, Allen Dulles, and Their Secret World War* (New York: Times Books, 2013).

72. Central Intelligence Agency, "Analysis of the Power of the Communist Parties of France and Italy and of Measures to Counter Them," cover note. U.S. officials expressed concerns similar to Dulles's continually. In 1953, the CIA compiled reports on "the continuing strength of the Italian Communist Party" and the "uncertain future" of De Gasperi's government. Another CIA memorandum, written a few years later, assessed the various sources of the Communist Party's strength in Italy, including its well-funded and "massive propaganda campaigns." See Central Intelligence Agency, "The Continuing Strength of the Italian Communist Party," May 28, 1953 (declassified Jan. 2002), www.cia.gov; Central Intelligence Agency, "The Italian Elections," June 9, 1953 (declassified Aug. 2000), www.cia.gov; Central Intelligence Agency, "Status and Strength of the Italian Communist Party (PCI)," exact date of issuance unclear (declassified July 2001), www.cia.gov.

73. Central Intelligence Agency, "Analysis of the Power of the Communist Parties of France and Italy and of Measures to Counter Them," cover note.

74. These figures and dates are from a memorandum that emerged while the U.S. Congress was investigating the CIA in the mid-1970s, taken from *CIA: The Pike Report* (Nottingham, U.K.: Spokesman, 1977), 204–6. Conversion information from U.S. Inflation Calculator, www.usinflation calculator.com, using a baseline of 1958.

75. Central Intelligence Agency, "Analysis of the Power of the Communist Parties of France and Italy and of Measures to Counter Them," exhibit 3.

76. William Colby, *Honorable Men: My Life in the CIA* (New York: Simon & Schuster, 1978), 109, 110, 116. Bobby Inman, the former CIA deputy director, told me that "Colby made his reputation in the Italian elections." While in Italy, Colby worked closely with Clare Boothe Luce, who became the U.S. ambassador there in 1953. Alessandro Brogi, "Ike and Italy: The Eisenhower Administration and Italy's 'Neo-Atlanticist Agenda,'" *Journal of Cold War Studies* 4, no. 3 (2002): 5–35; Inman, interview by author. For further reading on Colby's career, see John Prados, *Lost Crusader: The Secret Wars of CIA Director William Colby* (New York: Oxford University Press, 2003).

77. Fina, interview by Charles Kennedy, May 21, 1992, Association for Diplomatic Studies and Training, www.adst.org; Colby, *Honorable Men,* 119, in which he further explained, "Washington wanted the ability to place stories in non-American media around the world and then cause its other 'outlets' to pick up and publicize it."

78. Colby, *Honorable Men,* 120. Stansfield Turner, CIA director between 1977 and 1981, explained in his memoirs that cutouts enabled the agency to pass "funds to foreign groups that needed help without those groups knowing their source was the CIA." During his tenure, he continued, the CIA used cutouts to direct more than $10 million annually to "useful and friendly groups" overseas. Stansfield Turner, *Secrecy and Democracy: The CIA in Transition* (Boston: Houghton Mifflin, 1985), 77.

79. Dulles, "Analysis of the Power of the Communist Parties of France and Italy and of Measures to Counter Them," cover note. See also Mario Del Pero, "The United States and Psychological Warfare in Italy, 1948–1955," *Journal of American History* 87, no. 4 (2001): 1304–34.

80. Central Intelligence Agency, "Analysis of the Power of the Communist Parties of France and Italy and of Measures to Counter Them," exhibit 3.

81. Central Intelligence Agency, "Memorandum for the Record," Jan. 29, 1953 (declassified Aug. 2000), www.cia.gov.

82. Colby, *Honorable Men,* 114, 130. Indeed, Richard Drake writes, "For decades the Soviet Union gave more money to the [Italian Communist Party] than to any other non-ruling Communist party." Richard Drake, "The Soviet Dimension of Italian Communism," *Journal of Cold War Studies* 6, no. 3 (2004): 116.

83. "NSC 68," April 14, 1950, *FRUS*, 1950, vol. I, National Security Affairs;

Foreign Economic Policy, doc. 85, history.state.gov. For elaboration on NSC 68 and its impact, see Ken Young, "Revisiting NSC 68," *Journal of Cold War Studies* 15, no. 1 (2013): 3–33; Curt Caldwell, *NSC 68 and the Political Economy of the Early Cold War* (New York: Cambridge University Press, 2011); Ernest May, *American Cold War Strategy: Interpreting NSC 68* (Boston: St. Martin's, 1993).

84. While investigating the CIA decades later, a congressional committee found, "Covert action projects were first designed to counter the Soviet threat in Europe and were, at least initially, a limited and ad hoc response to an exceptional threat to American security. Covert action soon became a routine program of influencing governments and covertly exercising power—involving literally hundreds of projects each year. By 1953 there were major covert operations underway in 48 countries, consisting of propaganda, paramilitary and political action projects." U.S. Congress, Senate, *Foreign and Military Intelligence,* 153. For a general history of the CIA's Cold War operations, see James Callanan, *Covert Action in the Cold War: US Policy, Intelligence, and CIA Operations* (London: I. B. Tauris, 2009).

85. Miles Copeland, *Without Cloak or Dagger: The Truth About the New Espionage* (New York: Simon & Schuster, 1974), 11.

86. Shelton-Colby, interview by author, Washington, D.C., July 18, 2019.

CHAPTER 3: THE EXPLOSION

1. Robarge, interview by author, McLean, Va., July 19, 2019. See also note 21 of the introduction of this book.

2. Inman, interview by author, Austin, Tex., Nov. 2, 2018. For further consideration of Cold War power dynamics, see Robert Jervis, "Was the Cold War a Security Dilemma?," *Journal of Cold War Studies* 3, no. 1 (2001): 36–60; William C. Wohlforth, *The Elusive Balance: Power and Perceptions During the Cold War* (Ithaca, N.Y.: Cornell University Press, 1993).

3. Westad, *Cold War,* 627; Odd Arne Westad, *The Global Cold War: Third World Interventions and the Making of Our Times* (Cambridge, U.K.: Cambridge University Press, 2007), 3.

4. Muñoz, phone interview by author, July 20, 2019.

5. This figure became part of the public record after the Soviet Union collapsed, when Russian prosecutors investigated where the Soviet Politburo had directed state funds. See Celestine Bohlen, "Gorbachev Enabled Party Money to Be Invested, a Hearing Is Told," *New York Times,* Feb. 11, 1992, www.nytimes.com. Conversion information from U.S. Inflation Calculator, www.usinflationcalculator.com, using a baseline of 1985.

6. Andrew and Mitrokhin, *The Sword and the Shield,* 293–97, which further explains that Moscow's support did have its limits. In early 1972, Luigi Longo, Italy's Communist leader, requested increasingly more money as an election approached. In a personal reply, Leonid Brezhnev, the Soviet

leader, granted Longo another $500,000 while emphasizing "at the present time, there is no more that we can do."

Officials in Moscow also valued the influence they established over the foreign parties they funded. "The tight link between Moscow and the West European Communist parties required the parties to subordinate their interests to those of the Soviet Union," writes Silvio Pons in "Stalin, Togliatti, and the Origins of the Cold War in Europe," 5.

7. Andrew and Mitrokhin, *The Sword and the Shield,* 305, 451–55. For further reading on Marchais, see Jeffrey Vanke, "Georges Marchais and the Decline of French Communism," *Journal of Cold War Studies* 6, no. 1 (2004): 90–94.

8. Westad thus writes, "U.S. involvements were perceived in America as defensive interventions, mainly against left-wing or Communist movements," in *Global Cold War,* 111, regarding America's interventionist activities generally. The CIA was also active in the Soviet Union's sphere of influence, executing operations that had nothing to do with elections. For example, the CIA helped organize and fund Radio Free Europe, which broadcast pro-U.S. propaganda across the Eastern bloc. See A. Ross Johnson, *Radio Free Europe and Radio Liberty: The CIA Years and Beyond* (Stanford, Calif.: Stanford University Press, 2010); Sig Mickelson, *America's Other Voice: The Story of Radio Free Europe and Radio Liberty* (New York: Praeger, 1983). For more general reading, see Laura A. Belmonte, *Selling the American Way: U.S. Propaganda and the Cold War* (Philadelphia: University of Pennsylvania Press, 2008); Nicholas Cull, *The Cold War and the United States Information Agency: American Propaganda and Public Diplomacy, 1945–1989* (Cambridge, U.K.: Cambridge University Press, 2008).

9. "Editorial Note," *FRUS, 1964–1968,* vol. 29, pt. 2, *Japan,* doc. 1, history .state.gov; Robarge, interview by author.

10. Tim Weiner, "C.I.A. Spent Millions to Support Japanese Right in 50's and 60's," *New York Times,* Oct. 9, 1994, www.nytimes.com.

11. Dean Rusk, "Memorandum from Secretary of State Rusk to President Johnson," Feb. 6, 1964, *FRUS, 1964–1968,* vol. 32, *Dominican Republic; Cuba; Haiti; Guyana,* doc. 371, history.state.gov; "Editorial Note," *FRUS, 1964–1968,* vol. 32, *Dominican Republic; Cuba; Haiti; Guyana,* doc. 370, history.state.gov.

12. "Memorandum Prepared for the 303 Committee," March 17, 1967, *FRUS, 1964–1968,* vol. 32, *Dominican Republic; Cuba; Haiti; Guyana,* doc. 421, history.state.gov.

13. "Editorial Note," doc. 370; Richard Meislin, "Guyana's Leader Dies; Successor Is Sworn In," *New York Times,* Aug. 7, 1985, www.nytimes.com.

14. Henry Kissinger, "Memorandum for the President: Exploitation of Tensions in the Soviet Union and Eastern Europe," April 9, 1970, taken from CIA General Records (declassified Feb. 2010), www.cia.gov. For further reading on Kissinger, see Walter Isaacson, *Kissinger: A Biography* (New York: Simon & Schuster, 1992).

15. Henry Kissinger, "Memorandum from the President's Assistant for National Security Affairs (Kissinger) to President Nixon," n.d., *FRUS, 1969–1976,* vol. 12, *Soviet Union, January 1969–October 1970,* doc. 149.

16. Goss, interview by author, Florida Keys, Fla., Dec. 26, 2018.

17. "Allende, a Man of the Privileged Class Turned Radical Politician," *New York Times,* Sept. 12, 1973, timesmachine.nytimes.com; Simon Collier and William Sater, *A History of Chile, 1808–2002* (Cambridge, U.K.: Cambridge University Press, 2004), 258; Kristian Gustafson, *Hostile Intent: U.S. Covert Operations in Chile, 1964–1974* (Washington, D.C.: Potomac Books, 2007), 19–24. For further reading on the evolution of Allende and the Chilean left, see Peter Winn, *Weavers of Revolution: The Yarur Workers and Chile's Road to Socialism* (New York: Oxford University Press, 1986), chap. 3.

18. Ferocious critiques of American foreign policy followed in the public square. The CIA tracked these criticisms internally. For example, the agency cataloged an article published by Willard Barber, a former State Department official, titled "Are We Losing Latins to Reds?," in which he warned of "Russian and Chinese Communists efforts" to establish influence over countries like Chile. See Willard Barber, "Are We Losing Latins to Reds?," *Washington Post,* Jan. 6, 1963, taken from CIA General Records (declassified June 2000), www.cia.gov. Similarly, the CIA recorded a column by Robert Morris, a conservative politican, titled "Reds Map Plan to Win Latins," in which he complained about Washington's passive response to Moscow's plan "to conquer the world." According to an Eastern defector, Morris continued, Castro and Moscow had resolved to create "what is called in the Kremlin—the USRLA—the United Socialist Republics of Latin America." Within a few years, he went on, this leftist alliance would include Chile. See Robert Morris, "Reds Map Plan to Win Latins," publication unclear, Oct. 23, 1963, taken from CIA General Records (declassified March 2001), www.cia.gov. On international reactions to Castro's rise, see Tanya Harmer, "The 'Cuban Question' and the Cold War in Latin America, 1959–1964," *Journal of Cold War Studies* 21, no. 3 (2019): 114–51.

19. Kalugin, interview by author, Rockville, Md., Aug. 7, 2018; Tanya Harmer, *Allende's Chile and the Inter-American Cold War* (Chapel Hill: University of North Carolina Press, 2011), 21, 34, 36; Central Intelligence Agency, "Communist Penetration of Latin America," NSC Briefing, Dec. 15, 1959, www.cia.gov. On the differing strategies of Castro and Allende, see Jonathan Haslam, *The Nixon Administration and the Death of Allende's Chile: A Case of Assisted Suicide* (London: Verso Press, 2005), 30.

20. Robert A. Hurwitch, "Letter from the First Secretary of the Embassy in Chile (Hurwitch) to the President's Special Assistant for National Security Affairs (Bundy)," June 19, 1964, *FRUS, 1964–1968,* vol. 31, *South and Central America; Mexico,* doc. 259, history.state.gov; "Telegram from

the Embassy in Chile to the Department of State," April 22, 1964, *FRUS, 1964–1968*, vol. 31, *South and Central America; Mexico,* doc. 251, history.state.gov.

The CIA reported in a memorandum that Allende's Socialist Party "usually follows the Communist line," and forecast in the president's daily brief that "the Communists [would have] a large say" in an Allende-led government. See Central Intelligence Agency, "Current Intelligence Memorandum: Chilean Congressional Elections of 5 March 1961," Feb. 7, 1961 (declassified Aug. 2001), www.cia.gov; Central Intelligence Agency, "The President's Intelligence Checklist," March 17, 1964 (declassified July 2015), www.cia.gov.

21. U.S. Congress, Senate, Select Committee to Study Governmental Operations with Respect to Intelligence Activities, *Covert Action in Chile, 1963–1973,* 94th Cong., 1st sess., 1975, 4. John F. Kennedy had announced the Alliance for Progress in 1961, declaring in his inaugural address that it would "assist free men and free governments in casting off the chains of poverty." By 1964, America had directed more than $1.5 billion into this initiative. Chile received the most support per capita of any country in the region. In all, between 1962 and 1970, the United States provided Chile $1.2 billion in economic grants and loans, as well as $91 million in military aid. See John F. Kennedy, "Inaugural Address" (speech, Washington, D.C., Jan. 20, 1961), Avalon Project, avalon.law .yale.edu; "Fruitful Year Is Forecast for Alliance for Progress," *New York Times,* Jan. 17, 1964, www.nytimes.com; Peter Kornbluh, *The Pinochet File: A Declassified Dossier on Atrocity and Accountability* (New York: New Press, 2003), 5–6.

22. Hurwitch, "Letter from the First Secretary of the Embassy in Chile"; "Chile: The Crucial Choice," *Time,* April 17, 1964, taken from CIA General Records (declassified March 2012), www.cia.gov. From the perspective of the CIA, David Robarge writes, "US policymakers believed a socialist regime in Chile would give the Soviet Union a satellite in Latin America that potentially was more useful than Cuba for starting a radical 'chain reaction' in unstable countries in the region, including Argentina, Bolivia, Brazil, and Colombia." David Robarge, *John McCone as Director of Central Intelligence, 1961–1965* (Washington, D.C.: Central Intelligence Agency, published internally in 2005, declassified in April 2015), 286.

23. MITN 2/22, entries 343 and 368, Papers of Vasili Mitrokhin, Churchill College, Cambridge University.

24. Gustafson, *Hostile Intent,* 32.

25. MITN 2/22, entry 368, Papers of Mitrokhin.

26. Kalugin, interview by author.

27. Central Intelligence Agency, "The President's Intelligence Checklist," March 21, 1964 (declassified July 2015), www.cia.gov; Central Intelligence Agency, "The President's Intelligence Checklist," April 23, 1964 (declassified July 2015), www.cia.gov.

28. Robarge, *John McCone,* 284; U.S. Congress, Senate, *Foreign and Military Intelligence,* bk. 1, 46, 57, which found that fewer than one-fifth of all covert action projects reached the Special Group.

29. U.S. Congress, Senate, *Covert Action in Chile,* 5, 14; Ralph Dungan, "Memorandum from the President's Special Assistant (Dungan) to the President's Special Assistant for National Security Affairs (Bundy)," Jan. 18, 1964, *FRUS, 1964–1968,* vol. 31, *South and Central America; Mexico,* doc. 246, history.state.gov.

30. "Chile's Leftist Candidate Vows Legal Seizure of U.S. Concerns," *New York Times,* June 7, 1964, www.nytimes.com.

31. U.S. Congress, Senate, *Covert Action in Chile,* 15; Gustafson, *Hostile Intent,* 44; "Editorial Note," *FRUS, 1964–1968,* vol. 31, *South and Central America; Mexico,* doc. 258, history.state.gov.

32. Gordon Chase, "Memorandum from Gordon Chase of the National Security Council Staff to the President's Special Assistant for National Security Affairs (Bundy)," March 19, 1964, *FRUS, 1964–1968,* vol. 31, *South and Central America; Mexico,* doc. 249, history.state.gov.

    In 1962 and 1963, the Special Group had sanctioned one-off, non-attributable payments to Chile's Christian Democratic Party and the more reliably conservative Democratic Front. But in early 1964, the Democratic Front, made up of the Radical, Liberal, and Conservative Parties, disbanded. Frei, who identified as a non-Marxist, thus became the only viable alternative to a candidate whom Washington associated with Soviet influence. See U.S. Congress, Senate, *Covert Action in Chile,* 5, 15.

33. "Memorandum Prepared for the Special Group," April 1, 1964, *FRUS, 1964–1968,* vol. 31, *South and Central America; Mexico,* doc. 250, history.state.gov.

34. Ibid. In 1964, it seems, American officials would not consider supporting a military coup against a prospective Allende administration. The U.S. Congress later found, "On July 19, 1964, the Chilean Defense Council, which is the equivalent of the U.S. Joint Chiefs of Staff, went to [the outgoing Chilean president] to propose a coup d'état if Allende won. This offer was transmitted to the CIA Chief of Station, who told the Chilean Defense Council through an intermediary that the United States was absolutely opposed to a coup." U.S. Congress, Senate, *Covert Action in Chile,* 16–17.

35. Joseph Caldwell King, "Memorandum from the Chief of the Western Hemisphere Division (King) to Director of Central Intelligence McCone," Jan. 3, 1964, *FRUS, 1964–1968,* vol. 31, *South and Central America; Mexico,* doc. 245, history.state.gov.

36. "Memorandum Prepared for the Special Group," doc. 250.

37. U.S. Congress, Senate, *Covert Action in Chile,* 16.

38. "Transcript of Telephone Conversation Between Director of Central Intelligence McCone and the Assistant Secretary of State for Inter-American Affairs (Mann)," April 28, 1964, *FRUS, 1964–1968,* vol. 31, *South and Central America; Mexico,* doc. 252, history.state.gov; Thomas Mann,

"Memorandum from the Assistant Secretary of State for Inter-American Affairs (Mann) to Secretary of State Rusk," May 1, 1964, *FRUS, 1964–1968*, vol. 31, *South and Central America; Mexico*, doc. 253, history .state.gov.

39. "Telephone Conversation Between President Johnson and the Assistant Secretary of State for Inter-American Affairs (Mann)," June 11, 1964, *FRUS, 1964–1968*, vol. 31, *South and Central America; Mexico*, doc. 16, history.state.gov.

40. U.S. Congress, Senate, *Covert Action in Chile*, 9, 15.

41. Ibid., 15; Margaret Power, "The Engendering of Anticommunism and Fear in Chile's 1964 Presidential Election," *Diplomatic History* 32, no. 5 (2008): 933, 939, in which Power further explains that in the 1958 election "women's electoral preferences were decisive to determining which candidate won," and "this realization explains why the U.S. government viewed capturing women's votes as critical to winning the 1964 presidential election."

42. U.S. Congress, Senate, *Covert Action in Chile*, 7–8, 15.

43. Ibid., 16; "Editorial Note," doc. 258; "Editorial Note," *FRUS, 1964–1968*, vol. 31, *South and Central America; Mexico*, doc. 262, history .state.gov.

44. "Editorial Note," doc. 262. Bundy found some comfort in internal polling, informing Johnson, in July, that forecasts were promising but that victory still was not assured. "The Christian Democrats are coming from behind," Bundy warned. "They now have a good organization but they have to guard against over-confidence and fight all the way to the finish line if they hope to win." See McGeorge Bundy, "Information Memorandum from the President's Special Assistant for National Security Affairs (Bundy) to President Johnson," July 8, 1964, *FRUS, 1964–1968*, vol. 31, *South and Central America; Mexico*, doc. 261, history.state.gov.

45. U.S. Congress, Senate, *Covert Action in Chile*, 1, 9. Conversion to 2020 values executed by U.S. Inflation Calculator, www.usinflationcalculator .com.

46. McGeorge Bundy, "Memorandum from the President's Special Assistant for National Security Affairs (Bundy) to President Johnson," Aug. 13, 1964, *FRUS, 1964–1968*, vol. 31, *South and Central America; Mexico*, doc. 265, history.state.gov. In Washington, the CIA had forecast ahead of time that Chile might terminate its relations with Cuba before the election. See Central Intelligence Agency, "The President's Intelligence Checklist," Aug. 10, 1964, www.cia.gov.

47. Central Intelligence Agency, "The President's Intelligence Review," July 29–31, Aug. 26–28, and Aug. 29–Sept. 1, 1964 (declassified July–Aug. 2015), www.cia.gov; "Memorandum Prepared in the Central Intelligence Agency," Sept. 1, 1964, *FRUS, 1964–1968*, vol. 31, *South and Central America; Mexico*, doc. 268, history.state.gov. On the environment in Chile just before the election, see Henry Raymont, "Chile Acts to Insure

Orderly Presidential Voting," *New York Times,* Sept. 1, 1964, times
machine.nytimes.com; Henry Raymont, "Candidate Seeks Nonaligned
Chile," *New York Times,* Aug. 31, 1964, timesmachine.nytimes.com.

48. "Editorial Note," *FRUS, 1964–1968,* vol. 31, *South and Central America; Mexico,* doc. 269, history.state.gov; Central Intelligence Agency,
"The President's Intelligence Checklist," Sept. 5, 1964 (declassified July
2015), www.cia.gov; Henry Raymont, "Frei, a Moderate, Elected to the
Presidency of Chile," *New York Times,* Sept. 5, 1964, www.nytimes.com.

49. Thomas Hughes, "Intelligence Note from the Director of the Bureau of
Intelligence and Research (Hughes) to Secretary of State Rusk," Sept. 5,
1964, *FRUS, 1964–1968,* vol. 31, *South and Central America; Mexico,*
doc. 270, history.state.gov; Henry Raymont, "Frei, Victor in Chile, Vows
Cooperation with the U.S.," *New York Times,* Sept. 6, 1964, times
machine.nytimes.com; Henry Raymont, "Chileans Install Frei as President," *New York Times,* Nov. 4, 1964, timesmachine.nytimes.com.

50. Robarge, interview by author; Central Intelligence Agency, "The President's Intelligence Checklist," Sept. 5, 1964 (declassified July 2015), www
.cia.gov; "Editorial Note," doc. 269.

51. "Editorial Note," doc. 269; "Transcript of the President's News Conference on Foreign and Domestic Matters," *New York Times,* Sept. 6, 1964,
www.nytimes.com. See also Henry Raymont, "Prospect of a Marxist
Victory in Chilean Election Causes Wide Concern in Hemisphere," *New
York Times,* Sept. 3, 1964, timesmachine.nytimes.com.

52. McLaughlin, phone interview by author, Sept. 5, 2019.

53. Central Intelligence Agency, "The President's Intelligence Checklist,"
Sept. 3, 1964 (declassified July 2015), www.cia.gov; "Chile: The Cru-
cial Choice"; Raymont, "Frei, a Moderate, Elected to the Presidency of
Chile."

54. U.S. Congress, Senate, *Covert Action in Chile,* 54. Gustafson explains,
"The United States had effectively, and with consent, undermined the
credibility of the Frei government and the [Christian Democratic Party]
by aligning too closely with them." Gustafson, *Hostile Intent,* 49.

55. Tom Wicker, "Johnson Says He Won't Run," *New York Times,* April
1, 1968, timesmachine.nytimes.com; "Vietnam War Casualty Statistics,"
National Archives, accessed online; John Lewis Gaddis, *The Cold War:
A New History* (New York: Penguin Press, 2005), 133. On Moscow's
relationship with the Frei administration, see Rafael Pedemonte, "A Case
of 'New Soviet Internationalism': Relations Between the USSR and Chile's
Christian Democratic Government, 1964–1970," *Journal of Cold War
Studies* 21, no. 3 (2019): 4–25.

56. U.S. Congress, Senate, *Covert Action in Chile 1963–1973,* 57; "Memorandum for the 303 Committee, Final Report: March 1969 Chilean
Congressional Election," March 14, 1969, *FRUS, 1969–1976,* vol. 21,
Chile, 1969–1973, doc. 3, history.state.gov. The U.S. Senate further
found, "In the years between 1962 and 1969, Chile received well over

a billion dollars in direct, overt United States aid, loans and grants both included." U.S. Congress, Senate, *Covert Action in Chile,* 4. In addition to this overt aid, Kornbluh explains, the United States "pressured major U.S. corporations, particularly the two copper giants, Anaconda and Kennecott, which dominated the Chilean economy, to modernize and expand their investments and operations." Kornbluh, *Pinochet File,* 5.

57. Central Intelligence Agency, "The President's Daily Brief," Feb. 7, April 2, May 2, and July 24, 1968 (declassified July 2015), www.cia.gov; Central Intelligence Agency, "Intelligence Memorandum: The Chilean Economy: Trends Under Frei and Prospects for 1969–1970," April 1969 (declassified Jan. 2012), www.cia.gov.

58. Henry Kissinger, "Memorandum from the President's Assistant for National Security Affairs (Kissinger) to President Nixon," July 11, 1969, *FRUS, 1969–1976,* vol. 21, *Chile, 1969–1973,* doc. 17, history.state.gov; Central Intelligence Agency, "Chilean Problems and Frei's Prospects," March 4, 1968 (declassified Aug. 2006), www.cia.gov. According to the U.S. Senate, "To deal with the American copper companies, Frei proposed 'Chileanization,' by which the state would purchase majority ownership in order to exercise control and stimulate output. Frei's reforms, while impressive, fell far short of what he had promised." U.S. Congress, Senate, *Covert Action in Chile,* 5. See also John Fleming, "The Nationalization of Chile's Large Copper Companies in Contemporary Interstate Relations," *Villanova Law Review* 18, no. 4 (1973), digitalcommons.law.villanova.edu.

59. U.S. Congress, Senate, *Covert Action in Chile,* 20; "Editorial Note," *FRUS, 1964–1968,* vol. 31, *South and Central America; Mexico,* doc. 273, history.state.gov; "Memorandum for the 303 Committee," Jan. 25, 1965, *FRUS, 1964–1968,* vol. 31, *South and Central America; Mexico,* doc. 277, history.state.gov; William Broe, "Memorandum from the Chief of the Western Hemisphere Division (Broe) to the Deputy Director for Plans, Central Intelligence Agency (Karamessines)," April 26, 1968, *FRUS, 1964–1968,* vol. 31, *South and Central America; Mexico,* doc. 304, history.state.gov; "Memorandum for the 303 Committee," doc. 3.

60. "Memorandum for the 303 Committee," doc. 3; "Telegram from the Embassy in Chile to the Department of State," March 25, 1969, *FRUS, 1969–1976,* vol. 21, *Chile, 1969–1973,* doc. 5, history.state.gov; "Memorandum for the Record, Minutes of the Meeting of the 303 Committee, 15 April 1969," April 17, 1969, *FRUS, 1969–1976,* vol. 21, *Chile, 1969–1973,* doc. 7, history.state.gov.

61. "Chilean Left Finally Picks Allende to Run for President," *New York Times,* Jan. 23, 1970, www.nytimes.com; Central Intelligence Agency, "The President's Daily Brief," Jan. 24, 1970, www.cia.gov; "Memorandum for the 40 Committee, Political Action Related to 1970 Chilean Presidential Election," March 5, 1970, *FRUS, 1969–1976,* vol. 21, *Chile, 1969–1973,* doc. 29, history.state.gov.

Frei, term-limited, could not run for president in 1970. See Haslam, *The Nixon Administration*, 37.

62. "Memorandum for the 40 Committee," doc. 29.

63. "Memorandum for the Record, Discussion of U.S. Government Activities Leading Up to the Chilean Election in September 1970," Jan. 19, 1970, *FRUS, 1969–1976,* vol. 21, *Chile, 1969–1973,* doc. 28, history.state.gov.

64. Viron Vaky, "Memorandum by Viron P. Vaky of the National Security Council Staff," March 25, 1970, *FRUS, 1969–1976,* vol. 21, *Chile, 1969–1973,* doc. 30, history.state.gov; U.S. Congress, Senate, *Covert Action in Chile,* 43.

65. U.S. Congress, Senate, *Covert Action in Chile,* 21–22; Devine, interview by author, New York, Feb. 21, 2019.

66. Malcolm Browne, "Most Parties in Chile Find C.I.A. a Useful Target," *New York Times,* Dec. 24, 1969, www.cia.gov; "Memorandum for the 40 Committee," doc. 29.

67. Richard Helms, "Memorandum from Director of Central Intelligence Helms to the President's Assistant for National Security Affairs (Kissinger)," June 16, 1970, *FRUS, 1969–1976,* vol. 21, *Chile, 1969–1973,* doc. 34, history.state.gov; "Memorandum for the Record: Minutes of the Meeting of the 40 Committee," June 27, 1970, *FRUS, 1969–1976,* vol. 21, *Chile, 1969–1973,* doc. 41, history.state.gov; Viron Vaky, "Memorandum from Viron P. Vaky of the National Security Council Staff to the President's Assistant for National Security Affairs (Kissinger)," June 23, 1970, *FRUS, 1969–1976,* vol. 21, *Chile, 1969–1973,* doc. 39, history .state.gov.

68. Henry Kissinger, *White House Years* (New York: Simon & Schuster, 1979), 667.

69. U.S. Congress, Senate, *Covert Action in Chile,* 20. Helms, in his memoirs, wrote that "the cost and extent" of the CIA's electoral interference operation "was but a fraction of the Soviet and Cuban effort in Chile." Richard Helms, *A Look over My Shoulder: A Life in the Central Intelligence Agency* (New York: Random House, 2003), 400.

70. MITN 2/22, entry 368, Papers of Mitrokhin.

71. Christopher Andrew and Vasili Mitrokhin, *The World Was Going Our Way: The KGB and the Battle for the Third World* (New York: Basic Books, 2005), 72; MITN 2/22, entry 41, Papers of Mitrokhin.

72. MITN 2/22, entry 368, Papers of Mitrokhin.

73. Henry Kissinger, "National Security Study Memorandum 97," July 24, 1970, *FRUS, 1969–1976,* vol. 21, *Chile, 1969–1973,* doc. 46, history .state.gov.

74. "NSSM 97—Chile," *FRUS, 1969–1976,* vol. E-16, *Documents on Chile,* doc. 13, history.state.gov. NSSM 97 also contained a secret CIA annex analyzing whether and how to stage a coup d'état in Chile, were Allende to win. This annex concluded that this policy should be pursued only if the United States believed that Allende posed "a security threat . . . sufficiently great to justify a covert effort to overthrow him." See "Annex

NSSM 97," *FRUS, 1969–1976,* vol. E-16, *Documents on Chile,* doc. 14, history.state.gov.

75. Central Intelligence Agency, "The President's Daily Brief," Dec. 3, 1969, June 30, Sept. 3, and Sept. 4, 1970 (declassified April 2016), www.cia .gov.

76. Juan de Onis, "Allende, Chilean Marxist, Wins Vote for Presidency," *New York Times,* Sept. 6, 1970, www.nytimes.com; John Foran, *Taking Power: On the Origins of Third World Revolutions* (Cambridge, U.K.: Cambridge University Press, 2005), 163.

77. Central Intelligence Agency, "Intelligence Memorandum: Reactions in Latin America to Allende's Victory in Chile," Sept. 17, 1970 (declassified Feb. 2008), www.cia.gov. For elaboration on overseas reactions to Allende's triumph, see Sebastián Hurtado-Torres, "The Chilean Moment in the Global Cold War: International Reactions to Salvador Allende's Victory in the Presidential Election of 1970," *Journal of Cold War Studies* 21, no. 3 (2019): 26–55.

78. Robarge, interview by author; Devine, interview by author.

79. U.S. Congress, Senate, *Covert Action in Chile,* 54; Kissinger, *White House Years,* 669.

80. Of Nixon's immediate reaction to Allende's victory, Westad writes, "In Washington Allende's victory in the 1970 elections set off near panic. President Nixon thought Chile would develop into a second Cuba, with enormous consequences for Latin America and for the Cold War in the rest of the world. Détente with Moscow did not diminish this perspective. On the contrary, both Nixon and Kissinger believed that if Allende was able to succeed in Chile, then the Soviets would be less likely to cooperate with the United States elsewhere. With Allende's victory in a democratic election, the Soviets had a 'Red sandwich' between Havana and Santiago, which could engulf all of Latin America, Nixon asserted later." Westad, *Cold War,* 356.

81. "Minutes of a Meeting of the Special Review Group," Aug. 19, 1970, *FRUS, 1969–1976,* vol. 21, *Chile, 1969–1973,* doc. 53, history.state.gov.

82. Charles Meyer, "Memorandum from the Assistant Secretary of State for Inter-American Affairs (Meyer) to the Under Secretary of State for Political Affairs (Johnson)," Aug. 31, 1970, *FRUS, 1969–1976,* vol. 21, *Chile, 1969–1973,* doc. 58, history.state.gov.

83. On Alessandri, see Joseph Novitski, "Political Deal Urged in Chile to Keep Allende from the Presidency," *New York Times,* Sept. 12, 1970, timesmachine.nytimes.com; Central Intelligence Agency, "The President's Daily Brief," Sept. 11, 1970 (declassified April 2016), www.cia.gov. On Washington's decision making, see Edward Korry, "Telegram from the Embassy in Chile to the Department of State," Sept. 8, 1970, *FRUS, 1969–1976,* vol. 21, *Chile, 1969–1973,* doc. 68, history.state.gov; U.S. Congress, Senate, *Covert Action in Chile,* 23–25. Back in June, Korry had advocated authorizing funds for vote buying, but the 40 Committee had opted to delay "any decision on the buying of congressional votes"

until after the election, because "the risks in eventually embarking on this course were apparent." See "Memorandum for the Record," doc. 41; Viron Vaky, doc. 39.

84. "Memorandum for the Record, Discussion of Chilean Political Situation," Sept. 14, 1970, *FRUS, 1969–1976,* vol. 21, *Chile, 1969–1973,* doc. 89, history.state.gov. See also Joseph Novitski, "Chile's Christian Democrats Fail to Decide on Presidential Vote," *New York Times,* Oct. 5, 1970, timesmachine.nytimes.com.

    In a series of intelligence briefings between September 7 and 14, the CIA reported that Allende would almost certainly win the congressional vote. See Central Intelligence Agency, "The President's Daily Brief," Sept. 7, 8, and 14, 1970 (declassified April 2016), www.cia.gov.

85. U.S. Congress, Senate, *Covert Action in Chile,* 24.

86. "Memorandum for the Record, Minutes of the Meeting of the 40 Committee," Sept. 8, 1970, *FRUS, 1969–1976,* vol. 21, *Chile, 1969–1973,* doc. 70, history.state.gov.

87. "Telegram from the Central Intelligence Agency to the Station in Chile," Sept. 9, 1970, *FRUS, 1969–1976,* vol. 21, *Chile, 1969–1973,* doc. 72, history.state.gov.

88. "Transcript of a Telephone Conversation Between President Nixon and the President's Assistant for National Security Affairs (Kissinger)," Sept. 12, 1970, *FRUS, 1969–1976,* vol. 21, *Chile, 1969–1973,* doc. 82, history.state.gov.

89. "Transcript of a Telephone Conversation Between Secretary of State Rogers and the President's Assistant for National Security Affairs (Kissinger)," Sept. 14, 1970, *FRUS, 1969–1976,* vol. 21, *Chile, 1969–1973,* doc. 88, history.state.gov.

90. Viron Vaky, "Memorandum from Viron P. Vaky of the National Security Council Staff to the President's Assistant for National Security Affairs (Kissinger)," Sept. 14, 1970, *FRUS, 1969–1976,* vol. 21, *Chile, 1969–1973,* doc. 86, history.state.gov.

91. For a detailed account of CIA operations in Chile after Allende's victory in the 1970 election, see Gustafson, *Hostile Intent,* chaps. 3–7; Kornbluh, *The Pinochet File,* chap. 1–2.

92. "Editorial Note," *FRUS, 1969–1976,* vol. 21, *Chile, 1969–1973,* doc. 93, history.state.gov; U.S. Congress, Senate, *Covert Action in Chile,* 23.

93. "Telegram from the Central Intelligence Agency to the Station in Chile," Oct. 16, 1970, *FRUS, 1969–1976,* vol. 21, *Chile, 1969–1973,* doc. 154, history.state.gov; William V. Broe, "Memorandum for the Record," Sept. 16, 1970, *FRUS, 1969–1976,* vol. 21, *Chile, 1969–1973,* doc. 94, history.state.gov; U.S. Congress, Senate, *Covert Action in Chile,* 2.

94. Central Intelligence Agency, "CIA Activities in Chile," Sept. 18, 2000, www.cia.gov; U.S. Congress, Senate, *Covert Action in Chile,* 26.

95. Central Intelligence Agency, "CIA Activities in Chile." For the sequence of events that resulted in Schneider's death, see Haslam, *The Nixon Administration,* 70; Kornbluh, *Pinochet File,* 22–28. John Dinges further

explains, "The CIA provided three submachine guns to one group of plotters at 2 A.M. on the day of the kidnapping. The CIA has always insisted that the weapons were never used and that a different group killed Schneider. Weapons and money were also promised to that second group but were never delivered, according to the CIA. The distinction between the two groups seems insubstantial, however, since the CIA never abandoned the tactic of kidnapping the army chief and was providing support to plotters on the same day it actually happened. The United States thus gave its operational endorsement to acts of terrorism in furtherance of the cause of anti-Communism." John Dinges, *The Condor Years: How Pinochet and His Allies Brought Terrorism to Three Continents* (New York: New Press, 2004), 19.

96. Joseph Novitski, "Chile Buries General as Martyr," *New York Times,* Oct. 27, 1970, timesmachine.nytimes.com; Joseph Novitski, "Military Leader Dies in Santiago," *New York Times,* Oct. 26, 1970, timesmachine .nytimes.com.

97. Juan de Onis, "Rightist Withdraws in Chile, Endorsing Allende," *New York Times,* Oct. 20, 1970, timesmachine.nytimes.com; Joseph Novitski, "Allende, Marxist Leader, Elected Chile's President," *New York Times,* Oct. 25, 1970, timesmachine.nytimes.com; Juan de Onis, "3 Communists Given Key Economic Posts in Chilean Cabinet," *New York Times,* Oct. 31, 1970, timesmachine.nytimes.com; Juan de Onis, "Allende Sworn; Urges Sacrifice," *New York Times,* Nov. 4, 1970, timesmachine.nytimes .com.

    Later, in December 1970, the CIA reported that "in Chile, the Communist Party has publicly boasted of its important role in the Allende government." Central Intelligence Agency, "The President's Daily Brief," Dec. 1, 1970 (declassified June 2016), www.cia.gov.

98. U.S. Congress, Senate, *Covert Action in Chile 1963–1973,* 27. In February 1973, a besieged Allende hosted a KGB employee at his villa, where he described plans to reform Chile's security services so that their "main focus" would be "finding out about and suppressing American subversion." Of this meeting, the KGB archives continue, "Allende really counts on Soviet help in this matter. This information was relayed to [Leonid] Brezhnev." That month, Yuri Andropov, the head of the KGB, briefed his superiors on Allende. "Providing [Allende] with some monetary help, paying attention to him and executing his personal wishes," Andropov wrote, "helped strengthen the trusting relationship between our employee and Allende." See MITN 2/22, entries 77 and 377, Papers of Mitrokhin.

99. Devine, interview by author; Jack Devine and Vernon Loeb, *Good Hunting: An American Spymaster's Story* (New York: Farrar, Straus and Giroux, 2014), 43–44.

100. "Chilean Medical Report Calls Allende a Suicide," Reuters, Oct. 31, 1973, www.nytimes.com. On the Eastern bloc's interpretation of events in Chile, see Radoslav A. Yordanov, "Warsaw Pact Countries' Involvement

in Chile from Frei to Pinochet, 1964–1973," *Journal of Cold War Studies* 21, no. 3 (2019): 56–87. For further reading on the Pinochet regime, see Kornbluh, *Pinochet File;* Dinges, *Condor Years.*

101. Kornbluh, *Pinochet File,* 114.

102. U.S. Congress, Senate, Select Committee to Study Governmental Operations with Respect to Intelligence Activities, *Hearings Before the Select Committee to Study Governmental Operations with Respect to Intelligence Activities: Covert Action,* 94th Cong., 1st sess., Dec. 4 and 5, 1975, 62, www.intelligence.senate.gov.

CHAPTER 4: THE STASI CHANGES HISTORY

1. Westad summarizes the vision behind Brandt's Ostpolitik as follows: "A careful building of trust among governments in the east and west of Europe, which would enable disarmament, increased trade, travel, and cultural contacts, and, eventually, German reunification and the full removal of Europe's Cold War divides." Westad, *Cold War,* 385.

2. David Binder, "Brandt Defeats Move to Oust Him," *New York Times,* April 28, 1972, www.nytimes.com.

3. Kopp, interview by author, Berlin, Germany, July 26, 2017. I first reported on this in an article for *Foreign Affairs* ("A Cold War Case of Russian Collusion," *Foreign Affairs,* April 5, 2019, www.foreignaffairs.com).

4. Gregg, interview by author, Armonk, N.Y., March 17, 2018. Gregg worked for the CIA from 1951 to 1982, and then as national security adviser to Vice President George H. W. Bush, and as U.S. ambassador to South Korea.

5. Kopp, interview by author; Jens Gieseke, *The History of the Stasi: East Germany's Secret Police, 1945–1990* (Brooklyn: Berghahn, 2015), 155; "Der Deutsche Bundestag 1949 bis 1989 in den Akten des Ministeriums für Staatssicherheit (MfS) der DDR," Federal Commissioner for the Documents of the State Security Service of the Former German Democratic Republic, Berlin, March 2013.

6. Julius Steiner Dossier, Bundesbeauftragter für die Unterlagen des Staatssicherheitsdienstes der ehemaligen DDR, BStU, Berlin, 4 (hereafter cited as Steiner Dossier). This file was provided to the author by the Stasi Records Agency (the BStU) in Berlin, Germany, in response to an archival request. It includes 299 pages of materials on Steiner documented by the Stasi.

7. Leo Wagner Dossier, Bundesbeauftragter für die Unterlagen des Staatssicherheitsdienstes der ehemaligen DDR, BStU, Berlin, 21 (hereafter cited as Wagner Dossier). This file was provided to the author by the Stasi Records Agency (the BStU) in Berlin, Germany, in response to an archival request. It includes fifty-three pages of materials on Wagner documented by the Stasi.

8. Ibid.; "CSU-Spion enttarnt," *Der Spiegel,* Nov. 27, 2000, www.spiegel

.de; "Bis zu meinem Zusammenbruch," *Der Spiegel,* Oct. 20, 1980, www
.spiegel.de.

9. *Die Geheimnisse des Schönen Leo,* directed by Benedikt Schwarzer (Germany: Lichtblick Film & TV Produktion, 2019), copy provided to author
by director; "Bis zu meinem Zusammenbruch." Conversion information
for deutschemarks to dollars (1972) taken from Germany/U.S. Foreign
Exchange Rate, Federal Reserve Bank of St. Louis, fred.stlouisfed.org;
conversion information for dollar values (1972 to 2020) taken from U.S.
Inflation Calculator, www.usinflationcalculator.com.

10. *Die Geheimmissee des Schöner Leo,* directed by Schwarzer.

11. Kopp, interview by author; "CSU-Spion enttarnt."

12. Kopp, interview by author. A group of prosecutors, while investigating
Wagner years later, found that he had been living extravagantly since the
late 1960s, around when Fleissman began passing him cash and intelligence. See "Urteil," *Der Spiegel,* Dec. 29, 1980, www.spiegel.de.

13. *Die Geheimnisse des Schönen Leo,* directed by Schwarzer.

14. Kopp, interview by author.

15. Willy Brandt, *Begegnungen und Einsichten* (Hamburg: Hoffmann &
Campe, 1976), 198; Westad, *Cold War,* 365, 373–78; Gaddis, *The Cold
War: A New History,* 153; Harry Schwartz, "The Khrushchev/Brezhnev
Doctrine at Helsinki," *New York Times,* Aug. 5, 1975, www.nytimes
.com. See also Kieran Williams, *The Prague Spring and Its Aftermath:
Czechoslovak Politics, 1968–1970* (Cambridge, U.K.: Cambridge Uni-
versity Press, 1997), chaps. 4–5; Jussi Hanhimaki, *The Rise and Fall of
Détente: American Foreign Policy and the Transformation of the Cold
War* (Washington, D.C.: Potomac Books, 2013), chap. 2; Leonid Brezhnev,
On the Policy of the Soviet Union and the International Situation (New
York: Doubleday, 1973).

On Western reactions to the Prague Spring, see John G. McGinn, "The
Politics of Collective Inaction: NATO's Response to the Prague Spring,"
Journal of Cold War Studies 1, no. 3 (1999): 111–38. On the conception
and evolution of the Brezhnev Doctrine, see Matthew J. Ouimet, *The Rise
and Fall of the Brezhnev Doctrine in Soviet Foreign Policy* (Chapel Hill:
University of North Carolina Press, 2003). On détente, see Keith L. Nelson, *The Making of Détente: Soviet-American Relations in the Shadow
of Vietnam* (Baltimore: Johns Hopkins University Press, 1995). On the
similarities between Leonid Brezhnev and Vladimir Putin, see Snyder,
Road to Unfreedom, 46–48; Susan Glasser, "Putin the Great: Russia's
Imperial Imposter," *Foreign Affairs,* Sept./Oct. 2019, www.foreignaffairs
.com.

16. Wippl, phone interview by author, Nov. 8, 2018; Brandt, *Begegnungen
und Einsichten,* 343, 360; Gaddis, *Cold War,* chap. 3. See also Philip
Hanson, *The Rise and Fall of the Soviet Economy: An Economic History
of the USSR from 1945* (London: Longman, 2003).

17. In 1975, the Soviet Union, the United States, Canada, and nearly every

European state agreed to the Helsinki Final Act. Under the agreement, signatories pledged to respect the current European order and to "refrain from any intervention, direct or indirect, individual or collective, in the internal or external affairs falling within the domestic jurisdiction of another participating State" (a commitment, of course, that both of the superpowers had been violating, and would continue to do so, through covert electoral interference). Participating countries also agreed to "respect the territorial integrity of each of the participating states," highlighting the sanctity of territorial rather than electoral sovereignty. See Final Act of the Conference on Security and Co-operation in Europe, Helsinki, August 1, 1975, in U.S. Department of State, *Documents on Germany, 1944–1985* (Washington, D.C.: Government Printing Office, 1985), 1285. See also William J. Tompson, *The Soviet Union Under Brezhnev* (Abingdon, U.K.: Routledge, 2003), 48; Judt, *Postwar*, 501. On China, see Jeremi Suri, *Power and Protest: Global Revolution and the Rise of Détente* (Cambridge, Mass.: Harvard University Press, 2005), 226–45; Hanhimaki, *Rise and Fall of Détente*, 44; Brandt, *Begegnungen und Einsichten*, 300.

18. Judt, *Postwar*, 254. For further reading on Berlin as a Cold War hot spot, see Deborah Welch Larson, "The Origins of Commitment: Truman and West Berlin," *Journal of Cold War Studies* 13, no. 1 (2011): 180–212; David Coleman, "Eisenhower and the Berlin Problem, 1953–1954," *Journal of Cold War Studies* 2, no. 1 (2000): 3–34; David E. Murphy, Sergei A. Kondrashev, and George Bailey, *Battleground Berlin: CIA vs. KGB in the Cold War* (New Haven, Conn.: Yale University Press, 1997). Also, Douglas Selvage and Hope Harrison, in separate articles, analyze and contextualize pertinent primary source materials in "New Evidence on the Berlin Crisis, 1958–1962," *Cold War International History Project Bulletin* 11 (1998): 200–29.

19. Judt, *Postwar*, 27, 270.

20. Kopp, interview by author. In September 1969, just before the West German election, Moscow offered to open negotiations with Bonn. Egon Bahr, Brandt's foreign policy adviser, then drafted a working paper detailing a potential reconciliation agreement with the Soviet Union. See Timothy Garton Ash, *In Europe's Name: Germany and the Divided Continent* (London: Vintage, 1994), 67–68. For further reading on Ostpolitik, see Gottfried Niedhart, "Ostpolitik: Transformation Through Communication and the Quest for Peaceful Change," *Journal of Cold War Studies* 18, no. 3 (2016): 14–59.

21. Brandt, *Begegnungen und Einsichten*, 168.

22. Neil MacFarlane and Yuen Foong Khong aptly define the pursuit of security as a state seeking to minimize threats to its survival, welfare, and identity in *Human Security and the UN: A Critical History* (Bloomington: Indiana University Press, 2006), 2.

23. Brandt, *Begegnungen und Einsichten*, 169; "Bonn-Soviet Text Leaked to Paper," *New York Times*, June 13, 1970, timesmachine.nytimes.com.

Still, in conjunction with détente in Europe, competition for influence persisted across Africa, Asia, and Latin America. Westad explains, "The Soviets never intended détente with Washington to include an end to Moscow's support for movements and regimes in the Third World." Westad, *Global Cold War,* 195.

24. Julia Von Dannenberg, *The Foundations of Ostpolitik: The Making of the Moscow Treaty Between West Germany and the USSR* (New York: Oxford University Press, 2008), 164–65.

25. Bernard Gwertzman, "Treaty Initialed by Moscow and Bonn," *New York Times,* Aug. 8, 1970, www.nytimes.com.

26. Brandt, *Begegnungen und Einsichten,* 325–29. Additionally, the Moscow Treaty declared that each party sought "to maintain international peace and achieve détente," and had agreed to "settle their disputes exclusively by peaceful means" and to "regard the frontiers of all States in Europe as inviolable such as they are on the date of signature of the present Treaty, including the Oder-Neisse line." See Treaty Between the Federal Republic of Germany and the Soviet Union (the Moscow Treaty) of August 12, 1970, in U.S. Department of State, *Documents on Germany, 1944–1985,* 1103. West German negotiators had spent weeks tweaking the treaty's language, to keep the door open to peacefully adjusting frontiers and, therefore, to reunifying Germany. For example, the Soviets had asked that Europe's frontiers be labeled "unalterable"; West German negotiators successfully substituted "inviolable" in its place. See Garton Ash, *In Europe's Name,* 70–71.

27. Treaty between the Federal Republic of Germany and Poland Concerning the Basis for Normalizing Their Mutual Relations (the Treaty of Warsaw) of December 7, 1970, in U.S. Department of State, *Documents on Germany, 1944–1985,* 1125. On the consequences of recognizing Poland's western border, Brandt wrote, "Many of our German contemporaries accused us of being the first to crystallize what they refused to accept as an accomplished act and would rather have continued to ignore." Brandt, *Begegnungen und Einsichten,* 181.

28. Authoritative histories of this period highlight the importance of Brandt's gesture in Warsaw. Westad writes, "For Poles and others who watched in eastern Europe, it was a powerful symbol of a new German government intent on peace, headed by a man of a new generation who himself had no blame in Germany's wartime atrocities. It went further than any treaty in creating an image of a new West Germany for peoples in the east." Westad, *Cold War,* 386. Garton Ash likewise writes, "For many people around the world, Ostpolitik is Willy Brandt falling to his knees before the monument to the heroes of the Warsaw ghetto." Garton Ash, *In Europe's Name,* 298.

29. Brandt, *Begegnungen und Einsichten,* 332, 387; M. E. Sarotte, *Dealing with the Devil: East Germany, Détente, and Ostpolitik, 1969–1973* (Chapel Hill: University of North Carolina Press, 2001), 120–29, in which she also explains how the Quadripartite Agreement, finalized by

the United States, the United Kingdom, France, and the Soviet Union in 1971, enabled the transit accord.

30. John Kess, "Brandt Wins Nobel Prize for His Efforts for Peace," *New York Times,* Oct. 21, 1971, www.nytimes.com; "Memorandum of Conversation," Jan. 10, 1972, *FRUS, 1969–1976,* vol. 40, *Germany and Berlin, 1969–1972,* doc. 337, history.state.gov; Brandt, *Begegnungen und Einsichten,* 349; Sarotte, *Dealing with the Devil,* 130.

31. Brandt, *Begegnungen und Einsichten,* 356.

32. Wippl, interview by author. Article 67 reads, "The Bundestag may express its lack of confidence in the Federal Chancellor only by electing a successor by the vote of a majority of its Members and requesting the Federal President to dismiss the Federal Chancellor. The Federal President must comply with the request and appoint the person elected." See the Basic Law for the Federal Republic of Germany, May 8, 1949, art. 67, accessed through the Bundestag website, www.btg-bestellservice.de.

33. Rainer Barzel, *Die Tür blieb offen: Mein persönlicher Bericht über Ostverträge, Misstrauensvotum, Kanzlersturz* (Berlin: Bouvier, 1998), 54. See also John O. Koehler, *Stasi: The Untold Story of the East German Secret Police* (Boulder, Colo.: Westview Press, 1999), 69.

34. Kalugin, interview by author, Rockville, Md., Aug. 7, 2018; Markus Wolf and Anne McElvoy, *Man Without a Face: The Autobiography of Communism's Greatest Spymaster* (New York: Times Books, 1997), 135, 166–71.

35. "Telegram from the Embassy in Germany to the Department of State," April 14, 1972, *FRUS, 1969–1976,* vol. 40, *Germany and Berlin, 1969–1972,* doc. 354, history.state.gov; Wolfgang Mueller, "Recognition in Return for Détente? Brezhnev, the EEC, and the Moscow Treaty with West Germany, 1970–1973," *Journal of Cold War Studies* 13, no. 4 (2011): 79–100; Sarotte, *Dealing with the Devil,* 130–33. Barzel announced the vote of no confidence on April 24 after briefing his inner circle of his plans on April 19; see Barzel, *Die Tür blieb offen,* 97.

36. "Editorial Note," *FRUS, 1969–1976,* vol. 40, *Germany and Berlin, 1969–1972,* doc. 358, history.state.gov.

37. Brandt, *Begegnungen und Einsichten,* 336; "Editorial Note," doc. 358; Sarotte, *Dealing with the Devil,* 133.

38. Egon Bahr, *Zu meiner Zeit* (Berlin: Blessing, 1998), 383. Based on available sources, it is unclear whether authorities in Moscow briefed their counterparts in East Germany on this approach to Bahr.

39. M. E. Sarotte writes, based on her interview with Wolf, that he "remembered in 1996 that the instructions from Moscow at the time were clear: the [East German government] was to do everything possible to protect Brandt." Sarotte, *Dealing with the Devil,* 130. Christopher Andrew and Vasili Mitrokhin write that Wolf had Moscow's "blessing" in seeking to interfere in the vote. Andrew and Mitrokhin, *The Sword and the Shield,* 427.

40. Inman, interview by author, Austin, Tex., Nov. 2, 2018; Goss, interview

by author, Florida Keys, Fla., Dec. 26, 2018. See also Gieseke, *History of the Stasi,* chap. 6.

41. Koehler, *Stasi,* 3–4. On the evolution of the Stasi's domestic operations, see Gary Bruce, "The Prelude to Nationwide Surveillance in East Germany: Stasi Operations and Threat Perceptions, 1945–1953," *Journal of Cold War Studies* 5, no. 2 (2003): 3–31; David Childs and Richard Popplewell, *The Stasi: The East German Intelligence and Security Service* (London: Macmillan, 1996).

42. Kopp, interview by author. Conversion information for deutschemarks to dollars (1972) taken from Germany/U.S. Foreign Exchange Rate, Federal Reserve Bank of St. Louis, fred.stlouisfed.org; conversion information for dollar values (1972 to 2020) taken from U.S. Inflation Calculator, www.usinflationcalculator.com.

43. Kopp, interview by author; *Die Geheimnisse des Schönen Leo,* directed by Schwarzer.

44. Brandt, *Begegnungen und Einsichten,* 435. See also Hélène Miard-Delacroix, *Willy Brandt: Life of a Statesman* (London: I. B. Tauris, 2016), 130.

45. Binder, "Brandt Defeats Move to Oust Him"; *Die Geheimnisse des Schönen Leo,* directed by Schwarzer.

46. Sarotte, *Dealing with the Devil,* 133.

47. "Der Deutsche Bundestag 1949 bis 1989 in den Akten des Ministeriums für Staatssicherheit (MfS) der DDR."

48. "West Germany's Treaties with Soviet and Poland Win Bundestag Approval," *New York Times,* May 18, 1972, www.nytimes.com; "Exit Mr. Barzel," *New York Times,* May 10, 1973, www.nytimes.com. On the subsequent evolution of the conservative bloc's foreign policy, see Clay Clemens, *Reluctant Realists: The Christian Democrats and West German Ostpolitik* (Durham, N.C.: Duke University Press, 1989).

49. David Binder, "Brandt Coalition Is Swept Back In for Second Term," *New York Times,* Nov. 20, 1972, www.nytimes.com.

50. Wippl, interview by author.

51. Garton Ash, *In Europe's Name,* 376.

52. Binder, "Brandt Defeats Move to Oust Him."

53. Wippl, interview by author.

54. Franz Josef Strauss, *Die Erinnerungen* (Berlin: Siedler, 1989), 398; Rainer Barzel, *Ein gewagtes Leben* (Berlin: Honenheim, 2001), 84; Brandt, *Begegnungen und Einsichten,* 435.

55. Steiner Dossier, 23; "Die sind ja alle so mißtrauisch," *Der Spiegel,* June 4, 1973, www.spiegel.de; "Der Deutsche Bundestag 1949 bis 1989 in den Akten des Ministeriums für Staatssicherheit (MfS) der DDR."

56. Steiner Dossier, 21–23; "Die sind ja alle so mißtrauisch." The Steiner Affair emerged just as the Watergate scandal—which caused Nixon to resign the presidency in August 1974—was escalating in the United States. On Watergate, see Keith W. Olson, *Watergate: The Presidential Scandal*

That Shook America (Lawrence: University Press of Kansas, 2003); Carl Bernstein and Bob Woodward, *All the President's Men* (New York: Simon & Schuster, 1974).

57. Steiner Dossier, 23, 35, 126; "Affäre Steiner: Rätsel über Rätsel," *Der Spiegel*, July 23, 1973, www.spiegel.de; Miard-Delacroix, *Willy Brandt*, 131.

58. Kopp, interview by author; "Der Deutsche Bundestag 1949 bis 1989 in den Akten des Ministeriums für Staatssicherheit (MfS) der DDR."

59. Steiner Dossier, 20–150. One of the articles in the Stasi's file poses the question—Watergate in Bonn?—in reference to the Steiner Affair, a common comparison at the time.

60. "Affäre Wienand: 'Der Kanzler hält sich raus,'" *Der Spiegel*, June 18, 1973, www.spiegel.de; Steiner Dossier, 26.

61. "Affäre Steiner: Rätsel über Rätsel"; Steiner Dossier, 23, 38. During the inquiry, many members of the CDU became attached to the allegation that Wienand had bribed Steiner, perhaps because this version of events most suited their political agenda; see Steiner Dossier, 76.

62. Steiner Dossier, 46; Detlef Kleinert, Wolfgang Schäuble, and Friedrich Shepherd, "Bericht und Antrag zu dem Antrag der Fraktion der CDU/CSU betr. Einsetzung eines Untersuchungsausschusses," Bundestag, March 3, 1974, dipbt.bundestag.de.

63. "Bonn Aide Admits He Withdrew Funds in Bribery Inquiry," *New York Times*, Sept. 6, 1973, www.nytimes.com.

64. "CSU-Spion enttarnt."

65. Kopp, interview by author; Wagner Dossier, 7. The entries, on pages 8 and 9, include "S7604981: Background on the restitution of the CSU parliamentary unit; SE7602099: Minutes for the 24th federal convention of the CDU—May 24th to 26th 1976; SE7602995: Visit of the Balkans by [whited out]; SE7604373: Background and documentation on CDU/CSU discussion."

66. Koehler, *Stasi*, 150–62, 200.

67. Kopp, interview by author.

68. "CSU-Spion enttarnt."

69. Ibid.; MITN 2/2, 52, Papers of Mitrokhin.

70. "CSU-Politiker Wagner soll Stasi-Spion gewesen sein," *Rheinische Post*, Nov. 25, 2000, www.rp-online.de; "CSU-Spion enttarnt"; Sarotte, *Dealing with the Devil*, 133.

71. "CSU-Spion enttarnt"; "CSU-Politiker Wagner lässt Ämter ruhen," German Press Agency, Nov. 27, 2000, www.schwaebische.de.

72. The German government found, "This leads to the conclusion that in 1972 Wagner was simply a corruptible parliamentarian whose financial problems the [Stasi] exploited through the journalist Georg Fleissman (IM 'Dürer'). The [Stasi] manipulated the vote of no confidence in 1972 by targeting corrupt members of parliament. . . . With all due prudence, it is assumed today that the deputies Steiner and Wagner were bribed by the [Stasi] in 1972 and led to the failure of Barzel's no-confidence vote. This

assumption is based on testimonies, self-accusations, reports by the Bundestag's investigative committee, the Federal Prosecutor's Office's insights from the espionage trials of the nineties, and accounts of those involved at the time." "Der Deutsche Bundestag 1949 bis 1989 in den Akten des Ministeriums für Staatssicherheit (MfS) der DDR."

73. Kopp, interview by author.

CHAPTER 5: THE KGB TARGETS AMERICA

1. Inman, interview by author, Austin, Tex., Nov. 2, 2018.
2. Kalugin, interview by author, Rockville, Md., Aug. 7, 2018. The Soviet Union was unique in that it consistently sought to interfere covertly in U.S. elections during the twentieth century, but it was not the only country to ever try. For example, Nazi Germany attempted—entirely ineffectively—to intervene covertly in America's 1940 presidential election. See Bradley Hart, *Hitler's American Friends: The Third Reich's Supporters in the United States* (New York: St. Martin's, 2018), chap. 5.
3. "The Kitchen Debate Transcript," July 24, 1959, taken from the CIA General Records, www.cia.gov.
4. Nikita Khrushchev, *Memoirs of Nikita Khrushchev: Statesman, 1953–1964,* ed. Sergei Khrushchev (University Park: Pennsylvania State University Press, 2007), 295. For further reading on Khrushchev's views of Nixon, see William Taubman, *Khrushchev: The Man and His Era* (New York: W. W. Norton, 2003), chap. 17.
5. Kalugin, interview by author.
6. Khrushchev, *Memoirs,* 295; Taubman, *Khrushchev,* 484; Kalugin, interview by author.
7. Taubman, *Khrushchev,* xix. On dynamics in Moscow following Stalin's death, see Mark Kramer's three-part series "The Early Post-Stalin Succession Struggle and Upheavals in East-Central Europe," *Journal of Cold War Studies* 1, no. 1–3 (1999). On Khrushchev's rise to power, see also Vladislav Zubok and Constantine Pleshakov, *Inside the Kremlin's Cold War: From Stalin to Khrushchev* (Cambridge, Mass.: Harvard University Press, 1997).
8. Khrushchev, *Memoirs,* 138.
9. This account of Stevenson's meeting with Menshikov as well as the text of the letter to Menshikov is based on a memorandum that Stevenson wrote on January 25, 1960, which can be found in Walter Johnson, *The Papers of Adlai E. Stevenson: Continuing Education and the Unfinished Business of American Society, 1957–1961* (Boston: Little, Brown, 1977), 386–89. On Stevenson's last-minute and failed attempt to win the nomination at the Democratic National Convention, see Jean H. Baker, *The Stevensons: A Biography of an American Family* (New York: W. W. Norton, 1996), 402–4.
10. Khrushchev, *Memoirs,* 295; Zubok and Pleshakov, *Inside the Kremlin's Cold War,* 238.

11. Kalugin, interview by author.

12. Lindesay Parrott, "U.S. Urges U.N. Vote Impartial Inquiry in Attack on RB-47," *New York Times,* July 26, 1960, timesmachine.nytimes.com. America's U-2 spy planes had, since 1956, been reporting back to Washington that Khrushchev did not possess the long-range missile capabilities about which he so frequently boasted; see Gaddis, *Cold War,* 72–74.

13. Khrushchev, *Memoirs,* 296; "U.S. Doubts Russians Will Free RB-47 Fliers," *New York Times,* Sept. 10, 1960, timesmachine.nytimes.com.

14. Taubman, *Khrushchev,* 484.

15. W. H. Lawrence, "Moscow Frees 2 RB-47 Survivors; Kennedy Calls Khrushchev Move a Step Toward Better Relations," *New York Times,* Jan. 26, 1961, timesmachine.nytimes.com; "Burial for Gary Powers Tomorrow," *New York Times,* Aug. 7, 1977, www.nytimes.com.

16. Kalugin, interview by author.

17. Khrushchev, *Memoirs,* 296.

18. "Racist Hate Note Sent to U.N. Aides," *New York Times,* Nov. 29, 1960, timesmachine.nytimes.com.

19. UN General Assembly Official Record, 15th Session, 944th Plenary Meeting, Agenda Item 87 (Dec. 13, 1960), legal.un.org.

20. Ibid.

21. MITN 1/6/5, p. 444, Papers of Mitrokhin.

22. Ibid., p. 432.

23. Kalugin, interview by author.

24. Ibid.; Kalugin, *Spymaster,* 54.

25. Kalugin, interview by author.

26. Ibid. On Brezhnev's interest in détente, see chapter 4 of this book. For Humphrey's reflections on his life and career generally, see Hubert H. Humphrey, *The Education of a Public Man: My Life and Politics* (Garden City, N.Y.: Doubleday, 1976).

27. Anatoly Dobrynin, *In Confidence: Moscow's Ambassador to Six Cold War Presidents* (Seattle: University of Washington Press, 2001), 176.

28. Ibid.

29. Ibid.

30. Westad writes, "If it had not been for the new Nixon Administration itself engaging in renewed efforts at détente with the Soviets, Brandt's policy could have been seen as positively treacherous in a NATO context." Westad, *Cold War,* 386. For further reading on Nixon, see Stephen Ambrose, *Nixon: The Triumph of a Politician, 1962–1972* (New York: Simon & Schuster, 1989); Melvin Small, *The Presidency of Richard Nixon* (Lawrence: University Press of Kansas, 1999).

31. Goss, interview by author, Florida Keys, Fla., Dec. 26, 2018; McLaughlin, phone interview by author, Sept. 5, 2019. On press coverage of the CIA during the early Cold War, see David P. Hadley, "A Constructive Quality: The Press, the CIA, and Covert Intervention in the 1950s," *Intelligence and National Security* 31, no. 2 (2016): 246–65. For further reading, see Loch K. Johnson, *America's Secret Power: The CIA in a Democratic*

Society (New York: Oxford University Press, 1989); David M. Barrett, *The CIA and Congress: The Untold Story from Truman to Kennedy* (Lawrence: University Press of Kansas, 2005); John Ranelagh, *The Agency: The Rise and Decline of the CIA* (New York: Simon & Schuster, 1986); Evan Thomas, *The Very Best Men: Four Who Dared: The Early Years of the CIA* (New York: Simon & Schuster, 1995).

32. Seymour Hersh, "C.I.A. Chief Tells House of $8-Million Campaign Against Allende in '70–73," *New York Times,* Sept. 8, 1974, www .nytimes.com; Brent Durbin, *The CIA and the Politics of US Intelligence Reform* (Cambridge, U.K.: Cambridge University Press, 2017), 135–37; Gustafson, *Hostile Intent,* 1–3.

33. Jeffreys-Jones, *CIA and American Democracy,* 198; "Editorial Note," *FRUS, 1969–1976,* vol. 38, pt. 1, *Foundations of Foreign Policy, 1973– 1976,* doc. 53, history.state.gov.

34. Seymour Hersh, "Huge C.I.A. Operation Reported in U.S. Against Anti-war Forces, Other Dissidents in Nixon Years," *New York Times,* Dec. 22, 1974, timesmachine.nytimes.com.

35. Jeffreys-Jones, *CIA and American Democracy,* 194.

36. Olav Njølstad, "The Carter Administration and Italy: Keeping the Communists Out of Power Without Interfering," *Journal of Cold War Studies* 4, no. 3 (2002): 56, 69, which further explains that an internal U.S. government memorandum, issued when Carter was president, said that his administration would reject "such actions as dictating to Italians how they should vote, seeking to manipulate political events in Italy, or financing Italian political parties or personalities." For further reading on foreign policy making during the Carter years, see Gaddis Smith, *Morality, Reason, and Power: American Diplomacy in the Carter Years* (New York: Hill and Wang, 1986); Jimmy Carter, *Keeping Faith: Memoirs of a President* (New York: Bantam, 1982); Zbigniew Brzezinski, *Power and Principle: Memoirs of the National Security Adviser, 1977–1981* (New York: Farrar, Straus and Giroux, 1983).

37. U.S. Congress, Senate, Select Committee to Study Governmental Operations with Respect to Intelligence Activities, *Hearings Before the Select Committee to Study Governmental Operations with Respect to Intelligence Activities: Covert Action,* 94th Cong., 1st sess., Dec. 4 and 5, 1975, 54, www.intelligence.senate.gov.

38. U.S. Congress, Senate, Select Committee to Study Governmental Operations with Respect to Intelligence Activities, *Alleged Assassination Plots Involving Foreign Leaders,* 94th Cong., 1st sess., 1975, www.intelligence .senate.gov; Executive Order 11905: United States Foreign Intelligence Activities, Feb. 18, 1976, www.fordlibrarymuseum.gov.

39. Oriana Fallaci, "What Did You Do to My Italy, Mr. Spy?," *Washington Star,* March 7, 1976, taken from CIA General Records (declassified May 2012), www.cia.gov.

40. Ibid.

41. Devine, interview by author, New York, Feb. 21, 2019; Ventresca, *From*

Fascism to Democracy, 20; Kaeten Mistry, "Approaches to Understanding the Inaugural CIA Covert Operation in Italy: Exploding Useful Myths," *Intelligence and National Security* 26, no. 2–3 (2011): 249–50.

42. Gaddis, *Cold War,* 217. On Reagan's presidency and character, see Lou Cannon, *President Reagan: The Role of a Lifetime* (New York: Simon & Schuster, 1991). For Reagan's and Ford's personal reflections, see Ronald Reagan, *An American Life* (New York: Simon & Schuster, 1990); Gerald R. Ford, *A Time to Heal: The Autobiography of Gerald R. Ford* (New York: Harper & Row, 1979).

43. Ronald Reagan, "To Restore America" (campaign address, California, March 31, 1976), Ronald Reagan Presidential Library & Museum, Simi Valley, Calif., www.reaganlibrary.gov.

44. Kalugin, interview by author.

45. MITN 1/6/5, p. 442, Papers of Mitrokhin.

46. Ford lost to Jimmy Carter, under whom détente collapsed anyway. For a primary source account, see James Hershberg, "U.S.-Soviet Relations and the Turn Toward Confrontation, 1977–1980: New Russian & East German Documents," *Cold War International History Project Bulletin,* no. 8–9 (1996/1997): 103–28. See also Odd Arne Westad, *The Fall of Détente: Soviet-American Relations During the Carter Years* (Oslo: Scandinavian University Press, 1997); James Blight and Janet Lang, "When Empathy Failed: Using Critical Oral History to Reassess the Collapse of U.S.-Soviet Détente in the Carter-Brezhnev Years," *Journal of Cold War Studies* 12, no. 2 (2010): 29–74; Raymond L. Garthoff, *Détente and Confrontation: American-Soviet Relations from Nixon to Reagan* (Washington, D.C.: Brookings Institution, 1994).

47. Andrew and Mitrokhin, *The Sword and the Shield,* 241–42.

48. MITN 1/6/5, p. 438, Papers of Mitrokhin.

49. Ibid., p. 439.

50. Ibid., pp. 439–40.

51. Ibid., p. 438.

52. Kalugin, interview by author.

53. Hannah Arendt, *The Origins of Totalitarianism* (New York: Schocken Books, 1951), 335. On the evolving use of the term "totalitarianism," see Abbot Gleason, *Totalitarianism: The Inner History of the Cold War* (New York: Oxford University Press, 1995).

54. MITN 1/6/5, pp. 439–40, Papers of Mitrokhin.

55. Ibid.

56. Ibid., p. 437.

57. Kalugin, interview by author.

58. MITN 1/6/5, p. 437, Papers of Mitrokhin.

59. Ibid., p. 432.

60. Ibid., p. 439.

61. Andrew and Mitrokhin, *The Sword and the Shield,* 237.

62. Fred Barbash, "U.S. Ties 'Klan' Olympic Hate Mail to KGB," *Washington Post,* Aug. 7, 1983, www.washingtonpost.com.

63. Andrew and Mitrokhin, *The Sword and the Shield,* 237.

64. Barbash, "U.S. Ties 'Klan' Olympic Hate Mail to KGB."

65. Jim Anderson, "U.S. Says Soviets Sent Leaflets," UPI Archives, July 11, 1984, www.upi.com; "Soviets Say 'Delirious Myths' in Reply to U.S. View KGB Wrote Klan Letters," *Philadelphia Inquirer,* Aug. 9, 1987, taken from CIA General Records (declassified June 2010), www.cia.gov.

66. John E. Haynes and Harvey Klehr, "'Moscow Gold,' Confirmed at Last?," *Labor History* 33, no. 2 (1992): 279–93; Andrew and Mitrokhin, *The Sword and the Shield,* 287–92.

67. Kalugin, interview by author; John Barron, *Operation Solo: The FBI's Man in the Kremlin* (Washington, D.C.: Regnery Publishing, 1996). Distrust of the CPUSA was center stage during the Second Red Scare in the immediate postwar period. In 1949, after a nine-month trial, a New York court convicted eleven of its leaders for conspiring to overthrow the U.S. government. "The Communist Party is an illegal conspiracy," Burr Harrison, a Democratic congressman, said at the time. See Russell Porter, "11 Communists Convicted of Plot," *New York Times,* Oct. 15, 1949, timesmachine.nytimes.com; Lewis Wood, "Capital Officials Hail U.S. Victory," *New York Times,* Oct. 15, 1949, timesmachine.nytimes.com.

68. Kalugin, interview by author. Trump has historically denied allegations that he has engaged in any such extracurricular activities while in Moscow. See Eric Beech, "Trump Calls Russia Reports 'Fake News—a Total Political Witch Hunt,'" Reuters, Jan. 11, 2017, www.reuters.com; Jim Comey, *A Higher Loyalty: Truth, Lies, and Leadership* (New York: Flatiron, 2018), 223–25. Of his 1987 trip to the Soviet Union, Trump writes, "In January 1987, I got a letter from Yuri Dubinin, the Soviet ambassador to the United States, that began: 'It is a pleasure for me to relay some good news from Moscow.' It went on to say that the leading Soviet state agency for international tourism, Goscomintourist, had expressed interest in pursuing a joint venture to construct and manage a hotel in Moscow. On July 4, I flew with Ivana, her assistant Lisa Calandra, and Norma to Moscow. It was an extraordinary experience. We toured a half dozen potential sites for a hotel, including several near Red Square. We stayed in Lenin's suite at the National Hotel, and I was impressed with the ambition of the Soviet officials to make a deal." Donald Trump and Tony Schwartz, *Trump: The Art of the Deal* (New York: Random House, 1987), 364.

69. Kalugin, interview by author. For example, in a 2017 survey, sixty-six percent of Americans said that Trump—by then the U.S. president—had done more to divide than unify the United States. See Gary Langer, "Trump Seen by 66 percent in US as Doing More to Divide Than Unite Country," *ABC News,* Sept. 24, 2017, abcnews.go.com.

70. See note 5 of chapter 3 of this book.

71. William M. LeoGrande, *Our Own Backyard: The United States in Central America, 1977–1992* (Chapel Hill: University of North Carolina Press, 1998), 160, 560; Philip Taubman, "C.I.A. Said to Aid Salvador Parties," *New York Times,* May 12, 1984, www.nytimes.com.

72. Shultz, phone interview by author, Dec. 10, 2018. For Shultz's personal recollections, see George P. Shultz, *Turmoil and Triumph: My Years as Secretary of State* (New York: Scribner's, 1993).

73. Philip Taubman, "C.I.A. Chief Tells of Attempt to Aid Salvador Vote," *New York Times,* July 30, 1982, www.nytimes.com. For elaboration on the 1984 election in El Salvador, and on the Reagan administration's posture toward Central America generally, see Evan McCormick, "Freedom Tide? Ideology, Politics, and the Origins of Democracy Promotion in U.S. Central America Policy, 1980–1984," *Journal of Cold War Studies* 16, no. 4 (2014): 60–109.

74. Taubman, "C.I.A. Said to Aid Salvador Parties."

75. Shultz, interview by author.

76. Goss, interview by author.

77. Inman, interview by author.

CHAPTER 6: DEMOCRACY PROMOTION

1. Andrew Rosenthal, "Yeltsin Cheered at Capitol As He Pledges Era of Trust and Asks for Action on Aid," *New York Times,* June 18, 1992, timesmachine.nytimes.com.

2. Literature on the end of the Cold War is boundless. For a synthetic account, see Jeremi Suri, "Explaining the End of the Cold War: A New Historical Consensus?," *Journal of Cold War Studies* 4, no. 4 (2002): 60–92. Of Gorbachev, the historian Vladislav Zubok concludes that his "personality had much to do with the peaceful death of communism in Eastern Europe (with the exception of Romania)." Vladislav Zubok, "New Evidence on the 'Soviet Factor' in the Peaceful Revolutions of 1989," *Cold War International History Project Bulletin,* no. 12/13 (2001): 5–24. For firsthand accounts, see Anatoly S. Chernyaev, *My Six Years with Gorbachev* (University Park: Pennsylvania State University Press, 2000); Mikhail Gorbachev, *Memoirs* (New York: Doubleday, 1995). For analysis of Gorbachev's decision making, see Andrew Bennett, "The Guns That Didn't Smoke: Ideas and the Soviet Non-use of Force in 1989," *Journal of Cold War Studies* 7, no. 2 (2005): 81–109, which is part of an illuminating special issue, co-edited by Nina Tannenwald and William Wohlforth, on this historical moment. Mark Kramer further analyzes how the collapse of the Eastern bloc contributed to the collapse of the Soviet Union in his three-part series, "The Collapse of East European Communism and the Repercussions Within the Soviet Union," *Journal of Cold War Studies* (Fall 2003, Fall 2004, Winter 2005). For further reading, see Walter Connor, "Soviet Society, Public Attitudes, and the Perils of Gorbachev's Reforms: The Social Context of the End of the USSR," *Journal of Cold War Studies* 5, no. 4 (2003): 43–80; Astrid Tuminez, "Nationalism, Ethnic Pressures, and the Breakup of the Soviet Union," *Journal of Cold War Studies* 5, no. 4 (2003): 81–136; Robert D. English, *Russia and the Idea*

of the West: Gorbachev, Intellectuals, and the End of the Cold War (New York: Columbia University Press, 2000).

3. On German reunification and its consequences, see Konrad Jarausch, *The Rush to German Unity* (New York: Oxford University Press, 1994); Philip Zelikow and Condoleezza Rice, *Germany Unified and Europe Transformed: A Study in Statecraft* (Cambridge, Mass.: Harvard University Press, 1995); Angela E. Stent, *Russia and Germany Reborn: Unification, the Soviet Collapse, and the New Europe* (Princeton, N.J.: Princeton University Press, 1999); Stephen Szabo, *The Diplomacy of German Unification* (New York: St. Martin's, 1992). On the dynamic between the White House and the Kremlin, see Michael Beschloss and Strobe Talbott, *At the Highest Levels: The Inside Story of the End of the Cold War* (Boston: Little, Brown, 1993).

4. On the dynamic between Gorbachev and Yeltsin, see Marc Zlotnik, "Yeltsin and Gorbachev: The Politics of Confrontation," *Journal of Cold War Studies* 5, no. 1 (2003): 128–64. For a firsthand account of U.S. policy making, see George Bush and Brent Scowcroft, *A World Transformed* (New York: Knopf, 1998). For further reading, see David Remnick, *Lenin's Tomb: The Last Days of the Soviet Empire* (New York: Random House, 1993); Vladislav M. Zubok, *A Failed Empire: The Soviet Union in the Cold War from Stalin to Gorbachev* (Chapel Hill: University of North Carolina Press, 2007).

5. Robert Pear, "Congress Approves Aid Plan of $852 Million for Poland," *New York Times,* Nov. 19, 1989, timesmachine.nytimes.com; George H. W. Bush, "Statement on Signing the FREEDOM Support Act," White House, Oct. 24, 1992, www.govinfo.gov.

6. Thomas Friedman, "Bill to Aid Former Soviet Lands Is Stuck in Capitol Hill Quagmire," *New York Times,* June 5, 1992, timesmachine.nytimes .com; James Baker, "What America Owes the Ex–Soviet Union," *New York Times,* Aug. 5, 1992, timesmachine.nytimes.com; Adam Clymer, "House Votes Billions in Aid to Ex-Soviet Republics," *New York Times,* Aug. 7, 1992, timesmachine.nytimes.com.

7. U.S. Congress, Senate, Freedom for Russia and Emerging Eurasian Democracies and Open Markets (FREEDOM) Support Act of 1992, S. 2532, 102nd Cong., introduced in Senate April 7, 1992, www.congress .gov; "Transcript of 2nd TV Debate Between Bush, Clinton, and Perot," *New York Times,* Oct. 16, 1992, www.nytimes.com.

8. Francis Fukuyama, *The End of History and the Last Man* (New York: Free Press, 1992).

9. Steinberg, phone interview by author, Oct. 30, 2019.

10. U.S. Congress, FREEDOM Support Act of 1992.

11. Marian L. Lawson and Susan B. Epstein, *Democracy Promotion: An Objective of U.S. Foreign Assistance* (Washington, D.C.: U.S. Library of Congress, Congressional Research Service, 2019), fas.org; Susan B. Epstein, *National Endowment for Democracy: Policy and Funding*

Issues, CRS Report for Congress (Washington, D.C.: U.S. Library of Congress, Congressional Research Service, 1999), www.everycrsreport .com.

12. "A National Security Strategy of Engagement and Enlargement," White House, Bill Clinton, mandated report, Feb. 1996.

13. While IRI and NDI receive the bulk of their funding from USAID, NED has long issued grants to each organization; between 2009 and 2018, NED gave both IRI and NDI an annual allocation ranging from $13.8 to $16.2 million. See Lawson and Epstein, *Democracy Promotion,* 16. On initial debates over, and the major components of, overt election assistance, see Thomas Carothers, *Aiding Democracy Abroad: The Learning Curve* (Washington, D.C.: Carnegie Endowment for International Peace, 1999), chap. 6.

14. USAID, *USAID Political Party Development Assistance,* Technical Publication Series (Washington, D.C.: USAID, Bureau for Global Programs, Field Support, and Research, Center for Democracy and Governance, 1999), 16–19, 41, www.usaid.gov.

15. Ibid., 20; 22 USC 4414: "Requirements Relating to the Endowment and Its Grantees," uscode.house.gov.

For example, Jon Finer, a former State Department chief of staff and director of policy planning, said that while some U.S. democracy promotion initiatives "provid[e] technical support and training for people who are participating in elections," a "condition of that is that it is offered to anybody across the political spectrum, that is how the United States gets around the notion that we are putting our thumb on the scale in an official capacity in an election: We say it's available to anybody." Jon Finer, interview by author, New York, Feb. 20, 2019.

16. USAID, *USAID Political Party Development Assistance,* 26, 33.

17. Nuland, interview by author, Washington, D.C., Feb. 22, 2019; Wollack, phone interview by author, Oct. 15, 2019.

18. USAID, *USAID Political Party Development Assistance,* 33; International Republican Institute, *Annual Report* (Washington, D.C., 1996), 7.

19. USAID, *USAID Political Party Development Assistance,* 36.

20. Milošević was the president of the Federal Republic of Yugoslavia, which included both Serbia and Montenegro. However, in accordance with other texts on this period, and because Montenegro boycotted the 2000 election, this book refers to the contest as involving Serbia specifically.

21. Jane Perlez, "NATO Authorizes Bomb Strikes; Primakov, in Air, Skips U.S. Visit," *New York Times,* March 24, 1999, timesmachine.nytimes .com; Michael Scharf, "Indicted for War Crimes, Then What?," *Washington Post,* Oct. 3, 1999, www.washingtonpost.com; Michael Dobbs, "Serbian Nationalism Lifts Milosevic," *Washington Post,* March 30, 1999, www.washingtonpost.com; Marlise Simons, "Court Declares Bosnia Killings Were Genocide," *New York Times,* Feb. 27, 2007, www .nytimes.com; Jane Perlez, " 'Ethnic Cleansing': Enormity of Atrocities Is Called 'Shocking' by Administration," *New York Times,* March 28,

1999, www.nytimes.com; Ian Traynor, "Russia Moves to Ditch Old Ally," *Guardian,* Sept. 26, 2000, www.theguardian.com.

For further reading on Milošević's atrocities and America's posture toward his regime, see Judt, *Postwar,* 665–85; Samantha Power, *"A Problem from Hell": America and the Age of Genocide* (New York: Basic Books, 2002), chaps. 9 and 12; Tim Judah, *The Serbs: History, Myth, and the Destruction of Yugoslavia* (New Haven, Conn.: Yale University Press, 1997); Richard Holbrooke, *To End a War* (New York: Modern Library, 1998); Madeleine Albright, *Fascism: A Warning* (New York: Harper-Collins, 2018), chap. 8; Ivo H. Daalder, *Getting to Dayton: The Making of America's Bosnia Policy* (Washington, D.C.: Brookings Institution, 2000).

22. Goss, interview by author, Florida Keys, Fla., Dec. 26, 2018; Panetta, phone interview by author, Nov. 12, 2019.

23. O'Brien, phone interview by author, April 23, 2019.

24. Roger Cohen, "Who Really Brought Down Milosevic?," *New York Times,* Nov. 26, 2000, www.nytimes.com. Of Milošević, Albright writes, "Milošević, who insisted that he was a democrat, harbored a peculiar notion of what that calling entailed. He exercised a despot's control over his country's media, repressed political opposition, and created a paramilitary force to intimidate domestic rivals. Even when fueling the terrible fighting in Bosnia, he claimed to want peace; and even amid the slaughter of civilians in Sarajevo, he insisted that Serbs were the primary victims. . . . Without warning, he ordered his security forces into Kosovo to burn houses, arrest political leaders and journalists, and sow panic. His goal was to drive Albanians out of the country so that they would no longer be the majority in Kosovo. Within weeks, hundreds of thousands had been compelled to leave by train, by truck, by car, or on foot and to find temporary shelter in the hastily constructed tent cities that sprouted in surrounding fields and hills. As we had threatened, NATO initiated air strikes to force the Serbs to back down. After two and a half months of fighting, the alliance prevailed, Milošević gave in, the refugees returned, and, with international help, the Kosovars set up their own government." Albright, *Fascism,* 103–4. For further reading on Albright, see Michael Dobbs, *Madeleine Albright: Against All Odds* (New York: Henry Holt, 1999); Thomas Lippman, *Madeleine Albright and the New American Diplomacy* (Boulder, Colo.: Westview Press, 2000).

25. O'Brien, interview by author. See also "Challenging Mr. Milosevic," *New York Times,* Aug. 5, 2000, timesmachine.nytimes.com.

26. Thomas Carothers, *Critical Mission: Essays on Democracy Promotion* (Washington, D.C.: Carnegie Endowment for International Peace, 2004), 54–55.

27. Wollack, interview by author; Michael Dobbs, "U.S. Advice Guided Milosevic Opposition," *Washington Post,* Dec. 11, 2000, www.washington post.com; Cohen, "Who Really Brought Down Milosevic?"; National Endowment for Democracy, *Annual Report* (Washington, D.C.: NED, 2000), 36, www.ned.org. See also Ray Salvatore Jennings, "Serbia:

Evaluating the Bulldozer Revolution," in Kathryn Stoner and Michael McFaul, *Transitions to Democracy: A Comparative Perspective* (Baltimore, Md.: Johns Hopkins University Press, 2013), 98.

28. Memorandum of Conversation between Presidents Clinton and Putin, Sept. 6, 2000 (New York City, Waldorf Astoria, President's Suite), National Security Council and NSC Records Management System, "Declassified Documents Concerning Russian President Vladimir Putin," Clinton Digital Library. For further reading, see Ivo Daalder and Michael O'Hanlon, *Winning Ugly: NATO's War to Save Kosovo* (Washington, D.C.: Brookings Institution, 2000); Tim Judah, *Kosovo: War and Revenge* (New Haven, Conn.: Yale University Press, 2000); David Halberstam, *War in a Time of Peace: Bush, Clinton, and the Generals* (New York: Scribner, 2001), chaps. 41–43.

29. International Republican Institute, *Annual Report* (Washington, D.C.: IRI, 2000), 8, www.iri.org.

30. O'Brien, interview by author.

31. Steven Erlanger, "Milosevic Concedes His Defeat; Yugoslavs Celebrate New Era," *New York Times,* Oct. 7, 2000, timesmachine.nytimes .com.

32. O'Brien, interview by author.

33. Clinton, phone interview by author, April 4, 2020.

34. Sipher, phone interviews by author, Oct. 18, 2019 and Feb. 3 and April 7, 2020.

35. Clinton, interview by author; Lott, phone interview by author, Oct. 31, 2019.

36. Hall, phone interview by author, Oct. 22, 2019.

37. Wise, phone interview by author, Oct. 21, 2019.

38. Sipher, interview by author; Wise, interview by author.

39. Wollack, interview by author; Wise, interview by author.

40. McLaughlin, phone interview by author, Sept. 5, 2019; O'Brien, phone interview by author, March 4, 2020.

41. Sipher, interview by author; Hall, interview by author; Wise, interview by author.

42. Clinton, interview by author.

43. David Sanger, "President Says Military Phase in Iraq Has Ended," *New York Times,* May 2, 2003, www.nytimes.com. For casualty statistics, see Elizabeth Flock, "Five American Soldiers Killed in Iraq: Iraq by the Numbers," *Washington Post,* June 6, 2011, www.washingtonpost.com; "Documented Civilian Deaths from Violence," Iraq Body Count, www .iraqbodycount.org. As the years progressed, the number of Iraqis killed as a result of this war, while contested, entered into the hundreds of thousands. See Philip Bump, "15 Years After the Iraq War Began, the Death Toll Is Still Murky," *Washington Post,* March 20, 2018, www.washington post.com.

44. George W. Bush, "Remarks by President George W. Bush at the 20th Anniversary of the National Endowment for Democracy" (speech, Nov. 6,

2003), National Endowment for Democracy, Washington, D.C., www .ned.org.

45. Shultz, phone interview by author, Dec. 10, 2018.

46. Muñoz, phone interview by author, July 20, 2019.

47. International Republican Institute, *Annual Report* (Washington, D.C.: IRI, 2004), 5–6, www.iri.org; National Democratic Institute, *Annual Report* (Washington, D.C.: NDI, 2005), 32, www.ndi.org; Larry Diamond, *Squandered Victory: The American Occupation and the Bungled Effort to Bring Democracy to Iraq* (New York: Henry Holt, 2005), 125–126.

48. McLaughlin, interview by author; Wise, interview by author. See also Thom Shanker and Steven R. Weisman, "Iran Is Helping Insurgents in Iraq, U.S. Officials Say," *New York Times,* Sept. 20, 2004, www.nytimes .com; John F. Burns and Robert F. Worth, "Iraqi Campaign Raises Question of Iran's Sway," *New York Times,* Dec. 15, 2004, www.nytimes.com.

49. Negroponte, phone interview by author, May 21, 2019; Powell, email correspondence with author, Dec. 2, 2019, and with author, Feb. 19, 2020.

50. Daschle, phone interview by author, Aug. 12, 2019.

51. David Ignatius, "Bush's Lost Iraq Election," *Washington Post,* Aug. 30, 2007.

52. Negroponte, interview by author; McLaughlin, interview by author; Muñoz, interview by author.

53. Daschle, interview by author.

54. Ignatius, "Bush's Lost Iraq Election."

55. Negroponte, interview by author.

56. McLaughlin, interview by author; Ignatius, "Bush's Lost Iraq Election."

57. On Election Day, threats of violence kept many Iraqis home, and a series of attacks, including nine suicide bombings, killed forty-four people. Even so, millions turned out to vote. See Dexter Filkins, "Defying Threats, Millions of Iraqis Flock to Polls," *New York Times,* Jan. 31, 2005, www .nytimes.com. On Iran's ties to the new government, see John F. Burns, "Registering New Influence, Iran Sends a Top Aide to Iraq," *New York Times,* May 18, 2005, www.nytimes.com; Edward Wong, "Allawi Tries to Regain Office with a Non-theocratic Bloc," *New York Times,* Oct. 31, 2005, www.nytimes.com.

58. Kalugin, interview by author, Rockville, Md., Aug. 7, 2018; Phil McCausland, "Putin Interview: Did Russia Interfere in the Election, Collect Info on Trump," NBC News, June 5, 2017, www.nbcnews.com.

59. Morell, phone interview by author, March 6, 2019; Petraeus, phone interview by author, Oct. 8, 2018; Cohen, interview by author, Washington, D.C., July 17, 2018; Brennan, interview by author, Washington, D.C., July 10, 2018.

60. McLaughlin, interview by author; Blinken, interview by author, Washington, D.C., Jan. 3, 2019; Haines, interview by author, New York, Feb. 23, 2019; Clapper, interview by author, Fairfax, Va., Jan. 3, 2019.

61. Panetta, interview by author; Muñoz, interview by author.

62. Panetta, interview by author.

63. Robarge, interview by author, McLean, Va., July 19, 2019; Negroponte, interview by author.

64. Goss, interview by author; Muñoz, interview by author. For further reading on the CIA in this transitional period, see George Tenet and Bill Harlow, *At the Center of the Storm: My Years at the CIA* (New York: HarperCollins, 2007).

65. Morell, interview by author; Hayden, interview by author, Washington, D.C., Nov. 5, 2018; McLaughlin, interview by author.

66. Petraeus, interview by author; Haines, interview by author.

67. McLaughlin, interview by author.

68. Petraeus, interview by author.

69. Goss, interview by author; Cohen, interview by author; Barack Obama, "Barack Obama: As Your Friend, Let Me Say That the EU Makes Britain Even Greater," *Telegraph,* April 23, 2016, www.telegraph.co.uk; Haines, interview by author.

70. Morell, interview by author; "National Endowment for Democracy (NED), NDI, IRI, CIPE, and Solidarity Center Welcome Increased Funding from Congress," National Endowment for Democracy, Dec. 21, 2019, ned.org. Lawson and Epstein, *Democracy Promotion,* 14–15; Hayden, interview by author.

71. Sarah Repucci, "Freedom in the World, 2020: A Leaderless Struggle for Democracy," Freedom House, freedomhouse.org.

72. For further consideration, see Richard Wike and Janell Fetterolf, "Liberal Democracy's Crisis of Confidence," *Journal of Democracy* 29, no. 4 (2018): 136–50; Roberto Stefan Foa, "Modernization and Authoritarianism," *Journal of Democracy* 29, no. 3 (2018): 129–40; Marc F. Plattner, "Illiberal Democracy and the Struggle on the Right," *Journal of Democracy* 30, no. 1 (2019): 5–19; William A. Galston, "The Populist Challenge to Liberal Democracy," *Journal of Democracy* 29, no. 2 (2018): 5–19. For analysis specific to Europe, see Anna Grzymala-Busse, "The Failure of Europe's Mainstream Parties," *Journal of Democracy* 30, no. 4 (2019): 35–47; Péter Krekó and Zsolt Enyedi, "Explaining Eastern Europe: Orbán's Laboratory of Illiberalism," *Journal of Democracy* 29, no. 3 (2018): 39–51; Jacques Rupnik, "Explaining Eastern Europe: The Crisis of Liberalism," *Journal of Democracy* 29, no. 3 (2018): 24–38. For analysis specific to Latin America, see Steven Levitsky, "Latin America's Shifting Politics: Democratic Survival and Weakness," *Journal of Democracy* 29, no. 4 (2018): 102–13. And for analysis specific to the former Soviet republics, see Henry E. Hale, "25 Years After the USSR: What's Gone Wrong?," *Journal of Democracy* 27, no. 3 (2016): 24–35.

CHAPTER 7: FROM YELTSIN TO PUTIN

1. Memorandum of Conversation between Presidents Clinton and Yeltsin, April 21, 1996 (Moscow, the Kremlin), National Security Council and

NSC Records Management System, "Declassified Documents Concerning Russian President Boris Yeltsin," Clinton Digital Library. On Yeltsin's domestic standing, see Carol J. Williams, "In Yeltsin vs. Parliament, the Likely Loser Is Russia," *Los Angeles Times,* June 25, 1995, latimes .com.

2. Memorandum of Conversation between Presidents Clinton and Yeltsin, May 10, 1995 (Moscow, the Kremlin), National Security Council and NSC Records Management System, "Declassified Documents Concerning Russian President Boris Yeltsin," Clinton Digital Library.

3. Talbott, phone interview by author, Oct. 16, 2019; Panetta, phone interview by author, Nov. 12, 2019; Steinberg, phone interview by author, Oct. 30, 2019.

4. For further reading on NATO enlargement, see James M. Goldgeier, *Not Whether but When: The U.S. Decision to Enlarge NATO* (Washington, D.C.: Brookings Institution, 1999). For a critical perspective, see John Lewis Gaddis, "The Senate Should Halt NATO Expansion," *New York Times,* April 27, 1998, www.nytimes.com. For a firsthand account, see Warren Christopher, *Chances of a Lifetime: A Memoir* (New York: Scribner, 2001), chap. 16.

5. Memorandum of Conversation between Presidents Clinton and Yeltsin, May 10, 1995. NATO next enlarged in 1999, with the additions of Hungary, Poland, and the Czech Republic. See Jane Perlez, "Poland, Hungary, and the Czechs Join NATO," *New York Times,* March 13, 1999, times machine.nytimes.com.

6. Ibid.; Memorandum of Conversation between Presidents Clinton and Yeltsin, April 21, 1996.

7. Memorandum of Telephone Conversation between Presidents Clinton and Yeltsin, April 9, 1996, National Security Council and NSC Records Management System, "Declassified Documents Concerning Russian President Boris Yeltsin," Clinton Digital Library.

8. Memorandum of Telephone Conversation between Presidents Clinton and Yeltsin, Jan. 26, 1996, National Security Council and NSC Records Management System, "Declassified Documents Concerning Russian President Boris Yeltsin," Clinton Digital Library.

9. Memorandum of Telephone Conversation between Presidents Clinton and Yeltsin, Feb. 21, 1996, National Security Council and NSC Records Management System, "Declassified Documents Concerning Russian President Boris Yeltsin," Clinton Digital Library.

10. Memorandum of Telephone Conversation between Presidents Clinton and Yeltsin, May 7, 1996, National Security Council and NSC Records Management System, "Declassified Documents Concerning Russian President Boris Yeltsin," Clinton Digital Library.

11. Pascual, phone interview by author, Nov. 20, 2019.

12. Summers, phone interview by author, Nov. 22, 2019.

13. Michael Gordon, "Russia and IMF Agree on a Loan for $10.2 Billion," *New York Times,* Feb. 23, 1996, www.nytimes.com.

14. Strobe Talbott, *The Russia Hand: A Memoir of Presidential Diplomacy* (New York: Random House, 2002), 205.

15. Ibid., 447; Dick Morris and Eileen McGann, *Because He Could* (New York: HarperCollins, 2001), chap. 8. For a detailed breakdown of the types of support the Clinton administration did and did not provide Yeltsin prior to the 1996 election—and of the negligible influence of the private American consultants—see James Goldgeier and Michael McFaul, *Power and Purpose: U.S. Policy Toward Russia After the Cold War* (Washington, D.C.: Brookings Institution Press, 2003), 147–156.

16. International Republican Institute, *Annual Report* (Washington, D.C.: IRI, 1996), 13–14, www.iri.org; Sarah E. Mendelson, "Democracy Assistance and Political Transition in Russia: Between Success and Failure," *International Security* 25, no. 4 (2001), 75–78; Goldgeier and McFaul, *Power and Purpose*, 154–155.

17. Clinton, phone interview by author, April 4, 2020; Panetta, interview by author. John Sipher and Steven Hall, two CIA operations officers stationed in Russia in the 1990s, also insisted that the agency did not assist Yeltsin's campaign. Hall said, "Based on my knowledge, that was not so." Sipher, likewise, said, "There was nothing, we didn't have a covert action finding, we did nothing from Moscow station to help support that election. . . . There was no actual clandestine covert means to support Yeltsin being elected." And James Steinberg, the director of policy planning in 1996, gave a similar denial. "To my knowledge we did not do that," he said. Sipher, Hall, and Steinberg, interviews by author.

18. Talbott papers, June 16, 1996 (provided to author by Talbott), minor spelling errors corrected by author.

19. Talbott, interview by author; Michael McFaul, *Russia's Unfinished Revolution: Political Change from Gorbachev to Putin* (Ithaca, N.Y.: Cornell University Press, 2001), 2. In February 2012, Dmitri Medvedev, the Russian president, allegedly told a private audience that Yeltsin did not really win the 1996 election. See Simon Shuster, "Rewriting Russian History: Did Boris Yeltsin Steal the 1996 Presidential Election?," *Time,* Feb. 24, 2012, content.time.com.

20. Memorandum of Telephone Conversation between Presidents Clinton and Yeltsin, July 5, 1996, National Security Council and NSC Records Management System, "Declassified Documents Concerning Russian President Boris Yeltsin," Clinton Digital Library.

21. Memorandum of Telephone Conversation between Presidents Clinton and Yeltsin, Dec. 5, 1996, National Security Council and NSC Records Management System, "Declassified Documents Concerning Russian President Boris Yeltsin," Clinton Digital Library.

22. Donilon, interview by author, Washington, D.C., July 16, 2018.

23. Erlanger, interview by author, Brussels, Belgium, Dec. 18, 2018.

24. Talbott, interview by author; Summers, interview by author. For further reading, see Jeffrey Sachs, "Russia's Failure to Reform," Project Syndicate, Aug. 30, 1999, www.project-syndicate.org.

25. Celestine Bohlen, "Yeltsin Resigns; Putin Takes Over; Elections in March," *New York Times,* Jan. 1, 2000, www.nytimes.com.

26. Memorandum of Conversation between Presidents Clinton and Yeltsin, Nov. 19, 1999 (Istanbul, Turkey), and Memorandum of Telephone Conversation between Presidents Clinton and Yeltsin, Dec. 31, 1999, National Security Council and NSC Records Management System, "Declassified Documents Concerning Russian President Boris Yeltsin," Clinton Digital Library; Memorandum of Telephone Conversation between President Clinton and Acting President Putin, Jan. 1, 2000, National Security Council and NSC Records Management System, "Declassified Documents Concerning Russian President Vladimir Putin," Clinton Digital Library.

27. Memorandum of Conversation between Presidents Clinton and Yeltsin, Nov. 19, 1999.

28. Talbott, interview by author.

29. Memorandum of Telephone Conversation between Sandy Berger and Vladimir Putin, June 15, 1999, National Security Council and NSC Records Management System, "Declassified Documents Concerning Russian President Vladimir Putin," Clinton Digital Library; Memorandum of Conversation between President Clinton and Prime Minister Putin, Sept. 12, 1999 (Aukland, New Zealand), National Security Council and NSC Records Management System, "Declassified Documents Concerning Russian President Vladimir Putin," Clinton Digital Library.

30. Memorandum of Conversation between Presidents Clinton and Putin, Nov. 15, 2000 (Brunei), National Security Council and NSC Records Management System, "Declassified Documents Concerning Russian President Vladimir Putin," Clinton Digital Library.

31. Memorandum of Conversation between President Clinton and Prime Minister Putin, Nov. 2, 1999 (Oslo, Norway), National Security Council and NSC Records Management System, "Declassified Documents Concerning Russian President Vladimir Putin," Clinton Digital Library.

32. Memorandum of Conversation between Presidents Clinton and Putin, Sept. 6, 2000, and Memorandum of Telephone Conversation between Presidents Clinton and Putin, Dec. 27, 2000, National Security Council and NSC Records Management System, "Declassified Documents Concerning Russian President Vladimir Putin," Clinton Digital Library.

33. Clinton, interview by author.

34. Vladimir Putin, *First Person: An Astonishingly Frank Self-Portrait by Russia's President,* with Nataliya Gevorkyan, Natalya Timakova, and Andrei Kolesnikov (New York: PublicAffairs, 2000), 4, 18–22.

35. Ibid., 22.

36. Ibid., 47–52, 66–70.

37. On the collapse of East Germany, see Hans-Hermann Hertle, "The Fall of the Wall: The Unintended Self-Dissolution of East Germany's Ruling Regime," *Cold War International History Project Bulletin,* no. 12/13 (2001): 131–64; Charles S. Maier, *Dissolution: The Crisis of Communism and the End of East Germany* (Princeton, N.J.: Princeton University

Press, 1997); A. James McAdams, *Germany Divided: From the Wall to Reunification* (Princeton, N.J.: Princeton University Press, 1993).

38. Putin, *First Person,* 76–78; Zubok, "New Evidence on the 'Soviet Factor' in the Peaceful Revolutions of 1989," 11–12.

39. Putin, *First Person,* 80, 82.

40. For further reading on the Soviet Union's security services and military toward the end of the Cold War, see *Journal of Cold War Studies 5,* no. 1 (2003), in which Amy Knight captures the role and work of the KGB between 1985 and 1991 in "The KGB, Perestroika, and the Collapse of the Soviet Union," 67–93; John Dunlop analyzes the failed coup d'état and its consequences in "The August 1991 Coup and Its Impact on Soviet Politics," 94–127; and Brian Taylor examines the restraint of the Soviet armed forces in "The Soviet Military and the Disintegration of the USSR," 17–66. See also Oleg Gordievsky, "The KGB After the Coup," *Intelligence and National Security* 8, no. 3 (1993): 68–71.

41. For further reading on Putin's rise, character, and worldview, see Fiona Hill and Clifford Gaddy, *Mr. Putin: Operative in the Kremlin* (Washington, D.C.: Brookings Institution Press, 2013); Angela Stent, *Putin's World: Russia Against the West and with the Rest* (New York: Twelve, 2019); Steven Lee Myers, *The New Tsar: The Rise and Reign of Vladimir Putin* (New York: Knopf, 2015); Masha Gessen, *The Man Without a Face: The Unlikely Rise of Vladimir Putin* (New York: Riverhead, 2012).

42. Sipher, phone interview by author, Oct. 18, 2019; Fuerth, phone interview by author, Oct. 31, 2019. On the sustained influence of Russia's security services, see Amy Knight, *Spies Without Cloaks: The KGB's Successors* (Princeton, N.J.: Princeton University Press, 1996); Andrei Soldatov and Irina Borogan, *The New Nobility: The Restoration of Russia's Security State and the Enduring Legacy of the KGB* (New York: PublicAffairs, 2010); Yuriy Felshtinsky and Vladimir Pribylovskiy, *The Corporation: Russia and the KGB in the Age of President Putin* (New York: Encounter Books, 2008).

43. Fuerth, interview by author. For an alternative view, see Vladislav Inozemtsev, "The Kremlin Emboldened: Why Putinism Arose," *Journal of Democracy* 28, no. 4 (2017): 80–85.

44. Michael McFaul, "Why Russia's Politics Matter," *Foreign Affairs,* January/February 1995, www.foreignaffairs.com; U.S. Department of State, Office of the Historian, "United States Relations with Russia after the Cold War," https://2001-2009.state.gov/r/pa/ho/pubs/fs/85962.htm. Goldgeier and McFaul further explain, "Especially in the early years of aid to Russia, the lion's share of Western assistance was devoted not to political reform but to economic reform. . . . Of the $5.45 billion in direct U.S. assistance to Russia between 1992 and 1998, only $130 million or 2.3 percent was devoted to programs involved directly in democratic reform." Goldgeier and McFaul, *Power and Purpose,* 114.

45. Steinberg, interview by author; Memorandum of Telephone Conversation between Presidents Clinton and Yeltsin, July 5, 1996.

46. Talbott papers, Aug. 31, 1998 (provided to author by Talbott).

47. Ibid.

48. Steinberg, interview by author; Summers, interview by author.

49. McFaul, *Russia's Unfinished Revolution,* 323–27; McFaul, *From Cold War to Hot Peace: An American Ambassador in Putin's Russia* (New York: Houghton Mifflin Harcourt, 2018), 41–47, 54. Of this period, Timothy Snyder writes, "The wealthy few around Yeltsin, christened the 'oligarchs,' wished to manage democracy in his favor and theirs." Snyder, *Road to Unfreedom,* 53. See also Anders Åslund, *Russia's Crony Capitalism: The Path from Market Economy to Kleptocracy* (New Haven, Conn.: Yale University Press, 2019), 19–25; Fareed Zakaria, *The Future of Freedom: Illiberal Democracy at Home and Abroad* (New York: W. W. Norton, 2003), chap. 3.

50. Talbott papers, Aug. 31, 1998 (provided to author by Talbott), minor spelling errors corrected by author. On Yeltsin and his presidency, see Timothy Colton, *Yeltsin: A Life* (New York: Basic Books, 2008); David Remnick, *Resurrection: The Struggle for a New Russia* (New York: Random House, 1997).

51. Panetta, interview by author.

52. McLaughlin, phone interview by author, Sept. 5, 2019; Fuerth, interview by author; Clinton, interview by author. Of this moment of transition, McFaul writes, "That the fate of Russian democracy in 2000 was so tied to the ideas and actions of one individual underscores the failure of Yeltsin and the democrats to institutionalize democracy." McFaul, *From Cold War to Hot Peace,* 56.

53. Summers, interview by author. Anne Applebaum made a similar case in 2014, arguing, "In truth, we've had very little influence on Russian internal politics since 1991, even when we've understood them. The most important changes—the massive transfer of oil and gas from the state to the oligarchs, the return to power of men formed by the KGB, the elimination of a free press and political opposition—took place against our advice. The most important military decisions—the invasions of Chechnya and Georgia—met with our protests." Anne Applebaum, "A Need to Contain Russia," *Washington Post,* March 20, 2014, www .washingtonpost.com.

54. Peter Pomerantsev, *Nothing Is True and Everything Is Possible: The Surreal Heart of the New Russia* (New York: PublicAffairs, 2014), Act I; William H. Cooper, *Russia's Economic Performance and Policies and Their Implications for the United States* (Washington, D.C.: U.S. Library of Congress, Congressional Research Service, 2009), fas.org; Snyder, *Road to Unfreedom,* chap. 2. On Putin's consolidation of power, see Peter Baker and Susan Glasser, *Kremlin Rising: Vladimir Putin's Russia and the End of Revolution* (New York: Scribner, 2005); Steven Fish, *Democracy Derailed in Russia: The Failure of Open Politics* (New York: Cambridge University Press, 2005).

   Putin, in these years, left the internet relatively unregulated, because it seemed relatively irrelevant. In 2005, just 15 percent of Russian citizens were using the internet, a strikingly low figure compared with the United States, where 68 percent of citizens were plugged into the web already. See "Russia Internet Users" and "United States Internet Users," Internet Live Stats, www.internetlivestats.com. It was China, not Russia, that pioneered the concept of "digital authoritarianism," defined as "the use of digital information technology by authoritarian regimes to surveil, repress, and manipulate domestic and foreign populations" by Alina Polyakova and Chris Meserole in "Exporting Digital Authoritarianism: The Russian and Chinese Models," Brookings Policy Brief (Washington, D.C.: Brookings Institution), Aug. 2019, www.brookings.edu. See also Xiao Qiang, "The Road to Digital Unfreedom: President Xi's Surveillance State," *Journal of Democracy* 30, no. 1 (2019): 53–67.

55. Kalugin, interview by author, Rockville, Md., Aug. 7, 2018.
56. Steven Lee Myers, "Pervasive Corruption in Russia Is 'Just Called Business,'" *New York Times,* Aug. 13, 2005, www.nytimes.com.
57. Credit Suisse, "Global Wealth Databook 2014," Oct. 2014, 125; Katy Barnato, "Russia Is the Most Unequal Major Country in the World," CNBC, Sept. 1, 2016, www.cnbc.com.
58. Mansur Mirovalev, "Putin's Best Friend Is at the Heart of Panama Papers Scandal," *Los Angeles Times,* April 4, 2016; Luke Harding, "Sergei Roldugin, the Cellist Who Holds the Key to Tracing Putin's Hidden Fortune," *Guardian,* April 3, 2016; Andrei Soldatov and Irina Borogan, *The Red Web: The Kremlin's Wars on the Internet* (New York: PublicAffairs, 2015), 312–19.
59. Karen Dawisha, *Putin's Kleptocracy: Who Owns Russia?* (New York: Simon & Schuster, 2014), 280. For additional interpretations, see Miriam Lanskoy and Dylan Myles-Primakoff, "The Rise of Kleptocracy: Power and Plunder in Putin's Russia," *Journal of Democracy* 29, no. 1 (2018): 76–85; Steven Fish, "The Kremlin Emboldened: What Is Putinism?," *Journal of Democracy* 28, no. 4 (2017): 61–75. On the concept and mechanics of kleptocracy, see Alexander Cooley, John Heathershaw, and J. C. Sharman, "The Rise of Kleptocracy: Laundering Cash, Whitewashing Reputations," *Journal of Democracy* 29, no. 1 (2018): 39–53; Oliver Bullough, "The Rise of Kleptocracy: The Dark Side of Globalization," *Journal of Democracy* 29, no. 1 (2018): 25–38; Christopher Walker and Melissa Aten, "The Rise of Kleptocracy: A Challenge for Democracy," *Journal of Democracy* 29, no. 1 (2018): 20–24.
60. Julie Ray and Neli Esipova, "Economic Problems, Corruption Fail to Dent Putin's Image," Gallup, March 28, 2017, news.gallup.com; "Russians Are Most Unhappy with Putin over Wealth Inequality—Poll," *Moscow Times,* May 7, 2018, www.themoscowtimes.com.
61. In interviews, former CIA directors and operations officers emphasized this aspect of Putin's worldview. For instance, Steven Hall, a former Moscow station chief, said, "Putin believes that the U.S. government writ large wants to do this, to foment a color revolution in the streets of Moscow,

and it's a conspiracy theory obviously, but I think Putin actually believes that it's true." Hall, phone interview by author, Oct. 22, 2019.

62. Sipher, interview by author; Hall, interview by author; McLaughlin, interview by author.

63. Wise, phone interview by author, Oct. 21, 2019; Hall, interview by author.

64. Memorandum of Telephone Conversation between Presidents Clinton and Putin, Sept. 30, 2000, National Security Council and NSC Records Management System, "Declassified Documents Concerning Russian President Vladimir Putin," Clinton Digital Library.

65. Andrew Higgins and Alan Cullison, "Russia Alienates an Ally by Hesitating in Yugoslavia," *Wall Street Journal,* Oct. 9, 2000, www.wsj.com.

66. Ibid.; Hall, interview by author.

67. Putin, interviewed by *Time* magazine, Dec. 12, 2007, en.kremlin.ru.

68. Ibid.

69. Martin Chulov, "Gaddafi's Last Moments: 'I Saw the Hand Holding the Gun and I Saw It Fire,'" *Guardian,* Oct. 20, 2012, www.theguardian.com.

70. Ellen Barry, "Putin Criticizes West for Libya Incursion," *New York Times,* April 26, 2011, www.nytimes.com.

71. Putin, interviewed by Charlie Rose, Sept. 29, 2015, en.kremlin.ru.

72. Steven Woehrel, *Ukraine's Political Crisis and U.S. Policy Issues* (Washington, D.C.: U.S. Library of Congress, Congressional Research Service, 2005), fas.org; Anne Applebaum, "Obama and Europe," *Foreign Affairs,* Sept./Oct. 2015, www.foreignaffairs.com. See also Stephen Shulman and Stephen Bloom, "The Legitimacy of Foreign Intervention in Elections: The Ukrainian Response," *Review of International Studies* 38, no. 2 (2012): 445–71.

73. Emily Tamkin, "10 Years After the Landmark Attack on Estonia, Is the World Better Prepared for Cyber Threats?," *Foreign Policy,* April 27, 2017, foreignpolicy.com; Snyder, *Road to Unfreedom,* 80. On Russia's evolving military strategy and cyber operations, see Michael Connell and Sarah Vogler, "Russia's Approach to Cyber Warfare," CNA, March 2017, www.cna.org.

74. David Sanger, *The Perfect Weapon: War, Sabotage, and Fear in the Cyber Age* (New York: Crown, 2018), xiv.

75. Of this shift, Timothy Snyder writes, "Killing the political future forced the political present to be eternal," and "making an eternity of the present required endless crisis and permanent threats." Snyder, *Road to Unfreedom,* 48.

76. Kathy Lally, "Russia Targets U.S.-Linked Election Monitor," *Washington Post,* Nov. 30, 2011, www.washingtonpost.com; David Herszenhorn, "Russia Takes Legal Action Against Election Monitors," *New York Times,* April 9, 2013, www.nytimes.com.

77. Ellen Barry, "Russian Authorities Pressure Elections Watchdog," *New York Times,* Dec. 1, 2011, www.nytimes.com; Michael Schwirtz and David Herszenhorn, "Voters Watch Polls in Russia, and Fraud Is What They See," *New York Times,* Dec. 5, 2011, www.nytimes.com.

78. Hall, interview by author.
79. Hillary Clinton, "Remarks at a Town Hall with Georgian Women Leaders," July 5, 2010, State Department, 2009–2017, state.gov; McFaul, *From Cold War to Hot Peace*, 96. For more on the reset, see McFaul, *From Cold War to Hot Peace,* chaps. 6–13.
80. Clinton, interview by author, New York, Dec. 4, 2019; Jo Becker and Scott Shane, "Hillary Clinton, 'Smart Power,' and a Dictator's Fall," *New York Times,* Feb. 27, 2016, www.nytimes.com.
81. Matt Spetalnick, Arshad Mohammed, and Andrew Quinn, "U.S. Voices 'Serious Concerns' About Russia Vote," Reuters, Dec. 5, 2011, www .reuters.com. In her interview with the author, Clinton characterized the election as "blatantly rigged."
82. Ellen Barry and David Herszenhorn, "Putin Contends Clinton Incited Unrest over Vote," *New York Times,* Dec. 8, 2011, www.nytimes.com. Lilia Shevtsova of Chatham House argues, "[Putin's] scramble for self-preservation also reaches beyond Russia's borders. To a larger extent than most authoritarian regimes, the regime has turned its survival into an international problem by using its foreign policy for domestic ends. Confronted by challenges at home, it manufactures external threats in an attempt to sweep these domestic issues under the rug." Lilia Shevtsova, "The Kremlin Emboldened: Paradoxes of Decline," *Journal of Democracy* 28, no. 4 (2017): 102. See also McFaul, *From Cold War to Hot Peace,* chap. 15.
83. Clinton, interview by author.
84. Steve Gutterman and Amie Ferris-Rotman, "Thousands of Russians Protest Against Putin," Reuters, Dec. 10, 2011, www.reuters.com.
85. Morell, phone interview by author, March 6, 2019; Hall, interview by author.
86. Clinton, interview by author.
87. Barry, phone interview by author, June 19, 2019. On Putin's hold over Russia, see Graeme Robertson and Samuel Greene, "The Kremlin Emboldened: How Putin Wins Support," *Journal of Democracy* 28, no. 4 (2017): 86–100.
88. David Herszenhorn and Ellen Barry, "Russia Demands U.S. End Support of Democracy Groups," *New York Times,* Sept. 18, 2012, www.nytimes .com; Susan Cornwell, "U.S. Pro-democracy Groups Pulling Out of Russia," Reuters, Dec. 14, 2012, www.reuters.com; "Russia Internet Blacklist Law Takes Effect," BBC, Nov. 1, 2012, www.bbc.com; "Overview: Russia," NDI.org.
89. In 2013, Victoria Nuland explained, "Since Ukraine's independence in 1991, the United States has supported Ukrainians as they build democratic skills and institutions, as they promote civic participation and good governance, all of which are preconditions for Ukraine to achieve its European aspirations. We have invested over $5 billion to assist Ukraine in these and other goals that will ensure a secure and prosperous and democratic Ukraine." See Katie Sanders, "The United States Spent $5 Billion on

Ukraine and Anti-government Riots," PolitiFact, March 19, 2014, www.politifact.com.

90. "Top U.S. Official Visits Protesters in Kiev as Obama Admin. Ups Pressure on Ukraine President Yanukovich," CBS News, Dec. 11, 2013, www.cbsnews.com; Andrew Higgins and Peter Baker, "Russia Claims U.S. Is Meddling over Ukraine," *New York Times,* Feb. 6, 2014, www.nytimes.com; Nuland, interview by author, Washington, D.C., Feb. 22, 2019.

91. Andrew Kramer and Andrew Higgins, "Ukraine's Forces Escalate Attacks Against Protesters," *New York Times,* Feb. 20, 2014, www.nytimes.com; Andrew Kramer and Andrew Higgins, "Archrival Is Freed as Ukraine Leader Flees," *New York Times,* Feb. 22, 2014, www.nytimes.com; Ivan Nechepurenko, "Ukraine's Ex-leader Regrets Not Breaking Up Protests That Led to His Fall," *New York Times,* Nov. 25, 2016, www.nytimes.com. For an especially vivid account of the movement against Yanukovych, see Marci Shore, *The Ukrainian Night: An Intimate History of Revolution* (New Haven, Conn.: Yale University Press, 2018).

92. Max Seddon, "Documents Show How Russia's Troll Army Hit America," *BuzzFeed News,* June 2, 2014, www.buzzfeednews.com.

93. Terrence McCoy, "Vladimir Putin Hates Everything About the Internet Except 'Website Vladimir,'" *Washington Post,* April 25, 2014, www.washingtonpost.com; "Vkontakte Founder Pavel Durov Learns He's Been Fired Through Media," *Moscow Times,* April 22, 2014, www.themoscowtimes.com; Amar Toor, "How Putin's Cronies Seized Control of Russia's Facebook," *Verge,* Jan. 31, 2014, www.theverge.com; Neil MacFarquhar, "Russia Quietly Tightens Reins on Web with 'Bloggers Law,'" *New York Times,* May 6, 2014, www.nytimes.com; Alexei Anishchuk, "Russia Passes Law to Force Websites onto Russian Servers," Reuters, July 4, 2014, www.reuters.com.

94. The journalist Adrian Chen explains, "Trolling has become a key tool in a comprehensive effort by Russian authorities to rein in a previously freewheeling Internet culture, after huge anti-Putin protests in 2011 were organized largely over social media. It is used by Kremlin apparatchiks at every level of government in Russia; wherever politics are discussed online, one can expect a flood of comments from paid trolls." Adrian Chen, "The Real Paranoia-Inducing Purpose of Russian Hacks," *New Yorker,* July 27, 2016. Leonid Volkov, a Russian opposition leader, told Chen that pro-Kremlin operatives infest social media to confuse rather than to change minds: "The point is to spoil it, to create the atmosphere of hate, to make it so stinky that normal people won't want to touch it."

95. Putin, interview by Kelly, March 1–2, 2018, en.kremlin.ru.

96. Burns, interview by author, Washington, D.C., July 9, 2018.

97. This zero-sum calculus is not new. In 1945, George Kennan, while stationed in Moscow, warned Secretary of State James F. Byrnes of a similar attitude within the Kremlin. He wrote, "There is nothing—I repeat nothing—in the history of the Soviet regime which could justify us in assuming that the men who are now in power in Russia, or even those

who have chances of assuming power within the foreseeable future, would hesitate for a moment to apply this power against us if by doing so they thought that they might materially improve their own power position in the world." See Gaddis, *George F. Kennan,* 207.

98. Panetta, interview by author.

99. Morell, interview by author. See also Snyder, *Road to Unfreedom,* chap. 5.

100. Morell, interview by author; Kalugin, interview by author. Lucas Kello of Oxford writes, "Russian strategists exhort actions that seek to deny adversaries the internal political cohesion necessary to act purposefully abroad. Cyberspace offers a rich plane onto which practitioners can extend this activity." Lucas Kello, *The Virtual Weapon and International Order* (New Haven, Conn.: Yale University Press, 2017), 227.

101. Vladislav Surkov, "Владислав Сурков: Долгое государство Путина," *Независимая газета,* Feb. 11, 2019, www.ng.ru.

102. Hayden, interview by author, Washington, D.C., Nov. 5, 2018. For Hayden's personal recollections, see Michael Hayden, *The Assault on Intelligence: American National Security in an Age of Lies* (New York: Penguin Press, 2018). Russia's intelligence services have struck abroad in other ways in recent years. See David V. Gioe, Michael S. Goodman, and David S. Frey, "Unforgiven: Russian Intelligence Vengeance as Political Theater and Strategic Messaging," *Intelligence and National Security* 34, no. 4 (2019): 561–75.

103. Tsybulska, interview by author, Kyiv, Ukraine, June 17, 2019.

CHAPTER 8: A NEW AGE

1. "Putin Describes Secret Operation to Seize Crimea," AFP, March 8, 2015, news.yahoo.com.

2. For further reading, see Snyder, *Road to Unfreedom,* chaps. 4 and 5; Lucan Ahmad Way, "Ukraine's Post-Maidan Struggles: Free Speech in a Time of War," *Journal of Democracy* 30, no. 3 (2019): 48–60; Joanna Rohozinska and Vitaliy Shpak, "Ukraine's Post-Maidan Struggles: The Rise of an 'Outsider' President," *Journal of Democracy* 30, no. 3 (2019): 33–47.

3. Vladimir Putin, "Address by President of the Russian Federation" (speech, March 18, 2014), en.kremlin.ru.

4. Alberto Nardelli, Jennifer Rankin, and George Arnett, "Vladimir Putin's Approval Rating at Record Levels," *Guardian,* July 23, 2015, www .theguardian.com. Leon Aron explains, "Faced with the need to revitalize his support, Putin seems to have made the most fateful choice of his political life: He sharply shifted the basis of his popularity—and thus his regime's legitimacy—from economic growth to patriotic mobilization." Leon Aron, "The Kremlin Emboldened: Putinism After Crimea," *Journal of Democracy* 28, no. 4 (2017): 76–79. For further reading, see Daniel Treisman, "Why Putin Took Crimea," *Foreign Affairs,* May/June 2016, www.foreignaffairs.com.

5. Steve Holland and Jeff Mason, "Obama, Merkel Vow Broader Russian

Sanctions if Ukraine Election Derailed," Reuters, May 2, 2014, af.reuters
.com.

6. Margaret Coker and Paul Sonne, "Ukraine: Cyberwar's Hottest Front," *Wall Street Journal,* Nov. 9, 2015, www.wsj.com; Mark Clayton, "Ukraine Election Narrowly Avoided 'Wanton Destruction' from Hackers," *Christian Science Monitor,* June 17, 2014, www.csmonitor.com; Laurens Cerulus, "How Ukraine Became a Test Bed for Cyberweaponry," *Politico Europe,* Feb. 14, 2019, www.politico.eu; Defense Intelligence Agency, "Russia Military Power: Building a Military to Support Great Power Aspirations," 2017, dia.mil.

Of the virus detected on Election Day, the SBU, Ukraine's security service, said in a statement that "offenders were trying by means of previously installed software to fake election results in the given region and in such a way to discredit general results of elections of the President of Ukraine." See Clayton, "Ukraine Election Narrowly Avoided 'Wanton Destruction' from Hackers."

7. Fedchenko, interview by author, Kyiv, Ukraine, June 17, 2019.

8. Oren Dorell, "Alleged Russian Political Meddling Documented in 27 Countries Since 2004," *USA Today,* Sept. 7, 2017, www.usatoday.com. See also U.S. Congress, Senate, Committee on Foreign Relations, *Putin's Asymmetric Assault on Democracy in Russia and Europe: Implications for U.S. National Security,* 115th Cong., 2nd sess., 2018, S. Rep. 115-21, www.foreign.senate.gov; Evan Osnos, David Remnick, and Joshua Yaffa, "Trump, Putin, and the New Cold War," *New Yorker,* Feb. 24, 2017, www.newyorker.com.

9. Schadlow, phone interview by author, Nov. 9, 2018. I first reported on this in an article for *The New Yorker* ("Smaller Democracies Grapple with the Threat of Russian Interference," *New Yorker,* Dec. 8, 2018, newyorker .com).

10. Gerasimov, "Value of Science Is in the Foresight."

11. Goss, interview by author, Florida Keys, Fla., Dec. 26, 2018; Heiestad, interview by author, Brussels, Belgium, Dec. 4, 2018.

12. Paul Sonne, "A Russian Bank Gave Marine Le Pen's Party a Loan. Then Weird Things Began Happening," *Washington Post,* Dec. 27, 2018, www .washingtonpost.com; Suzanne Daley and Maïa de la Baume, "French Far Right Gets Helping Hand With Russian Loan," *New York Times,* Dec. 1, 2014, www.nytimes.com.

13. Burns, interview by author.

14. Putin, interview by John Micklethwait, Sept. 1, 2016, en.kremlin.ru.

15. Đukanović, interview by author, Oxford, U.K., Nov. 26, 2018.

16. Aleksandar Vasovic, "Montenegro Opposition Rejects Election Outcome due to 'Atmosphere of Fear,'" Reuters, Oct. 18, 2016, www.reuters .com; Petar Komnenic, "Montenegro Begins Trial of Alleged Pro-Russian Coup Plotters," Reuters, July 19, 2017, www.reuters.com; Julian Barnes, "Ex–C.I.A. Officer's Brief Detention Deepens Mystery in Montenegro," *New York Times,* Nov. 23, 2018, www.nytimes.com; Ken Dilanian et

al., "White House Readies to Fight Election Day Cyber Mayhem," NBC News, Nov. 3, 2016, www.nbcnews.com; Michael Schwirtz, "Top Secret Russian Unit Seeks to Destabilize Europe, Security Officials Say," *New York Times,* Oct. 8, 2019, www.nytimes.com.

17. Đukanović, interview by author.

18. Wise, phone interview by author, Oct. 21, 2019; Nuland, interview by author, Washington, D.C., Feb. 22, 2019; Wallander, interview by author, Washington, D.C., July 17, 2019.

19. John McCain, "Why Should You Care About Russian Interference? Look No Further than the Attempted Coup in Montenegro," Medium, June 20, 2017, medium.com.

20. Đukanović, interview by author.

21. Santos, interview by author, Oxford, U.K., Nov. 13, 2018; Nicholas Casey and Susan Abad, "Colombia Elects Iván Duque, a Young Populist, as President," *New York Times,* June 17, 2018, www.nytimes.com; Azam Ahmed and Paulina Villegas, "López Obrador, an Atypical Leftist, Wins Mexico Presidency in Landslide," *New York Times,* July 1, 2018, www .nytimes.com.

22. On the causes and consequences of Brexit, see Anne Applebaum, "Britain After Brexit: A Transformed Political Landscape," *Journal of Democracy* 28, no. 1 (2017): 53–58; Robert Ford and Matthew Goodwin, "Britain After Brexit: A Nation Divided," *Journal of Democracy* 28, no. 1 (2017): 17–30. On Russia's tactics, see Snyder, *Road to Unfreedom,* 104–9, in which Snyder explains, "Brexit was a triumph for Russian foreign policy, and a sign that a cyber campaign directed from Moscow could change reality."

23. David D. Kirkpatrick, "Signs of Russian Meddling in Brexit Referendum," *New York Times,* Nov. 15, 2017, www.nytimes.com; Matthew Field and Mike Wright, "Russian Trolls Sent Thousands of Pro-Leave Messages on Day of Brexit Referendum, Twitter Data Reveals," *Telegraph,* Oct. 17, 2018, www.telegraph.co.uk; Snyder, *Road to Unfreedom,* 106.

24. Hannigan, interview by author, London, March 22, 2019.

25. On the covert nature of Russia's operation, Snyder writes, "About a third of the discussion of Brexit on Twitter was generated by bots—and more than 90% of the bots tweeting political material were not located in the United Kingdom. Britons who considered their choices had no idea at the time that they were reading material disseminated by bots, nor that the bots were part of a Russian foreign policy to weaken their country." Snyder, *Road to Unfreedom,* 106.

26. Clapper, interview by author, Fairfax, Va., Jan. 3, 2019.

27. Anton Troianovski and Karla Adam, "In Brexit, Putin Sees a Crisis of Democracy—Not That He Has Anything to Do with It," *Washington Post,* Dec. 20, 2018, www.washingtonpost.com.

28. Mark Landler and Stephen Castle, "U.K. Parliament Advances Brexit Bill in Lopsided Vote, All but Assuring January Exit," *New York Times,* Dec. 20, 2019, www.nytimes.com.

29. Hannigan, interview by author.

30. Wise, interview by author.

31. Erlanger, interview by author, Brussels, Belgium, Dec. 18, 2018.

32. On the decline of foreign reporting, see Justin D. Martin, "Loneliness at the Foreign 'Bureau,'" *Columbia Journalism Review,* April 23, 2012, archives.cjr.org; Jodi Enda, "Retreating from the World," *AJR,* Dec./Jan. 2011, ajrarchive.org.

33. Cohen, interview by author, Washington, D.C., July 17, 2018; Johnson, interview by author, New York, July 29, 2019; Hall, phone interview by author, Oct. 22, 2019.

34. Blinken, interview by author, Washington, D.C., Jan. 3, 2019.

35. Clapper, interview by author.

36. Andrei Soldatov and Irina Borogan, two Russian journalists, have explained that "Putin believed the Panama Papers attack was sponsored by Hillary Clinton's people—this, in a way, provided him with a 'justification' for a retaliatory operation." See Adam Taylor, "Putin Saw the Panama Papers as a Personal Attack and May Have Wanted Revenge, Russian Authors Say," *Washington Post,* Aug. 28, 2017, www.washington post.com.

37. Patrick O'Connor, "Hillary Clinton Exits with 69% Approval Rating," *Wall Street Journal,* Jan. 17, 2013, blogs.wsj.com; Hillary Rodham Clinton, *Hard Choices* (New York: Simon & Schuster, 2014), 215.

38. Philip Rucker, "Hillary Clinton Says Putin's Actions Are Like 'What Hitler Did Back in the '30s,'" *Washington Post,* March 5, 2014, www .washingtonpost.com; Liz Kreutz, "Vladimir Putin on Hillary Clinton: 'Better Not to Argue with Women,'" ABC, June 4, 2014, abcnews.go.com.

39. Hall, interview by author.

40. For further reading, see David Remnick, *The Bridge: The Life and Rise of Barack Obama* (New York: Knopf, 2010).

41. Barack Obama, speech in Chicago, Oct. 2, 2002, www.npr.org. In his inaugural address, Obama declared that "the state of our economy calls for action, bold and swift" and pledged to "begin to responsibly leave Iraq to its people and forge a hard-earned peace in Afghanistan." See Barack Obama, "Inaugural Address" (speech, Washington, D.C., Jan. 20, 2009), the Obama White House, obamawhitehouse.archives.gov.

42. "Transcript of the Third Presidential Debate," *New York Times,* Oct. 22, 2012, www.nytimes.com. Anne Applebaum traces the evolution in U.S.-Russian relations from the start of the Obama presidency through the Ukraine crisis in "Obama and Europe."

43. Marvin Kalb, "Stumbling Toward Conflict with Russia?," Brookings Institution, June 3, 2015, www.brookings.edu.

44. Petraeus, phone interview by author, Oct. 8, 2018; Joby Warrick, "More than 1,400 Killed in Syrian Chemical Weapons Attack, U.S. Says," *Washington Post,* Aug. 30, 2013, www.washingtonpost.com.

45. Ben Rhodes, "Inside the White House During the Syrian 'Red Line' Crisis," *Atlantic,* June 3, 2018, www.theatlantic.com.

46. Paul Nitze, a former deputy secretary of defense, captured the essence of escalation dominance when he said that a "copybook principle in strategy" is that "the advantage tends to go to the side in a better position to raise the stakes by expanding the scope, duration or destructive intensity of the conflict." See Robert Jervis, "The Madness Beyond MAD—Current American Nuclear Strategy," *PS* 17, no. 1 (1984): 34. On Nitze, see Strobe Talbott, *The Master of the Game: Paul Nitze and the Nuclear Peace* (New York: Knopf, 1988). Daniel Byman and Matthew Waxman define escalation dominance as "the ability to increase the threatened costs to the adversary while denying the adversary the opportunity to negate those costs or to counterescalate." Daniel Byman and Matthew Waxman, *The Dynamics of Coercion: American Foreign Policy and the Limits of Military Might* (Cambridge, U.K.: Cambridge University Press, 2002), 38. For further reading on escalatory concerns in foreign policy, see Richard Smoke, *War: Controlling Escalation* (Cambridge, Mass.: Harvard University Press, 1977).

47. Nuland, interview by author.

48. Peter Baker and Andrew Higgins, "U.S. and European Sanctions Take Aim at Putin's Economic Efforts," *New York Times,* Sept. 12, 2014, www.nytimes.com; Jeremy Herb, "Obama Pressed on Many Fronts to Arm Ukraine," *Politico,* March 11, 2015, www.politico.com.

49. Morell, phone interview by author, March 6, 2019.

50. Panetta, phone interview by author, Nov. 12, 2019.

51. Petraeus, interview by author.

52. Dina Smeltz and Ivo Daalder, "Foreign Policy in the Age of Retrenchment," Chicago Council on Global Affairs, 7, survey.thechicagocouncil.org.

53. Morell, interview by author.

54. *United States v. Internet Research Agency LLC,* 18 U.S.C. §§ 2, 371, 1349, 1028A (D.D.C. 2018), 6, www.justice.gov.

55. U.S. Congress, Senate, Select Committee on Intelligence, *Russian Efforts Against Election Infrastructure,* vol. 1 of *Report on Russian Active Measures Campaigns and Interference in the 2016 U.S. Election,* 116th Cong., 1st sess., 2019, S. Rep. 116-XX, 3, www.intelligence.senate.gov.

56. Office of the Director of National Intelligence, Intelligence Community Assessment, *Assessing Russian Activities and Intentions in Recent U.S. Elections,* Jan. 6, 2017, www.dni.gov.

57. Brennan, interview by author, Washington, D.C., July 10, 2018. For a typical article on Trump's campaign announcement, see Alex Altman and Charlotte Alter, "Trump Launches Presidential Campaign with Empty Flair," *Time,* June 16, 2015, time.com.

58. Alan Gilbert, "The Far-Right Book Every Russian General Reads," *Daily Beast,* Feb. 26, 2018, www.thedailybeast.com.

59. U.S. Department of Justice, Office of Special Counsel Robert S. Mueller III, *Report on the Investigation into Russian Interference in the 2016 Presidential Election* (hereafter cited as Mueller Report), March 2019,

70–71. For further reading on Trump's business pursuits in Russia, see David Ignatius, "A History of Donald Trump's Business Dealings in Russia," *Washington Post*, Nov. 2, 2017, www.washingtonpost.com; Megan Twohey and Steve Eder, "For Trump, Three Decades of Chasing Deals in Russia," *New York Times*, Jan. 16, 2017, www.nytimes.com/. For Trump's response, see Linda Qiu, "Trump Denies Business Dealings With Russia. His Former Lawyer Contradicts Him," *New York Times*, Nov. 29, 2018, www.nytimes.com.

60. Andrew Kramer, "Vladimir Putin Chides Turkey, Praises Trump, and Talks Up Russia's Economy," *New York Times,* Dec. 17, 2015, www.nytimes.com; Vladimir Putin, "Vladimir Putin's Annual News Conference," Dec. 17, 2015, en.kremlin.ru.

61. *United States v. Internet Research Agency LLC,* 18 U.S.C. §§ 2, 371, 1349, 1028A (D.D.C. 2018), 17, www.justice.gov.

62. Maggie Haberman, "Super Tuesday Takeaways: Trump and Clinton Sprint, While Others Stumble," *New York Times,* March 2, 2016, www.nytimes.com. Also in March, Trump hired Paul Manafort, a lobbyist who had made millions advising Viktor Yanukovych, the former Ukrainian president. Alexander Burns and Maggie Haberman, "Donald Trump Hires Paul Manafort to Lead Delegate Effort," *New York Times,* March 28, 2016, www.nytimes.com. For further reading on Manafort, see Steven Lee Myers and Andrew Kramer, "How Paul Manafort Wielded Power in Ukraine Before Advising Donald Trump," *New York Times,* July 31, 2016, www.nytimes.com; Andrew Kramer, Mike McIntire, and Barry Meier, "Secret Ledger in Ukraine Lists Cash for Donald Trump's Campaign Chief," *New York Times,* Aug. 14, 2016, www.nytimes.com; Franklin Foer, "The Plot Against America," *Atlantic,* March 2018; Simon Shuster, "How Paul Manafort Helped Elect Russia's Man in Ukraine," *Time,* Oct. 31, 2017, www.time.com.

63. Mueller Report, 37–38; U.S. Congress, Senate, Select Committee on Intelligence, *Hearings Before the Select Committee on Intelligence, Disinformation: A Primer in Russian Active Measures and Influence Campaigns* (testimony by Thomas Rid), 115th Cong., March 30, 2017, 4, www.intelligence.senate.gov.

64. Amita Kelly, "Donald Trump Clinches GOP Nomination," NPR, May 26, 2016, www.npr.org; Amy Chozick and Patrick Healy, "Hillary Clinton Has Clinched Democratic Nomination, Survey Reports," *New York Times,* June 6, 2016, www.nytimes.com.

65. Mueller Report, 72–78; Kalugin, interview by author, Rockville, Md., Aug. 7, 2018; note 59 of this chapter. For Trump's account of his 1987 trip to Moscow, see note 68 of chapter 5 of this book. Additionally, Robert Mueller, in his final report, concluded: "Although the investigation established that the Russian government perceived it would benefit from a Trump presidency and worked to secure that outcome, and that the Campaign expected it would benefit electorally from information stolen and released through Russian efforts, the investigation did not establish

that members of the Trump Campaign conspired or coordinated with the Russian government in its election interference activities." Mueller Report, 5. For foundational reporting on Russian interference in the 2016 election and on ties between Trump, his associates, and Russia, see David Corn and Michael Isikoff, *Russian Roulette: The Inside Story of Putin's War on America and the Election of Donald Trump* (New York: Twelve, 2018); Greg Miller, *The Apprentice: Trump, Russia, and the Subversion of American Democracy* (New York: Custom House, 2018).

66. Cohen, interview by author.

PART TWO: 2016

1. U.S. Congress, *Russian Efforts Against Election Infrastructure*, 3.
2. Pope, phone interview by author, June 26, 2019.
3. Andrew Perrin, "Social Media Usage: 2005–2015," Pew Research Center, Oct. 8, 2015, www.pewresearch.org; "Internet/Broadband Fact Sheet," Pew Research Center, June 12, 2019, www.pewresearch.org.

CHAPTER 9: DELAYING OFFENSE

1. In a PBS interview on August 9, 2017, Clapper said, "It was during the summer or so of 2015 that we began to see these indications, and certainly the hacking attempts at the DNC, which primarily involved the FBI and the Department of Homeland Security engaging with the DNC. Other things that began to unfold from then on through the election, of course, were the instances of what I would call reconnoitering by the Russian intelligence services into state-level databases, primarily voter registration rolls, in many cases maintained by contractor by each of the states. . . . [Obama] was thoroughly briefed up on this. And we had been doing PDB [President's Daily Brief] articles on this throughout, starting in 2015, about this activity as it unfolded and as we were able to understand it." See Clapper, interview by Jim Gilmore, Aug. 9, 2017, www.pbs.org. Clapper further said, in his interview with the author, "We had been reporting on [Russia's activities] throughout in the PDB and other intelligence, but it was all individual vignettes" rather than a complete picture.
2. Clapper, interview by author, Fairfax, Va., Jan. 3, 2019.
3. Hall, phone interview by author, Oct. 22, 2019; McLaughlin, phone interview by author, Sept. 5, 2019; Morell, phone interview by author, March 6, 2019.
4. "Increased Public Support for the U.S. Arming Ukraine," Pew Research Center, Feb. 23, 2015, www.people-press.org; Jeffrey Jones, "Americans Increasingly See Russia as Threat, Top U.S. Enemy," Gallup, Feb. 16, 2015, news.gallup.com; Kyle Dropp, Joshua Kertzer, and Thomas Zeitzoff, "The Less Americans Know About Ukraine's Location, the More They Want U.S. to Intervene," *Washington Post*, April 7, 2014, www.washingtonpost.com.

5. "Ukraine Crisis: Transcript of Leaked Nuland-Pyatt Call," BBC, Feb. 7, 2014, www.bbc.com.

6. Nuland, interview by author, Washington, D.C., Feb. 22, 2019.

7. Ellen Nakashima, "Russian Government Hackers Penetrated DNC, Stole Opposition Research on Trump," *Washington Post*, June 14, 2016, www.washingtonpost.com. See also Dmitri Alperovitch, "Bears in the Midst: Intrusion into the Democratic National Committee," CrowdStrike, June 15, 2016, www.crowdstrike.com; Sheera Frenkel, "Meet Fancy Bear, the Russian Group Hacking the US Election," *BuzzFeed News*, Oct. 15, 2016, www.buzzfeednews.com.

8. Mueller Report, 42–43; Monaco, interview by author, New York, Sept. 25, 2019.

9. Colin Wilhelm, "Sanders Taunts Clinton Again on Wall Street Ties," *Politico*, April 17, 2016, www.politico.com; Amy Chozick, Patrick Healy, and Yamiche Alcindor, "Bernie Sanders Endorses Hillary Clinton, Hoping to Unify Democrats," *New York Times,* July 12, 2016, www.nytimes .com.

10. Mueller Report, 45–46; Michael D. Shear and Matthew Rosenberg, "Released Emails Suggest the D.N.C. Derided the Sanders Campaign," *New York Times,* July 22, 2016, www.nytimes.com. On the GRU's social media activities, see Renée DiResta and Shelby Grossman, "Potemkin Pages & Personas: Assessing GRU Online Operations, 2014–2019," Stanford Cyber Policy Center, Nov. 2019, 8, 73, fsi-live.s3.us-west-1 .amazonaws.com.

11. Zakaria, phone interview by author, July 18, 2019.

12. Aaron Blake, "Here Are the Latest, Most Damaging Things in the DNC's Leaked Emails," *Washington Post,* July 25, 2016, www.washingtonpost .com; Alana Abramson and Shushannah Walshe, "The 4 Most Damaging Emails from the DNC WikiLeaks Dump," ABC News, July 25, 2016, abcnews.go.com; Eric Bradner, "Clinton's Campaign Manager: Russia Helping Trump," CNN, July 25, 2016, www.cnn.com.

13. There were exceptions—first among them, Anne Applebaum, who said in late July that the DNC hack and release was "exactly out of the Russian security service's playbook" and that "this is a very established Russian tactic that's been used multiple times in democratic elections, mostly in Europe." She similarly said, in another interview in late July, that the DNC release "looks like almost exactly the same pattern is now in play in the United States that we've seen play out in other European countries." Later, in September, Applebaum wrote a column elaborating upon what Russia's electoral interference operation could entail through Election Day, citing the experiences of various European countries. See Applebaum, interview by Jacob Weisberg, *Slate,* July 28, 2016, slate.com; Olivia Lazarus and T. J. Raphael, "Trump: The President Russia Wants?," PRI, July 26, 2016, www.pri.org; Anne Applebaum, "How Russia Could Spark a U.S. Electoral Disaster," *Washington Post*, Sept. 8, 2016, www .washingtonpost.com. On Ukraine, see note 6 of chapter 8 of this book.

14. Eliot Nelson, "Sanders Calls DNC Leak 'Outrageous,' Calls for New DNC Chair," *Huffington Post,* July 24, 2016, www.huffpost.com; Matt Flegenheimer, "Democratic Convention Day 4 Takeaways: Over? She's Just Starting," *New York Times,* July 28, 2016, www.nytimes.com; Anne Gearan, Philip Rucker, and Abby Phillip, "DNC Chairwoman Will Resign in Aftermath of Committee Email Controversy," *Washington Post,* July 24, 2016, www.washingtonpost.com; Will Drabold, "DNC Apologizes to Bernie Sanders and Supporters over Leaked Emails," *Time,* July 25, 2016, time.com.

15. Clinton, interview by author, New York, Dec. 4, 2019; Jake Rudnitsky, John Micklethwait, and Michael Riley, "Putin Says DNC Hack Was a Public Service, Russia Didn't Do It," *Bloomberg,* Sept. 2, 2016, www .bloomberg.com.

16. Department of Justice, Office of Special Counsel Robert Mueller, "Interview of Richard Gates 4/11/18," 21, released via FOIA on Nov. 1, 2019, www.documentcloud.org.

    Donald McGahn, counsel to the Trump campaign, declined to be interviewed for this book, saying that he did not know what he was at liberty to disclose. Reince Priebus, then the RNC chairman, did not respond to multiple interview requests.

17. Wise, phone interview by author, Oct. 21, 2019; Daniel, phone interview by author, July 19, 2019.

18. Johnson, interview by author, New York, July 29, 2019; Nuland, interview by author.

19. Johnson, interview by author; Daniel, interview by author. Brennan, in his testimony before Congress in May 2017, said, "When it became clear to me last summer that Russia was engaged in a very aggressive and wide-ranging effort to interfere in one of the key pillars of our democracy, we pulled together experts from CIA, NSA, and FBI in late July to focus on the issue, drawing in multiple perspectives and subject matter experts with broad expertise to assess Russian attempts to interfere in the U.S. presidential election." See Tim Hains, "Brennan: 'It Should Be Clear to Everyone That Russia Brazenly Interfered in Our 2016 Election,'" Real Clear Politics, May 23, 2017, www.realclearpolitics.com.

20. Rice, phone interview by author, Aug. 27, 2019; Blinken, interview by author, Washington, D.C., Jan. 3, 2019. Information warfare is defined as "a strategy for the use and management of information to pursue a competitive advantage, including both offensive and defensive operations." Catherine A. Theohary, *Defense Primer: Information Operations* (Washington, D.C.: U.S. Library of Congress, Congressional Research Service, 2018), R45142, fas.org.

21. Wallander, interview by author, Washington, D.C., July 17, 2019. For elaboration on the perceived significance of the DNC email release from inside the White House, see chapter 11 of this book.

22. David Sanger, "Harry Reid Cites Evidence of Russian Tampering in U.S. Vote, and Seeks F.B.I. Inquiry," *New York Times,* Aug. 29, 2016, www

.nytimes.com; Dustin Volz and Jim Finkle, "FBI Detects Breaches Against Two State Voter Systems," Reuters, Aug. 29, 2016, www.reuters.com.

23. U.S. Congress, *Russian Efforts Against Election Infrastructure,* 6, 22–24.

24. *United States v. Viktor Netyksho et al.,* 18 U.S.C. §§ 2, 371, 1030, 1028A (D.D.C. 2018), 26, www.justice.gov; Mueller Report, 50.

25. U.S. Congress, *Russian Efforts Against Election Infrastructure,* 22.

26. Monaco, interview by author; Daniel, interview by author; Pope, phone interview by author, June 26, 2019.

27. Rice, interview by author.

28. Wallander, interview by author; Daniel, interview by author; Nuland, interview by author.

29. Wallander, interview by author; Nuland, interview by author. On Putin's wealth, see Adam Taylor, "Is Vladimir Putin Hiding a $200 Billion Fortune? (And If So, Does It Matter?)," *Washington Post,* Feb. 20, 2015, www.washingtonpost.com; Adrian Blomfield, "$40bn Putin 'Is Now Europe's Richest Man,' " *Telegraph,* Dec. 21, 2007, www.telegraph.co.uk.

30. Nuland, interview by author.

31. Daniel, interview by author; Wallander, interview by author.

32. Haines, interview by author, New York, Feb. 23, 2019.

33. Clapper, interview by author.

34. Blinken, interview by author; Brennan, interview by author, Washington, D.C., July 10, 2018.

35. Blinken, interview by author; Johnson, interview by author.

36. Blinken, interview by author.

37. Ibid.

38. U.S. Congress, House, Help America Vote Act of 2002, H.R. 2395, 107th Cong., introduced in House Nov. 14, 2001, www.congress.gov.

39. Monaco, interview by author. Outside experts have also concluded that voter registration databases presented an accessible point of entry for Russia in 2016. Professor Charles Stewart III explains, "The rising number of centralized and Internet-reliant registration systems offers more targets for widespread attacks." Charles Stewart III, "The 2016 U.S. Election: Fears and Facts About Electoral Integrity," *Journal of Democracy* 28, no. 2 (2017): 58. See also Sarah Eckman, *Election Security: Voter Registration System Policy Issues* (Washington, D.C.: U.S. Library of Congress, Congressional Research Service, 2019), fas.org; Ben Buchanan and Michael Sulmeyer, "Hacking Chads: The Motivations, Threats, and Effects of Electoral Insecurity," Cybersecurity Project, Harvard Kennedy School, Oct. 2016, www.belfercenter.org.

40. Pope, interview by author; Blinken, interview by author; Brennan, interview by author.

41. Brennan, interview by author; Monaco, interview by author.

42. Clapper, interview by author.

43. Trump had introduced strongman tactics to Republican Party politics: mocking his primary opponents, developing a cult of personality, and embracing "Lock her up!" chants at his rallies. Beyond presidential

politics, event after event was tearing at the fabric of American society. On June 12, 2016, a gunman killed forty-nine people at a gay nightclub in Orlando, Florida, the latest of a years-long string of mass shootings in the United States. A little over a week later, Democratic lawmakers staged a twenty-five-hour sit-in on the floor of the House of Representatives, trying, to no avail, to persuade their Republican counterparts to vote on gun control legislation. On July 5 and 6, police officers fatally shot two black men, Alton Sterling and Philando Castile, in interactions that were filmed and posted online, prompting widespread protests against police shootings of black Americans. On July 7, a gunman in Dallas killed five police officers and injured nine more; he targeted white members of law enforcement in retaliation for the recent shootings of black Americans. See Manny Fernandez, Richard Pérez-Peña, and Jonah Engel Bromwich, "Five Dallas Officers Were Killed as Payback, Police Chief Says," *New York Times,* July 8, 2016, www.nytimes.com; Matt Furber and Richard Pérez-Peña, "After Philando Castile's Killing, Obama Calls Police Shootings 'an American Issue,' " *New York Times,* July 7, 2016, www.nytimes.com; Richard Fausset, Richard Pérez-Peña, and Campbell Robertson, "Alton Sterling Shooting in Baton Rouge Prompts Justice Dept. Investigation," *New York Times,* July 6, 2016, www.nytimes.com; Lizette Alvarez and Richard Pérez-Peña, "Orlando Gunman Attacks Gay Nightclub, Leaving 50 Dead," *New York Times,* June 12, 2016, www.nytimes.com; Peter W. Stevenson, "A Brief History of the 'Lock Her Up!' Chant by Trump Supporters Against Clinton," *Washington Post,* Nov. 22, 2016, www.washingtonpost.com; Jose A. Del Real, "Blasting 'Pathetic' Agreement, Trump Mocks and Taunts Rivals Cruz and Kasich," *Washington Post,* April 25, 2016, www.washingtonpost.com; David M. Herszenhorn and Emmarie Huetteman, "House Democrats' Gun-Control Sit-in Turns into Chaotic Showdown with Republicans," *New York Times,* June 22, 2016, www.nytimes.com.

44. Ashley Parker and David Sanger, "Donald Trump Calls on Russia to Find Hillary Clinton's Missing Emails," *New York Times,* July 27, 2016, www.nytimes.com.

45. Mueller Report, 49; Bannon, interview by author, New York, Sept. 21, 2019.

46. Tessa Berenson, "Donald Trump: 'The Election's Going to Be Rigged,' " *Time,* Aug. 1, 2016, time.com.

47. Pope, interview by author.

48. Obama's quotation about Clinton comes from former FBI director Jim Comey's memoir, *A Higher Loyalty: Truth, Lies, and Leadership* (New York: Flatiron, 2018), 190.

49. Daniel, interview by author.

50. McDonough, interview by author, Washington, D.C., July 17, 2018.

51. Pope, interview by author; Finer, interview by author, New York, Feb. 20, 2019.

52. Chris Kahn, "Clinton Leads Trump by 12 Points in Reuters/Ipsos Poll," Reuters, Aug. 23, 2016, www.reuters.com.

53. Johnson, interview by author; Clapper, interview by author; Sarah Bloom Raskin, phone interview by author, Feb. 3, 2020.

54. Wallander, interview by author; Wallander, phone interview by author, Jan. 24, 2020.

55. Monaco, interview by author; Haines, interview by author; Rice, interview by author.

CHAPTER 10: PLAYING DEFENSE

1. McDonough, interview by author, Washington, D.C., July 17, 2018; Monaco, interview by author, New York, Sept. 25, 2019.

2. Johnson, interview by author, New York, July 29, 2019.

3. Christina Cassidy, "AP Fact Check: Voter Registration Problems Do Not Equate to Fraud," PBS, Oct. 25, 2016, www.pbs.org; R. Sam Garrett, *Federal Role in U.S. Campaigns and Elections: An Overview* (Washington, D.C.: U.S. Library of Congress, Congressional Research Service, 2018), fas.org; White House, "Our Government: Elections & Voting," www.whitehouse.gov. See also note 5 of the introduction of this book.

4. Johnson, interview by author.

5. Daniel, phone interview by author, July 19, 2019; Pope, phone interview by author, June 26, 2019.

6. "Trust in Government: 1958–2015," Pew Research Center, Nov. 23, 2015, www.people-press.org. For further context, see Alec Tyson, "Obama Job Approval Higher, but Views of Him Are Still the Most Polarized in Recent History," Pew Research Center, Oct. 28, 2016, www.pewresearch.org; "Partisan Views of 2016 Candidates, Barack and Michelle Obama, Views of the Election," Pew Research Center, June 22, 2016, www.people-press .org.

7. Johnson, interview by author.

8. Anna Mulrine, "Homeland Security Chief Weighs Plan to Protect Voting from Hackers," *Christian Science Monitor,* Aug. 3, 2016, www.csmonitor .com.

9. Johnson, interview by author.

10. Department of Homeland Security, "Readout of Secretary Johnson's Call with State Election Officials on Cybersecurity," Aug. 15, 2016, www.dhs .gov.

11. Johnson, interview by author.

12. Rice, phone interview by author, Aug. 27, 2019.

13. Johnson, interview by author.

14. Miller, *Apprentice,* 149–54; Monaco, interview by author; Brennan, interview by author, Washington, D.C., July 10, 2018.

15. Federal Bureau of Investigation, "Flash: Targeting Activity Against State Board of Election Systems," Aug. 18, 2016, info.publicintelligence.net;

U.S. Congress, *Russian Efforts Against Election Infrastructure,* 7, 12; Michael Isikoff, "FBI says foreign hackers penetrated state election systems," Yahoo News, Aug. 29, 2016, www.yahoo.com; Daniel, interview by author.

16. Daniel, interview by author.
17. Monaco, interview by author; Eric Geller, "Elections Security: Federal Help or Power Grab?," *Politico,* Aug. 28, 2016, www.politico.com; Ali Breland, "State Declines DHS Security for Voting Machines," *Hill,* Aug. 26, 2016, thehill.com.
18. Johnson, interview by author; Rice, interview by author.
19. Pope, interview by author.
20. Panetta, phone interview by author, Nov. 12, 2019; Lott, phone interview by author, Oct. 31, 2019; David Rogers, "Some Good Old Boys Honor Trent Lott," *Politico,* Sept. 17, 2009, www.politico.com.
21. Glenn Kessler, "When Did McConnell Say He Wanted to Make Obama a 'One-Term President'?," *Washington Post,* Sept. 25, 2012, www .washingtonpost.com. The feeling was mutual. In 2013, just after winning reelection, Obama mocked McConnell at the White House Correspondents' Dinner: "Some folks still don't think I spend enough time with Congress. 'Why don't you get a drink with Mitch McConnell?' they ask. Really? Why don't *you* get a drink with Mitch McConnell? I'm sorry. I get frustrated sometimes." See "Transcript: Obama Speaks at WHCD," *Politico,* April 28, 2013, www.politico.com.
22. Burgess Everett and Glenn Thrush, "McConnell Throws Down the Gauntlet: No Scalia Replacement Under Obama," *Politico,* Feb. 13, 2016, www.politico.com; Mitch McConnell, *The Long Game: A Memoir* (New York: Sentinel, 2016), 185.
23. Jonathan Chait, "Five Days That Shaped a Presidency," *New York,* Oct. 3, 2016, nymag.com.
24. Brennan, interview by author. For the specific dates of Brennan's briefings to each member of the Gang of Eight, see U.S. Congress, Senate, Select Committee on Intelligence, *Report on Russian Active Measures Campaigns and Interference in the 2016 U.S. Election Volume 3: U.S. Government Response to Russian Activities,* 116th Congress, 2nd session, 2020, S. Report 116-XX, 13, s.wsj.net/public /resources /documents /Senate_Russia_Report_Volume3.pdf?mod=article_inline.
25. Brennan, interview by author.
26. Reid, interview by author, Las Vegas, July 24, 2019.
27. Reid to Comey, Aug. 27, 2016, www.documentcloud.org; David Sanger, "Harry Reid Cites Evidence of Russian Tampering in U.S. Vote, and Seeks F.B.I. Inquiry," *New York Times,* Aug. 29, 2016, www.nytimes .com.
28. Reid, interview by author.
29. Podesta, interview by author, Washington, D.C., June 15, 2018.
30. McDonough, interview by author; Haines, interview by author, New York, Feb. 23, 2019.

31. Reid, interview by author; Haines, interview by author.

32. McDonough, interview by author.

33. Johnson, interview by author.

34. Reid, interview by author.

35. Podesta, interview by author; Panetta, interview by author.

36. McDonough, interview by author.

37. Haines, interview by author.

38. "Transcripts: Intel Chief Testifies Amid New Russia Revelation," CNN, May 23, 2017, transcripts.cnn.com.

39. Johnson, interview by author; Blinken, interview by author, Washington, D.C., Jan. 3, 2019.

40. Haines, interview by author.

41. White House, "Press Conference by the President," Dec. 16, 2016, obama whitehouse.archives.gov.

42. Monaco, interview by author.

43. McDonough, interview by author; Wallander, interview by author, Washington, D.C., July 17, 2019; Morell, phone interview by author, March 6, 2019.

44. Blinken, interview by author; Monaco, interview by author; Wallander, interview by author; Daniel, interview by author.

45. Comey, *Higher Loyalty,* 190.

46. Haines, interview by author.

47. Johnson, interview by author.

48. Ibid.; Comey, *Higher Loyalty,* 189–90, in which he elaborates, "I also acknowledged to the president that an inoculation effort might accidentally accomplish the Russians' goal of undermining confidence in our election system. If you tell Americans that the Russians are tampering with the election, have you just sowed doubt about the outcome, or given one side an excuse for why they lost?" Ultimately, Comey declined to sign the statement alongside Johnson and Clapper. Of this decision, he writes, "A month later, in early October, the Obama team decided some kind of formal statement from the administration was in order after all. The director of national intelligence, Jim Clapper, and the secretary of Homeland Security, Jeh Johnson, were prepared to sign it. The FBI leadership team and I decided that there was not an adequate reason for us to also sign on." Comey, *Higher Loyalty,* 191. Of Comey's thinking at the time, then FBI deputy director Andrew McCabe later told the Senate, "Director Comey felt that [the op-ed] was important to do when he suggested it." However, "[b]y the time he kind of got around to thinking about it seriously, he felt like the opportunity had passed and we were too close [to the election] at that point to have the intended effect on the electorate." See U.S. Congress, *Report on Russian Active Measures Campaigns and Interference in the 2016 U.S. Election Volume 3: U.S. Government Response to Russian Activities,* 35.

49. Cohen, interview by author, Washington, D.C., July 17, 2018; Johnson, interview by author; Haines, interview by author.

50. Johnson, interview by author; Clapper, interview by author, Fairfax, Va., Jan. 3, 2019.

51. Johnson, interview by author.

52. Ibid.

53. Kathleen Hall Jamieson, *Cyberwar: How Russian Hackers and Trolls Helped Elect a President: What We Don't, Can't, and Do Know* (New York: Oxford University Press, 2018), 153–54. See also U.S. Department of Homeland Security, "Joint Statement from the Department of Homeland Security and Office of the Director of National Intelligence on Election Security," Oct. 7, 2016, www.dhs.gov; David A. Fahrenthold, "Trump Recorded Having Extremely Lewd Conversation About Women in 2005," *Washington Post,* Oct. 7, 2016, www.washingtonpost.com.

54. Rucker, phone interview by author, Sept. 2, 2018.

55. Clapper, interview by author; Johnson, interview by author.

56. Bannon, interview by author, New York, Sept. 21, 2019.

57. "Full Transcript: Third 2016 Presidential Debate," *Politico,* Oct. 20, 2016, www.politico.com.

58. Johnson, interview by author.

59. Blair, phone interview by author, May 27, 2019.

60. Comey, *Higher Loyalty,* 191.

61. Johnson, interview by author.

62. McDonough, interview by author.

63. John F. Kelly to Senator Claire McCaskill, June 13, 2017, www.hsgac .senate.gov.

64. Alexander Tin, "Ahead of Elections, States Reject Federal Help to Combat Hackers," CBS News, Oct. 28, 2016, www.cbsnews.com.

65. Mueller Report, 51; Patricia Mazzei, "Russians Hacked Voter Systems in 2 Florida Counties. But Which Ones?," *New York Times,* May 14, 2019, www.nytimes.com; Patricia Mazzei, "F.B.I. to Florida Lawmakers: You Were Hacked by Russians, but Don't Tell Voters," *New York Times,* May 16, 2019, www.nytimes.com; Dustin Volz, "Hackers Breached Voter Databases in Two Florida Counties Ahead of 2016 Election," *Wall Street Journal,* May 14, 2019, www.wsj.com.

66. Wallander, interview by author; Daniel, interview by author.

67. On Election Day concerns, see chapter 11 of this book.

CHAPTER 11: ELECTION DAY

1. Johnson, interview by author, New York, July 29, 2019.

2. Pope, phone interview by author, June 26, 2019.

3. Daniel, phone interview by author, July 19, 2019; Monaco, interview by author, New York, Sept. 25, 2019; Rice, phone interview by author, Aug. 27, 2019.

4. See chapter 8 of this book.

5. Brennan, interview by author, Washington, D.C., July 10, 2018; Pope, interview by author; Johnson, interview by author.

6. Johnson, interview by author; Haines, interview by author, New York, Feb. 23, 2019; Monaco, interview by author. Of this scenario, Monaco explained, "What I was very concerned about and what we spent a lot of time worrying about as a worst-case scenario was manipulation of voter registration databases such that what we were seeing was that they were obviously very diffuse and not subject to any kind of uniform set of cyber-security standards or controls. Encryption was spotty, not uniform. . . . We had seen Russia scanning and probing voter registration databases, and I think we were all worried again, as in any threat situation, what is it that we don't know? . . . My worst-case scenario was John Smith goes to vote on Election Day and appears at his polling place and says I am John Smith from First Street here to vote and on the database and on their records they have him listed somewhere else or don't have him."

7. Josh Katz, "Who Will Be President?," *New York Times,* Nov. 8, 2016, www.nytimes.com.

8. "Full Transcript: Third 2016 Presidential Debate."

9. McDonough, interview by author, Washington, D.C., July 17, 2018.

10. Pope, interview by author.

11. Clapper, interview by author, Fairfax, Va., Jan. 3, 2019.

12. Brennan, interview by author; Clinton, interview by author, New York, Dec. 4, 2019.

13. Wallander, interview by author, Washington, D.C., July 17, 2019.

14. Philip Bump, "Donald Trump Will Be President Thanks to 80,000 People in Three States," *Washington Post,* Dec. 1, 2016, www.washingtonpost .com.

15. Clapper, interview by author.

16. Reid, interview by author, Las Vegas, July 24, 2019.

17. Clapper, interview by author; Rice, interview by author; McDonough, interview by author.

18. "'This Week' Transcript: President Barack Obama," ABC News, Jan. 8, 2017, abcnews.go.com.

19. Nuland, interview by author, Washington, D.C., Feb. 22, 2019.

20. Wallander, interview by author; Comey, *Higher Loyalty,* 190; Haines, interview by author. Lucas Kello explores the intricacies of deterrence in the digital age in *Virtual Weapon and International Order,* chap. 7, in which he writes, "The principal problem with current doctrine is that it is designed to punish individual acts," and so, "when applied to the current context, adversaries understand that so long as no single cyber action unambiguously crosses the bar of war, they will escape its certain penalties."

21. Rice, interview by author.

22. Brennan, interview by author; Podesta, interview by author, Washington, D.C., June 15, 2018.

23. Miller, phone interview by author, July 11, 2019; Rucker, phone interview by author, Sept. 2, 2018.

24. Jamieson, *Cyberwar,* 150, 156.

25. Amy Chozick et al., "Highlights from the Clinton Campaign Emails: How to Deal with Sanders and Biden," *New York Times,* Oct. 10, 2016, www .nytimes.com. Other headlines included "Leaked Speech Excerpts Show a Hillary Clinton at Ease with Wall Street"; "Hillary Clinton Aides Kept de Blasio at Arm's Length, WikiLeaks Emails Show"; "Hacked Transcripts Reveal a Genial Hillary Clinton at Goldman Sachs Events"; "Email about Qatari Offer Shows Thorny Ethical Issues Clinton Foundation Faced"; "'We Need to Clean This Up': Clinton Aide's Newly Public Email Shows Concern"; "Donations to Foundation Vexed Hillary Clinton's Aides, Emails Show"; "Chelsea Clinton's Frustrations and Devotion Shown in Hacked Emails"; and "WikiLeaks Lays Bare a Clinton Insider's Emphatic Cheers and Jeers."

26. Sonne, phone interview by author, June 20, 2019.

27. Wallander, interview by author.

28. Eric Lipton, David Sanger, and Scott Shane, "The Perfect Weapon: How Russian Cyberpower Invaded the U.S.," *New York Times,* Dec. 13, 2016, www.nytimes.com.

29. Podesta, interview by author; Bannon, interview by author, New York, Sept. 21, 2019.

30. Mueller Report, 48; Goff, interview by author, New York, Aug. 22, 2019.

31. Podesta, interview by author.

32. Baker, phone interview by author, Oct. 17, 2018; Rucker, interview by author.

33. Clapper, interview by author.

34. Applebaum went on, "But whatever resources Putin wagered on Trump, they are paying off. For even if Trump never becomes president, his candidacy has already achieved two extremely important Russian foreign policy goals: to weaken the moral influence of the United States by undermining its reputation as a stable democracy, and to destroy its power by wrecking its relationships with its allies." Anne Applebaum, "How a Trump Presidency Could Destabilize Europe," *Washington Post,* July 21, 2016, www.washingtonpost.com.

35. Daniel, interview by author. In a statement provided to the U.S. Senate on March 1, 2019, the FBI said, "In October 2016, the Counterintelligence Division tasked a contractor to identify Russian influence activity on Twitter. The FBI contractor collected and analyzed a sample of Twitter activity conducted by an overtly pro-Russian network of 13 Twitter accounts and their followers, including automated accounts, which promoted US election-related news and leaked Democratic party emails published by WikiLeaks." See U.S. Congress, Senate, Select Committee on Intelligence, *Russia's Use of Social Media,* vol. 2 of *Report on Russian Active Measures Campaigns and Interference in the 2016 U.S. Election,* 116th Cong., 1st sess., 2019, S. Rep. 116-XX, 73, www.intelligence.senate .gov.

36. Cohen, interview by author, Washington, D.C., July 17, 2018; Brennan, interview by author.

37. Morell, phone interview by author, March 6, 2019; Wise, phone interview by author, Oct. 21, 2019; Panetta, phone interview by author, Nov. 12, 2019.

38. Nuland, interview by author.

39. Office of the Director of National Intelligence, *Assessing Russian Activities and Intentions in Recent U.S. Elections*, 1.

40. Sanger, "Obama Strikes Back at Russia for Election Hacking."

41. Wallander, interview by author; Morell, interview by author; Haines, interview by author.

42. Clapper, interview by author; Blinken, interview by author, Washington, D.C., Jan. 3, 2019; Sarah Bloom Raskin, phone interview by author, Feb. 3, 2020; Finer, interview by author, New York, Feb. 20, 2019.

43. Adam Entous, Elizabeth Dwoskin, and Craig Timberg, "Obama Tried to Give Zuckerberg a Wake-up Call over Fake News on Facebook," *Washington Post*, Sept. 24, 2017, www.washingtonpost.com.

44. " 'This Week' Transcript: President Barack Obama," Jan. 8, 2017.

CHAPTER 12: SOCIAL MEDIA

1. *United States v. Internet Research Agency LLC*, 18 U.S.C. §§ 2, 371, 1349, 1028A (D.D.C. 2018), 12–13.

2. Ibid., 6–7; U.S. Congress, *Russia's Use of Social Media*, 22–24. For further reading on Yevgeny Prigozhin, the Russian oligarch who bankrolled the IRA, see Neil MacFarquhar, "Yevgeny Prigozhin, Russian Oligarch Indicted by U.S., Is Known as 'Putin's Cook,' " *New York Times*, Feb. 16, 2018, www.nytimes.com.

3. Stamos, phone interview by author, May 28, 2018.

4. Adrian Chen, "The Agency," *New York Times*, June 2, 2015, www.nytimes.com. Even earlier, in 2014, *BuzzFeed* published an article about how the IRA, with a staff of more than six hundred people and a yearly budget of more than $10 million, was using social media to influence public opinion at home and abroad, including in the United States. See Seddon, "Documents Show How Russia's Troll Army Hit America."

5. By July 2016, Adrian Chen wrote, "The Internet Research Agency appears to have quieted down significantly." Chen, "Real Paranoia-Inducing Purpose of Russian Hacks."

6. Hall, phone interview by author, Oct. 22, 2019.

7. An indictment issued by the office of Robert Mueller described another aspect of the GRU's social media activities: "Unit 74455 assisted in the release of stolen documents through the DCLeaks and Guccifer 2.0 personas, the promotion of those releases, and the publication of anti-Clinton content on social media accounts operated by the GRU." See *United States v. Viktor Netyksho et al.*, 18 U.S.C. §§ 2, 371, 1030, 1028A (D.D.C. 2018), 5.

8. Officials at Twitter had a similar experience. The company's general counsel told the U.S. Senate, in January 2019, that "to the best of our

knowledge, Twitter received no information from the U.S. government in advance of the 2016 election about state sponsored information operations." See U.S. Congress, *Russia's Use of Social Media,* 73.

9. Stamos, interview by author; Gleicher, phone interview by author, Feb. 25, 2020. On those exceptions at Facebook, see David Smith, "How Key Republicans Inside Facebook Are Shifting Its Politics to the Right," *Guardian,* Nov. 3, 2019, www.theguardian.com. For one of the many speculative pieces about Sandberg's political future, see Ben White, "Sheryl Sandberg Rising in Treasury Watch," *Politico,* Sept. 15, 2016, www.politico.com. For Sandberg's public response, see Christina Passariello, "Facebook's Sheryl Sandberg Says She Won't Be Joining Government," *Wall Street Journal,* Oct. 11, 2016, www.wsj.com.

10. The U.S. Senate Select Committee on Intelligence concluded that "the Russian government tasked and supported the IRA's interference in the 2016 U.S. election," that "the IRA sought to influence the 2016 U.S. presidential election by harming Hillary Clinton's chances of success and supporting Donald Trump at the direction of the Kremlin," and that "IRA social media activity was overtly and almost invariably supportive of then-candidate Trump, and to the detriment of Secretary Clinton's campaign." See U.S. Congress, *Russia's Use of Social Media,* 4–5.

11. Stamos, interview by author.

12. Sandberg, interview by author, New York, June 2018. (Ms. Sandberg gave the author this brief remark spontaneously when asked at a coffee shop in Manhattan.) On Facebook's internal quarrels and decision-making process after the 2016 election, see Sheera Frenkel et al., "Delay, Deny, and Deflect: How Facebook's Leaders Fought Through Crisis," *New York Times,* Nov. 14, 2018, www.nytimes.com.

13. See U.S. Congress, *Russia's Use of Social Media,* 45–50, which further explains that on Facebook the 76.5 million engagements included 30.4 million shares, 37.6 million likes, 3.3 million comments, and 5.2 million reactions and that on Instagram almost half of the IRA's 133 accounts had more than 10,000 followers, and 12 had more than 100,000.

14. Renée DiResta et al., "The Tactics and Tropes of the Internet Research Agency," New Knowledge, Dec. 17, 2018, 7, www.newknowledge.com.

15. U.S. Congress, *Russia's Use of Social Media,* 59–62.

16. Stanford researchers found that across the GRU's Facebook accounts "engagement was minimal. Across all posts, there were 4,830 Likes, 5,469 reactions, 3,432 shares, and 902 comments. . . . While GRU-attributed Facebook posts spanned a period from 2014 to 2018—a time when the IRA was operational and actively spending money and effort on audience engagement—only one of the GRU-attributed Pages bought ads. . . . The effort expended on attracting audiences, even via obvious strategies like running ads, was conspicuously minimal; the marked lack of engagement is indeed somewhat perplexing. There are a few possible explanations for this: the first is that social influence was not the focus nor the goal of GRU activity, which was primarily concerned with media hacking. . . .

A second explanation is that they didn't fully understand the dynamics of social platforms. A third is that they were simply ineffectual or incompetent in their execution." On the IRA and GRU, the researchers conclude, "The extent of coordination between the various entities with influence operations capabilities—in this case, the GRU and the IRA—is an open question. . . . [T]here has been no concrete evidence of collaboration between the two entities." See DiResta and Grossman, "Potemkin Pages & Personas," 5, 7, 9, 91.

17. Goss, interview by author, Florida Keys, Fla., Dec. 26, 2018. Several former CIA officers have written about continuities in Russia's covert influence operations. See David V. Gioe, "Cyber Operations and Useful Fools: The Approach of Russian Hybrid Intelligence," *Intelligence and National Security* 33, no. 7 (2018): 954–73; John Sipher, "Russian Active Measures," *CHACR Global Analysis Programme Briefing* 14 (2018).

18. Haley, interview by author, Washington, D.C., July 23, 2018. (Ambassador Haley granted the author this brief comment spontaneously when asked at a restaurant in Foggy Bottom.)

19. Shannon Greenwood, Andrew Perrin, and Maeve Duggan, "Social Media Update 2016," Pew Research Center, Nov. 11, 2016, www.pewresearch .org. Michael Hayden, the NSA director from 1999 to 2005, told me that, at the turn of the twenty-first century, he expected a digitally connected world to "create a common dialogue and bring people together toward a middle, deeper, and richer understanding." Still, some thinkers, like Jack Goldsmith, Tim Wu, and Lawrence Lessig, sensed that a globalized internet, with all its potential, had much potential for abuse. "Everything you do on the Net produces data," Lessig wrote in 2006, "about what you do and what you say," which can be used to influence "you in a direct and effective way." See Lawrence Lessig, *Code: And Other Laws of Cyberspace, Version 2.0* (New York: Basic Books, 2006), 216. Goldsmith and Wu, in their 2006 book, warned that authoritarian countries like China would maintain a "model of political control" through a "sphere of influence over network norms," while the United States would adopt a "free and open model" of internet activity. As a result, Wu and Goldsmith forecast "a technological version of the cold war, with each side pushing its own vision of the Internet's future." See Jack Goldsmith and Tim Wu, *Who Controls the Internet? Illusions of a Borderless World* (New York: Oxford University Press, 2006), 101, 184.

20. Clapper, interview by author, Fairfax, Va., Jan. 3, 2019. Kira Vrist Rønn and Sille Obelitz Søe reflect on questions of privacy and social media platforms, arguing, "While they feel private to users, they are in fact public spaces." See Kira Vrist Rønn and Sille Obelitz Søe, "Is Social Media Intelligence Private? Privacy in Public and the Nature of Social Media Intelligence," *Intelligence and National Security* 34, no. 3 (2019): 363–78. On the undemocratic consequences of social media, see Ronald Deibert, "The Road to Digital Unfreedom: Three Painful Truths About Social Media," *Journal of Democracy* 30, no. 1 (2019): 25–39; Larry

Diamond, "The Road to Digital Unfreedom: The Threat of Postmodern Totalitarianism," *Journal of Democracy* 30, no. 1 (2019): 20–24.

21. Scott Detrow, "What Did Cambridge Analytica Do During the 2016 Election?," NPR, March 20, 2018, www.npr.org. Cecilia Kang and Sheera Frenkel, "Facebook Says Cambridge Analytica Harvested Data of Up to 87 Million Users," *New York Times,* April 4, 2018, www.nytimes.com.

22. Robert Bond et al., "A 61-Million-Person Experiment in Social Influence and Political Mobilization," *Nature* 489, no. 7415 (2012): 295–98, which concludes that "the results show that the messages directly influenced political self-expression, information seeking and real-world voting behavior of millions of people," and that "the messages not only influenced the users who received them but also the users' friends, and friends of friends." Also, prior to America's 2012 election, Facebook researchers manipulated the feeds of 1.9 million users to promote more "hard news" stories; those users subsequently demonstrated increased civic engagement and turnout on Election Day. See Micah Sifry, "Facebook Wants You to Vote on Tuesday. Here's How It Messed with Your Feed in 2012," *Mother Jones,* Oct. 31, 2014, www.motherjones.com.

For further reading on messaging in America's evolving information environment, see Bruce Hardy, Kate Kenski, and Kathleen Hall Jamieson, *The Obama Victory: How Media, Money, and Message Shaped the 2008 Election* (New York: Oxford University Press, 2010); Yue Tan and David H. Weaver, "Agenda Diversity and Agenda Setting from 1956 to 2004: What Are the Trends Over Time?" *Journalism Studies* 14, no. 6 (2013): 773–89; Richard Johnston, Michael Hagen, and Kathleen Hall Jamieson, *The 2000 Presidential Election and the Foundations of Party Politics* (New York: Cambridge University Press, 2004); Adam Kramer, Jamie Guillory, and Jeffrey Hancock, "Experimental Evidence of Massive-Scale Emotional Contagion Through Social Networks," *PNAS, Proceedings of the National Academy of Sciences of the United States of America* 111, no. 24 (2014): 8788–90.

23. Kate Kaye, "Data-Driven Targeting Creates Huge 2016 Political Ad Shift: Broadcast TV Down 20%, Cable and Digital Way Up," *AdAge,* Jan. 3, 2017, adage.com.

24. Bannon, interview by author, New York, Sept. 21, 2019; Goff, interview by author, New York, Aug. 22, 2019. On the persistent influence of TV news, see Hunt Allcott and Matthew Gentzkow, "Social Media and Fake News in the 2016 Election," *Journal of Economic Perspectives* 31, no. 2 (2017): 211–36.

25. Gottfried and Shearer, "News Use Across Social Media Platforms 2016."

26. Surkov, "Владислав Сурков."

27. Inman, interview by author, Austin, Tex., Nov. 2, 2018; Santos, interview by author, Oxford, U.K., Nov. 13, 2018.

28. *United States v. Internet Research Agency LLC,* 18 U.S.C. §§ 2, 371, 1349, 1028A (D.D.C. 2018), 6, 14. The Senate Select Committee on Intelligence concluded, "Analysis of the behavior of the IRA-associated social

media accounts makes clear that while the Russian information warfare campaign exploited the context of the election and election-related issues in 2016, the preponderance of the operational focus, as reflected repeatedly in content, account names, and audiences targeted, was on socially divisive issues—such as race, immigration, and Second Amendment rights—in an attempt to pit Americans against one another and against their government." U.S. Congress, *Russia's Use of Social Media,* 6.

29. Stamos, interview by author.
30. Soroush Vosoughi, Deb Roy, and Sinan Aral, "The Spread of True and False News Online," *Science* 359, no. 6380 (2018): 1146–51, science.sciencemag.org, in which the authors find that "falsehood diffused significantly farther, faster, deeper, and more broadly than the truth in all categories of information, and the effects were more pronounced for false political news." This pattern of behavior extended into 2016. See Craig Silverman, "This Analysis Shows How Viral Fake Election News Stories Outperformed Real News on Facebook," *BuzzFeed News,* Nov. 16, 2016, www.buzzfeednews.com.
31. McMaster, phone interview by author, Oct. 17, 2018.
32. DiResta et al., "Tactics and Tropes of the Internet Research Agency," 9, 21, 76–80, in which these researchers also explain that Clinton and Trump, while a persistent theme, were not the IRA's focus: Just 18 percent of its Instagram posts, 7 percent of its Facebook posts, and 6 percent of its tweets mentioned either candidate by name. The priority was to sow division, amass followers, and, at key moments, release election-related content.
33. *United States v. Internet Research Agency LLC,* 18 U.S.C. §§ 2, 371, 1349, 1028A (D.D.C. 2018), 17.
34. DiResta et al., "Tactics and Tropes of the Internet Research Agency," 56.
35. Jamieson, *Cyberwar,* 5, 68; Office of the Director of National Intelligence, *Assessing Russian Activities and Intentions in Recent U.S. Elections,* 3. Donald Trump, as a presidential candidate, granted an interview to RT during which he criticized the American press; see Adam Taylor and Paul Farhi, "A Trump Interview May Be Crowning Glory for RT, a Network Funded by the Russian Government," *Washington Post,* Sept. 9, 2016, www.washingtonpost.com. For further reading on RT and Sputnik, see Jim Rutenberg, "RT, Sputnik, and Russia's New Theory of War," *New York Times,* Sept. 13, 2017, www.nytimes.com.
36. Jamieson, *Cyberwar,* chap. 5; Philip Howard, Bharath Ganesh, Dimitra Liotsiou, John Kelly, and Camille François conclude, in their study of IRA-run accounts, that "it is evident that the campaigns sought to demobilize African Americans, LGBT, and liberal voters" and that "messaging to African Americans sought to divert their political energy away from established political institutions by preying on anger with structural inequalities faced by African Americans, including police violence, poverty, and disproportionate levels of incarceration. These campaigns pushed a message that the best way to advance the cause of the African American

community was to boycott the election and focus on other issues instead." Phil Howard et al., "The IRA, Social Media, and Political Polarization in the United States, 2012–2018," Computational Propaganda Research Project, Oxford Internet Institute, Dec. 2018, 19, 34.

37. *United States v. Internet Research Agency LLC,* 18 U.S.C. §§ 2, 371, 1349, 1028A (D.D.C. 2018), 18. The IRA also targeted Native Americans. See Ryan Brooks, "How Russians Attempted to Use Instagram to Influence Native Americans," *BuzzFeed News,* Oct. 23, 2017, www.buzzfeednews.com.

38. DiResta et al., "Tactics and Tropes of the Internet Research Agency," 85.

39. MITN 1/6/5, p. 436, Papers of Mitrokhin.

40. Stamos, interview by author. See also Ahmer Arif, Leo Graiden Stewart, and Kate Starbird, "Acting the Part: Examining Information Operations Within #BlackLivesMatter Discourse," *Proceedings of the ACM on Human-Computer Interaction* 2, no. CSCW (2018).

41. Seddon, "Documents Show How Russia's Troll Army Hit America"; Anton Troianovski, "A Former Russian Troll Speaks: 'It Was like Being in Orwell's World,'" *Washington Post,* Feb. 17, 2018, www.washingtonpost.com; Shaun Walker, "The Russian Troll Factory at the Heart of the Meddling Allegations," *Guardian,* April 2, 2015, www.theguardian.com.

42. *United States v. Internet Research Agency LLC,* 18 U.S.C. §§ 2, 371, 1349, 1028A (D.D.C. 2018), 14–15.

43. Troianovski, "Former Russian Troll Speaks."

44. U.S. Congress, *Russia's Use of Social Media,* 43–44. To examine actual IRA-run ads, see Scott Shane, "These Are the Ads Russia Bought on Facebook in 2016," *New York Times,* Nov. 1, 2017, www.nytimes.com.

45. U.S. Congress, *Russia's Use of Social Media,* 40, 77, in which Senate investigators found "that paid advertisements were not key to the IRA's activity, and moreover, are not alone an accurate measure of the IRA's operational scope, scale, or objectives. . . . The nearly 3,400 Facebook and Instagram advertisements the IRA purchased are comparably minor in relation to the over 61,500 Facebook posts, 116,000 Instagram posts, and 10.4 million tweets that were the original creations of IRA influence operatives, disseminated under the guise of authentic user activity."

46. DiResta, phone interview by author, May 22, 2019.

47. *United States v. Internet Research Agency LLC,* 18 U.S.C. §§ 2, 371, 1349, 1028A (D.D.C. 2018), 15.

48. Howard et al., "IRA, Social Media, and Political Polarization," 12; Craig Timberg and Shane Harris, "Russian Operatives Blasted 18,000 Tweets Ahead of a Huge News Day During the 2016 Presidential Campaign. Did They Know What Was Coming?," *Washington Post,* July 20, 2018, www.washingtonpost.com.

49. Tom Parfitt, "My Life as a Pro-Putin Propagandist in Russia's Secret 'Troll Factory,'" *Telegraph,* June 24, 2015, www.telegraph.co.uk.

50. Leon Yin et al., "Your Friendly Neighborhood Troll: The Internet Research Agency's Use of Local and Fake News in the 2016 U.S.

Presidential Campaign," SMaPP Lab, Nov. 19, 2018, www.nyu.edu. Spreading the content of news sources perceived as trustworthy has its advantage; MIT researchers have found that laypeople are "quite good at distinguishing between lower- and higher-quality sources" online. See Gordon Pennycook and David G. Rand, "Fighting Misinformation on Social Media Using Crowdsourced Judgments of News Source Quality," *PNAS, Proceedings of the National Academy of Sciences of the United States of America* 116, no. 7 (2019): 2521–26.

51. For example, as of November 2019, *The Hartford Courant*—the largest daily newspaper in Connecticut—had roughly 160,000 Twitter followers and 21,800 Instagram followers, the *San Francisco Chronicle* had 188,000 Twitter followers and 93,400 Instagram followers, and the *Pittsburgh Post-Gazette* had 166,500 Twitter followers and 54,300 Instagram followers.

52. U.S. Congress, *Russia's Use of Social Media,* 45, 49, 54.

53. *United States v. Internet Research Agency LLC,* 18 U.S.C. §§ 2, 371, 1349, 1028A (D.D.C. 2018), 14; Philip Bump, "At Least Five People Close to Trump Engaged with Russian Twitter Trolls from 2015 to 2017," *Washington Post,* Nov. 2, 2017, www.washingtonpost.com; Mueller Report, 28, 33–34.

54. Mike Glenn, "Dozens Turn Out to Support Houston Muslims," *Houston Chronicle,* May 21, 2016, www.chron.com. See also U.S. Congress, *Russia's Use of Social Media,* 47; Claire Allbright, "A Russian Facebook Page Organized a Protest in Texas. A Different Russian Page Launched the Counterprotest," *Texas Tribune,* Nov. 1, 2017, www.texastribune .org.

On the purpose of GRU-run social media accounts, one set of researchers found, "The operations were primarily focused on creating long-form state-aligned propaganda content and seeding it for distribution within other media properties, including authentic media in the local ecosystem. This is distinct from the social-media-first strategy of the International Research Agency (IRA) Pages, which focused primarily on memetic propaganda with high virality potential to attract the like-minded and facilitate tribalism. . . . The GRU narrative strategy also involved the creation of think tanks and 'alternative news' sites to serve as initial content drops, from which the content was syndicated or republished on other sites." DiResta and Grossman, "Potemkin Pages & Personas," 7.

55. Mueller Report, 29–31.

56. *United States v. Internet Research Agency LLC,* 18 U.S.C. §§ 2, 371, 1349, 1028A (D.D.C. 2018), 22–23, 29. Critically, Robert Mueller concluded, in his final report, that his team had "not identified evidence that any Trump Campaign official understood the requests were coming from foreign nationals." Mueller Report, 35.

57. Morgan, phone interview by author, May 3, 2019; DiResta et al., "Tactics and Tropes of the Internet Research Agency," 34; Stamos, interview by author.

58. *United States v. Internet Research Agency LLC,* 18 U.S.C. §§ 2, 371, 1349, 1028A (D.D.C. 2018), 13, 29.
59. DiResta et al., "Tactics and Tropes of the Internet Research Agency," 34–35. Still, Colin Stretch, a senior Facebook official, emphasized in his written testimony to the U.S. Senate that the IRA's method was in certain ways unsophisticated: "The targeting for the IRA ads that we have identified and provided to the Committee was relatively rudimentary, targeting broad locations and interests, and did not use a tool known as Contact List Custom Audiences." See U.S. Congress, *Russia's Use of Social Media,* 41.
60. Kalugin, interview by author, Rockville, Md., Aug. 7, 2018.
61. DiResta et al., "Tactics and Tropes of the Internet Research Agency," 91.
62. U.S. Congress, *Russia's Use of Social Media,* 6, which went on: "The Committee found that no single group of Americans was targeted by IRA information operatives more than African-Americans."
63. Ibid., 6, 61; DiResta et al., "Tactics and Tropes of the Internet Research Agency," 16. See also Arif, Stewart, and Starbird, "Acting the Part."
64. Kalugin, interview by author.
65. DiResta et al., "Tactics and Tropes of the Internet Research Agency," 72.
66. Robarge, interview by author, McLean, Va., July 19, 2019.
67. DiResta et al., "Tactics and Tropes of the Internet Research Agency," 69; David Weigel, "The Life and Death of the Seth Rich Conspiracy Theory," *Washington Post,* May 24, 2017, www.washingtonpost.com.
    The investigative reporter Michael Isikoff connects the genesis of the Seth Rich conspiracy theory to Russian intelligence, in "Exclusive: The True Origins of the Seth Rich Conspiracy Theory. A Yahoo News Investigation," Yahoo News, July 9, 2019, news.yahoo.com. For further reading on Russian efforts to foment fear and division around the safety of vaccines, see David A. Broniatowski et al., "Weaponized Health Communication: Twitter Bots and Russian Trolls Amplify the Vaccine Debate," *American Journal of Public Health* 108, no. 10 (2018): 1378–84.
68. DiResta et al., "Tactics and Tropes of the Internet Research Agency," 81–92.
69. Wallander, interview by author, Washington, D.C., July 17, 2019; Stamos, interview by author.
70. U.S. Congress, *Russia's Use of Social Media,* 34.
71. Jane Mayer, "How Russia Helped Swing the Election for Trump," *New Yorker,* Sept. 24, 2018, www.newyorker.com. See also Jamieson, *Cyberwar.*
72. James Clapper and Trey Brown, *Facts and Fears: Hard Truths from a Life in Intelligence* (New York: Viking, 2018), 395, in which Clapper argues, "Of course the Russian efforts affected the outcome. Surprising even themselves, they swung the election to a Trump win. To conclude otherwise stretches logic, common sense, and credulity to the breaking point. Less than eighty thousand votes in three key states swung the election. I have no doubt that more votes than that were influenced by this massive effort by the Russians."

73. Yochai Benkler, "Cautionary Notes on Disinformation and the Origins of Distrust," MediaWell, Oct. 22, 2019, mediawell.ssrc.org, in which he further writes, "Nonstop coverage of propaganda efforts and speculation about their impact, without actual evidence to support that impact, feeds the loss of trust in our institutions to a greater extent than the facts warrant." Stephen McCombie, Allon Uhlmann, and Sarah Morrison similarly argue that the IRA's impact on the outcome of the election was "minimal," but that the discovery of its operation has generated much discord inside the United States: "The Russian information operation—of which the IRA action was a major component—has served Russian goals indirectly by ostensibly failing to retain its cover and being perceived and presented as having played a potentially decisive role in the election." Stephen McCombie, Allon Uhlmann, and Sarah Morrison, "The U.S. 2016 Presidential Election & Russia's Troll Farms," *Intelligence and National Security* 35, no. 1 (2019): 95–114.

Several studies have examined the limited reach and impact of fake news on American discourse ahead of the 2016 election. See Allcott and Gentzkow, "Social Media and Fake News in the 2016 Election"; Andrew Guess, Jonathan Nagler, and Joshua Tucker, "Less than You Think: Prevalence and Predictors of Fake News Dissemination on Facebook," *Science Advances* 5, no. 1 (2019); Nir Grinberg et al., "Fake News on Twitter During the 2016 U.S. Presidential Election," *Science* 363, no. 6425 (2019): 374–78.

74. McMaster, interview by author.

75. DiResta, interview by author.

76. DiResta et al., "Tactics and Tropes of the Internet Research Agency," 93. The U.S. Senate, in its investigation of Russia's information warfare operation, found, "The data reveal increases in IRA activity across multiple social media platforms, post–Election Day 2016: Instagram activity increased 238 percent, Facebook increased 59 percent, Twitter increased 52 percent, and YouTube citations went up by 84 percent." U.S. Congress, *Russia's Use of Social Media*, 8.

77. Cohen, interview by author, Washington, D.C., July 17, 2018.

78. Sullivan, interview by author, New York, April 17, 2019.

79. Hannah Levintova, "Russian Journalists Just Published a Bombshell Investigation About a Kremlin-Linked 'Troll Factory,'" *Mother Jones,* Oct. 18, 2017, www.motherjones.com.

80. Inman, interview by author; Cohen, interview by author; Donilon, interview by author, Washington, D.C., July 16, 2018.

81. Reid, interview by author, Las Vegas, July 24, 2019; Stamos, interview by author.

82. Thomas Escritt, "Germany Fines Facebook for Under-reporting Complaints," Reuters, July 2, 2019, www.reuters.com; Natasha Singer, "Germany Restricts Facebook's Data Gathering," *New York Times,* Feb. 7, 2019, www.nytimes.com.

83. Hannigan, interview by author, London, March 22, 2019. On the liberal

and illiberal potential of social media, see Joshua A. Tucker et al., "From Liberation to Turmoil: Social Media and Democracy," *Journal of Democracy* 28, no. 4 (2017): 46–59. On the weaponization of social media abroad, see Samantha Bradshaw and Philip Howard, "Challenging Truth and Trust: A Global Inventory of Organized Social Media Manipulation," Computational Propaganda Research Project, the Oxford Internet Institute, July 20, 2018, comprop.oii.ox.ac.uk.

84. Brennan, interview by author, Washington, D.C., July 10, 2018.

85. Sullivan, interview by author; Stamos, interview by author; Schadlow, phone interview by author, Nov. 9, 2018.

CHAPTER 13: INACTION

1. For example, Peter Gourevitch, in a 1978 essay on external influences over domestic politics, labeled "meddling" as "obvious conceptually" and not "requir[ing] much investigation." He briefly mentioned instances of coup plotting, including in "Iran in 1954, Guatemala in the same year, [and] Chile in 1973." Gourevitch, like other thinkers, thus broached the subject of covert interference without mentioning the far more specific subject of covert *electoral* interference. See Peter Gourevitch, "The Second Image Reversed: The International Sources of Domestic Politics," *International Organization* 32, no. 4 (1978): 883.

2. Schadlow, phone interview by author, Nov. 9, 2018.

3. Brennan, interview by author, Washington, D.C., July 10, 2018.

4. "Full Transcript: Mueller Testimony Before House Judiciary, Intelligence Committees," NBC News, July 25, 2019, www.nbcnews.com; Doina Chiacu, "FBI Director Wray: Russia Intent on Interfering with U.S. Elections," Reuters, July 23, 2019, www.reuters.com.

5. Fiona Hill, "Opening Statement of Dr. Fiona Hill to the House of Representatives Permanent Select Committee on Intelligence," Nov. 21, 2019, s.wsj.net/public/resources/documents/hillopeningstatement1121.pdf.

6. Dan Mangan and Kevin Breuninger, "Trump Talked to Roger Stone About WikiLeaks, Rick Gates Says in Testimony Contradicting the President," CNBC, Nov. 12, 2019, www.cnbc.com.

7. Mueller Report, 5, 49.

8. Department of Justice, Office of Special Counsel Robert Mueller, "Interview of Hope Hicks 3/13/18," 583, released via FOIA on Dec. 2, 2019, www.cnn.com.

9. Philip Bump, "Actually, Trump Has Almost Never Blamed Russia Exclusively for 2016 Interference," *Washington Post,* July 19, 2018, www.washingtonpost.com.

10. McMaster, phone interview by author, Oct. 17, 2018; Mark Landler, "For McMaster, Pomp Under Bittersweet Circumstances," *New York Times,* April 6, 2018, www.nytimes.com.

11. Duke, interview by author, Washington, D.C., Nov. 5, 2018.

12. Jen Kirby, "Poll: Only 32 Percent of Republicans Think Russia Interfered in the 2016 Election," *Vox,* July 19, 2018, www.vox.com.

13. On investigations and reporting into Trump's ties to Russia, Trump's denials of any such ties, and the conclusions of the Mueller investigation, see note 65 of chapter 8 of this book.

14. McMaster, interview by author; Amy Held, "Trump Chides McMaster for Saying Evidence of Russian Interference 'Incontrovertible,'" NPR, Feb. 17, 2018, www.npr.org.

15. Duke, interview by author.

16. Michael Wines, "$250 Million to Keep Votes Safe? Experts Say Billions Are Needed," *New York Times,* Sept. 25, 2019, www.nytimes.com.

17. Wray, email correspondence with author, May 27, 2019.

18. Karen Yourish and Troy Griggs, "8 U.S. Intelligence Groups Blame Russia for Meddling, but Trump Keeps Clouding the Picture," *New York Times,* Aug. 2, 2018, www.nytimes.com.

19. U.S. Congress, *Russian Efforts Against Election Infrastructure,* 52; Ellen Nakashima, "U.S. Cyber Command Operation Disrupted Internet Access of Russian Troll Factory on Day of 2018 Midterms," *Washington Post,* Feb. 27, 2019, www.washingtonpost.com.

20. Office of the Director of National Intelligence, "Director of National Intelligence Daniel R. Coats Establishes Intelligence Community Election Threats Executive," July 19, 2019, www.dni.gov; McMaster, interview by author.

21. Abby Phillip, "Trump Signs What He Calls 'Seriously Flawed' Bill Imposing New Sanctions on Russia," *Washington Post,* Aug. 2, 2017, www.washingtonpost.com.

22. McMaster, interview by author.

23. "Read Trump's Phone Conversation with Volodymyr Zelensky," CNN, Sept. 26, 2019, www.cnn.com.

24. Adam Taylor, "Trump Has Spoken Privately with Putin at Least 16 Times. Here's What We Know About the Conversations," *Washington Post,* Oct. 4, 2019, www.washingtonpost.com.

25. For example, on January 11, 2017, Trump Tweeted: "Russia has never tried to use leverage over me. I HAVE NOTHING TO DO WITH RUSSIA - NO DEALS, NO LOANS, NO NOTHING!" Twitter user @realdonaldtrump, Jan. 11, 2017, www.twitter.com. For elaboration on Trump's business pursuits in Russia, see note 59 of chapter 8 of this book.

26. Carroll Doherty, "Key Findings on Americans' Views of the U.S. Political System and Democracy," Pew Research Center, April 26, 2018, www.pewresearch.org; "The Public, the Political System, and American Democracy," Pew Research Center, April 26, 2018, www.people-press.org.

27. Duke, interview by author.

28. Tom Stites, "About 1,300 U.S. Communities Have Totally Lost News Coverage, UNC News Desert Study Finds," Poynter, Oct. 15, 2018, www.poynter.org.

29. Goss, interview by author, Florida Keys, Fla., Dec. 26, 2018; Cohen, interview by author, Washington, D.C., July 17, 2018.

30. Aaron Zitner et al., "Democrats and Republicans Aren't Just Divided. They Live in Different Worlds," *Wall Street Journal,* Sept. 19, 2019, www.wsj.com.

31. Milan Svolik, "Polarization Versus Democracy," *Journal of Democracy* 30, no. 3 (2019): 20–32, in which he continues, "In sharply polarized electorates, even voters who value democracy will be willing to sacrifice fair democratic competition for the sake of electing politicians who champion their interests. When punishing a leader's authoritarian tendencies requires voting for a platform, party, or person that his supporters detest, many will find this too high a price to pay. Polarization thus presents aspiring authoritarians with a structural opportunity: They can undermine democracy and get away with it."

32. McMaster, interview by author; Rice, phone interview by author, Aug. 27, 2019.

33. Finer, interview by author, New York, Feb. 20, 2019.

34. Candace Smith, "Jeb Bush on Donald Trump: He's a 'Chaos Candidate' and He'd Be a 'Chaos President,'" ABC News, Dec. 15, 2015, abcnews.go.com; Glenn Thrush and Maggie Haberman, "Trump Gives White Supremacists an Unequivocal Boost," *New York Times,* Aug. 15, 2017, www.nytimes.com; Jonathan M. Katz and Farah Stockman, "James Fields Guilty of First-Degree Murder in Death of Heather Heyer," *New York Times,* Dec. 7, 2018, www.nytimes.com; Katie Rogers and Nicholas Fandos, "Trump Tells Congresswomen to 'Go Back' to the Countries They Came From," *New York Times,* July 14, 2019, www.nytimes.com; Kyle Balluck and Aris Folley, "Trump Suggests Pelosi Committed Treason, Should Be 'Immediately Impeached,'" *Hill,* Oct. 7, 2019, thehill.com.

35. Brennan, interview by author.

36. Blinken, interview by author, Washington, D.C., Jan. 3, 2019; Muñoz, phone interview by author, July 20, 2019.

37. Duke, interview by author; Wise, phone interview by author, Oct. 21, 2019.

38. "Public, the Political System, and American Democracy"; Richard Wike et al., "Democracy Widely Supported, Little Backing for Rule by Strong Leader or Military," Pew Research Center, Oct. 16, 2017, www.pewresearch.org. Americans are not unique in contemplating alternatives to the democratic model. See Wike and Fetterolf, "Liberal Democracy's Crisis of Confidence"; Richard Wike, Laura Silver, and Alexandra Castillo, "Dissatisfaction with Performance of Democracy Is Common in Many Nations," Pew Research Center, April 29, 2019, www.pewresearch.org.

39. Blinken, interview by author.

40. "It Was a Campaign Trap," *New York Times,* Nov. 7, 1888, timesmachine.nytimes.com. T. C. Hinckley, "George Osgoodby and the Murchison Letter," *Pacific Historical Review* 27, no. 4 (1958): 359–70.

41. Marco R. Newmark, "The Murchison Letter Incident," *Quarterly:*

Historical Society of Southern California 27, no. 1 (1945): 17–21; Robert Mitchell, "The Fake Letter Historians Believe Tipped a Presidential Election," *Washington Post,* June 21, 2018, www.washingtonpost.com.

42. Nicole Perlroth and David Sanger, "Iranian Hackers Target Trump Campaign as Threats to 2020 Mount," *New York Times,* Oct. 4, 2019, www.nytimes.com.

43. Goss, interview by author; Brennan, interview by author.

CONCLUSION: BREAKING THE SIEGE

1. Tony Judt and Timothy Snyder, *Thinking the Twentieth Century* (New York: Penguin, 2012), 306.

2. "Full Transcript: Mueller Testimony Before House Judiciary, Intelligence Committees."

3. Kenneth Waltz, *Man, the State, and War: A Theoretical Analysis* (New York: Columbia University Press, 1959), 149.

4. The Brennan Center concluded in August 2019 that it would cost roughly $2.15 billion, doled out over five years, for states to meet key election security needs, such as upgrading voter registration databases and voting machines. See Lawrence Norden and Edgardo Cortés, "What Does Election Security Cost?," Brennan Center for Justice, Aug. 15, 2019, www.brennancenter.org. Ahead of the 2020 election, it will cost just Pennsylvania roughly $150 million to replace its voting machines. See Sasha Hupka and Jonathan Lai, "After Pa. Gov. Tom Wolf Announces $90 Million to Upgrade Voting Machines, GOP Pushes Back," *Philadelphia Inquirer,* July 9, 2019, www.inquirer.com. See also Kate Rabinowitz, "Election Security a High Priority—Until It Comes to Paying for New Voting Machines," ProPublica, Feb. 20, 2018, www.propublica.org; Christopher R. Deluzio et al., "Defending Elections: Federal Funding Needs for State Election Security," Brennan Center for Justice, July 18, 2019, www.brennancenter.org.

5. Duke, interview by author, Washington, D.C., Nov. 5, 2018. For analysis of McConnell's position, see Amber Phillips, "Why Is Mitch McConnell Blocking Election Security Bills? Good Question," *Washington Post,* July 30, 2019, www.washingtonpost.com. On the uneven election security standards across states, see David Sanger, Reid J. Epstein, and Michael Wines, "States Rush to Make Voting Systems More Secure as New Threats Emerge," *New York Times,* July 26, 2019, www.nytimes.com.

6. Schadlow, phone interview by author, Nov. 9, 2018; Haines, interview by author, New York, Feb. 23, 2019; Johnson, interview by author, New York, July 29, 2019.

7. Carl Hulse, "After Resisting, McConnell and Senate G.O.P. Back Election Security Funding," *New York Times,* Sept. 19, 2019, www.nytimes.com.

8. The Help America Vote Act (HAVA) of 2002 included a series of

requirements for election administration, such as that states maintain a "single, uniform, official, centralized, interactive computerized statewide voter registration list." See U.S. Congress, House, Help America Vote Act of 2002, H.R. 2395.

Congress should, today, update those standards, in accordance with the digital age. The Securing America's Federal Elections (SAFE) Act, approved by the House in 2019, would install, per its official summary, "requirements for voting systems, including that systems (1) use individual, durable, voter-verified paper ballots; (2) make a voter's marked ballot available for inspection and verification by the voter before the vote is cast; (3) ensure that individuals with disabilities are given an equivalent opportunity to vote, including with privacy and independence, in a manner that produces a voter-verified paper ballot; (4) be manufactured in the United States; and (5) meet specified cybersecurity requirements, including the prohibition of the connection of a voting system to the internet." These criteria and more—designed to bolster the security both of voting systems and of voter registration databases—should be passed into law. See U.S. Congress, House, Securing America's Federal Elections Act, H.R. 2722, 116th Cong., introduced in House May 14, 2019, www.congress.gov.

On the politics of the SAFE Act, see Hailey Fuchs and Karoun Demirjian, "Divided House Passes Election Security Legislation over Republican Objections," *Washington Post,* June 27, 2019, www.washingtonpost.com. For additional recommendations, see National Academies of Sciences, Engineering, and Medicine, *Securing the Vote: Protecting American Democracy* (Washington, D.C.: National Academies Press, 2018), www .nap.edu.

9. Cohen, interview by author, Washington, D.C., July 17, 2018.

10. Rucker, phone interview by author, Sept. 2, 2018.

11. Baker, phone interview by author, Oct. 17, 2018.

12. Rachel Donadio, "Why the Macron Hacking Attack Landed with a Thud in France," *New York Times,* May 8, 2017, www.nytimes.com; Alex Hern, "Macron Hackers Linked to Russian-affiliated Group Behind US Attack," *Guardian,* May 8, 2017, www.theguardian.com; Mark Hosenball, "U.S. Increasingly Convinced that Russia Hacked French Election: Sources," Reuters, May 9, 2017, www.reuters.com.

13. Burns, interview by author, Washington, D.C., July 9, 2018.

14. Guy Rosen, Katie Harbath, Nathaniel Gleicher, and Rob Leathern, "Helping to Protect the 2020 U.S. Elections," Facebook, Oct. 21, 2019, about.fb.com. On an especially extensive network of Russian accounts across Africa, see Davey Alba and Sheera Frenkel, "Russia Tests New Disinformation Tactics in Africa to Expand Influence," *New York Times,* Oct. 30, 2019, www.nytimes.com. On the IRA's use of smaller platforms to test specific messaging strains, see Josephine Lukito, "Coordinating a Multi-platform Disinformation Campaign: Internet Research Agency Activity on Three U.S. Social Media Platforms, 2015 to 2017," *Political Communication* 37, no. 2 (2019): 238–55. On more recent Russian

activity on Reddit, see Madeleine Carlisle, "Reddit Says Leaked U.S.-U.K. Trade Documents Posted on the Site Are Linked to a Russian Information Campaign," *Time,* Dec. 7, 2019, time.com.

15. McMaster, phone interview by author, Oct. 17, 2018.

16. Stamos, phone interview by author, May 28, 2018; Gleicher, phone interview by author, Feb. 25, 2020.

17. Since 2016, lawmakers have passed no legislation in this space—not even the Honest Ads Act, a bill with bipartisan support that would require social media companies to disclose who paid for political advertisements, just as television, radio, and print providers do. See U.S. Congress, Senate, Honest Ads Act, S. 1989, 115th Cong., introduced in Senate Oct. 19, 2017, www.congress.gov. Senator Amy Klobuchar has further proposed U.S. Congress, Senate, Social Media Privacy Protection and Consumer Rights Act of 2019, S. 189, 116th Cong., introduced on Jan. 17, 2019, www.congress.gov. Another major bill on the Hill is the Bot Disclosure and Accountability Act, which would crack down on the use of automated bot accounts for political purposes; see Rachel Frazin, "Feinstein Introduces Bill to Prohibit Campaigns from Using Social Media Bots," *Hill,* July 16, 2019, thehill.com.

For a bipartisan set of recommendations, see U.S. Congress, *Russia's Use of Social Media,* 78–83. For additional recommendations, see McFaul, *Securing American Elections,* chaps. 3–5. Philip Howard, the director of the Oxford Internet Institute, recommends requiring technology companies to store all advertisements in a public archive, in "A Way to Detect the Next Russian Misinformation Campaign," *New York Times,* March 27, 2019, www.nytimes.com. And finally, Anne Applebaum makes an impassioned case for social media regulation in "Regulate Social Media Now. The Future of Democracy Is at Stake," *Washington Post,* Feb. 1, 2019, www.washingtonpost.com.

18. Clapper, interview by author, Fairfax, Va., Jan. 3, 2019.

19. For further reading on America's entrenched polarization and ways to alleviate it, see Nathaniel Persily, *Solutions to Political Polarization in America* (Cambridge, U.K.: Cambridge University Press, 2015).

20. Report for America, www.reportforamerica.org. Between 2008 and 2018, the number of newspaper newsroom employees in America declined from seventy-one thousand to thirty-eight thousand. Elizabeth Grieco, "U.S. Newsroom Employment Has Dropped by a Quarter Since 2008, with Greatest Decline at Newspapers," Pew Research Center, July 9, 2019, www.pewresearch.org. On the connection between a decline in local news and a rise in polarization, see Joshua Darr, Johanna Dunaway, and Matthew Hitt, "Want to Reduce Political Polarization? Save Your Local Newspaper," Nieman Lab, Feb. 11, 2019, www.niemanlab.org. See also Penelope Abernathy, "The Expanding News Desert," www.usnewsdeserts .com.

21. Ryan Foley, "Efforts Grow to Help Students Evaluate What They See Online," AP, Dec. 30, 2017, apnews.com.

22. Goss, interview by author, Florida Keys, Fla., Dec. 26, 2018; Hayden, interview by author, Washington, D.C., Nov. 5, 2018.

23. Eliza Mackintosh, "Finland Is Winning the War on Fake News. What It's Learned May Be Crucial to Western Democracy," CNN, May 2019, edition.cnn.com; Chris Good, "Ahead of Election, Sweden Warns Its Voters Against Foreign Disinformation," ABC News, Sept. 8, 2018, abcnews .go.com; Emma Charlton, "How Finland Is Fighting Fake News—in the Classroom," World Economic Forum, May 21, 2019, www.weforum.org.

24. Inman, interview by author, Austin, Tex., Nov. 2, 2018.

25. Blinken, interview by author, Washington, D.C., Jan. 3, 2019; McMaster, interview by author.

26. "Read Jim Mattis's Letter to Trump: Full Text," *New York Times*, Dec. 20, 2018, www.nytimes.com. In his memoirs, Mattis writes, "In my first dozen years in the Marines, I commanded two platoons and two companies, deploying to thirteen countries on a half dozen ships. Everywhere we sailed, at every landing and every exercise in foreign countries, I was introduced to the enormous value of allies." Jim Mattis and Bing West, *Call Sign Chaos: Learning to Lead* (New York: Random House, 2019), 9.

27. Haines, interview by author; Nuland, interview by author, Washington, D.C., Feb. 22, 2019.

28. Rice, phone interview by author, Aug. 27, 2019; McMaster, interview by author.

29. Sullivan, interview by author, New York, April 17, 2019; Morell, phone interview by author, March 6, 2019; Summers, phone interview by author, Nov. 22, 2019; Nuland, interview by author.

30. Nuland, interview by author.

31. McLaughlin, phone interview by author, Sept. 5, 2019; Reid, interview by author, Las Vegas, July 24, 2019; Panetta, phone interview by author, Nov. 12, 2019.

32. Petraeus, phone interview by author, Oct. 8, 2018; Finer, interview by author, New York, Feb. 20, 2019; Sullivan, interview by author.

33. Brennan, interview by author, Washington, D.C., July 10, 2018; Morell, interview by author.

34. Brennan, interview by author. Further, Harold Koh, a former dean of Yale Law School, argues that covert electoral interference violates international law: "Coercive interference in another country's electoral politics—including the deliberate spreading of false news—constitutes an intervention that violates international law." Harold Koh, *The Trump Administration and International Law* (New York: Oxford University Press, 2018), 83.

35. Hall, phone interview by author, Oct. 22, 2019; Schadlow, interview by author.

36. For further reading on the modern authoritarian challenge, see Christopher Walker, "The Authoritarian Threat: The Hijacking of 'Soft Power,'" *Journal of Democracy* 27, no. 1 (2016): 49–63; Ivan Krastev, "The Specter

Haunting Europe: The Unraveling of the Post-1989 Order," *Journal of Democracy* 27, no. 4 (2016): 88–98; Kagan, "Strongmen Strike Back."

37. McDonough, interview by author, Washington, D.C., July 17, 2018; Schadlow, interview by author.

38. Joshua Kurlantzick, "How China Is Interfering in Taiwan's Election," Council on Foreign Relations, Nov. 7, 2019, www.cfr.org; Ben Blanchard, "Taiwan President Says China Interfering in Election 'Every Day,'" Reuters, Nov. 19, 2019, www.reuters.com; Colin Packham, "Exclusive: Australia Concluded China Was Behind Hack on Parliament, Political Parties—Sources," Reuters, Sept. 15, 2019, www.reuters.com; John Garnaut, "How China Interferes in Australia," *Foreign Affairs*, March 9, 2018, www.foreignaffairs.com.

Index

A Note About the Author

DAVID SHIMER is pursuing a doctorate in international relations at the University of Oxford as a Marshall Scholar. His reporting and analysis have appeared in *The New York Times, The New Yorker,* and *Foreign Affairs.* He is an associate fellow of Davenport College at Yale University, where he received his undergraduate and master's degrees in history.

A Note on the Type

This book was set in Sabon, a typeface designed by Jan Tschichold (1902–1974). Designed in 1966 and based on the original designs by Claude Garamond (ca. 1480–1561), Sabon was named for the punch cutter Jacques Sabon, who brought Garamond's matrices to Frankfurt.

Composed by North Market Street Graphics
Lancaster, Pennsylvania

Printed and bound by Berryville Graphics
Berryville, Virginia

Designed by Michael Collica